MySQL® Database Design and Tuning

Robert D. Schneider

MySQL Press

800 East 96th Street, Indianapolis, Indiana 46240 USA

MySQL® Database Design and Tuning

International Standard Book Number: 0-672-32765-1

Library of Congress Catalog Card Number: 2004098791

Printed in the United States of America

First Printing: June 2005

08   07   06   05   4   3   2   1

Trademarks

All terms mentioned in this book that are known to be trademarks or service marks have been appropriately capitalized. Pearson cannot attest to the accuracy of this information. Use of a term in this book should not be regarded as affecting the validity of any trademark or service mark.

Warning and Disclaimer

Every effort has been made to make this book as complete and as accurate as possible, but no warranty or fitness is implied. The information provided is on an "as is" basis. The author and the publisher shall have neither liability nor responsibility to any person or entity with respect to any loss or damages arising from the information contained in this book.

Bulk Sales

Pearson offers excellent discounts on this book when ordered in quantity for bulk purchases or special sales. For more information, please contact

U.S. Corporate and Government Sales
1-800-382-3419
corpsales@pearsontechgroup.com

For sales outside of the U.S., please contact

International Sales
international@pearsoned.com

MySQL® Database Design and Tuning

ASSOCIATE PUBLISHER	MANAGING EDITOR	INDEXER	DESIGNER
Mark Taber	Charlotte Clapp	Chris Barrick	Gary Adair
ACQUISITIONS EDITOR	SENIOR PROJECT EDITOR	PROOFREADER	TECHNICAL EDITORS
Shelley Johnston	Matthew Purcell	Leslie Joseph	Philip Antoniades
DEVELOPMENT EDITOR		PUBLISHING	Dean Ellis
Damon Jordan	COPY EDITOR	COORDINATOR	Lachlan Mulcahy
	Karen Annett	Vanessa Evans	Trudy Pelzer
			Peter Zaitsev

MySQL® Press is the exclusive publisher of technology books and materials that have been authorized by MySQL AB. MySQL Press books are written and reviewed by the world's leading authorities on MySQL technologies, and are edited, produced, and distributed by the Que/Sams Publishing group of Pearson Education, the worldwide leader in integrated education and computer technology publishing. For more information on MySQL Press and MySQL Press books, please go to **www.mysqlpress.com**.

MYSQL HQ
MySQL AB
Bangårdsgatan 8
S-753 20 Uppsala
Sweden

UNITED STATES
MySQL Inc.
2510 Fairview Avenue East
Seattle, WA 98102
USA

GERMANY, AUSTRIA, AND SWITZERLAND
MySQL GmbH
Schlosserstraße 4
D-72622 Nürtingen
Germany

FINLAND
MySQL Finland Oy
Tekniikantie 21
FIN-02150 Espoo
Finland

FRANCE
MySQL AB (France)
123, rue du Faubourg St. Antoine
75011, Paris
France

MySQL® AB develops, markets, and supports a family of high-performance, affordable database servers and tools. MySQL AB is the sole owner of the MySQL server source code, the MySQL trademark, and the mysql.com domain. For more information on MySQL AB and MySQL AB products, please go to **www.mysql.com** or the following areas of the MySQL Web site:

- Training information: **www.mysql.com/training**
- Support services: **www.mysql.com/support**
- Consulting services: **www.mysql.com/consulting**

*To the Open Source movement, and the collaboration,
freedom, honesty, and pursuit of knowledge it
embodies and inspires.*

About the Author

Robert D. Schneider has more than 15 years of experience developing and delivering sophisticated software solutions worldwide. He has provided database optimization, distributed computing, and other technical expertise to a wide variety of enterprises in the financial, technology, and government sectors. Clients have included Chase Manhattan Bank, VISA, HP, SWIFT, and the governments of the United States, Brazil, and Malaysia.

He is the author of *Optimizing Informix Applications* and *Microsoft SQL Server: Planning and Building a High Performance Database*. He has also written numerous articles on technical and professional services topics. He can be reached at Robert.Schneider@Think88.com.

Acknowledgments

The author wants to acknowledge the following people for their invaluable assistance in creating and publishing this work. From Pearson Education: Shelley Johnston, Damon Jordan, Matthew Purcell, Vanessa Evans, Chris Barrick, Leslie Joseph, and Karen Annett. Technical editing by Philip Antioniades, Dean Ellis, Sara Golemon, Lachlan Mulcahy, Trudy Pelzer, and Peter Zaitsev. And last, but not least: Lynn Z. Schneider, Nicole Sierra Schneider, and Danielle Jolie Schneider for their patience and understanding.

Contents At a Glance

Table of Contents

We Want to Hear from You!

As the reader of this book, *you* are our most important critic and commentator. We value your opinion and want to know what we're doing right, what we could do better, what areas you'd like to see us publish in, and any other words of wisdom you're willing to pass our way.

You can email or write me directly to let me know what you did or didn't like about this book—as well as what we can do to make our books stronger.

Please note that I cannot help you with technical problems related to the topic of this book, and that due to the high volume of mail I receive, I might not be able to reply to every message.

When you write, please be sure to include this book's title and author as well as your name and phone number or email address. I will carefully review your comments and share them with the author and editors who worked on the book.

Email: mysqlpress@pearsoned.com

Mail: Mark Taber
           Associate Publisher
           Pearson Education/MySQL Press
           800 East 96th Street
           Indianapolis, IN 46240 USA

Introduction

The Purpose of This Book

MySQL is the foundation of many of today's highest quality, most robust database-driven solutions. However, users continually grow more demanding: A rich application that runs sluggishly is unacceptable, no matter what functionality it offers. Unfortunately, the cost of job cutbacks and outsourcing means that most overloaded IT professionals barely have enough time to deliver a minimal solution, much less master the minutiae of their database engine, which, in the case of MySQL, grows richer and more complex with each release.

Performance often takes a backseat to merely hitting the schedule. "Just ship it now and make it faster later" is a refrain heard around the world today. Regrettably, "later" rarely arrives, and designers, developers, and administrators end up delivering suboptimal solutions and then bracing themselves for the inevitable complaints from users. In many cases, these problems would never have come to pass if the overloaded designers and developers had enough time to fully research and exploit the numerous avenues to boost MySQL response. This book was written to help these beleaguered professionals jump-start their knowledge of MySQL performance tuning, letting them design, develop, and maintain the fastest MySQL solutions in the shortest amount of time.

Who Should Read This Book?

MySQL Database Design and Tuning is aimed at busy database designers, database and system administrators, webmasters, and developers who want to build, deploy, and manage the fastest possible solutions based on MySQL.

To take full advantage of this book, application developers should understand the following:

- **Standard Structured Query Language (SQL)**—Because SQL is the underpinning of MySQL database access, it's important that you at least comprehend basic SQL (simple queries, INSERT/UPDATE/DELETE operations, and so on).

- **A programming language such as Java, C++, and so on**—SQL is often paired with a procedural programming or scripting language to create MySQL-based applications. Although *MySQL Performance Optimization* is not a programming guide, it does discuss the performance interplay between the programming language and the MySQL engine.

Readers who are responsible for designing and/or administering databases should understand the following:

- **Basic relational database design theory**—To make the most of this book, you should be aware of how to design a simple database, as well as understand data normalization, constraints, and so on.

- **Intermediate or advanced SQL**—As a database administrator/analyst (DBA), you are often called on to produce more sophisticated SQL on behalf of your users. *MySQL Database Design and Tuning* will help you improve the responsiveness of your more complex join, subquery, index construction, and transactional challenges.

- **MySQL engine architecture**—This book does not expect you to have downloaded the MySQL source code or to construct hashing algorithms in your spare time. However, if you are familiar with the elegant MySQL product line architecture, you are likely to make better use of this book's recommendations.

System and web administrators should be familiar with the following:

- **MySQL's engine architecture**—Database performance issues are often misdiagnosed as hardware and/or operating system flaws. By understanding the components that make up the MySQL database, it's more likely that you will be able to accurately identify and fix (or even prevent) database response concerns.

- **Configuring server operating systems such as Windows and Linux**—There is interplay between the MySQL database and the underlying operating system. Fortunately, you can employ a number of operating system–specific settings to make your operating system more MySQL-friendly.

Finally, some words for the open source developer. Unlike any other widely available database, MySQL's open source architecture, customer-friendly licensing, and source code availability means that you can programmatically change the behavior of the engine itself. This book, however, focuses on using the commercially available versions of MySQL; this book does not expect any reader to have the time, skill, or inclination to alter MySQL's source code.

Benefits of Using This Book

Readers of *MySQL Database Design and Tuning* will help themselves and their organizations in at least five ways:

- **Simplicity**—There's a common belief that the simplest solution is by definition a slow solution. However, this is often incorrect. In fact, a well-designed, optimized database application is frequently cleaner and more elegant than an overengineered product. Good performance and simple design are rarely mutually exclusive. This book always opts for the simplest, fastest solution.

- **Productivity**—Database-centric applications often serve as the cornerstone of an organization's operations. A nonoptimized solution wastes each user's time. When multiplied by the large number of internal and external users affected by these delays, the cost to the organization's productivity can be staggering. *MySQL Performance Optimization* is filled with easily implemented tips and tricks that will have a dramatic, positive impact on performance.

- **Reliability**—Response and reliability problems often are mistaken for each other. For example, imagine that you are a user of a popular website that is built on MySQL. You have just submitted an e-commerce payment form. Unfortunately, the site database and application designers never planned for large numbers of users inserting information at the same time, so your browser appears to "hang" while waiting for a response. From the user's perspective, is this a flaw in response or reliability? It really doesn't matter because you now have an unhappy customer who thinks that your website is "buggy." Faster systems equal more reliable systems.

- **Cost control**—Hardware prices continue to fall; memory and disk drives are now so cheap that you might wonder if they will be offered in cereal boxes before too long. Nevertheless, many organizations that employ MySQL are cost conscious. Squeezing an extra 10% or 20% from your applications might spell the difference between your raise money being spent on you or on a new CPU.

- **User satisfaction**—Although your users will likely love your MySQL-based solutions, it's doubtful that they will want to spend any more time staring at their screens awaiting response than is absolutely necessary. Each year, users grow more sophisticated and less tolerant of delay. In some cases, a perfectly good system is abandoned because of performance problems. *MySQL Performance Optimization* is designed to help you delight your users by delivering the fastest, most reliable solutions.

How to Use This Book

This book is divided into six major sections:

- **Part I: Introduction**—This section describes how to get the most from this book, its structure and examples, and MySQL's architecture, as well as how to set up an optimization environment.

- **Part II: Advanced Database Design Concepts**—Your MySQL solution is only as solid and responsive as the database design upon which it rests. This section explores how to choose the correct options when designing your tables, the impact of constraints on response, the excellent diagnostics offered by the MySQL optimizer, and how to leverage indexes for exceptional performance.

- **Part III: Optimizing Application Code**—Your applications will likely interact with MySQL through one or more programming/scripting languages, even if it's just SQL. For that reason, this section examines how to write the most efficient SQL, as well as special considerations when using popular programming technologies, such as Java, C, ODBC, Perl, and so on. Because newer versions of MySQL offer stored procedures and triggers, this section also looks at how to make these exciting new technologies as speedy as possible.

- **Part IV: Optimizing and Tuning the MySQL Engine**—Administrators have dozens of choices to make when setting up and maintaining their MySQL environments. These choices range from engine and operating system parameters to disk management and bulk data operations. This section is devoted to helping these administrators make intelligent decisions when confronted with these situations.

- **Part V: Distributed Computing**—Replication and clustering are two key MySQL technologies for spreading your processing load among multiple computers. This section of the book examines when to deploy these powerful capabilities, as well as how to tune them for optimal performance.

- **Part VI: Case Studies**—The final section of this book ties the information found in the earlier chapters together in a series of multidimensional, real-world case studies.

Whether you choose to read all sections will likely be determined by your MySQL-oriented responsibility. For example, if you are an application developer, it's likely that you'll focus on Parts I, II, III, and V; you are probably not going to spend much time on Part IV's engine configuration. However, if you are tasked with tuning the database engine or the operating system, Part IV will be of supreme interest to you. In any case, the optimization techniques and examples have been purposely designed to be as independent of each other as possible.

Information About MySQL Software and Environments

The frequency with which MySQL AB releases new versions and products can be overwhelming. This book uses products from both the 4.1 series (versions 4.1.7 through 4.1.10), along with newer versions, from 5.0 through 5.0.3. When applicable, the performance-specific features of the 5.1 release are discussed. This book also highlights some of the excellent new graphical products, such as the MySQL Administrator and MySQL Query Browser.

MySQL's open source architecture means that the product runs on a tremendous variety of hardware and operating system environments. However, aside from the sections in which operating system tuning in a MySQL environment is discussed, this book always strives to make the examples as platform-independent as possible.

Information About Examples

Founded during the height of the dot-com boom in 1999, High-Hat Airways has grown into the world's largest airline. Its unique blend of hip, in-your-face marketing, low prices, and creative corporate accounting helped propel the airline past sluggish industry dinosaurs.

Its fleet has expanded from one 20-year-old rented Boeing 737 to more than 550 planes. During the next year, more than 275 million customers will board a High-Hat flight and be greeted by the familiar "Go sit down over there!" from a friendly flight attendant.

The year 2002 saw the indictments of the CEO and CFO, along with the mysterious disappearance of four members of the Board of Directors. However, these setbacks proved to be mere road bumps on the path to success: The value of High-Hat's stock has grown thirty-fold in less than three years.

As part of its ongoing commitment to cost control, High-Hat Airways has decided to convert all internal systems to open source. Naturally, MySQL will be a cornerstone of this new philosophy. However, the already overburdened IT staff has a monumental task ahead: to consolidate 27 internal applications running on 11 different database platforms. The most important applications are as follows:

- Reservations
- Flight logistics and scheduling
- Catering
- Luggage management
- Loyalty programs

To make matters worse, the CIO has promised both internal users and the general public that High-Hat's systems will have the fastest response time in the industry. The CIO is also refereeing a religious war between Microsoft zealots and Linux enthusiasts. The result is that the new solutions will be evenly split between the two operating systems.

As you proceed through this book, you'll notice it continually refers to the challenges faced by the High-Hat Airways IT staff as they struggle to deliver quality, high-performance solutions based on MySQL. Luckily, very simple, easily implemented changes can result in massive speed gains, and that is what this book plans to help you achieve.

To keep things simple, this book introduces High-Hat's new applications, database structures, and engine configurations on an as-needed basis, in concert with the specific performance concept being examined at the time. This means that you can focus on MySQL optimization, rather than becoming an expert in the internal systems of High-Hat Airways. Finally, the database design, SQL, and code examples are always as simple and to-the-point as possible while still conveying the appropriate performance messages.

Introduction

## 1

Setting Up an Optimization Environment

When users are filling your inbox and voice mail with urgent pleas for help in fixing performance problems on an existing system, it's natural to want to dive right in and start making things better. You might feel that any action is better than inaction. Regrettably, this often leads to more problems than it solves. To do this job right, you must follow a few crucial preparatory steps before you start changing things. Skipping these steps means that you run the very real risk of making incorrect judgments about your problems. You might then construct solutions that fail to address the underlying cause of the performance issues. In certain cases, this makes things worse, possibly by further degrading responsiveness or even damaging functionality. None of this will help your credibility with your users.

This chapter reviews the important steps you should follow before you start your performance testing. The steps are broken down into three major segments. The first segment examines what you should do before you even begin the testing process. This primarily deals with ensuring that the correct software, hardware, and operating system configurations are ready. In addition, this segment discusses the importance of being organized and following a plan before embarking on your optimization works.

The second segment helps you as your testing is under way. Although the most productive system performance experts follow their original investigation plan throughout the testing process, they also understand the importance of exploring new leads in the efforts to improve responsiveness.

The final segment discusses how to translate the valuable insights you learned during performance testing into real-world performance improvements.

If you are embarking on designing and developing a new system, you might wonder if this chapter will be useful for your situation. The answer is a definite yes: Applying the discipline and structure that this chapter advocates during the design process will go a long way toward helping you deliver a responsive system, one that will not need the performance retrofits that plague so many development efforts.

Pretesting Preparation

This section takes some time to review the important checkpoints you should complete before beginning your performance analysis.

Hardware

Each component in your hardware environment plays an important role in the responsiveness of your MySQL solutions. Ideally, your production and performance testing environments will match as many of the following items as closely as possible:

- **Processors**—Given the rapid increases in processor speed, you are likely to receive very different performance numbers if your production machine and test machine contain processors manufactured just one year apart. The same type of erroneous outcome will occur if your production machine has four processors and your testing machine only has one. This type of CPU disparity really becomes a problem when setting engine parameters.

- **Memory**—A 10-year-old computer with ample memory often outperforms a 10-day-old machine configured with insufficient memory. Prior to initiating your testing, it's crucial to ensure that the memory profiles of the production and test platforms are as similar as possible. If someone else sets up your hardware for you, be certain to examine the platform's configuration before starting: Don't take anything for granted, especially memory capacity and speed.

- **Mass storage**—Disk drive capacity and speed dramatically improve each year. You have many more choices when implementing your mass storage architecture. However, these choices can introduce anomalies when it comes to performance testing. For example, imagine that you want to examine why bulk data operations take so long on your production server. You don't have enough disk capacity on your test platform to unload/reload your 100-GB production data set, so you purchase an inexpensive 200-GB external drive. You then attach this device to your test machine using USB 1.1. Unfortunately, USB 1.1 is orders-of-magnitude slower than either USB 2.0 or internal storage. This means that any disk-based performance numbers you receive will not be meaningful, and could lead you to make incorrect assumptions.

- **Attached devices**—Every attached device (for example, printers, plotters, scanners, terminals) can exact a performance penalty on your MySQL production server. The same holds true for your test environment. Be careful that your test platform isn't serving double, triple, or even quadruple duty as a print server, firewall, and so on. These extra responsibilities can render any performance information useless.

In an ideal world, your test system will be a mirror image of your production server. Unfortunately, most readers will be fortunate if they even have a test machine, let alone a dedicated performance analysis platform. If this is the challenge you face, it makes more sense to run your tests on the production platform during periods of low activity.

Regrettably, this is likely to translate into a series of ruined nights and weekends for you. Testing on the production systems is discussed in the "Organizational Support" section later in this chapter.

Connectivity

Many MySQL installations service a wide cross section of users, including those connected via a local area network (LAN), a corporate wide area network (WAN), and over the Internet. Accurate performance testing demands that you attempt to replicate the connectivity profiles of all your users.

For example, suppose that remote users are connecting to your application via a web browser over the Internet and complaining of performance bottlenecks. To further complicate things, only a certain percentage of all remote browser users have performance complaints; the majority of the user community has no objections.

Before you even begin testing, you should do all that you can to describe and simulate all facets of the user experience, especially the connectivity components. You might be surprised to learn that the users who complain the most about browser access suffer from external performance impediments beyond your control, such as firewall issues, slow dial-up lines, proxy server problems, and so on. In certain cases, the users might even be running old, underpowered, or badly configured client machines. MySQL tuning will have little impact on these types of predicaments. Knowing these handicaps in advance will save you a tremendous amount of time, as well as greatly reduce the risk of taking action based on incorrect analysis.

Software

After you've obtained the right hardware and connectivity profile for your testing, the next step is to locate, install, and configure the correct software.

- **Database**—One of the most attractive aspects of MySQL's open source architecture is how frequently new releases and bug fixes are delivered to the marketplace. However, it's important to use the same version of MySQL in your test environment as in your production environment. MySQL releases can often change the underlying performance characteristics of an application as new features are provided and old features are made obsolete.

  For example, in versions prior to 4.1.4, launching the server with `mysqld` caused the engine to automatically start in debug mode. This consumed additional memory and CPU. From version 4.1.4 onward, the server now starts without debugging enabled; you use `mysql-debug` to launch the server with debugging turned on. This clearly has an impact on engine performance, and could skew your test results if your production and testing platforms differ. MySQL will also introduce new system and session variables, many of which might impact performance.

Speaking of system and session variables, be certain that your production and test platforms match as closely as possible; a difference in even a single setting can render all of your testing irrelevant.

Of course, after you have completed your performance testing, it is fine to upgrade your test server to a newer version of MySQL to see if this benefits responsiveness.

- **Application**—If you're using a packaged application (for example, enterprise software, web servers), try to have the same version of the software installed on your test platform. You should also apply whatever application patches are running in production onto your test server because these patches often affect responsiveness. Many enterprise software vendors allow you to run multiple instances of their products as long as the additional copies are not used for production. Try not to mix your development server with your test server: Development efforts can often interfere with scientific testing.

  Our earlier suggestion about keeping MySQL's settings consistent between production and test also applies here: Many application vendors offer numerous performance-related settings, which can introduce inconsistencies if they aren't kept in sync between the production and test environments.

- **Operating system**—MySQL's cross-platform portability is another benefit of its open source heritage. However, this portability can play havoc with determining the cause of performance issues. For example, assume that your production server is based on Windows Server 2003, whereas your testing server is running Linux. Given these differences, you can never be fully confident that the performance results you obtain from one platform will transfer to the other: There are obviously significant architectural and configuration differences between these operating systems that can affect MySQL application performance. The same holds true even for homogenous operating systems if they differ in installed patches or kernel modifications. To reduce the potential for confusion, try to have both platforms as similar as possible.

Data

At this point, you have done your best to replicate your production hardware, software, and connectivity profiles onto a test platform. Your next task is to come up with a data set for examining during the testing process. The ideal scenario is to replicate the entire production database, including tables, storage engine selection, indexes, views, triggers, and stored procedures.

Using the production schema with a small data set is a common error during testing. If your test database is too small, you might get an incorrect view of your true performance profile: The most inefficient database operation will blaze through a tiny set of information, even if the underlying database itself is poorly designed. In addition, the MySQL query optimizer might generate different plans for two identical databases if the number of rows is vastly different between them.

Fortunately, it's easy to make a full copy of a database. Use MySQL's `mysqldump` utility to export the data from the production instance to the test instance. Of course, if you're only concerned with a performance problem that affects a small subset of your production tables, it's probably safe to replicate only that portion of your database. However, it's still essential to duplicate the indexes, views, and so on.

Your Test Plan

Putting together a structured test plan takes time and discipline. You might feel that this work is a distraction from your performance-tuning tasks. However, if you invest the effort up front, you will realize significant benefits through the entire testing cycle. Your test plan will give you a clear sense of direction. If you have a multiperson testing team, a test plan is essential to bypassing the typical duplication of work and confusion that plague group performance analysis projects. This test plan will also form the nucleus of your report after you finish your analysis.

Test plans don't need to be masterpieces of design that take weeks to implement: You only need a road map that shows the steps you plan to take when conducting your experiments, along with any external assistance you might need.

For example, look at these entries from a sample test plan:

```
Test #:             203
Date:               5-October-2005
Start time:         11:14
Finish time:        11:19
Platform:           Production 2
Action:             Changed join syntax between 'customer' and 'problem' table
Special needs:      None
Test dependencies:  175, 182
Team members:       Bernard Bernbaum, Edward Dane
Test status:        Complete
Test results:       Query response improved 27%


Test #:             204
Date:               6-October-2005
Start time:         09:29
Finish time:        09:47
Platform:           Testing 1
Action:             Raised 'sort_buffer_size' by 25%; reran marketing's problem
                    'ORDER BY'
Special needs:      None
Test dependencies:  201
Team members:       Tom Reagan
Test status:        Complete
Test results:       No impact on problem query
```

```
Test #:              205
Date:                17-October-2005
Start time:          17:00
Finish time:         18:00
Platform:            Production 1
Action:              Create additional index on 'salesProbability' column; rerun
                     problem query
Special needs:       May impact reports
Test dependencies:   <None>
Team members:        Dale Levander, John Caspar
Test status:         <not yet started>
Test results:        <not completed>
```

You can store your test plan in a spreadsheet or within a MySQL database for widespread access.

Change One Variable at a Time

The fastest way to an ulcer is to attempt to make sense of your results after changing two, three, or even more performance-related variables at one time. Your testing experience will be much more successful and pleasant if you methodically change one variable at a time, run your test(s), record results, and then move on to the next candidate.

For example, suppose that you are faced with a transaction that takes too long to complete. You suspect a number of problems, including the following:

- Excessive indexing
- Incorrect database memory parameters
- An overloaded server
- Suboptimal SQL

In your eagerness to fix all of these problems at once, you make radical alterations in each of the preceding areas. You are happy to see a dramatic boost in responsiveness of your slow transaction. Your glee is short-lived, however: Your changes have damaged performance for other types of operations. You must now go back and undo your changes, and determine which ones heightened performance and which ones caused collateral damage. It would have been far better to make one change and then measure its impact before proceeding.

Organizational Support

By this time, it's fairly safe to say that you've invested a significant amount of effort obtaining and configuring hardware, installing the correct software and patches, ensuring connectivity, and building your test plan. The last hurdle is often the most difficult to overcome: gaining sufficient operational support for your performance-tuning efforts.

Management might be reluctant to grant you adequate time and resources. Users might be unwilling to help isolate a system performance problem, even though their daily lives are negatively impacted by these types of issues. The original designers and developers of the MySQL-based solution might assemble roadblocks, fearing the ramifications of your report on their careers. These obstacles might be magnified if the solution was provided by a third-party vendor.

Your performance testing and tuning mission will fail without ample support from all of these communities. Before beginning your work, you have the right to ask for assistance in each of these areas:

- **User cooperation**—You will always get a more realistic picture of a performance problem by witnessing it in action: Lab replication only goes so far. Sitting next to a user who is dealing with live response problems might save you days of labor. Bring a stopwatch, listen, and watch carefully. After you have implemented your performance solution(s), you should also observe the user to see if it really made an impact. Sometimes, the mere act of watching a user work convinces them that you have performed magic and solved their problem, when, in fact, all you have done is listen to them.

- **System load and processing profile**—If your production environment supports thousands of worldwide users running an application during office hours from Monday through Friday, performance testing on a quiet Saturday morning cannot possibly replicate the real-world conditions. If at all possible, try to either replicate the system load during your testing or gain access to the production system during live activity hours.

- **Production system access**—In the absence of a similarly configured, dedicated test bed, you might have no alternative but to run your research on the production system. If management is unenthusiastic about granting you access to these resources, point out the continued productivity drain caused by these performance problems. The sooner you conduct your experiments, the sooner you will be able to make the necessary corrections and move on.

- **Peer support**—Chances are you will need the cooperation from your fellow IT professionals. Alas, this support is often withheld from people tasked with resolving performance problems. This is especially true if you are an external consultant who was engaged specifically for this job. It's an unfortunate fact that a significant percentage of these types of projects degenerate into blame-shifting and political quagmires.

The only way for you to minimize these types of situations is to conduct yourself with a positive attitude and complete professionalism. Requirements often change from the time a system was designed to the current moment. Many times, these changes cause performance degradation that could not have been predicted. As the person tasked with fixing things, you are not trying to assign guilt or shame to anyone. Instead, you are simply trying to improve the working life of your customer: the user of the MySQL-based solution.

After Testing Is Under Way

Suppose that you are in the middle of your test plan when you realize that there is a completely different set of experiments that should be run. Should you walk away from your well-designed plan? Should you only add some new tests to the end of the plan and continue on the original path?

Creativity is greatly underestimated during performance testing and tuning; the best course is one of flexibility within certain constraints. Make careful note of your insights and ideas during this process—write them down as soon as they appear. There's no need to scrap all of the work you devoted to creating your test plan and performing your experiments. These new ideas can serve as a valuable addition to your well-designed plan.

For example, take a look at one of the tests from the preceding listing, along with the new test that it spawned:

```
Test #:            204
Date:              6-October-2005
Start time:        09:29
Finish time:       09:47
Platform:          Testing 1
Action:            Raised 'sort_buffer_size' by 25%; reran marketing's problem
'ORDER BY'
Special needs:     None
Test dependencies: 201
Team members:      Tom Reagan
Test status:       Complete
Test results:      No impact on problem query
```

Although this test did not improve the performance problem, during the course of your testing, you learned that the query sorted the result set by a column that had no index. This led to a new test:

```
Test #:            363
Date:              16-October-2005
Start time:        13:18
Finish time:       13:21
Platform:          Testing 1
Action:            Added index to 'secondary_region'column in 'marketing_
                   programs'table
Special needs:     None
Test dependencies: None
Team members:      Tom Reagan
Test status:       Complete
Test results:      Results came back in 11 seconds vs. 65 seconds. See test 204
```

Posttesting Implementation

By now, you probably have had enough of preparation and testing, and are ready to get started making things better. The following sections look at what to do next.

Recording Your Results

After the hard work of designing and conducting your tests, you should take the time to commit your results to paper. This is true even in the unfortunate and unlikely circumstance of complete failure. Why is this so important?

- **Future testing**—Even if you eliminated all performance problems, the odds are that you will someday need to decipher additional issues for new or altered systems. By documenting your efforts during this round, you can significantly reduce the amount of preparation for the next time you're faced with these kinds of challenges.

- **Essential feedback**—You asked your management, users, and peers for assistance before you began your research. It's important that you let them know what you learned—especially if you're still mystified by the performance problems. You don't need to write a 700-page novel to summarize your findings; a one- or two-page write-up will demonstrate your thoroughness and professionalism, as well as earn you good will for future testing. And if you don't summarize things and achieve closure, everyone will wonder what you actually did.

- **Helping new hires**—With turnover rates high, there's a good chance that you'll soon be called on to mentor new employees or contractors. Well-documented test plans and result reports will reduce the amount of time you need to spend educating your new peers.

Making Improvements

Many developers or analysts emerge from their testing with the confidence to make numerous performance-enhancing changes. However, in their eagerness to solve these problems, they often implement too many alterations at once, without allowing adequate time between the modifications. This can easily result in bugs, data integrity problems, and even degraded performance. Instead of rushing into potentially irreversible modifications, take the time to weigh the possible consequences of these amendments.

Generally, it's best to first implement the simplest corrections, such as engine parameter modifications. Should something go wrong, you can always switch back to the parameters' original values. If these first changes improve things, you can then move on to more complex changes, including those that affect SQL, application code, operating system, and database structure. Continue with your measured approach to alterations, and you will end up with a stable, better-performing solution.

## 2

Performance Monitoring Options

The preceding chapter discussed how essential it is to follow a well-defined, scientific process when analyzing your MySQL environment. Luckily, many automated tools, reports, and monitors are available that you can use to make your performance analysis and testing as productive and accurate as possible.

This chapter looks at two classes of performance monitoring utilities. The first section reviews MySQL's own utilities, logs, and reports; the second section surveys operating system–specific tools.

MySQL Tools and Utilities

In the past, administrators typically used character-based tools and utilities to examine their MySQL environment. This software is still available, but a new class of graphical technologies makes it even easier to gain insight into MySQL's performance profile. The next two sections examine these tools and utilities, from a character-based as well as a graphical viewpoint.

Character-Based Tools and Utilities

Over the years, MySQL AB has continually improved the number of character-based database tools and diagnostics found in the MySQL products. Many of these data can be used to help determine and correct performance anomalies. The following sections look at each command in more detail, beginning with the `mysqladmin` utility, followed by several flavors of the `SHOW` command that specifically report performance-related information.

mysqladmin

`Mysqladmin` provides a host of administrative and diagnostic functions for maintaining and tuning your MySQL database server. The following lists some of the commands that `mysqladmin` offers from a performance monitoring and management perspective:

extended-status	Show system status
flush-hosts	Flush all cached hosts
flush-logs	Flush all logs
flush-status	Clear status variables
flush-tables	Flush all tables
flush-threads	Flush the thread cache
flush-privileges	Reload grant tables (same as reload)
kill id,id,...	Kill mysql threads
processlist	Show list of active threads in server
refresh	Flush all tables and close and open logfiles
variables	Prints variables available

Specific use cases for these commands are cited throughout the book.

SHOW ENGINES

As you'll soon see, MySQL offers database developers and administrators a wide variety of storage engines. The situations in which each engine is appropriate are discussed as part of Chapter 4, "Designing for Speed," a detailed discussion on designing for speed. For now, to see the engines supported by MySQL's port for your operating system, run the SHOW ENGINES command:

```
mysql> SHOW ENGINES;
+------------+---------+---------------------------------------------------------+
| Engine     | Support | Comment                                                 |
+------------+---------+---------------------------------------------------------+
| MyISAM     | YES     | Default engine as of MySQL 3.23 with great performance  |
| HEAP       | YES     | Alias for MEMORY                                        |
| MEMORY     | YES     | Hash based, stored in memory, useful for temporary tables |
| MERGE      | YES     | Collection of identical MyISAM tables                  |
| MRG_MYISAM | YES     | Alias for MERGE                                        |
| ISAM       | NO      | Obsolete storage engine, now replaced by MyISAM        |
| MRG_ISAM   | NO      | Obsolete storage engine, now replaced by MERGE         |
| InnoDB     | DEFAULT | Supports transactions, row-level locking, and foreign keys|
| INNOBASE   | YES     | Alias for INNODB                                       |
| BDB        | YES     | Supports transactions and page-level locking          |
| BERKELEYDB | YES     | Alias for BDB                                          |
| NDBCLUSTER | NO      | Clustered, fault-tolerant, memory-based tables         |
| NDB        | NO      | Alias for NDBCLUSTER                                   |
| EXAMPLE    | NO      | Example storage engine                                |
| ARCHIVE    | NO      | Archive storage engine                                |
| CSV        | NO      | CSV storage engine                                    |
+------------+---------+---------------------------------------------------------+
```

In addition to this information, MySQL reports on your current default storage engine. This is the engine setting that all new tables will have unless explicitly specified otherwise when creating the table.

SHOW VARIABLES

MySQL is highly configurable: Administrators have dozens of settings to tinker with to affect a host of database behaviors, including performance. To see your current settings, run SHOW VARIABLES, as shown in Figure 2.1.

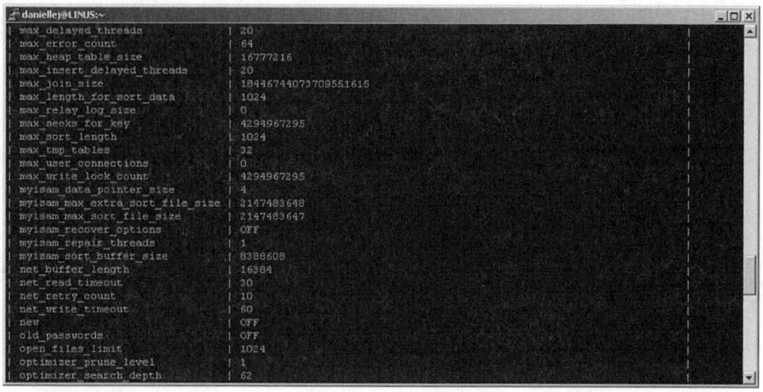

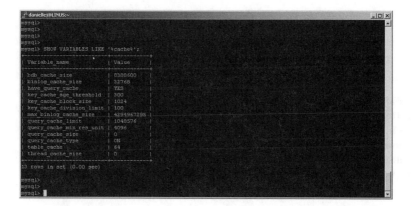

FIGURE 2.1   A selection of output from the SHOW VARIABLES command.

As you can see from this small subset, the amount of information can be overwhelming, especially if you're looking for a particular variable's value. You can narrow the scope of SHOW VARIABLES by including the LIKE option, as shown in Figure 2.2.

FIGURE 2.2   A more restrictive collection of SHOW VARIABLES output.

The differences between SESSION and GLOBAL variables are described a little later; in addition, many of these settings are discussed throughout the book.

SET/SELECT @@

The SHOW VARIABLES command doesn't tell the whole story: A number of system variables are viewed and set via SQL. Performance-affecting variables include the following:

- AUTOCOMMIT
- BIG_TABLES
- FOREIGN_KEY_CHECKS
- SQL_BIG_SELECTS
- SQL_BUFFER_RESULT
- SQL_LOG_BIN
- SQL_LOG_OFF
- SQL_LOG_UPDATE
- SQL_SELECT_LIMIT
- UNIQUE_CHECKS

How these variables affect performance is explored throughout the rest of the book.

SHOW STATUS

MySQL captures copious real-time statistics in addition to the dozens of database server-controlling variables that you just saw. To view these statistics, run the SHOW STATUS command:

```
mysql> SHOW STATUS;
+------------------------+----------+
| Variable_name          | Value    |
+------------------------+----------+
| Aborted_clients        | 2        |
| Aborted_connects       | 0        |
...
...
| Handler_read_first     | 2        |
| Handler_read_key       | 8        |
| Handler_read_next      | 8        |
| Handler_read_prev      | 0        |
| Handler_read_rnd       | 4        |
| Handler_read_rnd_next  | 30       |
...
...
| Qcache_free_blocks     | 0        |
| Qcache_free_memory     | 0        |
```

```
| Qcache_hits             | 0      |
| Qcache_inserts          | 0      |
| Qcache_lowmem_prunes    | 0      |
| Qcache_not_cached       | 0      |
| Qcache_queries_in_cache | 0      |
| Qcache_total_blocks     | 0      |
| Questions               | 104391 |
...
...
| Threads_created         | 3142   |
| Threads_running         | 175    |
| Uptime                  | 202083 |
+-------------------------+--------+
157 rows in set (0.00 sec)
```

You can also reduce the volume of this report with the LIKE option:

```
mysql> SHOW STATUS LIKE 'KEY%';
+-----------------------+--------+
| Variable_name         | Value  |
+-----------------------+--------+
| Key_blocks_not_flushed | 0     |
| Key_blocks_used       | 790    |
| Key_blocks_unused     | 6458   |
| Key_read_requests     | 283615 |
| Key_reads             | 791    |
| Key_write_requests    | 100177 |
| Key_writes            | 100177 |
+-----------------------+--------+
7 rows in set (0.00 sec)
```

SHOW PROCESSLIST

To retrieve a report of all active threads and user connections, along with the active database operation, run SHOW PROCESSLIST, as shown in Figure 2.3.

Armed with this information, you can elect to (carefully) kill a thread that is consuming too many system resources.

SHOW TABLES/SHOW TABLE STATUS

To get a simple list of the tables in your environment, just run SHOW TABLES:

```
mysql> SHOW TABLES;
+---------------------+------------+
| Tables_in_high_hat  | table_type |
+---------------------+------------+
| awards              | BASE TABLE |
```

```
| awards_pre_2000     | BASE TABLE |
| ...                 | ...        |
| ...                 | ...        |
| v_customer          | VIEW       |
| v_customer_europe   | VIEW       |
| ...                 | ...        |
| ...                 | ...        |
+---------------------+------------+
52 rows in set (0.00 sec)
```

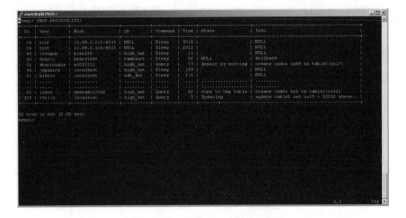

FIGURE 2.3   Output from the SHOW PROCESSLIST command.

However, adding STATUS to this command retrieves a much more comprehensive report. Append \G to make the report display vertically:

```
mysql> SHOW TABLE STATUS \G
*************************** 1. row ***************************
          Name: awards
        Engine: MyISAM
       Version: 9
    Row_format: Fixed
          Rows: 98483
Avg_row_length: 22
   Data_length: 2166626
Max_data_length: 94489280511
  Index_length: 808960
     Data_free: 0
Auto_increment: 98484
   Create_time: 2003-07-22 06:25:17
   Update_time: 2005-12-10 16:28:37
    Check_time: 2005-11-19 11:13:06
     Collation: latin1
      Checksum: NULL
```

```
   Create_options:
          Comment:
...
...
*************************** 7. row ***************************
            Name: lost_luggage
          Engine: InnoDB
         Version: 9
      Row_format: Fixed
            Rows: 46748
  Avg_row_length: 56
     Data_length: 2637824
 Max_data_length: NULL
    Index_length: 0
       Data_free: 0
  Auto_increment: 46364
     Create_time: NULL
     Update_time: NULL
      Check_time: NULL
       Collation: latin1
        Checksum: NULL
   Create_options:
          Comment: InnoDB free: 29696 kB
...
...
*************************** 10. row ***************************
            Name: v1
          Engine: NULL
         Version: NULL
      Row_format: NULL
            Rows: NULL
  Avg_row_length: NULL
     Data_length: NULL
 Max_data_length: NULL
    Index_length: NULL
       Data_free: NULL
  Auto_increment: NULL
     Create_time: NULL
     Update_time: NULL
      Check_time: NULL
       Collation: NULL
        Checksum: NULL
   Create_options: NULL
          Comment: view
```

SHOW INDEX

Chapter 6, "Understanding the MySQL Optimizer" and Chapter 7, "Indexing Strategies," conduct detailed explorations of the MySQL optimizer and indexing, respectively. For now, you can look at the results of the SHOW INDEX command for several tables, as shown in Figure 2.4.

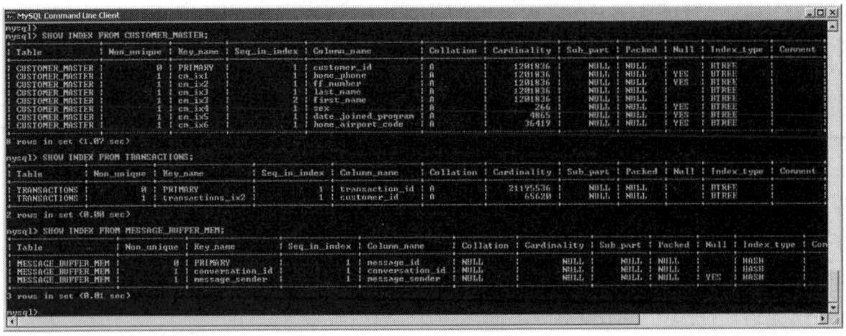

FIGURE 2.4   Output from the SHOW INDEX command for several tables.

As you'll see in a little while, these results are vitally important factors to help us determine the correct indexing strategy.

SHOW INNODB STATUS

The InnoDB storage engine adds great value to the MySQL product line. Transactional support and enhanced concurrency are just two of its powerful capabilities. InnoDB also provides extensive configuration alternatives and status reports. Running SHOW INNODB STATUS yields abundant information:

```
mysql> SHOW INNODB STATUS \G
*************************** 1. row ***************************
Status:
=====================================
051217 18:23:21 INNODB MONITOR OUTPUT
=====================================
Per second averages calculated from the last 6 seconds
----------
SEMAPHORES
----------
OS WAIT ARRAY INFO: reservation count 8296, signal count 8263
Mutex spin waits 18975, rounds 93704, OS waits 368
RW-shared spins 15507, OS waits 7344; RW-excl spins 463, OS waits 444
------------
TRANSACTIONS
------------
Trx id counter 0 3254792
```

```
Purge done for trx's n:o < 0 3250733 undo n:o < 0 0
Total number of lock structs in row lock hash table 947
LIST OF TRANSACTIONS FOR EACH SESSION:
---TRANSACTION 0 0, not started, process no 30901, OS thread id 1538513840
MySQL thread id 125, query id 124924 localhost daniellej
SHOW INNODB STATUS
---TRANSACTION 0 3254645, not started, process no 30901, OS thread id 1556286384
MySQL thread id 122, query id 124343 localhost jdpassos
---TRANSACTION 0 3250651, not started, process no 30901, OS thread id 1554172848
MySQL thread id 36, query id 104360 10.68.0.136 root
---TRANSACTION 0 0, not started, process no 30901, OS thread id 1538919344
...
...
MySQL thread id 34, query id 102148 10.68.0.136 root
---TRANSACTION 0 3254791, ACTIVE 1 sec, process no 30901, OS thread id 1547549616
1 lock struct(s), heap size 320, undo log entries 1
MySQL thread id 86, query id 124923 localhost fflukee
---TRANSACTION 0 3250519, ACTIVE 2145 sec, process no 30901, OS thread id 1556622256
948 lock struct(s), heap size 109888, undo log entries 560
MySQL thread id 123, query id 107797 localhost rschneider
--------
FILE I/O
--------
I/O thread 0 state: waiting for i/o request (insert buffer thread)
I/O thread 1 state: waiting for i/o request (log thread)
I/O thread 2 state: waiting for i/o request (read thread)
I/O thread 3 state: waiting for i/o request (write thread)
Pending normal aio reads: 0, aio writes: 0,
 ibuf aio reads: 0, log i/o's: 0, sync i/o's: 0
Pending flushes (fsync) log: 0; buffer pool: 0
3949 OS file reads, 9852 OS file writes, 7675 OS fsyncs
0.00 reads/s, 0 avg bytes/read, 4.17 writes/s, 3.33 fsyncs/s
-------------------------------------
INSERT BUFFER AND ADAPTIVE HASH INDEX
-------------------------------------
Ibuf for space 0: size 1, free list len 0, seg size 2, is empty
Ibuf for space 0: size 1, free list len 0, seg size 2,
0 inserts, 0 merged recs, 0 merges
Hash table size 34679, used cells 13138, node heap has 17 buffer(s)
1.83 hash searches/s, 0.00 non-hash searches/s
---
LOG
---
Log sequence number 0 276377354
Log flushed up to   0 276377304
Last checkpoint at  0 276377039
```

```
0 pending log writes, 0 pending chkp writes
6744 log i/o's done, 3.00 log i/o's/second
----------------------
BUFFER POOL AND MEMORY
----------------------
Total memory allocated 13459410; in additional pool allocated 356480
Buffer pool size    512
Free buffers        0
Database pages      489
Modified db pages   4
Pending reads 0
Pending writes: LRU 0, flush list 0, single page 0
Pages read 31241, created 2033, written 26128
0.00 reads/s, 0.00 creates/s, 1.00 writes/s
Buffer pool hit rate 1000 / 1000
--------------
ROW OPERATIONS
--------------
0 queries inside InnoDB, 0 queries in queue
Main thread process no. 30901, id 1529514928, state: sleeping
Number of rows inserted 88877, updated 727017, deleted 0, read 1747870
1.83 inserts/s, 0.00 updates/s, 0.00 deletes/s, 0.00 reads/s
--------------------------
END OF INNODB MONITOR OUTPUT
============================
```

Chapter 12, "InnoDB Parameters and Tuning," which provides guidance on tuning the InnoDB engine, illustrates how to interpret these results.

Graphical Tools

With the release of the MySQL Administrator and MySQL Query Browser, MySQL has come a long way toward matching the graphical tools offered by other major database platforms. The following sections explore each of these tools in more detail.

MySQL Administrator

This tool has many database management and monitoring capabilities. Database administrators can use the MySQL Administrator for a broad range of tasks, from setting server parameters and monitoring activity to backing up data, viewing logs, and examining performance. Its graphs and reports are also highly customizable and configurable; this capability is often overlooked by administrators who are just starting out with the tool.

The remainder of this book continually refers to MySQL Administrator. For now, the following figures show a few selected performance-monitoring-specific examples of its output.

Figure 2.5 examines the hit rates for the query and index cache.

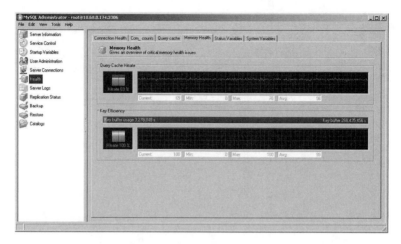

FIGURE 2.5   Query cache and key buffer diagnostics from MySQL
Administrator.

Figure 2.6 examines the actions of a particular database user. You have the option of looking at all threads for all users, or reviewing only the threads for one particular user.

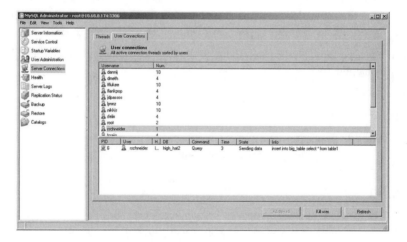

FIGURE 2.6   User-specific output from MySQL Administrator.

Finally, Figure 2.7 reviews server status variables to get a better idea of the load on our system.

You have dozens of available ways to use the MySQL Administrator to understand and tune your system. These concepts are all reviewed in more detail later in this book.

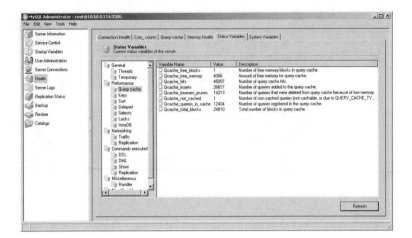

FIGURE 2.7   Server status variables as reported by MySQL Administrator.

MySQL Query Browser

Prior to the availability of this graphical tool, your options to view a query's results were limited to the character-based mysql utility, or a third-party graphical tool such as Microsoft Access or one of many independent database query tools. This has changed; you can now use the MySQL Query Browser to perform a wide variety of database operations.

From a tuning perspective, the tool's ability to display query plans and result sets side by side is very helpful.

Figure 2.8 looks at a relatively simple query plan.

Figure 2.9 reviews the results of another query.

Finally, Figure 2.10 splits the query screen and has rerun the query with more restrictive criteria. The split screen lets us compare the results.

Logging

MySQL offers numerous logging options to help developers and administrators investigate performance and other problems. This section takes a look at how you can use these logging settings to get more information about your environment. This section looks at both character output and graphic output from the MySQL Administrator.

FIGURE 2.8 A query plan as reported by the MySQL Query Browser.

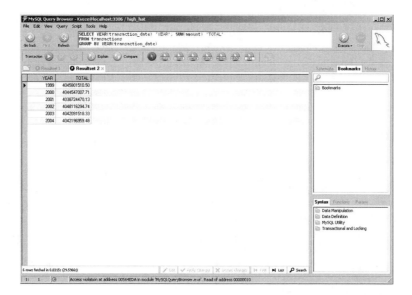

FIGURE 2.9 Results from a query as reported by the MySQL Query Browser.

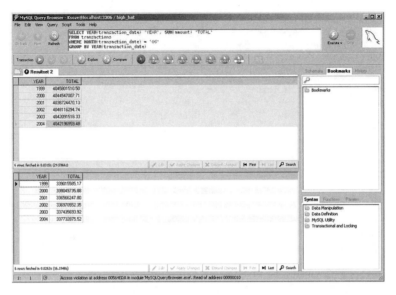

FIGURE 2.10   Comparing the results from two different queries within the
MySQL Query Browser.

General Query Log

The general query log tracks information about all queries that have been submitted to the
MySQL server. Start mysqld with the –1 option, or set the system variable log to ON. You
can also specify a filename to track the output. The following is an example of one minute's
worth of data:

```
051018 14:39:00
        4 Init DB     high_hat
        4 Query       SELECT * FROM table3 WHERE col1 BETWEEN 296561 AND 296584
       12 Init DB     high_hat
       12 Query       SELECT * FROM table3 WHERE col1 BETWEEN 192416 AND 192449
        1 Init DB     high_hat
        1 Query       SELECT * FROM table3 WHERE col1 BETWEEN 208225 AND 208251
        2 Init DB     high_hat
        2 Query       SELECT * FROM table3 WHERE col1 BETWEEN 41257 AND 41271
       12 Init DB     high_hat
       12 Query       SELECT * FROM table3 WHERE col1 BETWEEN 354771 AND 354793
       24 Query       COMMIT
       28 Init DB     high_hat
       28 Query       BEGIN
       28 Query       INSERT INTO table5 (col3) values (852031872)
        2 Init DB     high_hat
        2 Query       SELECT * FROM table3 WHERE col1 BETWEEN 383676 AND 383687
       10 Init DB     high_hat
```

```
    10 Query       SELECT * FROM table3 WHERE col1 BETWEEN 17865 AND 17879
     9 Query       SHOW STATUS
     9 Query       SHOW INNODB STATUS
     4 Init DB     high_hat
     4 Query       SELECT * FROM table3 WHERE col1 BETWEEN 50275 AND 50287
    14 Init DB     high_hat
    14 Query       SELECT * FROM table3 WHERE col1 BETWEEN 244074 AND 244107
  1419 Query       BEGIN
  1419 Query       DELETE FROM TABLE4 WHERE COL1 =  397967
  1419 Query       COMMIT
```

As you can see, this file has the potential to become very large. However, you have control over its size.

First, you can disable logging for a particular client simply by setting the SQL_LOG_OFF setting for that session to 1. This is particularly useful if you don't suspect a particular client (or set of clients) of causing a performance bottleneck; there's no need to intermingle their activity with that of potential problem clients.

You can also create a log rotation plan or just flush the contents periodically via the FLUSH LOGS command. The latter gives you the option of simply overlaying the existing log, or incrementing the name by one and creating a new log.

Slow Query Log

This log file captures information about queries that take longer than a predefined number of seconds to complete. MySQL tracks this information if you launch mysqld with --log-slow-queries or set the system variable log_slow_queries to the filename where you want the information stored.

You can define the threshold via the long_query_time system variable, which can be set at both the GLOBAL and SESSION levels. The information found in the slow query log is a great start toward finding and fixing performance problems, in many cases before users even notice the issues. The following is some sample output from the slow query log:

```
/usr/local/mysql/bin/mysqld, Version: 5.0.1-alpha-max-log. started with:
Tcp port: 3306  Unix socket: /var/lib/mysql/mysql.sock
Time                Id Command    Argument
# Time: 051211 14:21:07
# User@Host: [gperez] @ tty-3392 []
# Query_time: 4  Lock_time: 0  Rows_sent: 0  Rows_examined: 18701182
use high_hat;
insert into report_gperez select * from flights where flight_code like '%aa%';
# Time: 041211 15:19:55
# User@Host: [rfelix] @ bellmr11710 []
# Query_time: 3  Lock_time: 0  Rows_sent: 0  Rows_examined: 0
use high_hat;
ROLLBACK;
```

```
# Time: 041211 15:21:51
# User@Host: [fsanford] @ crensha291 []
# Query_time: 312  Lock_time: 0  Rows_sent: 0  Rows_examined: 8609600
insert into daily_rept_fsanford select * from awards;
```

Binary Log

The binary log, which replaces the earlier update log, serves many purposes. These include assisting in restoration, replication, as well providing a record of all changes that were made to the database. To enable the binary log, start mysqld with --log-bin, or set the GLOBAL variable log_bin to the filename where you want the information stored. The following shows some sample information from this log file, courtesy of the mysqlbinlog utility:

```
...
...
high_hat
BEGIN
high_hat
INSERT INTO table5 (col3) values (1887016705)
high_hat
COMMIT
high_hat
UPDATE table5 SET col2 = 21818 WHERE col1 = 1475
high_hat_dev
BEGIN
high_hat_dev
INSERT INTO table5 (col3) values (282253923)
high_hat
COMMIT
...
...
```

Error Log

The error log keeps a record of major events such as server start/stop, as well as any serious errors:

```
Version: '5.0.1-alpha-max-log'  socket: '/var/lib/mysql/mysql.sock'  port: 3306
051216 06:29:36  mysqld started
051216  6:29:36  Warning: Changed limits: max_open_files: 1024
max_connections: 250  table_cache: 382
051216  6:29:36  InnoDB: Database was not shut down normally!
InnoDB: Starting crash recovery.
InnoDB: Reading tablespace information from the .ibd files...
InnoDB: Restoring possible half-written data pages from the doublewrite
InnoDB: buffer...
051216  6:29:36  InnoDB: Starting log scan based on checkpoint at
InnoDB: log sequence number 0 3204554816.
```

```
InnoDB: Doing recovery: scanned up to log sequence number 0 3204554816
InnoDB: Last MySQL binlog file position 0 95, file name ./HAL9000-bin.000025
051216  6:29:36  InnoDB: Flushing modified pages from the buffer pool...
051216  6:29:36  InnoDB: Started; log sequence number 0 3204554816
051216  6:29:37  Warning: Can't open time zone table:
Table 'mysql.time_zone_leap_second' doesn't exist trying to live without them
/usr/local/mysql/bin/mysqld: ready for connections.
```

Operating System Tools

No MySQL instance exists in isolation; there are always potential interactions with the operating system. Consequently, it behooves database administrators to understand the obtainable performance monitoring tools for their operating system–specific environment. The following sections briefly look at the major choices available for the Windows and Linux/Unix operating systems.

Windows

Most modern versions of Microsoft Windows, including server- and client-based platforms, now sport very advanced graphical monitoring tools. These include the Windows Task Manager, which provides detailed data about the current activity level on a system, as well as the much more sophisticated performance monitoring capabilities of the Microsoft Management Console (MMC).

Figure 2.11 shows an example of the Performance tab of the Windows Task Manager.

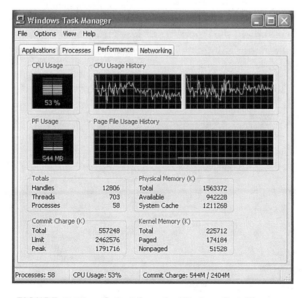

FIGURE 2.11   Output from the Windows Task Manager.

Other tabs describe the current state of the network, all processes, and any running applications.

For much more robust reporting, including the ability to save information for further analysis, the MMC Performance Monitor is essential (shown in Figure 2.12).

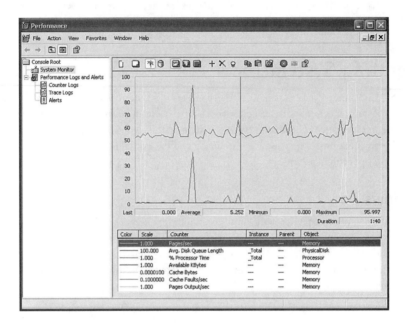

FIGURE 2.12   Output from the MMC Performance Monitor.

This example has customized the report to provide details about the current CPU activity, along with memory and disk utilization. This represents a minute fraction of the hundreds of possible statistics that you can track.

Chapter 14, "Operating System, Web Server and Connectivity Tuning," which provides details on operating system, Web, and connectivity tuning, discusses specific examples of how these tools can help us research, isolate, and correct performance bottlenecks.

Linux/Unix

Traditionally, Linux and Unix platforms have been less graphically rich than their Windows-based cousins. This is changing: Increasing numbers of both open source and commercial utilities provide detailed yet easily understood performance and status reporting.

Red Hat Linux offers a basic performance monitor, as shown in Figure 2.13.

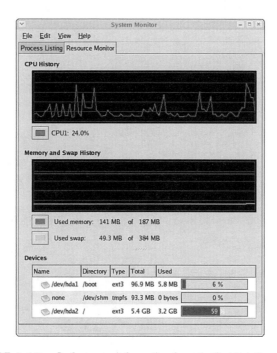

FIGURE 2.13   Performance information from the Red Hat Linux System Monitor.

For more sophisticated performance monitoring, IBM has done a nice job with its server-based `rmfpms` data gatherer and Windows or Linux-based `rmf pm` client (both available for download from IBM), as shown in Figure 2.14.

This utility is highly configurable. For example, you can track some metrics for the Apache HTTP server, as shown in Figure 2.15.

The following section briefly examines some of the character-based utilities that you can exploit to receive performance information about your system. The most commonly used utilities are covered briefly, and are covered in more detail later in Chapter 14.

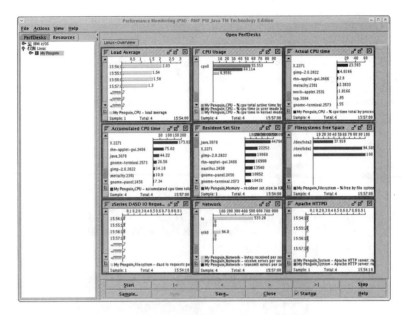

FIGURE 2.14   Output from the Performance Monitoring (rmfpms) utility from IBM.

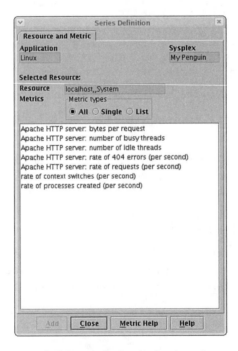

FIGURE 2.15   Defining metrics for the Apache web server within the Performance Monitoring utility.

Activity-Reporting Utilities

The ps and top utilities, provided by the Linux and Unix operating systems, return information, in static and dynamic format respectively, about current process activity on your system. You can pass numerous switches to these utilities to customize your monitoring. The following shows two examples:

```
[clafong@WEBSERVER1 clafong]$ ps eaxf
  PID TTY      STAT   TIME COMMAND
    1 ?        S      0:04 init [5]
    2 ?        SW     0:00 [migration/0]
...
    9 ?        SWN    0:00 [ksoftirqd/3]
   10 ?        SW<    0:00 [events/0]
   11 ?        SW<    0:00 [events/1]
 6407 ?        SW     0:01  \_ [pdflush]
...
 2549 ?        S      0:00 /usr/sbin/sshd
15321 ?        S      0:00  \_ sshd: weisenhard [priv]
15323 ?        S      0:00  |   \_ sshd: weisenhard@pts/24
15324 pts/24   S      0:00  |       \_ -bash USER=rarons LOGNAME=rarons
15410 pts/24   S      0:00  |           \_ su
15411 pts/24   S      0:00  |               \_ bash
15431 pts/24   S      0:00  |                   \_ su daniellej
15432 pts/24   S      0:00  |                       \_ bash
15450 pts/24   S      0:03  |                           \_ php cust_lookup.php
...
 6504 ?        S      0:00 /bin/sh /usr/bin/mysqld_safe
 6527 ?        S      0:00  \_ /usr/local/mysql/bin/mysqld
--basedir=/usr/local/mysql -data

[clafong@WEBSERVER1 clafong]$ top
top - 23:30:11 up 3 days,  8:04,  2 users,  load average: 4.40, 3.97, 2.33
Tasks:  96 total,   1 running,  95 sleeping,   0 stopped,   0 zombie
Cpu(s): 42.9% us, 29.7% sy,  0.0% ni, 25.4% id,  2.0% wa,  0.0% hi,  0.0% si
Mem:   2074924k total,  2064436k used,    10488k free,   209500k buffers
Swap:  2040244k total,        0k used,  2040244k free,  1453200k cached

  PID USER      PR  NI  VIRT  RES  SHR S %CPU %MEM    TIME+  COMMAND
15456 danielle  15   0 21540 7876  16m S 59.1  0.4  6:29.60 php
15459 danielle  16   0 20196 7780  16m S 58.7  0.4  6:20.78 php
15462 danielle  16   0 27060  14m  16m S 53.2  0.7  6:17.57 php
15450 danielle  16   0 19384 6328  16m S  1.7  0.3  0:09.34 php
15458 danielle  16   0 19924 6252  16m S  0.1  0.3  0:01.09 php
15464 danielle  16   0 19000 6252  16m S  0.1  0.3  0:01.06 php
 6527 mysql     16   0  384m 234m 7460 S  0.1 11.6  0:00.87 mysqld
15323 rschneid  15   0  8648 2296 6856 S  0.1  0.1  0:00.31 sshd
```

```
15457 danielle  16    0 18692 6204  16m S  0.1  0.3   0:00.63 php
15461 danielle  16    0 19724 6320  16m S  0.1  0.3   0:01.16 php
 3433 root      15    0 93332 8196  84m S  0.0  0.4   3:42.95 X
15460 danielle  16    0 19380 6284  16m S  0.0  0.3   0:00.65 php
```

The mpstat utility provides helpful information about processor activity, with special value for multi-CPU machines:

```
[clafong@WEBSERVER1 clafong]$ mpstat
Linux 2.6.5-1.358smp (WEBSERVER1)    2/18/2006

11:36:56 PM  CPU   %user  %nice %system %iowait   %irq   %soft   %idle   intr/s
11:36:56 PM  all    2.38   8.03    0.60    0.86   0.01    0.01   88.11  1019.03
```

The highly configurable sar utility helps track, over time, a number of critical performance details about your system:

```
[clafong@WEBSERVER1 clafong]$ sar

12:00:00 AM    CPU    %user    %nice   %system   %iowait    %idle
...
...
11:10:00 PM    all     0.05     0.00      0.01      0.00    99.94
11:20:01 PM    all     2.68    16.01      2.01      0.60    78.69
11:30:00 PM    all    44.30     0.00     31.64      2.42    21.64
11:40:00 PM    all    43.98     0.00     31.34      1.14    23.54
```

Finally, you should note the contents of the /proc directory, which are an enormous, virtual collection of information about the current state of your system, including kernel configuration, processor activity, memory utilization, network operations, and so on. The following is just one small sample:

```
[jbishop@WEBSERVER1 jbishop]$ cat /proc/stat
cpu   2988575 9278095 871824 101906758 994740 8505 15503
cpu0 336920 2325449 185697 25921556 246029 76 296
cpu1 181478 2308893 137074 26154657 221931 4299 7658
cpu2 1895367 2333828 376550 24146295 252279 4129 7541
cpu3 574808 2309924 172502 25684249 274499 0 7
intr 295688116 290125508 12 0 3 3 0 4 0 1 0 0 0 117 0 492 5197266
...
ctxt 38515831
btime 1103153119
processes 16169
procs_running 4
procs_blocked 0
```

Memory-Reporting Utilities

The free utility delivers a status update on the current state of physical memory and caching:

```
[clafong@WEBSERVER1 clafong]$ free
              total       used       free     shared    buffers     cached
Mem:        2074924    2060688      14236          0     153436    1502764
-/+ buffers/cache:      404488    1670436
Swap:       2040244          0    2040244
```

The vmstat utility describes the current state of virtual memory:

```
[clafong@WEBSERVER1 clafong]$ vmstat
procs -----------memory---------- ---swap-- -----io---- --system-- ----cpu----
 r  b   swpd   free   buff  cache   si   so    bi    bo   in    cs us sy id wa
 3  0      0  23756 163668 1492272   0    0    10    23   32    31 10  1 88  1
```

You'll spend significant time later in the book analyzing how MySQL itself uses memory to boost performance, along with the interplay between MySQL's memory usage and that of the operating system.

Network-Reporting Utilities

System and network administrators make great use of netstat, which provides a tremendous variety of insight into all aspects of your system's networking profile:

```
Active Internet connections (w/o servers)
Proto Recv-Q Send-Q Local Address          Foreign Address         State
tcp        0      0 ::ffff:20.69.21.174:ssh ::ffff:20.69.21.115:4823 ESTABLISHED
tcp        0      0 ::ffff:20.69.21.174:ssh ::ffff:20.69.21.115:4824 ESTABLISHED
Active UNIX domain sockets (w/o servers)
Proto RefCnt Flags       Type       State         I-Node Path
unix  13     [ ]         DGRAM                    3594   /dev/log
unix  2      [ ]         DGRAM                    1180   @udevd
unix  4      [ ]         STREAM     CONNECTING    0      /var/lib/mysql/mysql.sock
unix  3      [ ]         STREAM     CONNECTED     150634
...
...
unix  2      [ ]         DGRAM                    3813
unix  2      [ ]         DGRAM                    3656
unix  2      [ ]         DGRAM                    3604
unix  2      [ ]         DGRAM                    1163
```

Disk-Reporting Utilities

The iostat utility helps administrators gain a truer picture of what is happening with their file systems and other storage devices:

```
[sbooth@SNA-R379 sbooth]$ iostat
Linux 2.6.5-1.358smp (SNA-R379)     11/12/2005

avg-cpu:  %user   %nice   %sys %iowait   %idle
           2.45    8.02   0.68    0.86   87.99

Device:            tps   Blk_read/s   Blk_wrtn/s   Blk_read   Blk_wrtn
sda               0.00         0.02         0.00       4662        768
sdb              17.92        79.32       477.19   22947706  138060952
```

## 3

MySQL Overview and New Performance-Related Features

With an ever-growing market share and a continual stream of new software and functionality, MySQL AB's products have made a dramatic impact on the technology industry. New versions, features, and functions are arriving at an increasing pace, but database designers, developers, and administrators might feel overwhelmed by the sheer number of products, along with how frequently they're updated.

Although the primary purpose of this book is to help you coax the most performance out of your MySQL installation, you should first get the lay of the land of MySQL's entire product suite. To help make things clear, each of the major products can be classified into a small group of categories. In addition, this chapter describes how they are covered within this book, and also mentions some helpful performance-related tools that now ship with the products.

After reviewing the product line, this chapter briefly calls out the versions that are covered in this book, along with some of the platforms that we tested when making our recommendations.

Finally, this chapter lists all of MySQL's major performance enhancements beginning with version 4.0. This list might help you determine when it's time to upgrade (if you're an existing user) or which version to choose (if you're new to MySQL).

MySQL Products

To help make the most sense of MySQL AB's broad, rapidly growing product suite, these products are classified into the following categories:

- MySQL Core Technologies
- Database Storage Engines and Table Types
- Distributed Computing Technologies

- Graphical Tools and Assistants
- Connectors
- APIs
- Utilities

Each of these categories are explained in the following sections. In addition to these products, MySQL's website features hundreds of partner solutions (commercial, shareware, and freeware) that add value throughout the database design, development, deployment, and management cycles; there are also many applications built using MySQL technology.

MySQL Core Technologies

As the foundation of the entire product line, these technologies span a wide range of functionality, from MySQL's implementation of SQL to its query optimizer to memory management and communication. This book continually points out ways to improve these components' performance. Specifically, chapters are dedicated to making the most of your SQL statements, MySQL's query optimizer, general database server engine settings, and other core technology-related features.

Database Storage Engines and Table Types

Responsible for accumulating and retrieving information, the database storage engine lies at the heart of your MySQL installation. When it comes to picking a specialized storage engine or table type, MySQL offers database designers and administrators a surfeit of choices. This book spends considerable time discussing the following:

- **MyISAM**—Fast, compressible, and FULLTEXT-searchable, this is the default MySQL engine.
- **InnoDB**—Robust, transaction-ready, with strong referential integrity, this storage engine is often used to support complex, high-volume applications, in which transactional guarantees are essential.
- **MERGE**—By creating a single view of multiple identical MyISAM tables, this storage engine is essential to feed reporting or Decision Support System (DSS)/Online Analytical Processing (OLAP) tools.
- **MEMORY**—Previously known as HEAP, its tables are memory-based, extremely fast and easy to configure, letting developers leverage the benefits of in-memory processing via a standard SQL interface.
- **ARCHIVE**—As its name indicates, this storage engine is aimed at applications with very large volumes of infrequently-or-never updated information. Its tables are parsimonious in their consumption of disk resources.
- **CSV**—By creating comma-separated files (.csv), this storage engine makes it very easy for developers to feed other applications that consume these kinds of files with MySQL-based data.

- **FEDERATED**—Define and access remote tables as if they were hosted locally.

- **NDB Cluster**—As the underlying storage engine technology of MySQL Cluster, NDB Cluster makes it possible for multiple computers to keep their in-memory data in sync, leading to dramatic scalability and performance improvements.

Of the preceding list, the MyISAM and InnoDB storage engines see the most usage, which is one reason why this book has chapters dedicated to each of them, along with a chapter exploring MySQL Cluster (Chapter 17, "Clustering and Performance").

MySQL offers several additional storage engines that are not covered in this book. These include the following:

- `ISAM`—Although this is the original MySQL storage engine, the MyISAM engine has superseded this product; in fact, it will no longer be distributed from version 5.0. Nevertheless, many of the suggestions for improving MyISAM response might also apply for legacy ISAM tables.

- **Berkeley Database (BDB)**—This was the first MySQL storage engine to offer transactional support, among many other advanced features. However, the InnoDB storage engine has garnered, by far, the higher market share for this kind of storage engine, so this book primarily focuses on InnoDB.

- `EXAMPLE`—This is not a storage engine per se; instead, it can best be thought of as a template that shows MySQL's worldwide development community how to write a storage engine.

- **MaxDB**—This is not a storage engine, but a separate product, originally developed by Adabas, and then overseen by SAP. It's used by thousands of SAP customers today. Given the different lineages of the main MySQL product line and MaxDB, it is not covered in this book. However, many of the general-purpose recommendations (for example, designing for speed, indexing, and overhead reduction) made in this book are also applicable to MaxDB.

Distributed Computing Technologies

Replication and MySQL Cluster are the two foremost MySQL distributed computing technologies. Replication refers to the act of keeping multiple "slave" computers in sync with a "master" server. Because this is such a simple yet powerful way to increase throughput, Chapter 16, "Optimal Replication," is dedicated to replication best practices.

MySQL Cluster leverages multiple computers into a single team; this yields impressive performance and reliability gains, and is only limited by the amount of hardware you have at your disposal. This topic also merits its own chapter. Chapter 17 explores scenarios in which clustering makes good performance sense.

Graphical Tools and Assistants

From the beginning, MySQL products have typically been configured, monitored, and managed from the command line. However, several MySQL offerings now provide an easy-to-use, graphical interface:

- **MySQL Administrator**—Makes it possible for administrators to set up, evaluate, and tune their MySQL database server. This is intended as a replacement for `mysqladmin`.

- **MySQL Query Browser**—Provides database developers and others with a graphical database operation interface. It is especially useful for seeing multiple query plans and result sets in a single user interface.

- **Configuration Wizard**—Makes it easy for administrators to pick and choose from a predefined list of optimal settings, or create their own.

- **MySQL System Tray**—Provides Windows-based administrators a single view of their MySQL instance, including the ability to start and stop their database servers. It is similar to tools offered by other database vendors.

These important capabilities are referred to throughout the book. The Configuration Wizard is examined later in this chapter.

Connectors

Connectors provide database application developers and third-party tools with packaged libraries of standards-based functions to access MySQL. These libraries range from Open Database Connectivity (ODBC) technology through Java and .NET-aware components.

By using the ODBC connector to MySQL, any ODBC-aware client application (for example, Microsoft Office, report writers, Visual Basic) can connect to MySQL without knowing the vagaries of any MySQL-specific keyword restrictions, access syntax, and so on; it's the connector's job to abstract this complexity into an easily used, standardized interface.

Chapter 9, "Developing High Speed Applications," coverage of optimizing application logic discusses how to streamline ODBC access to MySQL.

APIs

MySQL AB and several third parties provide application programming interface (API) libraries to let developers write client applications in a wide variety of programming languages, including the following:

- C (provided automatically with MySQL)
- C++
- Eiffel
- .NET

- Perl
- PHP
- Python
- Ruby
- Tcl

Currently, C, PHP, and Perl represent the most widely used APIs from the preceding list, with ODBC connector-using client application development tools also seeing extensive usage. Although this book is not meant to be a detailed programming guide for any particular language, it does discuss the interplay between your chosen API and MySQL performance in Chapter 9.

Utilities

MySQL's primarily character-based utilities cover a broad range of database management tasks, including the following:

- Exporting information (`mysqldump`)
- Importing information (`mysqlimport`)
- Entering SQL statements, either interactively or via script (`mysql`)
- Checking MyISAM table integrity (`myisamchk`)
- Working with the binary log (`mysqlbinlog`)
- Compressing MyISAM tables (`myisampack`)

Where applicable, this book points out how to use these tools to boost performance. For example, the `mysqldump` utility is covered in great detail in Chapter 15, "Improving Import and Export Operations."

Performance-Related Tools

MySQL ships a number of tools that can help database administrators configure, test, and tune their MySQL installations. Some of these tools are aimed at people interested in source code, whereas others are aimed at a broader audience. Each of these tools are briefly examined in the following sections.

Benchmark Suite

MySQL's benchmark suite, available for download from their website, is a useful set of automated tests to help determine overall system performance for a broad collection of common database-oriented tasks. For example, the following is a snippet of Perl code that tests inserting new rows into a table:

```
...
...
for ($i=0 ; $i < $opt_row_count ; $i++)
{
  $query="insert into bench values ( " . ("$i," x ($opt_start_field_count-1)) .
  "$i)";
  $dbh->do($query) or die $DBI::errstr;
}

if ($opt_fast && $server->{transactions})
{
  $dbh->commit;
  $dbh->{AutoCommit} = 1;
}

$end_time=new Benchmark;

print "Time for insert ($opt_row_count)",
  timestr(timediff($end_time, $loop_time),"all") . "\n\n";
...
...
```

Although these tests don't help you determine the optimal database schema design, query construction, or application logic practices, they are useful for testing the before-and-after impact of changes to your MySQL server configuration settings. Just be certain that you take overall system load into consideration when evaluating the results.

BENCHMARK() Function

The built-in BENCHMARK() function is useful for running raw timing tests on various computational functions within MySQL. The results of these tests can help you:

- Compare MySQL's processing capabilities for disparate operations.
- Compare the same operations on different hardware/OS platforms.

For example, you can compare how long it takes MySQL to calculate the MD5 128 bit checksum for a randomly generated number on a modern, multiprocessor Linux machine versus a five-year-old, single-CPU desktop computer. This actually tests two MySQL functions: MD5() and RAND().

You could perform this test by hand, time the results, and write them down on paper:

```
...
mysql> SELECT MD5(RAND());
+--------------------------------+
| MD5(RAND())                    |
+--------------------------------+
```

```
| 165d139c2e6b40a5e476ecbba1981cc3 |
+----------------------------------+
1 row in set (0.00 sec)

mysql> SELECT MD5(RAND());
+----------------------------------+
| MD5(RAND())                      |
+----------------------------------+
| 0774e12a284887041f60223e134d01a1 |
+----------------------------------+
1 row in set (0.00 sec)
...
```

This might get a little tedious after a while, so it's best to use the BENCHMARK() function. To make the numbers significant, you can have MySQL perform the operation 500,000 times:

New, expensive Linux server:

```
mysql> SELECT BENCHMARK(500000,MD5(rand()));
+------------------------------+
| BENCHMARK(500000,MD5(rand())) |
+------------------------------+
|                            0 |
+------------------------------+
1 row in set (2.18 sec)
```

History museum-ready desktop:

```
mysql> SELECT BENCHMARK(500000,MD5(rand()));
+------------------------------+
| BENCHMARK(500000,MD5(rand())) |
+------------------------------+
|                            0 |
+------------------------------+
1 row in set (33.27 sec)
```

Notice the difference in how long it took to return the results: This is the number you should watch.

You can use this function to test the amount of time necessary to complete any expression. Note that BENCHMARK(), although valuable, does not tell you whether a particular query is efficient. For that kind of task, use the EXPLAIN statement, which is reviewed in great detail during Chapter 6, "Understanding the MySQL Optimizer," study of the MySQL query optimizer.

Configuration Wizard

Recent versions of MySQL now offer an optional Configuration Wizard, typically launched upon installation. This section takes a look at the sequence of steps followed by this wizard, along with how these topics are addressed throughout the book.

Note that this wizard is quite dynamic, so your experience might be different from the one presented here (see Figure 3.1).

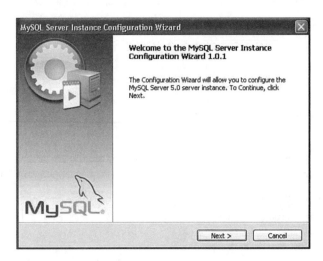

FIGURE 3.1   The launch screen for the MySQL Configuration Wizard.

Your first decision is to choose either a boilerplate ("standard") or customized ("detailed") installation process. Don't underestimate the value of the boilerplate configuration; it has been well thought out, and represents a good catch-all setup (see Figure 3.2).

FIGURE 3.2   Choose between a customized or general-purpose configuration.

If you choose the customized path, the first decision you must make is to select the type of database server that you are configuring as shown in Figure 3.3.

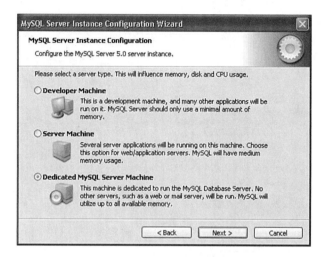

FIGURE 3.3   Choose one of three possible server configurations.

There are marked differences in memory caching and other key server settings depending on the server's role. These distinctions are continually cited throughout the book.

After you've chosen a server type, you must then categorize your typical processing profile (see Figure 3.4).

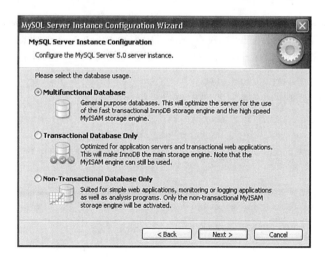

FIGURE 3.4   Pick the dominant processing profile for this server.

This is an important decision because the workloads experienced by transactional and decision support database servers are quite different, meaning that their respective configurations need to reflect this diversity.

This book keeps this diversity in mind throughout, and makes recommendations accordingly.

The wizard next provides a choice on how to configure the initial InnoDB tablespace (see Figure 3.5).

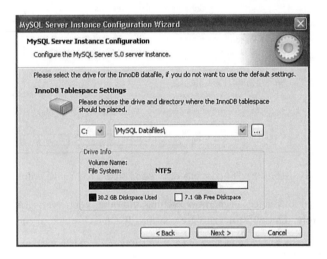

FIGURE 3.5   Initial InnoDB configuration.

Enhancing InnoDB performance is explored in Chapter 12, "InnoDB Parameters and Tuning"; disk-specific considerations are covered as part of Chapter 13, "Improving Disk Speed," general-purpose data storage review.

Configuring the correct number of concurrent sessions, network protocols, and character sets are your next assessments, as shown in Figures 3.6, 3.7, and 3.8.

The impact of connectivity and network settings on performance are examined as part of several chapters, including those on general engine tuning, optimal application development, and network configuration. However, character set issues are not part of the subject matter in this book.

The wizard then gives us a choice on how the database server will be started, as well as security alternatives (see Figures 3.9 and 3.10).

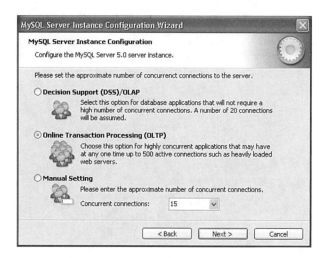

FIGURE 3.6   Specifying the number of server connections.

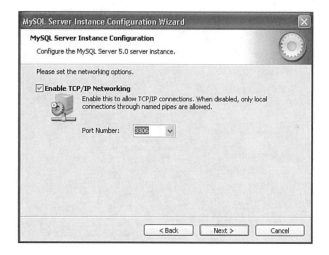

FIGURE 3.7   Enabling TCP/IP support along with its port number.

Because a Windows server is running for this example, MySQL provides Windows-specific options. The interplay between MySQL and its host operating system is explored in Chapter 14, "Operating System, Web Server and Connectivity Tuning"; aside from the performance degradation inherent in overly complex permission schemes, security is largely a peripheral topic for this book.

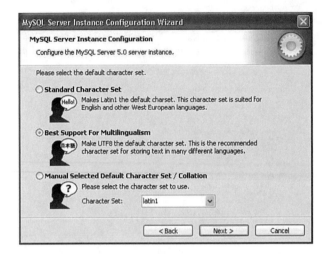

FIGURE 3.8   Choosing a character set.

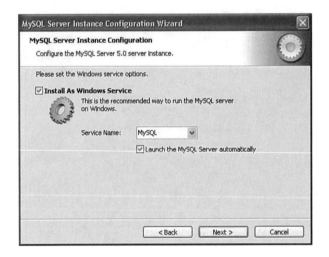

FIGURE 3.9   Setting operating-specific database service launch variables.

After answering the final questions, the wizard automatically generates the configuration file, and starts the server (see Figures 3.11 and 3.12).

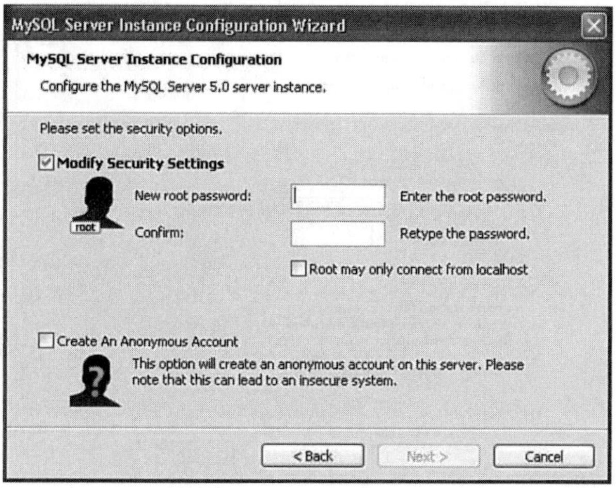

FIGURE 3.10   Implementing security preferences.

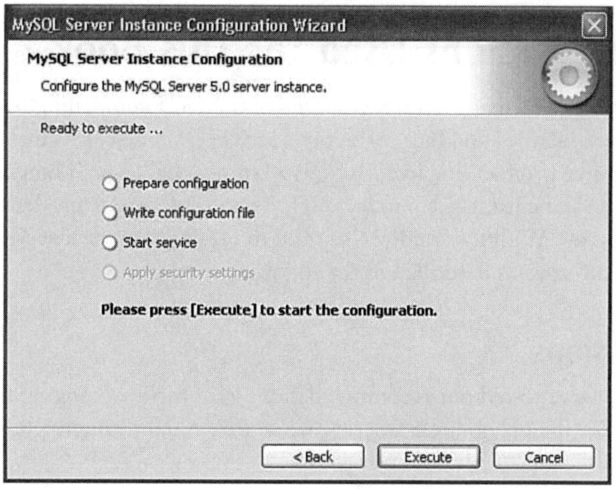

FIGURE 3.11   Preparing to write the site-specific configuration.

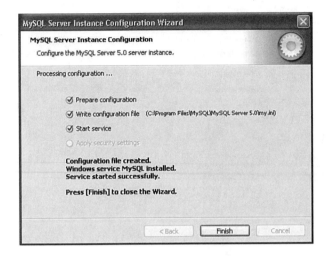

FIGURE 3.12   Configuration written, MySQL service started.

About the Versions Used for This Book

Open source software has many advantages. One of the most compelling benefits is the speed at which new features and bug corrections arrive. Of course, this makes writing a book about an open source product line like MySQL a bit of a challenge: Things change so rapidly that what is true and cutting-edge today might be the software equivalent of a leisure suit or pet rock tomorrow. With that said, we've tried to use the most recent MySQL versions on a variety of platforms, as described in the following sections.

MySQL Versions

In the 4.1 series, we've tested our recommendations with versions ranging from 4.1.6 through 4.1.11. For the upcoming 5.0 series, we've used 5.0.0 through 5.0.4.

Operating Systems

Unlike MySQL products, operating systems move at a slower release pace. For this book, we've installed MySQL products on Windows XP, Windows Server 2003, Red Hat Fedora Linux, and Debian Linux.

Performance-Boosting Features from Version 4.0 Onward

MySQL AB excels at rapidly fixing issues and introducing new features to the entire product line. Many of these new features have a significant impact on performance. Unfortunately, for the average overworked, underpaid database developer or administrator, it can be difficult to keep up with all of these new capabilities. In fact, in some cases it's likely that beneficial upgrades are put off because the administrator is unaware of the advantages of upgrading.

Because this book focuses on advancing MySQL performance, some of the major database speed augmentations provided in MySQL versions beginning with 4.0 are listed. These product enrichments show a clear pattern of continual performance-related improvements over time.

For brevity's sake, other enhancements that don't really impact system response are omitted. Internal engine improvements and bug fixes are also skipped, unless they provide direct, controllable access to developers. Finally, note that each of the topics listed in Table 3.1 are covered in the appropriate chapter.

TABLE 3.1   MySQL Performance-Related Features by Version

Version	Feature	Description
4.0	HANDLER interface	This feature provides a fast interface to MyISAM tables, letting developers directly position and move anywhere within the table, and then operate on rows accordingly.
4.0	FULLTEXT variables	Several server variables give administrators more control over how FULLTEXT indexes are built and managed.
4.0	UNION support	Improved SQL capability also yields potentially better index utilization.
4.0	Row estimation	Two new features (SQL_CALC_FOUND_ROWS, FOUND_ROWS()) give developers better visibility into costs and expected results from a query.
4.0.1	Query cache	You can cache queries and their results, which adds value to your applications regardless of your chosen storage engine.
4.0.1	Thread control	This feature introduces the innodb_thread_concurrency server setting, improving the speed of parallel operations for the InnoDB storage engine.
4.0.2	Track long queries	This feature adds the long_query_time configuration setting to provide better log tracking of problem queries. Queries that exceed this threshold are logged.
4.0.2	Improved ORDER BY	Indexes are now more efficiently used for additional sorting scenarios.
4.0.3	Faster reads	The added read_buffer_size setting gives administrators more control over sequential read performance.
4.0.4	Smarter loading	This feature reduces the amount of index creation work performed by LOAD DATA INFILE if data is already present in table.
4.0.5	Better concurrency	Four transaction isolation levels are now available for developers to control concurrency.

TABLE 3.1   **Continued**

Version	Feature	Description
4.0.5	Deadlock detection	InnoDB now has improved deadlock avoidance and detection algorithms.
4.0.6	Query cache details	The `Qcache_lowmem_prunes` indicator tells administrators how often contents of the query cache had to be removed because of insufficient memory.
4.0.9	Avoid table scans	Developers can now use the `FORCE INDEX` syntax to override the optimizer's query plan, thus going even further to avoid a costly table scan.
4.0.10	FULLTEXT control	Administrators can now define their own lists of words to be ignored in FULLTEXT searches via the `--ft-stopword-file` option.
4.0.13	MyISAM and threading	New parallel table repair and index creation features (configured via new `myisam_repair_threads` setting) introduce potential for significant index creation speed improvements.
4.0.13	InnoDB buffer pool	You can now specify how many pages in the InnoDB buffer pool are allowed to be dirty (that is, have altered data or index information) by setting `innodb_max_dirty_pages_pct`.
4.0.13	Limit thread delay	The new `max_delayed_threads` variable controls how many threads are allowed to queue to perform their inserts.
4.0.14	Guide optimizer	The `max_seeks_for_key` setting helps drive the optimizer toward choosing an index-based query plan, even if the index holds very duplicate information.
4.0.14	Slave control	The `--read-only` parameter for `mysqld` prevents inadvertent writes to a slave server.
4.0.16	Buffer control	Five new server variables let administrators more accurately allocate buffer memory. Variables include `transaction_alloc_block_size`, `transaction_prealloc_size`, `range_alloc_block_size`, `query_alloc_block_size`, and `query_prealloc_size`.
4.0.22	InnoDB deadlocks	Administrators can now tune the new `innodb_table_locks` session variable to reduce the likelihood of deadlocks.
4.1	MEMORY B-tree index	Database designers can now elect to use a B-tree index on a MEMORY table, instead of the default hash index.
4.1	Windows memory	MySQL now supports the extended (up to 64GB) memory capabilities (AWE) on Windows servers.
4.1	Detailed EXPLAIN	The EXPLAIN query report now provides additional data useful in helping determine if a query is as efficient as possible.

TABLE 3.1   Continued

Version	Feature	Description
4.1	Better `mysqldump`	Running `mysqldump` now disables foreign key checks automatically when generating a load file, helping to speed the reloading process.
4.1	Improved MyISAM	Several new important features for the MyISAM engine are now available. First, administrators can now use symbolic links for MyISAM tables, which lets tables be spread among multiple disk drives if desired.
		Next, key cache performance has been boosted by allowing for midpoint insertions, as well as permitting multiple threads to simultaneously access the cache.
4.1	Temp round robin	Administrators can now configure several directories to serve as temporary storage for MySQL by setting the `tmpdir` parameter. This can help to balance the disk load among multiple drives.
4.1.1	Key caching/indexes	You can now create multiple, specialized instances of the MyISAM performance-enhancing key cache. The new `preload_buffer_size` setting lets administrators configure memory when preloading indexes.
4.1.1	Filesort behavior	The new `max_length_for_sort_data` setting helps MySQL determine what kind of file sort algorithm to use when processing an `ORDER BY`.
4.1.2	Index enhancements	You can now specify up to 1,000 bytes for a MyISAM table's index key; you can create up to 64 indexes per table for InnoDB and MyISAM.
4.1.2	Large table support	You can now set MyISAM's row pointer size (`myisam_data_pointer_size`), which lets you address very large tables.
4.1.5	InnoDB expansion	The new `innodb_autoextend_increment` setting lets you control much additional disk space InnoDB requests when growing a tablespace.
4.1.6	Purge control	The `innodb_max_purge_lag` setting lets you control what happens when there is a significant amount of information to purge from internal InnoDB logs.
4.1.8	Better mysqldump	New parameters now let you use MySQL to generate a point-in-time InnoDB backup.
5.0.0	Index merge	The MySQL optimizer is now able to create query plans that use multiple indexes to satisfy an `OR` clause.
5.0.0	Stored procedures	You can now create server-side stored procedures, helping to remove workload from clients as well as centralize software development.

TABLE 3.1 Continued

Version	Feature	Description
5.0.1	Views	Views provide numerous benefits for administrators, including letting them define relationships among multiple tables, specify filter criteria, and present a simpler data interface to developers.
5.0.1	Optimizer tuning	The `optimizer_prune_level` and `optimizer_search_depth` settings let you dictate how you want the MySQL optimizer to examine potential query plans. Also, you can use the new `Last_query_cost` indicator to get an idea of the price of your most recent query.
5.0.2	InnoDB indicators	Many new indicators for InnoDB report on its current status and workload.
5.0.2	View control	The `updateable_views_with_limit` setting helps prevent a runaway update of a view when `LIMIT` is specified.
5.0.2	Server-side cursors	This feature lets you define structures to hold retrieved information. Typically used in conjunction with stored procedures, they add significant processing flexibility to your applications.
5.0.2	Triggers	Triggers let you define data-driven events that will kick off activities on the server.
5.0.3	FEDERATED engine	This feature defines table structures and operates upon data in remote locations as if they were local.

II

Advanced Database Design Concepts

This section explores how to design and configure your MySQL database to be as fast as possible.

Chapter 4, "Designing for Speed," begins by examining the various types of MySQL storage engines, as well as how they should be selected for optimal speed. This chapter also assesses a number of performance-related table configuration parameters, as well as how you can use views to speed and simplify your application. Finally, the chapter discusses situations in which you might want to denormalize your database.

MySQL offers a collection of constraints that you can use to help improve performance. These include PRIMARY, FOREIGN, ENUM, and SET constraints. Chapter 5, "Using Constraints to Improve Performance," reviews how to employ these constraints in your applications.

Chapter 6, "Understanding the MySQL Optimizer," investigates the MySQL optimizer, including a detailed review of the EXPLAIN command, which provides valuable information about how the optimizer processes requests. It also explores the ANALYZE TABLE and OPTIMIZE TABLE commands. Finally, Chapter 6 discusses how to give the optimizer hints on how you want it to behave.

Without a doubt, proper indexing can spell the difference between a sluggish application and one that works well. Chapter 7, "Indexing Strategies," provides extensive coverage of best practices for indexing. It reviews how MySQL structures and stores indexes, as well as which types of indexes to use for various situations and storage engines.

Designing for Speed

Choosing the Right Storage Engine and Table Type

MySQL's rich functionality and flexibility can be overwhelming: You have so many choices when constructing your MySQL-based solution. This is especially true when designing your database. MySQL offers an ever-increasing number of different storage engines and table types. This section reviews the various types of engines, along with how to select the best-performing option for your specific situation.

Before beginning the examination of your options, keep in mind one important MySQL flexibility feature: You can employ a mixture of different storage engine and table type configurations at the same time, usually without needing to make changes to your queries to cope with your unique combination. This allows you to experiment with varying engine arrangements to determine the best profile for your needs.

To select a storage engine for your table, you have at least two options:

1. Specify your choice of engine as part of your SQL data definition language (DDL):

```
CREATE TABLE INNODB_EXAMPLE (FIELD1 INT, FIELD2 VARCHAR(30)) ENGINE = INNODB;
CREATE TABLE MY_ISAM EXAMPLE (FIELD1 INT, FIELD2 VARCHAR(30)) ENGINE = MYISAM;
```

Note that you can interchange TYPE with ENGINE, although the latter is the preferred option for newer versions of MySQL beginning with versions 4.0.18/4.1.2. In fact, the TYPE keyword will disappear in versions 5.1.0 and beyond, so it's a good idea to get used to ENGINE instead.

2. Choose the appropriate option in the MySQL Table Editor from within MySQL Query Browser or MySQL Administrator, as shown in Figure 4.1.

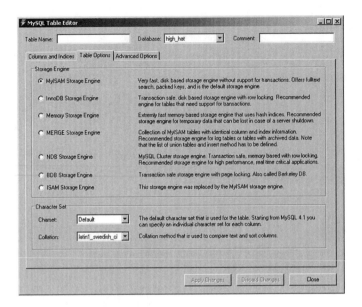

FIGURE 4.1   Options in the MySQL Table Editor.

InnoDB

First offered in source-code form in version 3.23.34a and binary distribution 4.0, InnoDB is MySQL's high-performance, transaction-safe engine. It provides advanced multiuser concurrency capabilities by allowing you to lock individual rows rather than entire tables.

Consider using InnoDB as your engine for those tables that will participate in critical transactions—those operations in which you must guarantee that data alterations are performed in one unit. InnoDB is also a wise choice when you are faced with the need to store very large amounts of data in a table. In fact, InnoDB tables can even exceed the caps placed on file size by the file system. Note that InnoDB tables generally consume more disk space than the other most popular engine, MyISAM.

Selecting InnoDB as your database engine brings some additional configuration responsibilities, especially with regard to data and log file settings. You'll explore making the most of InnoDB's copious tuning options in Part IV.

For now, let's look at a scenario in which InnoDB is the right choice. Suppose that developers for High-Hat Airways are designing a MySQL-based online reservation system. When customers place reservations, they also request a seat assignment. This operation updates two key tables: `reservations` and `seats`, both of which are expected to become very large over time. To ensure data integrity, it's imperative that these tables are both updated together if the transaction succeeds, or both returned to their original state should the transaction fail.

In this case, it makes sense to utilize the InnoDB engine for both tables, and create a transaction to combine the separate operations into one unit. In addition, it is wise to separate the tables and their indexes onto directories located on different disk drives. Note that this separation might not be possible on some operating systems; check your MySQL documentation to be certain.

MyISAM

MyISAM is a direct descendant of the ISAM database engine—the original product from MySQL. On some platforms, it is the default engine when you create a new table (unless you specify otherwise via the --default-storage-engine parameter). Among its many advantages, it excels at high-speed operations that don't require the integrity guarantees (and associated overhead) of transactions.

To illustrate this performance difference between InnoDB and MyISAM, the following are two basic sample tables, identical in all ways except for their MySQL engine:

```
CREATE TABLE SAMPLE_INNODB (
    col1 INT NOT NULL AUTO_INCREMENT PRIMARY KEY,
    col2 VARCHAR(255),
    col3 CHAR(80),
    col4 DATETIME,
    col5 FLOAT
) ENGINE = INNODB;

CREATE TABLE SAMPLE_MYISAM (
    col1 INT NOT NULL AUTO_INCREMENT PRIMARY KEY,
    col2 VARCHAR(255),
    col3 CHAR(80),
    col4 DATETIME,
    col5 FLOAT
) ENGINE = MYISAM;
```

Next, we repeatedly ran an ODBC-based program to insert large numbers of rows containing random data into each table. The results were conclusive: On average, the insert operations took 20% longer to complete for the InnoDB table than for the MyISAM table. This isn't surprising when you consider the overhead that InnoDB's transaction support adds to these kinds of operations. Of course, there are ways to optimize InnoDB in these kinds of situations, but it is still worthwhile to see the difference between the two engines.

MyISAM further boosts system response by letting administrators place their data and index files in separate directories, which can be stored on different disk drives. Again, check the version of MySQL for your operating system to be certain that it supports this separation. The full performance implications of disk drive management are discussed later in Part IV.

Finally, MyISAM tables offer more sophisticated indexing capabilities, including index support for BLOB and TEXT columns.

Continuing with the High-Hat Airways example, suppose that part of the customer support application will collect comments from clients about their High-Hat experience. Customers might telephone these comments, or might enter them via the website. Periodically, management wants to run queries against the comments to gauge customer opinions and search for particular problems. These queries will be free-form; there's no way to come up with a concrete set of query parameters.

In this case, it would be astute to use the MyISAM engine's full-text searching capabilities to give users the power to construct fast, flexible queries. A (simplified) version of the table would look like this:

```
CREATE TABLE customer_feedback (
    feedback_id INT NOT NULL AUTO_INCREMENT PRIMARY KEY,
    feedback_text TEXT,
    feedback_date DATETIME,
    FULLTEXT (feedback_text)
) ENGINE = MYISAM;
```

Users can now construct powerful searches against customer comments:

```
SELECT * FROM customer_feedback WHERE match(feedback_text) AGAINST('irate')
SELECT * FROM customer_feedback WHERE match(feedback_text) AGAINST('+luggage
    +lawyer' IN BOOLEAN MODE)
```

Chapter 11, "MyISAM Performance Enhancement," spends much more time investigating how to keep full-text searches as fast as possible.

MEMORY

Choosing the MEMORY engine option (formerly known as HEAP) allows you to create high-speed, memory-resident tables that are accessible to other authorized users for as long as the MySQL server is running. As an added benefit, you can select either a hash or b-tree index for each of your MEMORY tables. Indexing options are discussed in more detail in Chapter 7, "Indexing Strategies."

MEMORY tables offer a fast, simple way to perform sophisticated interprocess communication. The following explores a sample scenario in which this is the right engine for the task at hand.

High-Hat Airways' CIO has just promised a new chat system that must tie into the online reservation application. This new system will provide access to live operators for real-time chat and support. The MEMORY option makes it much easier to develop this potentially complicated feature.

```
CREATE TABLE conversation (
    conversation_id INT UNSIGNED AUTO_INCREMENT PRIMARY KEY,
    conversation_start DATETIME,
    conversation_end DATETIME
) ENGINE = MEMORY;
```

```
CREATE TABLE message_buffer (
    message_id INT NOT NULL AUTO_INCREMENT PRIMARY KEY,
    conversation_id INT NOT NULL,
    message_sender VARCHAR(255),
    message_text VARCHAR(255),
    message_date DATETIME,
    INDEX (conversation_id),
    INDEX (message_sender)
) ENGINE = MEMORY;
```

Each chat client would use this table as the communication interface. To keep the table from growing indefinitely, you would also write a simple process to purge the table of old conversations. This is far simpler than the effort involved in writing and using other interprocess methods.

In this example, three main drawbacks are associated with MEMORY tables:

- If the MySQL server goes down, it wipes out all active chat sessions. However, this is not likely to be a big issue given the stability of MySQL combined with the transient nature of these types of conversations.

- You cannot use BLOB or TEXT columns in MEMORY tables, but VARCHAR columns are supported as of MySQL version 5.0.3.

- If the max_heap_table_size parameter is not set correctly, you run the risk of consuming too much memory. You can also control MEMORY table size with the MAX_ROWS option when creating the table.

As mentioned earlier, MEMORY tables are fast. How fast? To get an idea of the speed of memory versus disk access, we created three identical copies of the message_buffer table, with the only difference being the storage engine; we selected the MYISAM, INNODB, and MEMORY options, respectively.

After the tables were created, we loaded large blocks of random data into each one. On average, these operations finished 33% faster with the MEMORY table than the MYISAM table, and 50% faster than the INNODB table.

We also constructed an identical, terribly inefficient table-scan query against each table. The results were consistent with the data insert process: The MEMORY table was significantly faster than its peers.

MERGE

MERGE tables are great for spreading the processing load from a single table onto a set of identical subtables. The chief downsides to this approach are fairly minimal:

- MERGE tables must use the MYISAM engine, so they are not transaction-safe.

- By definition, each subtable must have the same structure as all of its peers.

- Because information is spread among subtables, there are certain situations in which the MySQL engine must perform significant additional index processing to return a result set.

- Each subtable requires that the MySQL engine allocate a file descriptor for each client process that needs access to the table. File descriptors aren't free, so this might also negatively affect performance.

Despite these drawbacks, there are situations in which you will want to select a MERGE table as the optimal solution for your processing needs. The following example identifies a situation in which this would come in handy.

High-Hat Airways processes tens of millions of ticket purchase transactions each month. Periodically, a customer will call the reservation center and inquire about an old transaction. Transactions are kept in the live system database for 12 months before being archived. Unfortunately, even though the table that holds the purchase records is structured correctly and indexed appropriately, there is still a problem with latency.

In this case, a MERGE table might be the simplest way of eliminating unnecessary processing. This month's transactions would be kept in a dedicated table:

```
CREATE TABLE current_month (
    transaction_id INT NOT NULL AUTO_INCREMENT PRIMARY KEY,
    customer_id INT,
    transaction_date DATETIME,
    amount FLOAT,
    INDEX(customer_id)
) ENGINE = MYISAM;
```

Transactions for earlier months would be stored in separate tables:

```
CREATE TABLE january (
    transaction_id INT NOT NULL AUTO_INCREMENT PRIMARY KEY,
    customer_id INT,
    transaction_date DATETIME,
    amount FLOAT,
    INDEX(customer_id)
) ENGINE = MYISAM;

CREATE TABLE february (
    transaction_id INT NOT NULL AUTO_INCREMENT PRIMARY KEY,
    customer_id INT,
    transaction_date DATETIME,
    amount FLOAT,
    INDEX(customer_id)
) ENGINE = MYISAM;
…
…
…
```

```
CREATE TABLE december (
    transaction_id INT NOT NULL AUTO_INCREMENT PRIMARY KEY,
    customer_id INT,
    transaction_date DATETIME,
    amount FLOAT,
    INDEX(customer_id)
) ENGINE = MYISAM;
```

At the end of each month, you would run a batch process to move the information into the correct tables. To further boost performance, these tables could be positioned on different disk drives and compressed using the myisampack utility.

Finally, you would create a MERGE table that would present a virtual view of the information found in these tables:

```
CREATE TABLE transaction_history (
    transaction_id INT NOT NULL AUTO_INCREMENT,
    customer_id INT,
    transaction_date DATETIME,
    amount FLOAT,
    INDEX(transaction_id),
    INDEX(customer_id)
) ENGINE = MERGE UNION=(current_month, january, february, … , december)
    INSERT_METHOD = LAST;
```

After the MERGE table is in place, you simply run standard SQL against the new table:

```
SELECT transaction_id, customer_id, transaction_date, amount
FROM transaction_history
WHERE customer_id = 19443;
```

MySQL will locate all relevant records from the monthly tables and present the results to you in a single set.

CSV

If you have enabled the CSV engine, MySQL lets you create tables that store information in comma-separated-value (CSV) format on the file system. These tables are not typically used for enhancing performance, and they have a number of important restrictions (for example, only SELECT and INSERT are available, and you cannot create indexes). However, when used properly, they can greatly simplify the process of exporting data to other applications.

For example, suppose that High-Hat's business analysts want to perform some spreadsheet-based number crunching on a particular set of information. If these analysts work against live data, this work has the potential to bog down your database server. Consequently, you need to come up with an alternative process. You have numerous options, from creating temporary tables to off-loading information to different servers. In this case, however, it might be easiest to just create a CSV table and populate it with the raw data, assuming that the data set isn't too large. You could then have the analysts load the information into their spreadsheets and work with it on their client machines.

ARCHIVE

This recently added engine option is used chiefly for creating large, compressed tables that will not need to be searched via indexes. In addition, you cannot use any data alteration statements, such as UPDATE or DELETE, although you are free to use SELECT and INSERT. Keep in mind that a SELECT statement performs an expensive full table scan.

There are relatively few situations in which you would make use of an ARCHIVE table. Consider using them in cases in which disk space is at a premium but you need live (albeit slow) search capabilities to infrequently updated data.

BerkeleyDB (BDB)

The BerkeleyDB (BDB) engine is developed and maintained by Sleepycat Software. You'll find it included with the MySQL-Max binary distribution. Tables created with the BDB engine option provide sophisticated transaction support, as well as page-level locking. As with the InnoDB engine, BDB administrators have some additional configuration and tuning responsibilities.

BDB was available before InnoDB, so developers who needed transactions initially chose this engine. However, in most cases today, database developers employing transactions will likely opt for the InnoDB engine. This is not a criticism of BDB; it just reflects the current market reality.

MaxDB

Previously known as SAP DB, MaxDB is typically found in large SAP installations. Because this book is aimed at a more general audience, it does not devote large amounts of time to covering this product. However, our suggestions on table design, indexing, and good query processing apply to this engine as well.

NDB

MySQL's new clustering capabilities rely on the NDB storage engine. By spreading the data and processing load over multiple computers, clustering can greatly improve performance and reliability.

Clustering is explored in much more detail in Part V. For now, just remember that if you want a table to participate in clustering, you need to have clustering support enabled, and then specify the NDB storage engine when creating the table:

```
CREATE TABLE cluster_example (
    col1 INT NOT NULL AUTO_INCREMENT PRIMARY KEY,
    …
    …
) ENGINE = NDBCLUSTER;
```

FEDERATED

MySQL version 5.0.3 introduces a new storage engine designed for distributed computing. Specifying the FEDERATED option when creating your table tells MySQL that the table is actually resident in another database server (even if it is running on the same computer). Currently, this server must be running MySQL, but in the future other database engines will be supported.

You may wonder how MySQL knows where the remote table lives, and how it is accessed. First, you use an URL-like formatted string to tell MySQL the location of the remote table as part of the COMMENT portion of your CREATE TABLE statement. Note that the usage, format, security, and location of this connection string will likely be enhanced in future versions.

Next, MySQL reads your SQL statements, performs some internal transformations, and then accesses the FEDERATED table via its client API. The results are then presented to you as if the query was executed locally.

Optimizing Table Structure

MySQL lets you specify a number of performance-related settings when you create or alter a table. You can do this in two ways:

- Via SQL in the CREATE TABLE or ALTER TABLE command
- Via the MySQL Table Editor from within MySQL Query Browser or MySQL Administrator, as shown in Figure 4.2

The following sections take a look at some of these options.

Specifying Row Format

When you create or modify a table using the MyISAM engine, you can request that the engine store rows in fixed or dynamic format. If your table contains no TEXT or BLOB columns, MySQL chooses the fixed option by default, which automatically converts VARCHAR columns to CHAR. On the other hand, if you select dynamic, MySQL converts all columns of type CHAR to VARCHAR. As a third choice, running the myisampack command instructs MySQL to compress the table into a smaller, read-only format.

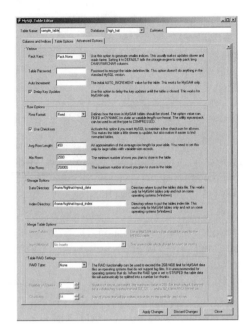

FIGURE 4.2   Specifying performance-related issues.

Because of their consistent row size, fixed format tables translate to less work (and better response) for the MySQL engine when accessing, caching, and updating information. They are also less likely to become corrupted. If disk space is not at a premium, fixed format tables are probably the best choice.

Conversely, dynamic tables use less space, but run the risk of fragmentation and/or eventual corruption. The OPTIMIZE TABLE command is reviewed in Chapter 6, "Understanding the MySQL Optimizer," to see how to correct fragmentation problems. Note that if your table has any columns of type TEXT, BLOB, or VARCHAR, MySQL automatically chooses this option.

Finally, compressed tables use the least amount of space.

The following examines the storage implications of these types of tables. We created two identical tables, except for their ROW_FORMAT, and then inserted 100,000 rows of random data:

```
CREATE TABLE fixed_demo (
    col1 INT NOT NULL AUTO_INCREMENT PRIMARY KEY,
    col2 VARCHAR(255),
    col3 CHAR(40),
    col4 INT,
    INDEX (col2),
    INDEX (col3)
) ENGINE = MYISAM ROW_FORMAT = FIXED;
```

```
CREATE TABLE dynamic_demo (
    col1 INT NOT NULL AUTO_INCREMENT PRIMARY KEY,
    col2 VARCHAR(255),
    col3 CHAR(40),
    col4 INT,
    INDEX (col2),
    INDEX (col3)
) ENGINE = MYISAM ROW_FORMAT = DYNAMIC;
```

As expected, the fixed_demo table used significantly more disk space than dynamic_demo (29MB data and 48MB index versus 15.5MB data and 23.3MB index).

We then ran a simple query against both tables:

```
SELECT COUNT(*) FROM fixed_demo WHERE col4 > 345 AND col4 < 1099;
SELECT COUNT(*) FROM dynamic_demo WHERE col4 > 345 AND col4 < 1099;
```

Both queries ran in less than a quarter second. However, the dynamic table query took approximately 50% longer than the fixed table query. For more complex operations, the fixed table savings could be dramatic.

Finally, we ran myisampack against the fixed_demo table. This reduced the table to 18.8MB data and 37.8MB index. Rerunning the SELECT COUNT(*) query against this newly compressed table returned results 10% faster than before compression.

Specifying Table Size

When you're using a dynamic, MyISAM table, you can use the AVG_ROW_LENGTH and MAX_ROWS options to tell MySQL how large you expect your table to be. Knowing this value helps the engine construct index keys in a more optimal way. This can translate into faster performance, especially in large tables.

To test the performance benefits of specifying table size, we created two sample tables, one of which included instructions on expected table size:

```
CREATE TABLE size_defined (
    col1 INT NOT NULL AUTO_INCREMENT PRIMARY KEY,
    col2 VARCHAR(255),
    col3 CHAR(40),
    col4 INT,
    INDEX (col2),
    INDEX (col3)
) ENGINE = MYISAM ROW_FORMAT = DYNAMIC AVG_ROW_LENGTH = 200 MAX_ROWS = 250000;

CREATE TABLE size_not_defined (
    col1 INT NOT NULL AUTO_INCREMENT PRIMARY KEY,
    col2 VARCHAR(255),
    col3 CHAR(40),
    col4 INT,
```

```
    INDEX (col2),
    INDEX (col3)
) ENGINE = MYISAM ROW_FORMAT = DYNAMIC;
```

We then loaded 100,000 rows of random data into each table. They both consumed the same amount of disk space, but simple queries ran approximately 10% faster against the size-defined table versus the size-undefined table.

Index Key Compression

When using MyISAM tables, you can request that the engine compress index keys by specifying the PACK_KEYS option when creating a table. You might find that your application's read operations improve; there might be an offsetting added cost for write operations.

Compressing index keys can save substantial disk space. To demonstrate, we created the following tables:

```
CREATE TABLE pack_keys_demo (
    col1 INT NOT NULL AUTO_INCREMENT PRIMARY KEY,
    col2 VARCHAR(255),
    col3 INT,
    INDEX (col2),
    INDEX (col3)
) ENGINE = MYISAM PACK_KEYS = 1;

CREATE TABLE pack_keys_demo_no (
    col1 INT NOT NULL AUTO_INCREMENT PRIMARY KEY,
    col2 VARCHAR(255),
    col3 INT,
    INDEX (col2),
    INDEX (col3)
) ENGINE = MYISAM PACK_KEYS = 0;
```

We then inserted 100,000 rows of random data into each table. For this test, we made the data in col2 highly random while the data in col3 was highly duplicate: Its values only ranged between 1 and 10.

After the tables were loaded, the pack_keys_demo table consumed 13.6MB and 20.6MB of storage for data and indexes, respectively. The pack_keys_demo_no table used 13.6MB and 43.9MB of storage for data and indexes, respectively.

The impact of index compression is discussed as part of our detailed review of indexing later in this section.

Checksum Integrity Management

If you choose MyISAM for a particular table, you might elect to have MySQL compute a checksum for each row. This adds slight overhead to data update operations, but helps you locate (and then correct) corrupted tables. This value is then used by the CHECKSUM TABLE command:

```
mysql> CHECKSUM TABLE checksum_demo;
+--------------------+-----------+
| Table              | Checksum  |
+--------------------+-----------+
| demo.checksum_demo | 544091798 |
+--------------------+-----------+
1 row in set (0.00 sec)
```

To test the overhead of this option, we created two identical tables, and asked MySQL to track a checksum for only one:

```
CREATE TABLE checksum_demo (
    col1 INT NOT NULL AUTO_INCREMENT PRIMARY KEY,
    col2 VARCHAR(255)
) ENGINE = MYISAM CHECKSUM = 1;

CREATE TABLE checksum_demo_no (
    col1 INT NOT NULL AUTO_INCREMENT PRIMARY KEY,
    col2 VARCHAR(255)
) ENGINE = MYISAM;
```

We then repeatedly ran tests that inserted 1,000 rows of random data into each table. The overhead averaged less than 5% for the first table: This is a small price to pay to improve data integrity.

Alternatively, you can still run CHECKSUM TABLE for a table without this option set. However, MySQL takes some time to process the results.

Column Types and Performance

The decisions you make regarding column types can have a significant impact on performance. MySQL offers numerous choices within each major column class (string, numeric, and date/time). Although it is assumed that you already understand the difference between these data types, as well as which ones to use for your application, this section takes a few moments to focus on the interplay of column type and responsiveness.

Making the right choice when deciding how to store dates and times can be confusing: The combination of the various column types, system settings, and date/time-specific SQL can be intimidating. However, because this book is focused on performance, a detailed discussion of the nuances of storing and calculating dates is avoided. Instead, this section reviews only string and numeric column-type considerations.

Before we begin, let's review a very handy utility provided by MySQL both as an example for open source developers who want to write functions to extend the product, as well as a tool for database designers to help pick optimal column types. The analyse() procedure takes the output of a SELECT statement and returns a report detailing the information shown in Table 4.1 for each column.

Table 4.1   PROCEDURE analyse() Results

Column	Purpose
field_name	The name of the returned column
min_value	The smallest value in the result set for this column
max_value	The largest value in the result set for this column
min_length	The smallest number of bytes in the result set for this column
max_length	The largest number of bytes in the result set for this column
empties_or_zeros	The number of returned rows with either an empty field or zero value in this column
nulls	The number of returned rows with nulls in this column
avg_value_or_avg_length	For numeric columns, the average value in the result set for this column; for string columns, the average length of all the values in this column for the result set
std	The standard deviation for the result set for this column, assuming it is a numeric column
optimal_fieldtype	The MySQL-preferred data type for this column, based on the data sample contained in the result set

For example, take a look at the following table:

```
CREATE TABLE demo_pa (
    col1 INT UNSIGNED AUTO_INCREMENT PRIMARY KEY,
    col2 SMALLINT,
    col3 CHAR(10),
    col4 VARCHAR(40)
) ENGINE = INNODB;
```

After loading 10,000 rows of random data into the table and running the following SQL statement:

```
SELECT * FROM demo_page PROCEDURE analyse(4);
```

The first parameter for analyse() refers to the number of columns to process. Optionally, you can also specify a maximum memory that MySQL can allocate to finding unique values in each column. The results are shown in Figure 4.3.

What did you learn about the table from this report, based on the sample data set?

1. col1 can probably be shortened from INT to SMALLINT.

2. col2 can also be shortened, from SMALLINT to TINYINT.

3. col3 can likely be specified with an ENUM list because only four distinct values are in the table. ENUM is discussed in more detail in Chapter 5, "Using Constraints to Improve Performance."

4. col4 is probably set just right.

FIGURE 4.3   MySQL can allocate memory to finding unique values.

Try experimenting with analyse() for your database; you might be surprised with what you learn.

String Considerations

MySQL offers database designers a rich choice of options when storing text and binary-based information. The following list explores the performance implications of these choices.

- CHAR versus VARCHAR—Database designers face a never-ending struggle when trying to decide between the disk space savings of storing strings as VARCHAR and the improved performance of using fixed CHAR columns. Remember that, as discussed earlier in this chapter, this decision is taken out of your hands if you choose a dynamic row format for a MyISAM table: MySQL automatically converts CHAR columns to VARCHAR. On the other hand, certain fixed row format MyISAM tables see all of the VARCHAR columns converted to CHAR.

Despite these limitations, and given the ever-decreasing cost of disk space, it's probably best to opt for the improved speed of the CHAR type whenever possible. As an added benefit, you are less likely to experience costly data fragmentation with fixed record tables.

- CHAR BINARY versus VARCHAR BINARY—Although these columns hold binary information, you can apply the same decision criteria as you do for CHAR versus VARCHAR when deciding which option to select.

- BLOBs and TEXT—Binary large objects (BLOBs) typically hold images, sound files, executables, and so on. This column type is further subdivided into TINYBLOB, BLOB, MEDIUMBLOB, and LONGBLOB. Maximum storage for these columns ranges from 257 bytes for TINYBLOBs all the way up to nearly 4.3GB for LONG-BLOB. TEXT columns follow a similar nomenclature and storage profile as BLOB columns, with the chief differences being that TEXT columns are processed using their character set for searching and collation.

Database administrators are often torn between stowing BLOBs and TEXT data in the MySQL database versus placing the information on the file system and simply storing a link to it in the database. There are arguments in favor of both approaches from the perspective of optimal performance.

You might find that your MySQL-driven applications bog down under the increased processing and storage costs of BLOBs and TEXT, especially if that data is merely ancillary to your primary database operations. Storing variable-length information also leads to eventual fragmentation, and you might also experience data truncation if you undersize your BLOB and/or TEXT columns.

On the other hand, keeping your BLOBs and TEXT data inside MySQL lets you take advantage of its backup/restore and replication features. In addition, you now can create indexes on these types of columns. You must use prefixes to make searches that employ these indexes meaningful. To improve sorting speed, you can configure the max_sort_length option. Indexing is reviewed in Chapter 6, "Understanding the MySQL Optimizer," and engine parameters are discussed in Chapter 10, "General Server Performance and Parameters Tuning," Chapter 11, "MyISAM Performance Enhancement," and Chapter 12, "InnoDB Performance Enhancement."

Numeric Considerations

After struggling through the decisions among all of the string options, you'll be relieved to know that making a choice among the numeric column options requires much less mental exertion.

A good general rule of thumb is to use the smallest numeric type that suits your needs; this helps conserve space and can also make some joins and searches more efficient. The following lists some examples.

- **Integers**—When you need to store an integer (that is, a number with no potential fractional/decimal values), MySQL gives you a choice of five options: TINYINT, SMALLINT, MEDIUMINT, INT, and BIGINT, along with the ability to declare them SIGNED or UNSIGNED. Storage requirements for each type range from a single byte for TINYINT with a possible range of values from either 0 to 255 or –127 to +127 all the way up to eight bytes for BIGINT with a possible range from either 0 to approximately 1.8442E+19 or –9.22E+18 to +9.22E+18.

- **Decimals**—Your choices are somewhat less dramatic for decimal-based columns (that is, numbers with potential fractional/decimal values). Your options include DECIMAL/NUMERIC, FLOAT, and DOUBLE. Just selecting FLOAT or DOUBLE without specifying a precision consumes four bytes and eight bytes, respectively. You also have the opportunity to specify a precision (on both sides of the decimal place) for the DECIMAL type. This directly determines storage consumption. For example, if you define a column of type DECIMAL(10,2), you consume at least 10 bytes, along with anywhere between 0 and 2 additional bytes, depending on if there is a fraction or sign involved.

With this many choices, many database designers fall into the expedient trap of just picking a numeric type that they've used many times before, regardless of the application's needs.

For example, suppose that High-Hat Airways' customer_master table includes a field that stores the customer's age. The database designer defines this column as an INT. However, because there are not many members of the flying public greater than 255 years old, an UNSIGNED TINYINT would suffice for this column, and save three bytes per record. Considering that the table will hold tens of millions of rows, the savings could be substantial, especially if the column were used in queries, joins, and groupings.

Using Views to Boost Performance

MySQL implemented views beginning with version 5.0. Most database administrators and developers don't normally think of views as a performance enhancer, but these database structures can add tremendous value to your applications. This section explores how you can take advantage of views to boost responsiveness.

Reduced Returned Columns

Retrieving information via SELECT * is second nature for most database administrators and developers, and is often baked in to many general-purpose data access products. Unfortunately, this often returns extra columns that are not of primary interest at the moment. When these kinds of queries are run en masse, it can negatively affect performance by increasing engine load, as well as consuming extra bandwidth between the client and database server. In situations like this, it's a better idea to create a view that returns only those columns that are absolutely necessary for the current task.

For example, suppose that one small part of High-Hat Airways' web-based client portal lets customers view and update their mailing address from the `customer_master` table. Given the millions of High-Hat customers, it's likely that this operation will be run thousands of times per week. You could construct your SQL statement as follows:

```
SELECT * FROM customer_master WHERE…
```

and then ignore any columns that aren't related to the customer's address. However, this extracts and sends unnecessary columns to the requesting application. You could also modify your SQL statement to something similar to the following:

```
SELECT address1, address2, city, province, postal_code… FROM customer_master WHERE…
```

but this is somewhat tedious and potentially error-prone. In this case, it's probably worth the effort to construct a view that just returns the right columns for the job:

```
CREATE VIEW V_CUSTOMER_ADDRESS AS
SELECT address1, address2, …
FROM customer_master
WHERE…
WITH CHECK OPTION
```

Adding the `WITH CHECK OPTION` at the end of the statement forces updates to the view to undergo validity checks before being accepted into the database. This is discussed in more detail momentarily.

Reduced Returned Rows

Views are also great for reducing the number of potential returned rows when performing a query. Many users (especially those using end-user reporting tools) issue blanket queries that result in sequential reads through very large tables. This is very inefficient and possibly dangerous for performance.

To help reduce the prospect of these kinds of unnecessary gargantuan data sets, you can employ views with more restrictive `WHERE` clauses. For example, suppose that users in High Hat's marketing department want to use a business intelligence tool to research the traveling habits of the most frequent customers who normally fly from Chicago's O'Hare airport. You could allow them unrestricted access to the appropriate tables. However, this is a recipe for disaster: It's quite likely that the users will construct extremely wasteful queries, no matter how advanced the business intelligence tool.

Instead, it is smarter to create a customized view:

```
CREATE VIEW V_FREQUENT_TRAVELERS_OHARE AS
SELECT first_name, last_name, …
FROM customer_master, flight_history,..
WHERE customer_master.account_balance > 50000
AND flight_history.departure_airport = 'ORD'
```

By directing your users at this view, you're much less likely to encounter performance-draining open queries.

Reduced Inefficient Joins

As a database administrator, you know that it's often difficult to construct efficient queries, even with your expertise in SQL. It's much harder for untrained developers and end users (with direct or indirect SQL access). These people often inadvertently submit horrendous queries that might overwhelm your MySQL server.

This problem is even more troubling when you realize that many queries invoke joins between two or more tables, which can cause performance to become exponentially worse. Fortunately, views provide you with defense against these kinds of issues.

If you have the authority, you can create a set of views that is designed with efficiency in mind. By understanding your users' needs, consulting the results of MySQL's EXPLAIN command, and experimenting, it's likely that you'll design views that are as efficient as possible. You can then require that end users and developers work through your views, rather than against the base tables.

Simpler Updating with Integrity Checking

MySQL 5.0 introduces updateable views. These can be very handy when developing applications because they let you update data in the same location as you found it (that is, you don't need to update base tables when you just found the information in the view).

In addition, from version 5.0.2 onward, appending WITH CHECK OPTION to your view creation statement enforces database engine validation of data modifications.

As shown earlier in this chapter, for example, the High-Hat Airways customer_master table serves as the foundation of all customer information. Suppose that you create a view to return the names and club status of only those lucky travelers who have reached the pinnacle of their Mad-Hatter Club (High-Hat Airways' award-winning frequent flyer program) membership:

```
CREATE VIEW V_HATTER_CLUB_BEST AS
SELECT first_name, last_name, club_level, home_airport
FROM customer_master
WHERE club_level = 'Top-Hat'
WITH CHECK OPTION
```

Next, you want to create an additional view that returns a subset of the first view. In particular, you only want to see those customers who have indicated JFK as their home airport:

```
CREATE VIEW V_HATTER_CLUB_BEST_JFK AS
SELECT first_name, last_name, club_level, home_airport
FROM V_HATTER_CLUB_BEST
WHERE home_airport = 'JFK'
WITH CASCADED CHECK OPTION
```

If a user attempts to insert a record into the V_HATTER_CLUB_BEST_JFK table and does not assign a club_level of 'Top-Hat', MySQL returns an error message (and blocks the insert) because this violates the rules that created the underlying V_HATTER_CLUB_BEST. This is a very simple example, but the concept is very powerful. Updateable views combined with cascaded checks can reduce the amount of validation that you must perform in your programs, while helping increase data integrity. Constraints are discussed in more detail in Chapter 5.

When Not to Normalize

Although relational database design theory is not part of this book's scope, it's worth taking a few moments to explore a particular scenario in which you might be justified in disobeying the normally inviolate three-normal-form rules.

Typically, it's unwise to store calculated information (for example, averages, sums, minimums, maximums) in your tables. Instead, users will receive more accurate information (and you will be in compliance with solid database design theory) if you compute the requested results at runtime, when the query is executed. However, if you are faced with a very large set of data that doesn't change very often, you might want to consider performing your calculations in bulk during off-hours, and then storing the results.

For example, let's look at how Mad-Hatter Club members interact with one MySQL-based solution. Customers might elect to either call a toll-free phone number or log in to High-Hat's website to check their mileage balance. However, this can cause enormous processing backlogs given the cost of traversing the billions of detailed transactions stored in the database multiplied by the thousands of queries being run at the same time. In cases like this, it is prudent to consider an alternative method to providing customers with this information.

You could use the MERGE table option to partition and compress data, but there is a simpler solution: Instead of wading through mounds of data in real time, why not add a column to the customer master table and store the mileage total in that convenient location? You could then run a daily batch operation during off-hours to update the totals.

Another trap that overzealous database designers fall into is the practice of creating lookup tables for columns that have fewer than five different values stored in small columns. This commonly happens for columns that store information from small potential pools, such as eye color, gender, seat preference (for example, window or aisle), and so on.

For example, suppose that the reservations table tracks the customer's preference for seating, as follows:

```
CREATE TABLE reservations (
    reservation_id INT UNSIGNED AUTO_INCREMENT PRIMARY KEY,
    …
    seat_pref_id INT NOT NULL,
    …
);
```

The next table holds a grand total of two rows, one for 'Window' and one for 'Aisle':

```
CREATE TABLE seat_pref_lookup (
    seat_pref_id INT UNSIGNED AUTO_INCREMENT PRIMARY KEY,
    seat_pref_description CHAR(40)
);
```

To get a meaningful seating preference value when viewing data from the `reservations` table, you must join the two tables together. These kinds of joins can add up and add unnecessary complexity to your database. For situations like this, it is better to simply store the actual seating preference value in the main `reservations` table, even though this is technically a violation of good database design theory.

To enforce the data integrity of the `reservations` table, you could then use the `ENUM` restriction when creating the table:

```
CREATE TABLE reservations (
    reservation_id INT UNSIGNED AUTO_INCREMENT PRIMARY KEY,
...

    seat_pref_description ENUM ('Window', 'Aisle')
...
);
```

Chapter 5 reviews `ENUM` along with all of MySQL's other constraints.

Using Constraints to Improve Performance

Simply defined, constraints are rules that a database designer specifies when setting up a table. MySQL enforces these rules when changes are made to information stored in the database. These changes usually occur via INSERT, UPDATE, or DELETE statements, although they can also be triggered by structural alterations to the tables themselves.

MySQL offers the following constraints:

- UNIQUE—Guarantees that there will be no duplicate values in a column
- PRIMARY KEY—Identifies the primary unique identifier of a row
- FOREIGN KEY—Codifies and enforces the relationships among two or more tables with regard to appropriate behavior when data changes
- DEFAULT—Provides an automatic value for a column if a user omits entering data
- NOT NULL—Forces users to provide information for a column when inserting or updating data
- ENUM—Allows you to set a restricted list of values for a particular column, although it is not a true constraint
- SET—Allows you to store combinations of predefined values within a string column, although it is not a true constraint

Constraints benefit your organization in several ways, including the following:

- **Data consistency/organizational policy enforcement**—As a centralized set of rules that are processed for all changes by all users to a given table, constraints greatly reduce the chances that someone will mistakenly introduce a data integrity problem.

    This can also help implement your organization's operational policies. For example, your organization might not allow a customer to be created without a valid phone number. A NOT NULL constraint on the relevant column in the appropriate table(s) blocks any invalid entries into the database.

- **Performance**—Constraints run on the database server. In most cases, this is faster than manually coding and downloading (or installing) the same logic on a client.
- **Developer time and productivity**—Reuse is a foundation of good software design practices. By using constraints, you are reducing the amount of time that developers need for these types of tasks, as well as helping cut down on potential errors. This lets the developers spend their valuable time building the core value of their applications.

The following sections look at each of these constraints to see how you can use them to achieve the benefits listed previously. To keep the examples consistent, we refer to the challenges faced by the designers of High-Hat Airways' new lost luggage application.

UNIQUE **Constraints**

When you specify a UNIQUE constraint for a column, MySQL generates an index (UNIQUE) and blocks any attempts to enter or update data so that more than one row has the same value in that column. If you attempt to duplicate a value, you receive an error:

```
Duplicate entry 'Late check-in' for key 1
```

PRIMARY KEY

A primary key is really a type of UNIQUE constraint that identifies one or more columns that uniquely locate a single row within a given table. When you create a primary key, MySQL builds an index (PRIMARY), thus guaranteeing that no two rows will ever have the same values in that key. If you attempt to violate this constraint via an INSERT or UPDATE, the engine returns an error to your application.

Primary keys are essential for maintaining database integrity, and they also help speed things up for queries and other operations that need to find a row quickly.

You have at least three methods to define a primary key:

- Directly via SQL: If the primary key contains more than one column, you must specify this at the end of your CREATE/ALTER TABLE statement.

```
CREATE TABLE checked_luggage (
    luggage_check_id INT AUTO_INCREMENT PRIMARY KEY,
    flight_id INT
…

…
);


CREATE TABLE checked_luggage (
    luggage_check_id INT AUTO_INCREMENT,
```

```
    flight_id INT,
...

...

    PRIMARY KEY (luggage_check_id, flight_id)
);
```

- Implicitly, by creating a unique index:

```
CREATE TABLE checked_luggage (
    luggage_check_id INT UNIQUE,
    flight_id INT
...

...

);
```

- Via the MySQL Table Editor (see Figure 5.1):

FIGURE 5.1   Using the MySQL Table Editor to define a primary key.

What is the difference between a primary key and a unique constraint? Both serve to identify one and only one row in a table. However, primary keys can consist of multiple columns that, when grouped together, form a unique value. On the other hand, a unique constraint can apply to only one column at a time.

You might encounter situations in which a table contains a system-generated value, which serves as a primary key, and another user-supplied value that is also unique. An example is a customer table in which the system generates primary key values using the AUTO_INCREMENT option in the CREATE TABLE statement while also storing a unique external value, such as a Social Security number or other government-generated value.

FOREIGN KEY

After your primary key is in place, you can turn your attention to foreign keys. Foreign key constraints typically are used to define relationships among two or more tables, usually in the context of "parent-child" or "header-detail" associations. In addition to enforcing data integrity, MySQL lets you use foreign keys to specify actions to take when rows are modified or deleted. This saves your developers from having to code those rules into their applications; it also improves performance because the rules can be run on the server immediately. These actions include the following:

- CASCADE
- RESTRICT
- SET NULL
- NO ACTION
- SET DEFAULT

Note that some versions of MySQL might not yet support all of the preceding actions. In addition, MySQL is always introducing new features, so be certain to check the documentation for your version to see if new foreign key actions have been implemented.

To use foreign keys, your database must satisfy the following criteria:

- Use the InnoDB storage engine.
- Have indexes in place on the appropriate columns.
- Match data types for the related columns. If the related columns are dissimilar, MySQL has no way to join them and enforce the constraint.

In the case of High-Hat Airways' new lost luggage application, suppose that you want to create a table (`missing_luggage`) to hold records of misplaced luggage to complement the `checked_luggage` table you created earlier in this chapter.

After consulting with your customers (the users of the application), you realize that these two tables have a parent-child relationship: No records can exist in `missing_luggage` without a corresponding parent in `checked_luggage`. Thus, your SQL to create the child table looks like this:

```
CREATE TABLE missing_luggage(
    missing_luggage_id INT AUTO_INCREMENT PRIMARY KEY,
    luggage_check_id INT,
...
...

    FOREIGN KEY (luggage_check_id) REFERENCES checked_luggage(luggage_check_id)
) ENGINE = INNODB;
```

You can use the MySQL Table Editor to view this foreign key, as shown in Figure 5.2.

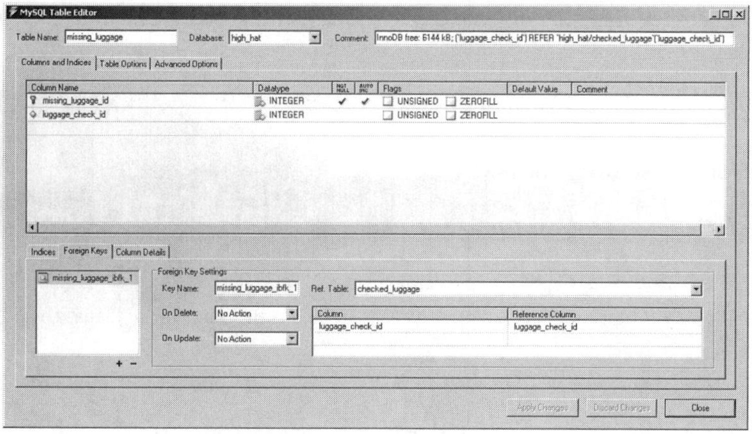

FIGURE 5.2   Using the MySQL Table Editor to view foreign key details.

As the constraint currently stands, MySQL returns an error if users attempt to enter a child record without a corresponding parent record in checked_luggage:

```
ERROR 1216 (23000): Cannot add or update a child row: a foreign key constraint fails
```

This helps improve performance and improve integrity at the same time. Unfortunately, this is not enough for one of the new hotshot MBAs brought in after the indictments of the CEO and CFO. She has a new idea for an application feature: What if High-Hat could simply purge its database of all missing luggage every so often? This would certainly improve the results of internal missing luggage reports, and could help her achieve her next promotion.

You could code this operation in SQL, but it's much easier to associate ON DELETE CASCADE with MySQL's foreign key constraints to take care of this task. Setting a cascading delete means that whenever a parent row (that is, a record in checked_luggage) is deleted, MySQL will employ the foreign key constraint to find all relevant child records (that is, related rows in missing_luggage), and then delete them.

```
CREATE TABLE missing_luggage(
    missing_luggage_id INT AUTO_INCREMENT PRIMARY KEY,
    luggage_check_id INT,
...
...
    FOREIGN KEY (luggage_check_id) REFERENCES checked_luggage(luggage_check_id)
ON DELETE CASCADE
) ENGINE = INNODB;
```

Several weeks later, the hotshot MBA is fired when her database manipulations are brought to light by an anonymous informant. Her replacement wants you to simply disassociate, rather than delete, child records from their parent when the parent is removed. This is much less likely to result in his termination and/or indictment.

In this case, you might use the ON DELETE NULL option as part of your foreign key declaration:

```
CREATE TABLE missing_luggage(
    missing_luggage_id INT AUTO_INCREMENT PRIMARY KEY,
    luggage_check_id INT,
…

…

    FOREIGN KEY (luggage_check_id) REFERENCES checked_luggage(luggage_check_id)
ON DELETE SET NULL
) ENGINE = INNODB;
```

This type of foreign key constraint sets the child's related column(s) to NULL when a parent row is removed. The child still remains, but it is now an orphan.

Let's spend a few moments discussing what happens when constraints such as UNIQUE, PRIMARY KEY, and FOREIGN KEY are violated. If you really want your operations to proceed despite these violations, you can use the IGNORE keyword when running your statement. You can also use the SHOW WARNINGS statement to learn what has happened. Note that constraint violation behavior might differ if you are using the InnoDB storage engine or the MyISAM engine. Optimal transaction planning is discussed in Chapter 9, "Developing High-Speed Applications."

Finally, be careful when setting up foreign key constraints: It is possible to create a circular reference. For example, table A might reference table B, which might, in turn, reference table C, which unwisely references table A. MySQL has defenses against the infinite loops that this might cause, but it's still a good idea to design these constraints cautiously.

DEFAULT and NOT NULL

Choosing a default value for a column saves you the effort of manually entering (or coding) a value if none is entered by a user, as well as sending this data from the client application to the database server. If you find that a table has fields that are usually filled with the same values, consider prepopulating them by using the DEFAULT constraint.

Be certain that you specify the NOT NULL constraint when creating the table if your application demands that a column is never left empty.

For example, suppose that you need a table to hold point-in-time snapshots of the airline's efforts to find a missing piece of luggage. One of the columns in the table will track the type of update that's being entered (for example, data entered by the airline, a phone call from the customer). If most of the entries in this table are generated by other programs (that is, entered by the airline), you could simply set the default for the column to be "Automatic update: High-Hat."

```
CREATE TABLE missing_luggage_tracking (
    missing_luggage_tracking_id INT AUTO_INCREMENT PRIMARY KEY,
    missing_luggage_id INT,
    entry_type VARCHAR(30) NOT NULL DEFAULT 'Automatic update: High-Hat',
...
...
    FOREIGN KEY (missing_luggage_id) REFERENCES missing_luggage(missing_luggage_id)
ON
DELETE CASCADE
) ENGINE = INNODB;
```

MySQL's Table Editor will show the constraints you've placed on the entry_type column, as shown in Figure 5.3.

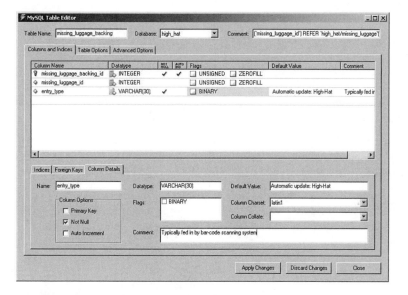

FIGURE 5.3   Using the MySQL Table Editor to set a default value.

Your INSERT statement now does not need to even mention this column unless you have a different value to insert. If there is also a human interface working against this table, that application could provide its own values in SQL (for example, 'Customer phone call'), which would override the default:

```
INSERT INTO missing_luggage_tracking (missing_luggage_id) VALUES (29320);

INSERT INTO missing_luggage_tracking (missing_luggage_id, entry_type)
VALUES (29320, 'Customer phone call');
```

ENUM

Applying the ENUM option to a column helps guarantee that any data placed into the column is one of a predefined set of values. In the case of the missing_luggage table you saw earlier, suppose that you want to add a new column to track the reason for the luggage's mysterious disappearance. You also need to restrict the reason to any one of a specific list of causes instead of letting users enter whatever they feel like. This is a good time to use the ENUM option:

```
CREATE TABLE missing_luggage (
    missing_luggage_id INT AUTO_INCREMENT PRIMARY KEY,
    luggage_id INT NOT NULL,
    missing_reason ENUM ('Airline error', 'Late checkin', 'Possible theft',
'Unknown'),
...
...

    FOREIGN KEY (luggage_id) REFERENCES checked_luggage(luggage_id) ON
DELETE CASCADE
) ENGINE = INNODB;
```

Should a user or application attempt to place an invalid value in the missing_reason column, MySQL blocks the incorrect entry and places a NULL in the column.

Be aware that MySQL sorts ENUM columns based on the order in which you entered your values in the column definition. Consequently, be certain to place your ENUM values in alphabetical order.

Finally, although this book does not focus on relational database theory best practices, sharp-eyed readers will spot a violation in the preceding table creation example. To those readers: Please excuse this unpleasant rule infringement in the interest of simplicity and clarity for our examples.

SET

Suppose that there can be multiple reasons for a piece of luggage to go missing. Perhaps it was checked in late, the airline misrouted it from London, UK, to London, Ontario, and then the suitcase was stolen in a daring, armed raid on a baggage cart at the London, Ontario, airport.

This is an example of a one-to-many relationship (that is, one piece of luggage can have many misfortunes). You would typically split the reasons off into their own table, and then create a row for each reason in that table. However, you could also use the SET attribute as follows:

```
CREATE TABLE missing_luggage (
    missing_luggage_id INT AUTO_INCREMENT PRIMARY KEY,
    luggage_id INT NOT NULL,
```

```
    missing_reason SET ('Airline error', 'Late check in', 'Possible theft',
    'Unknown'),
…
…
    FOREIGN KEY (luggage_id) REFERENCES checked_luggage(luggage_id) ON
DELETE CASCADE
) ENGINE = INNODB;
```

This lets you create very handy SQL for inserting or updating values into the missing_reason column. You can use integers to set the bits for the possible values, which translates to all possible permutations for missing_reason.

In this case, the possible values would translate to the following:

Value	Decimal	Binary
'Airline error'	1	0001
'Late check in'	2	0010
'Possible theft'	4	0100
'Unknown'	8	1000

With up to 64 possible values, you can represent many potential SET permutations with simple SQL:

```
INSERT INTO missing_luggage (missing_reason) VALUES (1)
```

This inserts a row and sets the missing_reason column to 'Airline error' only.

```
INSERT INTO missing_luggage (missing_reason) VALUES (7)
```

This inserts a record that matches the unfortunate piece of luggage described earlier: The check in was late (2), the airline made an error (1), and then the luggage was stolen (4).

If using these kinds of numeric values is not clear enough for you, you can also define mnemonic values in your application code. Your compiler will then swap these more readable values for the numeric settings listed previously. You can also provide a comma-separated list when inserting this type of information.

You can use the same syntax when searching for matching records:

```
SELECT * FROM missing_luggage WHERE missing_reason = 9
```

This returns all missing luggage in which the reason is both 'Airline error' and 'Unknown.'

If you don't want to use that style of query, you can use the LIKE '%value%' syntax or the FIND_IN_SET() function.

Note that MySQL always sorts the results in the order in which they were entered as possible SET values when the table was created, not the order in which they were entered into the table as data.

6

Understanding the MySQL Optimizer

What Is an Optimizer?

When you submit a request to the MySQL database engine, it must select one of many potential strategies to give you your requested results. These approaches often follow very different processing steps, yet all must arrive at the same results.

A good real-world analogy is to imagine that you are beginning a journey by car. If you only need to drive from your house to the one next door, you don't need to do much route planning: There's only one reasonable way to get there. However, suppose that you want to visit four friends, each of whom lives in a different city, all of whom are spread several hundred kilometers apart. It doesn't matter which friend you visit first, but you must see them all. There are dozens of streets and roads interlacing these cities: Some are high-speed freeways, whereas others are meandering country lanes. Unfortunately, you have very limited time to visit all of these friends, and you've heard rumors that traffic and construction are very bad on some of these roads.

If you were to sit down and map out all potential routes from the thousands of possible permutations, it's likely that it would take you longer to complete your mapping than if you simply picked one friend to visit at random, followed by another, and so on. Despite this overwhelming task, you do need some sort of plan, so the most logical thing to do is to obtain the most recent maps and quickly chart out the best possible course so that you visit all four friends as quickly as possible. When not considering information about construction and traffic, you would likely choose the high-speed freeways over alternate routes so that you could visit each friend as quickly as possible.

In a relational database management system like MySQL, the optimizer is responsible for charting the most efficient course to achieve your results. It must weigh many factors, such as table size, indexes, query columns, and so on before it can generate an accurate query plan.

For example, imagine that you issue a simple query that joins data from a table containing customer records with data from a table containing technical support entries. You ask the engine to find you all customers who live in Belgium (the country field in the customer records table) and have submitted a tech support case within the last six months (the date_registered field in the tech support table). Furthermore, suppose that there is an index in place on the customer records table's country field but not one on the tech support table's date_registered field.

How should the query proceed? Should it first scan all rows in the tech support table to find records with date_registered in the last six months and then use the index to search the customer records table on the country field? Or, should it do the opposite by first finding Belgians, and then finding appropriately time-stamped records from that group?

This is the kind of work that optimizers do: Using all available information about the table(s), pick an action plan that correctly satisfies the user's request in the most efficient way. However, optimizers are not flawless: They often require assistance and maintenance from database administrators, and can also take suggestions from developers on how best to achieve their results.

This chapter examines much more about MySQL's optimizer. First, this chapter explores how to provide the optimizer with the most up-to-date information so it can make the best decisions. Next, it discusses how to enable and interpret the extensive reporting that is available from the optimizer. The chapter then discusses how to give hints to the optimizer and override the automatically generated query plans.

Although there's an obvious interplay among your table design, index structure, and queries, this chapter focuses on the optimizer itself. Best practices for indexes and SQL are explored in Chapters 7 and 8 ("Indexing Strategies" and "Advanced SQL Tips"), respectively.

Optimizer Diagnostics and Tuning

MySQL offers an array of diagnostic information from the optimizer, as well as commands that you can use to help tune and guide this vital engine component. Most database administrators and developers will want to rush right in and start using the EXPLAIN command. However, EXPLAIN does not exist in a vacuum: There are complex interrelationships with other optimizer management commands, such as ANALYZE TABLE and OPTIMIZE TABLE. The following sections look at these first and then turn the attention to EXPLAIN.

The ANALYZE TABLE Command

The optimizer relies on accurate, up-to-date information to make its decisions. Statistics about indexes, including their keys, distribution, and structure, are critical factors in determining the most optimal results. For the InnoDB, MyISAM, and BDB engines, MySQL offers the ANALYZE TABLE command to calculate and store this information:

```
mysql> ANALYZE TABLE customer_master;
+-------------------------+---------+----------+----------+
| Table                   | Op      | Msg_type | Msg_text |
+-------------------------+---------+----------+----------+
| high_hat.customer_master | analyze | status   | OK       |
+-------------------------+---------+----------+----------+
1 row in set (0.47 sec)
```

It's a good idea to run this command periodically, especially for those tables subject to frequent updates that involve indexed columns.

To help you in choosing when to run the command, note that the engine places a read lock on the table for the duration of the study. However, if there are no changes to the underlying table, MySQL simply skips the analysis.

The OPTIMIZE TABLE Command

The storage advantages of variable-length rows were discussed earlier in the book. At that time, fragmentation was also cited as a potential performance risk. Fortunately, MySQL's OPTIMIZE TABLE command can defragment these tables, thereby restoring them to a more efficient structure while sorting any necessary indexes at the same time:

```
mysql> OPTIMIZE TABLE customer_master;
+-------------------------+----------+----------+----------+
| Table                   | Op       | Msg_type | Msg_text |
+-------------------------+----------+----------+----------+
| high_hat.customer_master | optimize | status   | OK       |
+-------------------------+----------+----------+----------+
1 row in set (3 min 51.78 sec)
```

Note that like its cousin ANALYZE TABLE, this command locks a table for the duration of processing. However, because it often restructures the table, OPTIMIZE TABLE generally takes much longer to complete, so be careful when selecting your launch time.

Disk management best practices are reviewed in more detail later in the book, especially in Chapter 13, "Improving Disk Speed." For now, take a look at a specific example of how OPTIMIZE TABLE can affect the disk usage and index structure of a table. For this example, we created a sample table as follows:

```
CREATE TABLE optimize_example
(
    col1 INT AUTO_INCREMENT PRIMARY KEY,
    col2 VARCHAR(30),
    col3 VARCHAR(100),
    col4 VARCHAR(255)
) ENGINE = INNODB;
```

We then loaded one million rows of random data into this table, followed by creating an index on col2:

```
CREATE INDEX opt_ix1 ON optimize_example(col2);
```

After building the index, MySQL reported this table's size at 215.8MB, and the indexes consumed a further 37.6MB.

Next, to simulate significant changes to the quantity of data in the table and index, we deleted every fifth row:

```
DELETE FROM optimize_example WHERE mod(col1,5) = 0;
```

After these large-scale deletions, MySQL continues to report this table's size at 215.8MB and the indexes at 37.6MB.

We then loaded 250,000 more rows of random data. The reported size is now 218.8MB of data and 35.6MB of index.

At this point, we ran the OPTIMIZE TABLE command to defragment the table and re-sort its indexes:

```
mysql> OPTIMIZE TABLE optimize_example;
+-------------------------+----------+----------+----------+
| Table                   | Op       | Msg_type | Msg_text |
+-------------------------+----------+----------+----------+
| high_hat.optimize_example | optimize | status   | OK       |
+-------------------------+----------+----------+----------+
1 row in set (4 min 56.69 sec)
```

After the command ran, the sample table had been compressed to 175.7MB of data and 33.6MB of index: a significant size reduction and defragmentation.

The EXPLAIN Command

Database designers and developers use MySQL's EXPLAIN in one of two ways:

1. To get a list of columns for the table. This is the same as running the DESCRIBE command, as shown in Figure 6.1.

2. To understand how MySQL processes a query against one or more tables. This usage is much more interesting from an optimization perspective. Beginning with version 5.0.1, MySQL now offers a status variable to help you compare the costs of different query plans. Use the last_query_cost indicator when you are trying to decide between two or more approaches to write the same query.

The first question about EXPLAIN is simple: When should you use it? Fortunately, the answer is simple as well. You should use this command whenever you are designing queries against a large and/or complex database, because you may elect to use the results to alter your indexing strategy or even override the optimizer's query plan.

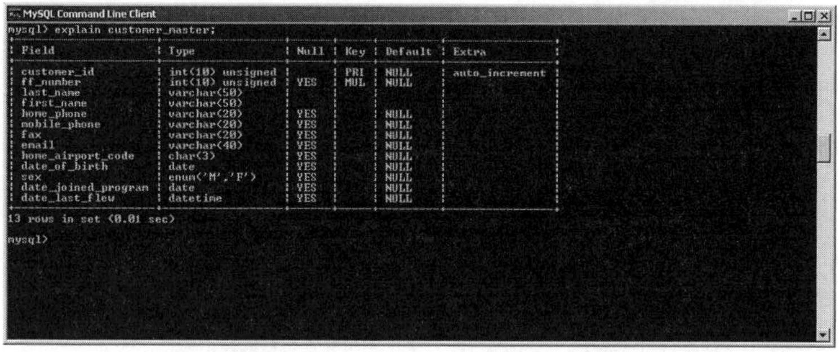

MySQL Command Line Client

mysql> explain customer_master;

Field	Type	Null	Key	Default	Extra
customer_id	int(10) unsigned		PRI	NULL	auto_increment
ff_number	int(10) unsigned	YES	MUL	NULL	
last_name	varchar(50)				
first_name	varchar(50)				
home_phone	varchar(20)	YES		NULL	
mobile_phone	varchar(20)	YES		NULL	
fax	varchar(20)	YES		NULL	
email	varchar(40)	YES		NULL	
home_airport_code	char(3)	YES		NULL	
date_of_birth	date	YES		NULL	
sex	enum('M','F')	YES		NULL	
date_joined_program	date	YES		NULL	
date_last_flew	datetime	YES		NULL	

13 rows in set (0.01 sec)

mysql>

FIGURE 6.1 Viewing EXPLAIN results for a table.

Next, how do you launch EXPLAIN? Whether you're using the command-line interface or the MySQL Query Browser, simply prefix your SQL SELECT statement with EXPLAIN. The optimizer then returns a detailed report on the suggested query plan. Let's review these reports in more detail.

Before beginning, use the following tables and related indexes throughout the balance of this chapter to help illustrate our examples:

```
CREATE TABLE customer_master
(
    customer_id INT UNSIGNED AUTO_INCREMENT PRIMARY KEY,
    ff_number CHAR(10),
    last_name VARCHAR(50) NOT NULL,
    first_name VARCHAR(50) NOT NULL,
    home_phone VARCHAR(20),
    mobile_phone VARCHAR(20),
    fax VARCHAR(20),
    email VARCHAR(40),
    home_airport_code CHAR(3),
    date_of_birth DATE,
    sex ENUM ('M','F'),
    date_joined_program DATE,
    date_last_flew DATETIME
) ENGINE = INNODB;
CREATE INDEX cm_ix1 ON customer_master(home_phone);

CREATE TABLE customer_address
(
    customer_id INT UNSIGNED NOT NULL,
    customer_address_seq SMALLINT(2) UNSIGNED NOT NULL,
    address1 VARCHAR(50),
    address2 VARCHAR(50),
    address3 VARCHAR(50),
    city VARCHAR(50),
```

```
        state VARCHAR(50),
        country VARCHAR(70),
        postal_code VARCHAR(20),
        PRIMARY KEY (customer_id, customer_address_seq)
) ENGINE = INNODB;
CREATE INDEX ca_ix1 ON customer_address(postal_code);
CREATE INDEX ca_ix2 ON customer_address(country);

CREATE TABLE transactions
(
        transaction_id INT UNSIGNED AUTO_INCREMENT PRIMARY KEY,
        transaction_date DATETIME NOT NULL,
        customer_id INT NOT NULL,
        amount DECIMAL (5,2) NOT NULL,
        transaction_type ENUM ('Purchase','Credit')
) ENGINE = MYISAM;
CREATE INDEX tr_ix2 on transactions(customer_id);

CREATE TABLE airports
(
        airport_id INT UNSIGNED AUTO_INCREMENT PRIMARY KEY,
        airport_code CHAR(3) NOT NULL,
        airport_name VARCHAR(40),
        vip_club SMALLINT(1),
        club_upgrade_date DATE
) ENGINE = INNODB;
CREATE UNIQUE INDEX air_ix1 ON airports(airport_code);

CREATE TABLE flights
(
        flight_id INT UNSIGNED AUTO_INCREMENT PRIMARY KEY,
        flight_number SMALLINT UNSIGNED NOT NULL,
        flight_date DATE NOT NULL,
        flight_departure_city CHAR(3),
        flight_arrival_city CHAR(3)
) ENGINE = INNODB;

CREATE TABLE customer_flights
(
        customer_flight_id INT UNSIGNED AUTO_INCREMENT PRIMARY KEY,
        customer_id INT UNSIGNED NOT NULL,
        flight_id SMALLINT UNSIGNED NOT NULL,
        FOREIGN KEY (customer_id) REFERENCES customer_master(customer_id),
        FOREIGN KEY (flight_id) REFERENCES flights(flight_id)
) ENGINE = INNODB;
```

Figure 6.2 shows a sample query as well as its related EXPLAIN output.

FIGURE 6.2   Sample query and its EXPLAIN output.

How can you interpret these results? This section first looks at a field list of the returned information, and then provides a detailed explanation of each value, along with examples.

Table 6.1 lists the columns returned by the EXPLAIN command, along with each column's purpose.

TABLE 6.1   *EXPLAIN* Result Columns

Column	Purpose
id	The step sequence number for this statement.
select_type	The kind of SELECT statement to be processed.
table	The table to be processed for this statement.
type	The type of join to be performed.
possible_keys	The available potential keys if the query is able to use an index.
key	The key that the optimizer chose from all the potential keys.
key_len	The length of the selected key.
ref	The values or columns that will be fed to the selected key.
rows	The optimizer's best estimate of the number of rows to be searched in this table for this query.
extra	Additional useful information from the optimizer. If this column states Impossible WHERE noticed after reading const tables, this means that your query criteria returned no rows; the optimizer is unable to provide any diagnostic information in this case.

The following sections look at each of the columns in more detail.

id

Remember that MySQL processes tables in the order in which they are listed in the EXPLAIN output. As you evaluate the proposed query plan and ponder making adjustments, keep an eye on the sequence number for each table.

select_type

Depending on query structure, SELECT statements are classified as one of the following:

- SIMPLE—This is a basic SELECT statement, with no subqueries or UNION:

```
SELECT * FROM customer_master WHERE last_name = "SIERRA";
```

- PRIMARY—This is the highest level SELECT statement. In the following two table–join examples, the customer_master table has this select_type:

```
SELECT cm.last_name, cm.first_name
FROM customer_master cm
WHERE cm.customer_id IN
(
        SELECT ca.customer_id
        FROM customer_address ca
        WHERE ca.country = "Canada"
);
```

- UNION—If the optimizer reports a UNION, this is any SELECT below the top level. In the following example, the second SELECT is identified as having a select_type of UNION:

```
SELECT cm.customer_id FROM CUSTOMER_MASTER cm
WHERE cm.date_joined_program > "2002-01-15" AND cm.home_airport_code = 'SEA'
UNION
SELECT cm1.customer_id FROM CUSTOMER_MASTER cm1 WHERE cm1.sex = 'M';
```

- DEPENDENT UNION—This is similar to the preceding UNION example, except it relies on the results of an outer subquery. In the following example, the second customer_master reference (cm1) is classified as DEPENDENT UNION:

```
SELECT ca.customer_id FROM customer_address ca
WHERE ca.country = "United States" AND ca.customer_id IN
(
        SELECT cm.customer_id FROM CUSTOMER_MASTER cm
        WHERE cm.date_joined_program > "2002-01-15" AND cm.home_airport_code =
        'SEA'
        UNION
        SELECT cm1.customer_id FROM CUSTOMER_MASTER cm1 WHERE cm1.sex = 'M'
);
```

- SUBQUERY—If the query includes a subquery, the first SELECT in the subquery is identified as SUBQUERY. In the following case, the customer_flights table is chosen for that categorization:

```
SELECT f.flight_id, f.flight_number, f.flight_date
FROM flights f
WHERE f.flight_id =
(
        SELECT cf.flight_id
```

```
        FROM customer_flights cf
        WHERE cf.customer_flight_id = 2291443
);
```

- DEPENDENT SUBQUERY—If the subquery relies on information from an outer subquery, the first SELECT statement inside the subquery is identified as a DEPENDENT SUBQUERY. In this example, as shown earlier, the subquery from the customer_address table is cited as a DEPENDENT SUBQUERY:

```
SELECT cm.last_name, cm.first_name
FROM customer_master cm
WHERE cm.customer_id IN
(
        SELECT ca.customer_id
        FROM customer_address ca
        WHERE ca.country = "Canada"
);
```

- UNION RESULT—When the optimizer needs to create a temporary intermediate table to hold the results of a UNION, it reports UNION RESULT:

```
SELECT * FROM customer_master99 WHERE first_name LIKE 'Bill%'
UNION
SELECT * FROM customer_master99 WHERE email LIKE '%@mysql.com';
```

- DERIVED—If a query involves a derived table (including a view), MySQL assigns the DERIVED select_type (see Figure 6.3).

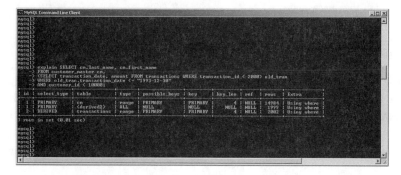

FIGURE 6.3   EXPLAIN output showing a DERIVED select_type.

table

MySQL cites the table name for each step of the query plan. Derived tables are identified as such; tables to hold the results of UNIONs are prefixed with union.

type

As you saw earlier, type refers to the kind of join that MySQL performs to retrieve your information. This is crucial to estimating performance because a bad join strategy can really bog down your application.

The following list looks at each of the potential values for this column, along with the scenarios that trigger the result. Because the goal is optimization, the list begins with the most sluggish values, and then works its way toward the fastest. As you experiment with your queries, always strive to achieve values toward the end of this list:

- ALL—This value means that the optimizer is forced to perform a table scan and read all rows in a table to find your results. This often happens when you are missing an index or are querying on substrings that can't be indexed:

```
SELECT mobile_phone
FROM customer_master
WHERE mobile_phone LIKE "%1212%";
```

  For small tables, this is not usually a problem but suppose that in this case the customer_master table has 75 million rows. ALL means that every one of these rows will be looked at to find matching mobile phone numbers. The problem becomes much more dramatic when the query has joins among numerous tables and also involves multiple table scans.

- index—Although similar to a table scan, these types of queries mean that MySQL is able to read the index to retrieve the data, rather than the underlying table. In the preceding example, suppose that you placed an index on the mobile_phone column and then ran the query again:

```
SELECT mobile_phone
FROM customer_master
WHERE mobile_phone LIKE "%1212%";
```

  The primary savings from this type of search is that the index is generally smaller than the data; otherwise, it's still a very inefficient query because all entries need to be read. Furthermore, if you request other columns than those in the index, MySQL is forced to read the table itself.

- range—Range queries make use of indexes to find data within the range specified by the query:

```
SELECT ca.*
FROM customer_address ca
WHERE ca.postal_code BETWEEN "11561" AND "11710";
```

  The efficiency of these types of queries is highly dependent on the breadth of the search, as well as the cardinality (degree of uniqueness) of the index.

- index_subquery—This kind of query takes advantage of an index to speed results on a subquery:

```
SELECT cm.last_name, cm.first_name
FROM customer_master cm
WHERE cm.customer_id IN
(
        SELECT ca.customer_id
        FROM customer_address ca
        WHERE ca.postal_code = "TVC15-3CPU"
);
```

In the preceding example, MySQL performs a table scan on `customer_master`, and for each located row uses the index on the `postal_code` field in the `customer_address` to complete the join.

- `unique_subquery`—Just like the previous example of `index_subquery`, this kind of query utilizes an index to quickly find the right information in a subquery. However, it's even faster because it is able to use a unique index or primary key to get to the data.

```
SELECT ca.country
FROM customer_address ca
WHERE ca.customer_id in
(
        SELECT cm.customer_id
        FROM customer_master cm
        WHERE cm.ff_number LIKE "%AAA-%"
);
```

In fact, this kind of search doesn't even read the subqueried table itself, but instead returns results directly from the index—the `customer_master.customer_id` field in this case.

- `index_merge`—Prior to version 5.0, MySQL could only employ one index when processing a table. On the other hand, many queries contain criteria that can be rapidly located via two or more indexes. Versions 5.0 and later can now potentially make use of multiple indexes on the same table, greatly reducing query time. The EXPLAIN command shows a type of `index_merge` when MySQL is able to leverage two or more indexes on a single table.

This concept is discussed more a little later in this chapter.

- `ref/ref_or_null`—These types of searches use a nonunique index to find one to potentially many rows from a table:

```
SELECT ca.*
FROM customer_address ca
WHERE ca.postal_code = "11561";
```

If `ref_or_null` is returned, it means that the query is also looking for null values from an index column:

```
SELECT ca.*
FROM customer_address ca
WHERE ca.postal_code = "11561"
OR ca.postal_code IS NULL;
```

- eq_ref—These types of searches first take data from an initial query and then use an index to find subsequent information. However, eq_ref searches are able to employ unique indexes or primary keys, making these joins much faster:

```
SELECT cm.last_name, cm.first_name, ca.city
FROM customer_master cm, customer_address ca
WHERE ca.city = "Honolulu"
AND ca.customer_id = cm.customer_id;
```

In this example, MySQL first interrogates the customer_address table (via a highly inefficient table scan) to find records from Honolulu. It then takes these results and searches for records in the customer_master table using the primary key, customer_id. Fortunately, this second search goes very fast: One and only one row will have a particular customer_id.

- const—The query will have a type of const (that is, constant value) if the optimizer is able to fully use a unique index or primary key to satisfy your search:

```
SELECT address1, address2, address3
FROM customer_address ca
WHERE ca.customer_id = 3484
AND ca.customer_address_seq = 1;
```

This is the fastest possible query; MySQL only needs to read one row to find your result. Note that if you're reading a system table with only one row, the optimizer classifies this as system instead of const.

possible_keys and key

MySQL often has multiple indexes at its disposal when trying to decide on a query plan. Viewing possible_keys lets you see the full list of potential indexes that the optimizer is evaluating, whereas the key value tells you what MySQL ended up choosing, as shown in Figure 6.4.

In this case, MySQL had a choice between the primary key (customer_id) and the ca_ix2 index (country). The optimizer selected the primary key.

If you're curious to learn more about how the optimizer chooses a plan, try experimenting with queries. For example, observe what happens when you change one word in the query (from AND to OR), as shown in Figure 6.5.

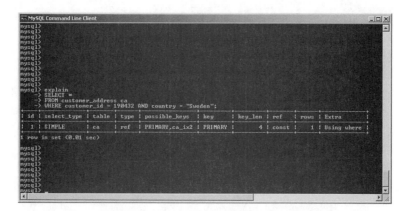

FIGURE 6.4   EXPLAIN output for a query that uses the primary key.

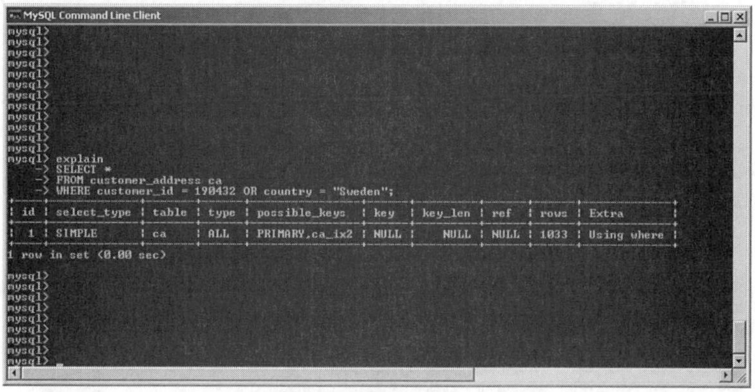

FIGURE 6.5   Query plan radically changed by substitution of OR for AND.

What happened? Why can't MySQL use our well-thought-out indexes? In this case, the search is written with an OR clause that refers to a single table. This forces the engine into a sequential table scan (ALL), or at least it did until version 5.0. MySQL version 5.0 features much more robust optimizer algorithms that can speed these kinds of queries. Figure 6.6 shows the same query after version 5.0.

With version 5.0, MySQL can now make use of multiple indexes on a single table to speed results. These new algorithms are explored a little later in this chapter. You'll also examine how to override the optimizer's analysis. Finally, Chapter 7, "Indexing Strategies," spends much more time probing indexing strategies.

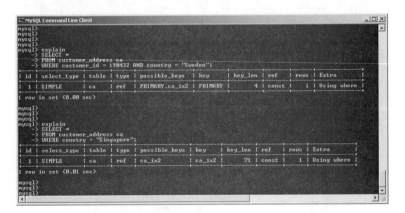

FIGURE 6.6   Version 5.0 now uses the `index_merge` algorithm to avoid a table scan by taking advantage of multiple indexes.

key_len

After MySQL has selected a key, this field shows the length of the chosen option. The example shown in Figure 6.7 uses the integer-based primary key for the `customer_address` table, which is four bytes in length. The second example searches on an indexed string field.

```
SELECT *
FROM customer_address ca
WHERE customer_id = 190432 OR country = "Sweden";
```

```
SELECT *
FROM customer_address ca
WHERE country = "Singapore";
```

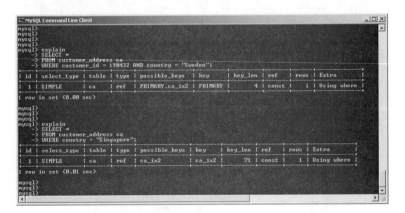

FIGURE 6.7   Different query plans based on the type of index key chosen.

MySQL reports the length of the field if it's a single field. For a multifield index, MySQL reports the full length of all fields (working from left to right) that will be used.

For example, suppose you create a multifield index (`ca_ix3`) on the `customer_address city` and `state` columns and then query against those values, as shown in Figure 6.8.

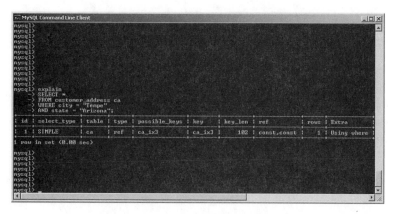

FIGURE 6.8   Query that uses a new multifield index.

As you can see, MySQL was able to use the multifield index to satisfy the query; the key length is the sum of the two fields (50 + 50), plus one overhead byte per field.

ref

This field tracks the values or columns that will be used to look for the row(s), as shown in Figure 6.9.

FIGURE 6.9   Query plan showing candidate columns for searching.

In this example, MySQL is able to filter the customer_address table on the newly created index, and then use the customer_id field as the lookup field for the second part of the query: matching the customer_address rows with their counterparts in customer_master.

It might be somewhat difficult to analyze and understand the results in this field because there will be times that MySQL reports NULL on a search when you might expect a const instead, as shown in Figure 6.10.

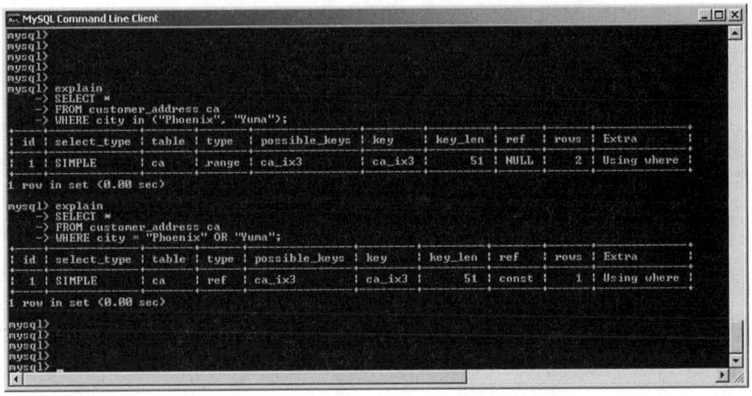

FIGURE 6.10   Two similar queries with different types of **ref** results.

The first query performs a **range** search, which results in NULL in the **ref** column:

```
SELECT *
FROM customer_address ca
WHERE city in ("Phoenix", "Yuma")
```

The second search performs a **ref** search, so you see **const** in the **ref** column:

```
SELECT *
FROM customer_address ca
WHERE city = "Phoenix" OR "Yuma"
```

rows

MySQL uses its internal table and index statistics to provide this number, which is its best estimate of the quantity of records that should be read to produce the results. Pay attention to very large numbers in this column: It usually indicates a table scan or highly duplicate index. As you saw earlier, this can become an even bigger problem when many tables in the query require the reading of large numbers of rows.

To keep MySQL's statistics up to date, it's also important to run ANALYZE TABLE or OPTIMIZE TABLE for those tables that change frequently.

Extra

The EXPLAIN command offers additional diagnostic information on top of the helpful data you've seen so far. These messages are placed in the extra column, and can include one or more of the following:

- Impossible WHERE noticed after reading const tables—As mentioned earlier, this message means that you have supplied search criteria that returns no rows. For example, you will see this message if you test a query that searches on a nonexistent value from an indexed column. If this happens, try rewriting your query with more inclusive criteria so that the EXPLAIN command can properly analyze your search.

- Using where—This is likely to be the most commonly encountered message in this section. You'll usually see it when you specify a WHERE clause to filter the number of potential rows.

- Distinct—The optimizer reports this condition when it determines that the first row that matches the query criteria will suffice, and there is no need to check additional rows.

- Not exists—There are certain situations when joining two or more tables in which MySQL detects the impossibility of finding more than one row in a table other than the leftmost table. This usually happens because additional rows would violate a primary key or NOT NULL constraint. When this condition is triggered, MySQL reports Not exists in the extra column.

- Range checked for each record—In certain situations, such as range queries combined with nonselective indexes, the optimizer reports this condition. It then attempts to resolve the query via the most useful key.

- Using filesort—The optimizer uses a filesort if your query conditions require MySQL to first identify the requested rows and then sort them without the benefit of an index:

```
SELECT *
FROM customer_address ca
ORDER BY ca.state;
```

Recall that the customer_address table does not have an index in which state is the leftmost (or only) component. That means that the existing multipart index on city, state is of no use in processing this query, thereby necessitating the filesort.

Fortunately, from version 4.1 onward, MySQL uses a much more sophisticated caching mechanism that reduces the amount of disk processing necessary when a filesort is mandated.

- Using index—You'll see this message for those times that MySQL can return your results by simply reading the index without having to read the table itself. For example, for the following two query plans shown in Figure 6.11, only the first is displayed as using index.

```
SELECT flight_id
FROM flights
WHERE flight_id = 8321;

SELECT flight_id, flight_date
FROM flights
WHERE flight_id = 8321;
```

The second query forces MySQL to read the row itself because the flight_date column is not indexed.

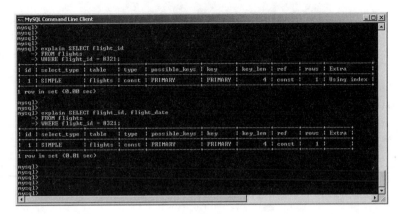

FIGURE 6.11   Using index is displayed when all requested information is found within the index.

- Using temporary—You'll receive this message if your query requires MySQL to store intermediate results in a temporary storage table before returning the final answer to you. In many cases, you will see this combined with the filesort message.

- Using index for group-by—In certain cases, MySQL might be able to consult an index to facilitate a GROUP BY request, rather than retrieving data from the underlying table.

As you saw earlier in the discussion on the type portion of EXPLAIN's output, MySQL's optimizer features enhanced algorithms beginning with version 5.0. These new capabilities let MySQL exploit two or more indexes on a single table to speed queries.

The following list looks at how the extra portion of the EXPLAIN command reports on these new algorithms.

- Using intersect—MySQL is able to use the index merge intersect algorithm when you create a query that employs ranges on a primary key and also includes a search on a value that is covered by a secondary index in the same table and related to the first part of the search with an AND.

  If these conditions are met, MySQL works in parallel to process the table using more than one index, and then merges the products back into a complete resultset.

  Look at some sample queries to see the difference between MySQL version 5.0 and earlier. Before beginning, assume that you add the following index to the customer_master table described earlier in the chapter:

  CREATE INDEX cm_ix6 ON customer_master(home_airport_code);

  Now, you can evaluate a query on the customer_master table that attempts to find a range of rows on the primary key, and also provides a value for the indexed home_airport_code column. In pre-5.0 MySQL, note the optimizer's report on this query, as shown in Figure 6.12.

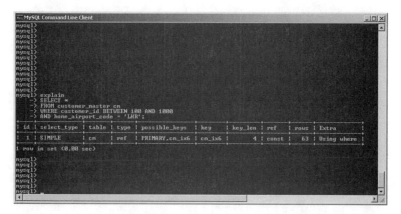

FIGURE 6.12   Pre-5.0 query plan: Only one index per table can be processed.

The optimizer correctly detected the relevant indexes, and picked one to retrieve data. In version 5.0 and beyond, the optimizer's report is different, as shown in Figure 6.13.

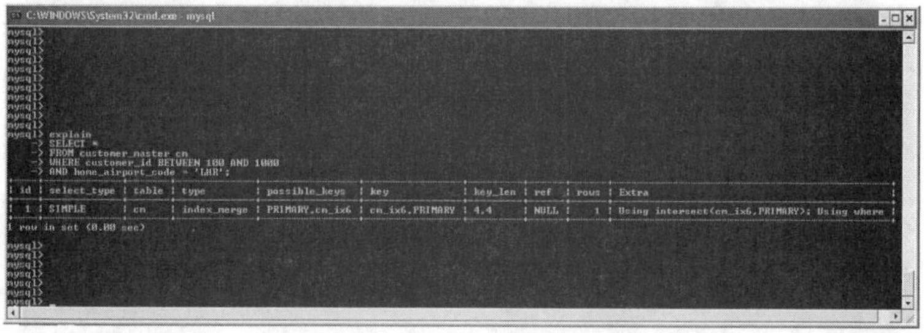

FIGURE 6.13   Post-5.0 query plan: Index merge algorithm can take advantage of multiple indexes per table.

The query and database remain the same, yet the query plan has changed. Why? MySQL is now able to use the index_merge algorithm to speed through the table by using the primary key index as well as the index on home_airport_code. At the end, it merges the two resultsets to give you a final answer.

Note that if the range is very large, even the 5.0 optimizer might elect to avoid using this algorithm because the index on the range column(s) isn't selective enough. Instead, MySQL simply drops back to a more traditional ref search, as shown in Figure 6.14.

- Using union—Just as with the using intersect result, using union is the outcome when you specify a range search on a primary key and include a search on a column that is also indexed. The chief difference between these two results is that using intersect combines the two search criteria with an AND, whereas using union creates a union between the two resultsets by employing OR. Figure 6.15 shows what you receive from EXPLAIN prior to version 5.0.

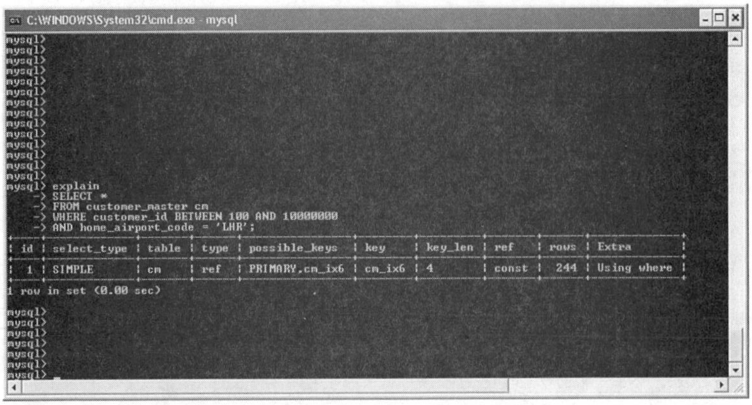

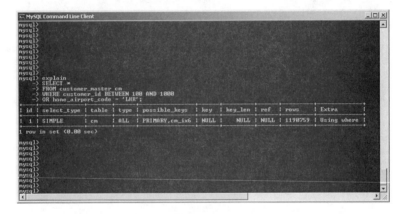

FIGURE 6.14   A too-large range may force a ref search instead of using the
index merge algorithm.

FIGURE 6.15   Expensive table scan forced prior to version 5.0.

This is a very expensive table scan; the OR sees to that. Observe the results for 5.0,
however, in Figure 6.16.

This should run much faster: MySQL is able to use two indexes rather than slogging
through the entire data set with a table scan.

- Using sort_union—As you would expect from the name, the chief difference between a
report of this option and using union is that using sort union indicates that MySQL
first has to sort the individual resultsets (using their rowids) and then merge them
together before giving you an answer.

Suppose that you place an index on the customer_master's date_joined_program column:

```
CREATE INDEX cm_ix5 ON customer_master(date_joined_program);
```

FIGURE 6.16   Much more efficient multiindex query plan in version 5.0 and beyond.

Now, suppose you create two range queries on the same table and combine them with an OR. Figure 6.17 shows the report prior to version 5.0.

FIGURE 6.17   Expensive table scan forced prior to version 5.0.

Again, this is a very costly table scan as MySQL works through the entire table to locate your results. It's a different story with version 5.0, as shown in Figure 6.18.

If the optimizer determines that neither index is selective enough, however, even version 5.0 falls back to a slow table scan, unless you specify FORCE INDEX with your query. This option is investigated later in the chapter.

As you experiment with your queries, see if you can construct your indexes and searches to take advantage of these new 5.0 features.

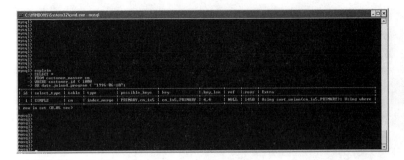

FIGURE 6.18   Much more efficient multiindex query plan in version 5.0 and beyond.

Helping the Optimizer

As you've seen, MySQL's optimizer conducts a sophisticated analysis of the facts before coming up with a query plan. However, it is not infallible, and there might be times when it could use your help. This section investigates several ways to provide assistance to the optimizer.

Remember that it's always a good idea to take a scientific approach to your query tuning, and track the impact your suggestions have on query plans and actual response. Also, remember that this section only looks at ways to directly affect the optimizer's behavior (including query plan choice). In particular, this section examines SELECT STRAIGHT_JOIN and USE INDEX, IGNORE INDEX, and FORCE INDEX.

You'll look at ways to tune your SQL statements and engine behavior in later chapters. These optimizer-affecting SQL statement options include the following:

- SELECT HIGH_PRIORITY
- SELECT SQL_BIG_RESULT
- SELECT SQL_SMALL_RESULT
- SELECT SQL_BUFFER_RESULT
- SELECT SQL_CACHE
- SELECT SQL_NO_CACHE
- LIMIT
- SQL_CALC_FOUND_ROWS

SELECT STRAIGHT_JOIN

For a multitable join, you might elect to change the order in which the optimizer joins your tables. By specifying STRAIGHT_JOIN in your SQL, MySQL is forced to join the tables in the order in which they're specified in your query. Note that this is an extension by MySQL to standard SQL.

You can look at a few examples to see when this might help (or even hurt!) performance. For simplicity, let's not consider the impact of query caching, memory, or other engine configuration.

First, suppose you want to perform a very simple join between the `customer_master` and `customer_address` tables:

```
SELECT cm.last_name, cm.first_name, ca.postal_code, ca.country
FROM customer_master cm, customer_address ca
WHERE cm.customer_id = ca.customer_id;
```

For this join, MySQL first performs a table scan through the `customer_address` table. It reads each row, and then performs an `eq_ref` join to the `customer_master` table, using its primary key `customer_id` field.

Assuming that the `customer_master` table has four million rows, the total number of rows read for this query is more than eight million: four million rows read from the `customer_address` table via a table scan, and one `customer_master` row read via the primary key per returned row.

Suppose, however, that the `customer_master` table is only one fourth as large as `customer_address`, and only contains one million rows. How could this be? Perhaps each customer has multiple addresses (home, office, billing, warehouse, and so on). In any case, what would happen if you forced the optimizer to first look at the `customer_master` table and then join to `customer_address`?

```
SELECT STRAIGHT_JOIN cm.last_name, cm.first_name, ca.postal_code, ca.country
FROM customer_master cm, customer_address ca
WHERE cm.customer_id = ca.customer_id;
```

In this case, MySQL churns through the one million row `customer_table`, picking up rows one-by-one and then performing a rapid lookup into the `customer_address` table, using the indexed `customer_id` field. The number of rows read for this query is approximately five million: one million table-scanned rows from `customer_master` and an average of four `customer_address` rows to match the indexed join.

For this example, it might be worth it to force MySQL first to read through the smaller table and then do an indexed lookup. Unfortunately, it's easy to imagine a scenario in which you damage performance by incorrectly forcing a straight join, so be careful when experimenting.

Let's look at an experiment gone wrong: a badly designed optimizer override. Suppose that you want to retrieve a list of all customers, along with the name of their home airport:

```
SELECT cm.last_name, cm.first_name, ai.airport_name
FROM airports ai, customer_master cm
WHERE cm.home_airport_code = ai.airport_code;
```

Note that the `airport_code` field is uniquely indexed in the `airports` table (but not in the `customer_master` table), and this table has 1,000 rows. For this query, MySQL correctly performs a table scan on the `customer_master` table, reading its four million rows one-by-one and then performing a single read into the `airports` table for each `customer_master` record.

What happens if you change the query to force MySQL to first read the `airports` table?

```
SELECT STRAIGHT_JOIN cm.last_name, cm.first_name, ai.airport_name
FROM airports ai, customer_master2 cm
WHERE cm.home_airport_code = ai.airport_code;
```

MySQL dutifully reads a row from the `airports` table, and then runs a table scan to read every one of the four million row `customer_master` table. After the table scan finishes, MySQL reads the next row from `airports`, and starts the table scan again to look for a new match.

This is hundreds of times slower than if you had just left it alone. Of course, this query would run much more efficiently if the `airport_code` field was indexed in `customer_master`, but this isn't the case in the example.

So far, you've looked at simple, two-table queries. Imagine the amount of time needed to study the potential impact (good or bad) of forcing straight joins on a five, six, or more table join. How would you know which table should go first, second, and so on? The number of permutations that you would need to test could become enormous. This is why, in most cases, it's a good idea to just let the optimizer do its job, unless you really do know better.

Forcing Index Selection

It's quite likely that many of your queries will access tables with multiple indexes. Generally, MySQL's optimizer uses its internal statistics to identify and choose the most efficient index. However, there might be situations in which you need to override this behavior. This section reviews several options that you can use in your SELECT statements to control how the optimizer picks an index. Recall that we're only looking at how to affect the optimizer's choice of index; Chapter 7 delves much more deeply into best practices for indexing.

To keep this as simple as possible, this example only looks at a single-table query; MySQL uses this index selection to find rows in a particular table, and only then processes any subsequent joins. To save you the effort of flipping pages, the `customer_master` table is redisplayed here, along with some additional indexes:

```
CREATE TABLE customer_master
(
    customer_id INT UNSIGNED AUTO_INCREMENT PRIMARY KEY,
    ff_number CHAR(10),
    last_name VARCHAR(50) NOT NULL,
    first_name VARCHAR(50) NOT NULL,
    home_phone VARCHAR(20),
    mobile_phone VARCHAR(20),
```

```
    fax VARCHAR(20),
    email VARCHAR(40),
    home_airport_code CHAR(3),
    date_of_birth DATE,
    sex ENUM ('M','F'),
    date_joined_program DATE,
    date_last_flew DATETIME
) ENGINE = INNODB;
CREATE INDEX cm_ix1 ON customer_master(home_phone);
CREATE INDEX cm_ix2 ON customer_master(ff_number);
CREATE INDEX cm_ix3 ON customer_master(last_name, first_name);
CREATE INDEX cm_ix4 ON customer_master(sex);
CREATE INDEX cm_ix5 ON customer_master(date_joined_program);
CREATE INDEX cm_ix6 ON customer_master(home_airport_code);
```

USE INDEX/FORCE INDEX

It's quite possible that MySQL will need to choose from a candidate pool of more than one index to satisfy your query. If, after reading the EXPLAIN output, you determine that MySQL is picking the wrong index, you can override the index selection by adding either USE INDEX or FORCE INDEX to the query. Take a look at some examples.

First, suppose that you want to issue a search to find all customers who have a home phone number in the city of Boston, and whose home airport is Boston Logan, as shown in Figure 6.19.

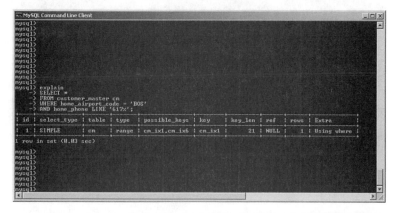

FIGURE 6.19   Optimizer correctly chooses between two candidate indexes to process a query.

What does this tell us? MySQL correctly identified two candidate indexes to speed the search: cm_ix1 (on home_phone) and cm_ix6 (on home_airport_code). In the end, it chose the index on home_phone (because it is much more selective than the home_airport_code field).

However, what if you wanted to force MySQL to use the index on `home_airport_code`? You would specify the `USE INDEX` option in your SQL statement, as shown in Figure 6.20.

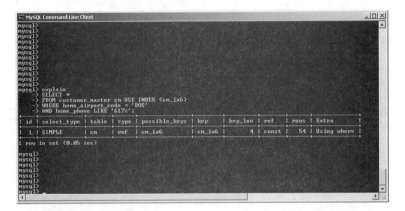

FIGURE 6.20   User intervention to force selection of a particular index to process a query.

Observe that MySQL no longer even reports the availability of the cm_ix1 key; it only specifies the key you requested. What happens if you mistype the key (see Figure 6.21)?

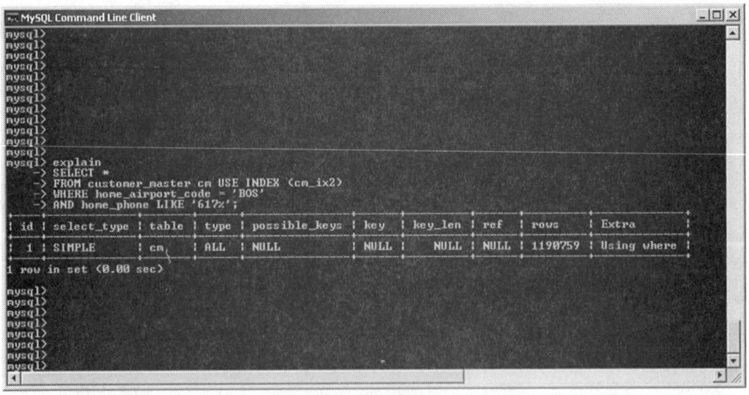

FIGURE 6.21   A typo produces an expensive table scan.

This is a costly mistake: MySQL does not warn us that this index is irrelevant for this query, and instead performs a table scan because of our typing error. The moral here is to pay attention when you override the optimizer!

Where does `FORCE INDEX` fit in? `FORCE INDEX` (first enabled in version 4.0.9) is very similar to `USE INDEX`; the main difference between the two options is that `FORCE INDEX` demands that MySQL use the index (if possible) in lieu of a more expensive table scan, whereas `USE INDEX` still allows the optimizer to choose a table scan.

IGNORE INDEX

Sometimes, tables are overindexed, and might confuse the optimizer into choosing an inefficient query plan. Fortunately, MySQL lets you "hide" certain indexes from the optimizer.

Suppose you put the query shown in Figure 6.22 to MySQL.

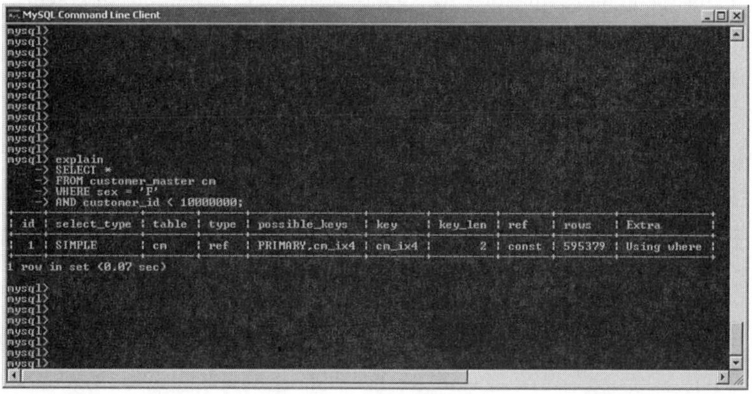

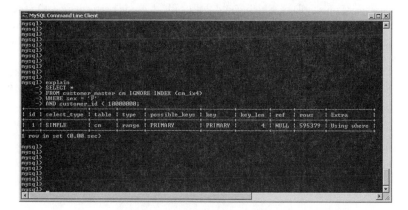

FIGURE 6.22 Optimizer chooses a very nonselective index.

MySQL has correctly identified two candidates indexes—the primary key (`customer_id`) and cm_ix4 (`sex`)—and has chosen the latter. Unfortunately, this is not a very selective index, and probably shouldn't even exist. Chapter 7 discusses indexing in much more detail, but for now, you can use the `IGNORE KEY` option to tell the optimizer to avoid this key, as shown in Figure 6.23.

FIGURE 6.23 Removing an index from consideration by the optimizer.

It's important to understand that overriding the optimizer will be a rare event as long as you keep your data and index statistics up to date (via `ANALYZE TABLE` and/or `OPTIMIZE TABLE`).

Optimizer Processing Options

Recall that it's the job of the optimizer to select the best plan among all possible alternatives. For relatively simple queries, the number of different choices might not be too large. But what happens if you construct very complex queries, involving more than a dozen large tables and very intricate search criteria? In these kinds of situations, it's possible that MySQL might spend more time picking a query plan from the millions of potential permutations than actually executing the query!

Fortunately, versions 5.01 and beyond offer two system variables that give the database developer some control over how much time the optimizer spends calculating its query plan.

optimizer_prune_level

The optimizer_prune_level variable, set to 1 (enabled) by default, tells the optimizer to avoid certain query plans if it determines that the number of rows processed per table will be excessive.

If you are confident that this avoidance is hurting performance and that MySQL should examine more query plans, set the variable to zero (disabled). Of course, this kind of experiment is a much better candidate for your performance testing platform, rather than your production system.

optimizer_search_depth

As you saw earlier, queries that touch numerous tables can cause the optimizer to spend more time calculating the query plan than actually running the query. Setting the optimizer_search_depth system variable lets you control how exhaustive these computations will be.

If you make this number large (close to the actual number of tables in the search), MySQL checks many more query plans, which could drastically degrade performance. On the other hand, a small number causes the optimizer to come up with a plan much faster, at the risk of skipping a better plan. Finally, setting this value to zero lets the optimizer make its own decision, and is probably the safest course of action in most cases.

7

Indexing Strategies

Like beauty, the most attractive indexing strategy is very much in the eye of the beholder. After indexes are in place for primary, join, and filter keys (a universal standard of indexing beauty, perhaps?), what works for application A might be the wrong approach for application B.

Application A might be a transactional system that supports tens of thousands of quick interactions with the database, and its data modifications must be made in milliseconds. Application B might be a decision support system in which users create an ample assortment of server-hogging queries. These two applications require very different indexing tactics.

In addition, MySQL's optimizer always tries to use the information at hand to develop the most efficient query plans. However, requirements change over time; users and applications can introduce unpredicted requests at any point. These requests might include new transactions, reports, integration, and so forth.

As a database designer or administrator, it's your job to continually examine your database and its indexes, being prepared to make alterations when applicable. The good news is that with the exception of server parameters, indexes are the easiest database structures to modify without causing havoc in your applications. If you forget an index prior to going into production, it's a relatively simple manner to add it without changing a line of code (although there might be a time cost to generating indexes on large tables).

This chapter investigates MySQL's index capabilities. It begins by reviewing how indexes work, as well as their structure. Next, it reviews indexing features specific to each of the major MySQL data storage engines. This chapter does not spend much time on actually tuning the storage engines' index capabilities; this comes later in the chapters dedicated to each of these engines.

This chapter then examines a broad range of situations in which indexes might help speed up your application. In addition to examining how indexes can be of assistance, this chapter also discusses circumstances in which indexes might actually damage performance.

Before commencing the analysis, let's review the example strategy. As described previously, this book always strives to make the examples as simple as possible while still illustrating a particular point. This means that for clarity's sake, some of the examples might violate suggestions made in different parts of the chapter and book. However, every example is relevant for the topic under review.

Index Key Terms and Concepts

Before proceeding into a discussion of optimal indexing, this section quickly discusses several crucial key terms and structures. To make the illustrations as clear as possible, you can first create, populate, and index a very simple table:

```
CREATE TABLE sample_names
(
    id INT UNSIGNED PRIMARY KEY AUTO_INCREMENT,
    last_name CHAR(30) NOT NULL,
    age SMALLINT NOT NULL,
    INDEX (last_name)
);
```

Now, Figure 7.1 looks at proceedinga simplified diagram showing the structure of the last_name index.

Figure 7.1 represents a B-tree index, which is the index format MySQL uses for all of its data types (including those that may be used in FULLTEXT indexes) and storage engines, with two exceptions:

1. The MEMORY (also known as HEAP) storage engine gives you the option to use hash indexes instead. These very fast indexes are discussed a little later.

2. The spatial data types use a specialized version of the B-tree index, known as an R-tree index.

You can gain several very important insights by examining Figure 7.1:

1. In the case of the MyISAM storage engine, MySQL separates its data from its indexes. That is, the contents of the indexes are stored in a different physical location than the actual data. In certain situations, you might place indexes and data on different disk drives, which might greatly help performance. This possibility is discussed later.

2. If you run a query that retrieves last_name only, MySQL can get everything it needs just by reading this index.

3. Typically, some free space is available within both the index and data pages. In addition, MySQL offers you the option to compress keys: For clarity's sake, this is omitted from this diagram.

4. The leftmost structures are nonleaf nodes. They can contain pointers to either other nonleaf nodes or leaf nodes. A leaf node is the lowest-level node, and contains the pointers to the actual data.

5. This index is relatively shallow: It doesn't have that many levels of nonleaf nodes. Figure 7.2 shows a deeper index.

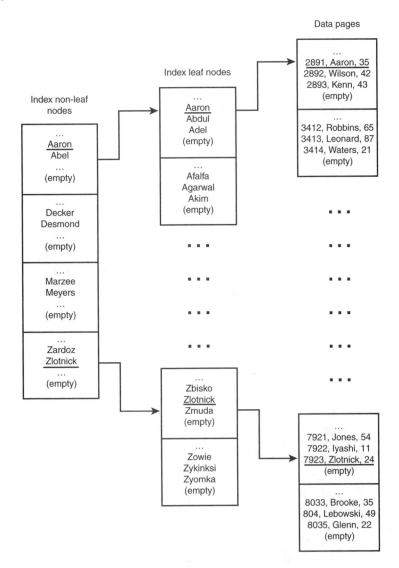

FIGURE 7.1   Structure of the B-tree index on the `last_name` column.

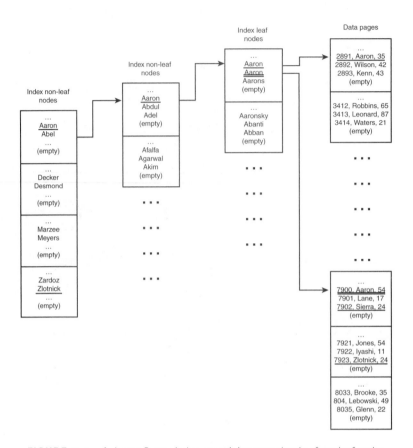

FIGURE 7.2 A deeper B-tree index, containing more levels of nonleaf nodes.

In the previous examples, the data is not stored in the order of the last_name index. However, it is stored in primary key order, so take a look at Figure 7.3, a diagram of the index on id.

As you can see, the actual data is stored in id order. That is, each page contains a group of rows that have nothing in common other than each row's id number is one less than the one that preceded it. The pages themselves are sequenced by the values of their rows' id field. A little later, you'll see how you can change the physical order of your data.

Next, suppose that you used the MEMORY storage engine for this table and requested a hash index:

```
CREATE TABLE sample_names
(
    id INT UNSIGNED PRIMARY KEY AUTO_INCREMENT,
    last_name CHAR(30) NOT NULL,
    age SMALLINT NOT NULL,
    INDEX USING HASH (last_name)
) ENGINE = MEMORY;
```

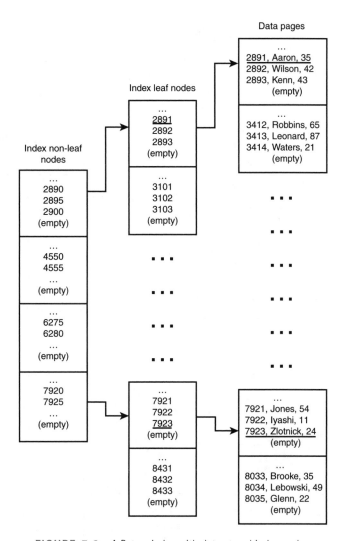

FIGURE 7.3 A B-tree index with data stored in key order.

Hash indexes provide very fast access to information but are a little harder to visualize (see Figure 7.4).

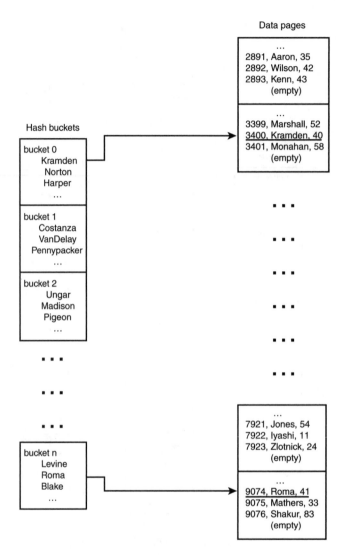

FIGURE 7.4 Hash index structure.

Without going into deep technical detail on the algorithms used to build these structures, understand that when you generate the index or insert a new row into the table, MySQL maps the index key into a hash bucket (which is a memory structure, not a container for breakfast or recreational drugs). The hash bucket then contains pointers to the data itself. Depending on the amount of available memory and other factors, MySQL generates a number of these hash buckets. Internal algorithms then determine which entries are then placed into the buckets. Generally, these algorithms have little to do with the data itself, but are instead focused on implementing a round-robin or other distribution strategy so that no particular bucket gets overloaded.

Notice how the data itself is stored in the order of the primary key (id), just as it would have been for a B-tree.

When it comes time to find the row (during a query or other operation), MySQL takes the lookup criteria, runs it through the hashing function, locates the correct hash bucket, finds the entry, and then retrieves the row.

For added speed and flexibility, MySQL uses dynamic hashing. However, as you can see from the diagram, there is no correlation between the order of entries in the hash index and their physical location on disk. This means that a hash index can't increase the performance of an ORDER BY.

Index Reports and Utilities

MySQL offers a collection of helpful reports and utilities that help developers and administrators gain insight into the indexing profile and needs for their own environments. The following sections consider several of these practical tools.

SHOW INDEX

The SHOW INDEX command returns a list of valuable data about indexes for a particular table. Because it's vital that you understand the output from this command to help you plan new tables or analyze your existing ones, this section spends some time reviewing how to interpret this information.

Before beginning, let's create a sample table containing a variety of data types:

```
CREATE TABLE demo_show_index
(
    col1 INT UNSIGNED AUTO_INCREMENT PRIMARY KEY,
    col2 VARCHAR(30) NOT NULL,
    col3 DATE NOT NULL,
    col4 ENUM ('Mercury', 'Venus', 'Mars', 'Earth', 'Jupiter') NOT NULL,
    col5 TEXT NOT NULL,
    col6 DATETIME NOT NULL,
    col7 BLOB NOT NULL,
    INDEX (col2),
    INDEX (col3),
    INDEX (col4),
    FULLTEXT (col5),
    INDEX (col6),
    INDEX (col7(150)),
    INDEX (col3,col2)
) ENGINE = MYISAM;
```

An assortment of indexes have been placed on all columns to make the SHOW INDEX output more interesting. Figure 7.5 shows what the table looks like when created and populated.

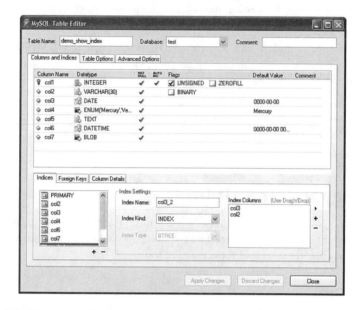

FIGURE 7.5   A view of the new table's data and index structure from within the MySQL Query Browser.

We then loaded 1,250,000 rows of random information into the table, and then ran OPTIMIZE_TABLE to update MySQL's internal statistics:

```
mysql> OPTIMIZE TABLE demo_show_index;
+---------------------+----------+----------+----------+
| Table               | Op       | Msg_type | Msg_text |
+---------------------+----------+----------+----------+
| test.demo_show_index | optimize | status   | OK       |
+---------------------+----------+----------+----------+
1 row in set (45 min 16.09 sec)
```

Notice how long it took to optimize the table; this is not something you would want to run in the middle of your busiest day. For administrators of the MyISAM storage engine, don't forget that you can elect to use the myisamchk command to perform the same table analysis and defragmentation; this command is discussed in Chapter 11, "MyISAM Performance Enhancement."

Now, take a look at the output of SHOW INDEX for this table:

```
mysql> SHOW INDEX FROM demo_show_index\G
*************************** 1. row ***************************
        Table: demo_show_index
```

```
    Non_unique: 0
      Key_name: PRIMARY
   Seq_in_index: 1
    Column_name: col1
      Collation: A
    Cardinality: 1250000
       Sub_part: NULL
         Packed: NULL
           Null:
     Index_type: BTREE
        Comment:
*************************** 2. row ***************************
          Table: demo_show_index
     Non_unique: 1
       Key_name: col2
   Seq_in_index: 1
    Column_name: col2
      Collation: A
    Cardinality: 2000
       Sub_part: NULL
         Packed: NULL
           Null:
     Index_type: BTREE
        Comment:
*************************** 3. row ***************************
          Table: demo_show_index
     Non_unique: 1
       Key_name: col3
   Seq_in_index: 1
    Column_name: col3
      Collation: A
    Cardinality: 2158
       Sub_part: NULL
         Packed: NULL
           Null:
     Index_type: BTREE
        Comment:
*************************** 4. row ***************************
          Table: demo_show_index
     Non_unique: 1
       Key_name: col4
   Seq_in_index: 1
    Column_name: col4
      Collation: A
    Cardinality: 5
       Sub_part: NULL
```

```
          Packed: NULL
            Null:
      Index_type: BTREE
         Comment:
*************************** 5. row ***************************
           Table: demo_show_index
      Non_unique: 1
        Key_name: col6
    Seq_in_index: 1
     Column_name: col6
       Collation: A
     Cardinality: 1250000
        Sub_part: NULL
          Packed: NULL
            Null:
      Index_type: BTREE
         Comment:
*************************** 6. row ***************************
           Table: demo_show_index
      Non_unique: 1
        Key_name: col7
    Seq_in_index: 1
     Column_name: col7
       Collation: A
     Cardinality: 1250000
        Sub_part: 150
          Packed: NULL
            Null:
      Index_type: BTREE
         Comment:
*************************** 7. row ***************************
           Table: demo_show_index
      Non_unique: 1
        Key_name: col3_2
    Seq_in_index: 1
     Column_name: col3
       Collation: A
     Cardinality: 2158
        Sub_part: NULL
          Packed: NULL
            Null:
      Index_type: BTREE
         Comment:
*************************** 8. row ***************************
           Table: demo_show_index
      Non_unique: 1
        Key_name: col3_2
```

```
 Seq_in_index: 2
 Column_name: col2
    Collation: A
  Cardinality: 1250000
     Sub_part: NULL
       Packed: NULL
         Null:
   Index_type: BTREE
      Comment:
*************************** 9. row ***************************
        Table: demo_show_index
   Non_unique: 1
     Key_name: col5
 Seq_in_index: 1
  Column_name: col5
    Collation: NULL
  Cardinality: 144
     Sub_part: NULL
       Packed: NULL
         Null:
   Index_type: FULLTEXT
      Comment:
```

Table 7.1 explains each of the columns in the report.

TABLE 7.1 **SHOW INDEX Output**

Column	Purpose
Table	The name of the table being reviewed.
Non_unique	1 if the index can hold duplicates, 0 if not.
Key_name	The name assigned to the index.
Seq_in_index	The position of the column in the index if this is a multicolumn index. The first column will be set to 1.
Column_name	The name of the column.
Collation	The method of index sorting. For now, it can only be 'A' (ascending) or NULL. In future releases, it might also indicate descending indexes.
Cardinality	A count of the unique values for the index. A low number in comparison to the number of rows means that this is a highly duplicate index; a high number means that this index is more unique. Higher values translate into more likely selection by the optimizer when building a query plan.
Sub_part	The value that shows the number of characters that have been placed into the index, if the column is only partially indexed.
Packed	A description of how the index is packed. If not packed, NULL will be displayed.

TABLE 7.1   **Continued**

Column	Purpose
Null	Columns that may potentially hold NULL values are indicated with a YES.
Index_type	The type of index (RTREE, FULLTEXT, HASH, BTREE).
Comment	A placeholder that contains information from earlier versions that are now given their own column(s).

How can you interpret the results of SHOW INDEX for the sample table? A few facts jump out:

- The primary key has all unique values because its cardinality is equal to the number of rows in the table. Of course, this is expected from a primary key.

- Columns six and seven are also completely unique. Why is that? As it turns out, col6 is defined as DATETIME, so the values that the random data loader inserted happened to be completely unique. Col7 is a BLOB, and it too was given completely unique values by the random data creator.

- Col4 has a very low cardinality (five) in contrast to the number of rows in the table (1.25 million). Why is this? Recall that this column was defined as an ENUM, with only five potential values: Mercury, Venus, Earth, Mars, and Jupiter. This translates to a cardinality of five.

- Our multicolumn index (col3, col2), although containing two relatively nonunique columns, is itself unique. If you multiply the cardinality of these two columns (2,158 x 2,000), you receive a result much higher than the number of rows in this table.

If you've chosen the MyISAM storage engine, you can also use the myisamchk utility to get additional details. This utility is explored in Chapter 11's review of the MyISAM engine.

Assisting the Optimizer with Indexes

Chapter 6, "Understanding the MySQL Optimizer," examines the MySQL optimizer and reviews how this vital technology determines the processing steps that the database engine takes to return the results for a query. Generally, the optimizer makes the correct decision with no intervention from the developer.

However, there are some situations, generally driven by a low index cardinality value, in which the optimizer might elect to perform an expensive table scan rather than employing an existing index. For circumstances like this, you can set the max_seeks_for_key parameter (either globally or for one session) to a low value. When this setting is low, the MySQL optimizer believes that the number of key seeks will not exceed this value, despite what its internal index statistics state. This assumption then forces an index lookup, rather than the more expensive table scan.

Index-Related Logging

Chapter 2, "Performance Monitoring Options," appraises MySQL's logging capabilities. You can use these logs to get a better understanding of any problem queries, particularly those that are running without the benefits of indexes. To do so, enable the --log-queries-not-using-indexes server parameter (new as of version 4.1; older versions used --log-long-format instead), and ensure that the --log-slow-queries flag is also enabled. With both these flags set, MySQL logs both slow queries as well as queries that do not make use of an index. For example, look at the following snippet of data from the slow queries log:

```
# Time: 051224 16:52:20
# User@Host: [Ksoze] @ client88 [204.11.13.187]
# Query_time: 0  Lock_time: 0  Rows_sent: 1  Rows_examined: 5000000
select count(*) from customer_address where address1 = '111 Wilson Street';
# Time: 051224 16:52:59
# User@Host: [Bedelman] @ belserv29 [10.82.17.170]
# Query_time: 4  Lock_time: 1  Rows_sent: 1  Rows_examined: 390463
select count(*) from customer_address where address1 = '43 Boyd Street';
# Time: 051224 16:55:15
# User@Host: [NSierra] @ mtnview19 [203.19.11.7]
# Query_time: 46  Lock_time: 0  Rows_sent: 1  Rows_examined: 21195536
select avg(amount) from transactions where transaction_id between 1 and 4000000;
```

Note that the long_query_time setting specifies the threshold above which any slow-running queries will be logged. For example, if this variable is set to 5 seconds, only those queries that took longer than 5 seconds are logged.

The server parameters are discussed in greater detail in Chapters 10, 11, and 12, "General Server Performance Parameters and Tuning," "MyISAM Performance Enhancement," "InnoDB Performance Enhancement," respectively.

MyISAM Indexing Features

This section devotes attention to some special performance-related features offered by the MyISAM engine. These include the key cache, which is an in-memory cache designed to reduce the need for costly disk access, the myisamchk utility, as well as a number of options to change the physical structure of a table.

Key Cache

Indexes speed access to information by providing "shortcuts" to data. For example, an index on last names is sorted alphabetically, which means you can use this sorted list to navigate very quickly to a particular name, or even a range of names.

MySQL takes these already-fast data access shortcuts and speeds them even further by giving administrators the option to store frequently used indexes in memory. Because in-memory operations are usually 10 times (or more) faster than disk operations, the savings can really add up. For the MyISAM storage engine, these cached indexes are held in a structure called the key cache. Unlike the InnoDB buffer pool, MyISAM offers no internal memory caching structures for data per se; the operating system's buffering features usually look after that responsibility. In fact, if you disable the key cache, you will still usually benefit from the built-in operating system–based caching found on most modern systems.

The myisamchk Utility

MySQL provides the myisamchk utility to let database administrators perform a wide variety of vital administration tasks, including the following:

- Integrity checking
- Repair
- Analysis
- Restructuring
- Optimization

Chapter 11, dedicated to the MyISAM storage engine, examines both the key cache (including how you can configure and affect its behavior) as well as using the myisamchk utility to boost performance.

Index and Table Compression

MyISAM helps conserve disk space by automatically compressing CHAR and VARCHAR columns; you can also request numeric column compression by specifying PACK_KEYS=1 when generating your table. If disk space is truly at a premium, and you aren't performing any data modifications, you can use myisampack to compress an entire table.

InnoDB Indexing Features

The InnoDB storage engine has its own set of index-related internal structures, caches, and features. This section briefly examines these capabilities; Chapter 12 discusses how to configure, monitor, and tune these capabilities.

Index Structure and Storage

The index structure diagrams displayed earlier in the chapter are still applicable for InnoDB. However, InnoDB includes a number of additional index storage and performance concepts:

- InnoDB actually stores each row's data in an internal structure known as a clustered index. The table is physically stored in the order of this index.
- When a primary key exists for your table, the clustered index is equivalent to the primary key, so the rows are stored physically in the order of the primary key.

- In the absence of a primary key, MySQL itself looks for another unique index to assign as the clustered index. The first unique index that consists of non-null columns will be chosen.

- If there are no qualified indexes, InnoDB generates its own internal index, along with a 6-byte unique row identifier known as the rowID. This approach leaves the rows physically stored in the order in which they were inserted. Note that you cannot see this index via the SHOW INDEX command or through the MySQL Administrator.

- All other indexes for the table include the value of the primary key along with their other index details. This value is then used to point back to the clustered index, which in turn yields the data.

Buffer Pool

The InnoDB buffer pool caches indexes as well as the underlying data, unlike MyISAM's key cache, which only stores index key information in a memory buffer.

Administrators have considerable control over the buffer pool and other InnoDB memory structures, including defining its capacity via the innodb_buffer_pool_size setting, whether it takes advantage of extended memory on Windows-based servers, and how frequently the log buffer is synchronized to disk. All of these, and many other InnoDB-specific topics, are explored later in Chapter 12.

Memory Pool

The memory pool is a RAM-based cache that holds information about internal MySQL structures as well as data dictionary information. Administrators can define the initial size of this cache via the innodb_additional_mem_pool_size server variable.

Adaptive Hash Index

As you saw earlier in this chapter, hash indexes provide extremely fast access to information, especially when combined with memory-resident data. InnoDB features an adaptive hash index algorithm, which examines access patterns for your data. If InnoDB detects the right kind of pattern, it automatically constructs a hash index. Aside from allocating enough memory to InnoDB for caching, there's nothing you need to do to enable this functionality; it builds the index without administrative intervention.

To determine if your server is benefiting from an adaptive hash index, simply run SHOW INNODB STATUS and locate the section containing the relevant details:

```
-------------------------------------
INSERT BUFFER AND ADAPTIVE HASH INDEX
-------------------------------------
Ibuf for space 0: size 1, free list len 397, seg size 399, is empty
Ibuf for space 0: size 1, free list len 397, seg size 399,
```

```
0 inserts, 0 merged recs, 0 merges
Hash table size 34679, used cells 1, node heap has 1 buffer(s)
1880.28 hash searches/s, 81.23 non-hash searches/s
```

In this example, these indexes are aiding a high percentage of searches.

Automatic Foreign Key Index Generation

The benefits of foreign key constraints were discussed earlier in the book. To make these constraints possible, it's important that the proper indexes are in place. As of version 4.1.2, InnoDB now automatically generates these indexes when you specify your foreign constraints.

Indexing Scenarios

This section assesses an array of circumstances in which indexing can add impressive speed to your MySQL-based applications.

PRIMARY KEY

As you saw earlier, a primary key is defined as one or more column(s) that uniquely identify every row in a table. MySQL can use this information as a shortcut to finding the row with as little effort as possible, as well as a safeguard against duplicate data.

With very few exceptions, all of your tables should have primary keys. If you can't identify one or more columns that can serve as a primary key, it's a good idea to simply create a single numeric column and let MySQL populate it with unique data:

```
CREATE TABLE pk_demo
(
    id INT UNSIGNED AUTO_INCREMENT PRIMARY KEY,
    col1 VARCHAR(10),
    ...
    ...
);
```

In the preceding example, id serves as the primary key. MySQL creates a unique index for this column, and prevents duplicate entries:

```
INSERT INTO pk_demo VALUES (1, 'Original');
INSERT INTO pk_demo VALUES (1, 'Duplicate');
ERROR 1062 (23000): Duplicate entry '1' for key 1
```

Each time you insert a row, MySQL increments this value by one. You should note the following two points about system-generated primary keys:

1. You have control over the starting point of this value. As of version 5.0.3, MyISAM and InnoDB both support the AUTO_INCREMENT directive, which lets you specify the first number in your sequence. For example, the next SQL statement will start the sequence at 1,000:

```
CREATE TABLE auto_inc_demo
(
    col1 INTEGER PRIMARY KEY AUTO_INCREMENT,
    col2 CHAR(10)
)  AUTO_INCREMENT = 1000 ENGINE = INNODB;
```

2. Don't make the system-generated primary key field any larger than necessary, but be certain you allocate enough room, especially if joins are involved. For example, if you define one table's primary key as SMALLINT and another's as TINYINT(2), the latter table can only hold 255 rows; additional row insert attempts receive a duplicate key error, and joins might be difficult between the two tables.

Finally, what if you *can* identify one or more columns that could serve as a primary key, but these columns are large and/or not numeric? In this case, you should probably still create a primary key and let MySQL fill it in with unique values. These values will come in handy when you try to speed the joins of this table to others; the benefits of numeric versus nonnumeric joins are discussed later. If you still want to create a multifield primary key, use the following syntax:

```
CREATE TABLE pk_demo_multi
(
    pk_field1 INT,
    pk_field2 VARCHAR(10),
    ...
    ...
    PRIMARY KEY (pk_field1, pk_field2)
);
```

Note that when your primary key is made up of multiple columns, it is the combination that must be unique; there can be many duplicate values in each column as long as the whole key is unique.

Filter Columns

Filter columns help speed the results of your database operations by reducing the number of potential rows that MySQL must process to satisfy your request. In the absence of an index, MySQL must perform a table scan to look at each row to see if it matches your criteria. On a large table, this can take a tremendous amount of time. To make matters worse, these costs are borne by statements in addition to SELECT, such as UPDATE and DELETE.

As a simple example, suppose that you have two sample tables defined as follows:

```
CREATE TABLE sample_customers
(
    customer_id INT,
    last_name VARCHAR(30),
    first_name VARCHAR(30),
    city VARCHAR(30)
);

CREATE TABLE city_customer_count
(
    city VARCHAR(30),
    customer_count INT
);
```

This table will likely be very large, holding many millions of rows. Users are expected to submit scores of queries that filter on the last_name, as well as numerous updates that find rows for a particular city and then revise related records in other tables:

```
SELECT customer_id, last_name, first_name
FROM sample_customers sc
WHERE last_name = 'Lebowski';

UPDATE city_customer_count ccc
SET customer_count =
(
    SELECT COUNT(*) FROM sample_customers
    WHERE city = 'Personville'
)
WHERE ccc.city = 'Personville';
```

These types of operations can take a very long time to complete when there are no indexes in place on filter columns. Luckily, it's very simple to place indexes on these frequently filtered columns; dramatic performance improvements usually follow these kinds of enhancements:

```
CREATE INDEX sc_ix1 ON sample_customers(last_name);
CREATE INDEX sc_ix2 ON sample_customers(city);
CREATE INDEX ccc_ix1 ON city_customer_count(city);
```

Both of these operations should run much more quickly now. MySQL can use the new indexes to rapidly locate the correct rows in either table.

It's important to understand that no index, including those on filters, is free. It's true that indexes consume additional disk space, but their true cost is often measured in the extra amount of time it takes for the database engine to update these indexes whenever a change (new row, updated row, deleted row) is made to the table. Over-indexed tables translate into slower data modifications, so be mindful of the benefits *and* costs of these crucial database structures.

Join Columns

When you join information between two or more tables, MySQL looks for any available indexes to help it locate the correct set of rows. In the absence of any indexes on join columns, MySQL is often forced to perform an expensive table scan of every row in an attempt to complete the join and locate your answer. This means that wherever possible, you should place indexes on join columns.

For example, suppose that you want to run a query to find all customers who joined the frequent flyer program during the month of December 2000 who have also redeemed an award during July 2006. First, take a look at the two tables in question:

```
CREATE TABLE customer_master
(
    customer_id INT UNSIGNED AUTO_INCREMENT PRIMARY KEY,
    ff_number CHAR(10),
    last_name VARCHAR(50) NOT NULL,
    first_name VARCHAR(50) NOT NULL,
    home_phone VARCHAR(20),
    mobile_phone VARCHAR(20),
    fax VARCHAR(20),
    email VARCHAR(40),
    home_airport_code CHAR(3),
    date_of_birth DATE,
    sex ENUM ('M','F'),
    date_joined_program DATE,
    date_last_flew DATETIME
) ENGINE = INNODB;

CREATE TABLE customer_awards
(
    award_id INT UNSIGNED AUTO_INCREMENT PRIMARY KEY,
    ff_number CHAR(10) NOT NULL,
    award_type_code TINYINT(2) NOT NULL,
    mileage_redeemed SMALLINT NOT NULL,
    date_redeemed DATE NOT NULL
) ENGINE = MYISAM;
```

Next, the following is the query to locate this information:

```
SELECT cm.ff_number, cm.last_name, cm.first_name,
ca.award_type_code, ca.date_redeemed
FROM customer_master cm INNER JOIN customer_awards ca ON cm.ff_number = ca.ff_number
AND cm.date_joined_program BETWEEN '2000-12-01' AND '2000-12-31'
AND ca.date_redeemed BETWEEN '2006-07-01' AND '2006-07-31';
```

Several problems with these tables were defined previously. Of immediate concern in this section is the lack of an index on the ff_number column in the customer_awards; the importance of indexing filter columns was discussed earlier in this chapter.

No matter what else happens in the query, this missing join index might translate into a table scan to find rows to join to the customer_master table. Placing an index on this column is easy and can have a dramatic effect on query performance.

You should note that placing an index on a join column is not a magic bullet: In its absence, MySQL might well determine a different but equally valid, fast query plan. However, it's still a good idea to help the database engine by indexing these kinds of columns—just be aware that they might not always solve all performance problems.

Composite indexes (that is, indexes that are made up of more than one column) are also a potential solution here. These indexes are discussed later in this chapter.

Finally, you can tune several server parameters to help boost join performance. These include join_buffer_size and max_join_size. All performance-related server parameters are reviewed later in the book.

Index Cardinality

As you saw earlier, MySQL's SHOW INDEX command returns details about the cardinality, or uniqueness, of the columns that make up an index. You should strive to make these values as high as possible to avoid highly duplicate indexes.

A highly duplicate index can be thought of as an index that only has a handful of potential key values. In many cases, it's worse to have a highly duplicate index than to have no index at all.

For example, suppose you added the following indexes to the customer_master example from earlier in this chapter:

```
CREATE INDEX cm_ix1 ON customer_master (last_name, first_name);
CREATE INDEX cm_ix2 ON customer_master (date_joined_program);
CREATE INDEX cm_ix3 ON customer_master (sex);
```

The first two indexes make sense: They contain keys that are likely to be quite distinct. However, because the sex column will only contain either 'M' or 'F,' the third index will be highly duplicated.

When you add a row into a table with a highly duplicate index, the engine must work through the myriad of index pages containing the highly duplicate entry to find the correct place to register the new row. This degrades performance by requiring additional I/O with minimal benefit to your application. For filtering or joining, it's probably just as simple for MySQL to use a table scan because the index is so nonselective.

If you find yourself with a highly duplicate index and you still need to search or sort on the value, consider creating a new multicolumn index that combines the highly duplicate column with a more unique column. Remember that to correctly take advantage of a multi-column index, your database operation must always include the leftmost column(s). This is discussed in more detail a little later in this chapter.

Hash Columns

Although a unique index or primary key is the best way to create a unique value, another approach to managing low cardinality situations is to take advantage of the MD5 hashing function to create a higher cardinality value from the concatenation of two or more columns, and then index this column.

For example, suppose that High-Hat Airways' catering department wants to maintain a system to track the inventory of all of their meals over time. In keeping with their ruthless cost-cutting policies, only a few different meal combinations (composed of type and size) are available, yet these two not-very-unique values will form the primary lookup criteria for queries. However, by setting aside and maintaining a hash column, the designers of the system make it easier to use an index to find the correct rows. The main table looks like this:

```
CREATE TABLE meal_choices
(
    meal_date DATE NOT NULL,
    meal_count SMALLINT(5) NOT NULL,
    meal_type CHAR(20) NOT NULL,
    meal_size CHAR(20) NOT NULL,
    meal_hash_code CHAR(32),
    INDEX (meal_hash_code)
);
```

Now, when new rows are inserted to this table, the INSERT statement looks like this:

```
INSERT INTO meal_choices
VALUES (
'2006-06-10',250,'Vegetarian','Large',MD5(concat('Vegetarian','Large'))
);
```

The meal_hash_code column could also be periodically populated via an UPDATE statement. In any case, the MD5 function is of use when querying the table because it will take advantage of the index:

```
SELECT *
FROM meal_choices
WHERE meal_hash_code = MD5(concat('Low sodium','Small'));
```

The benefits of hashing only go so far: It would not be possible, for example, to utilize the index for a range query. The goal of this example was simply to highlight hash lookups and demonstrate how to use them.

Character Versus Numeric Indexes

When compared with character-based indexes, numeric indexes often offer faster access to information. As you analyze your tables, see if you can find a character-based, indexed column that contains exclusively numeric information. If you discover such a column, consider dropping the index and then changing the column's type to the following:

- TINYINT if the numeric value for this column will never surpass 255 UNSIGNED, or will range between -128 and +128 if SIGNED

- SMALLINT(2) if the numeric value will never surpass 65535 UNSIGNED, or will range between -32,767 and +32,767 SIGNED

- INTEGER, which will consume 4 bytes to hold the data for the column. Values can range up to approximately 4 billion if UNSIGNED, or between approximately -2 billion and +2 billion if SIGNED

If you determine that some of the data includes decimal values, simply set the column type to match the table's information.

For example, we created two very simple tables to test the impact of numeric indexes versus character indexes:

```
CREATE TABLE char_test
(
    col1 char(10),
    col2 char(10),
    INDEX (col1)
);

CREATE TABLE numeric_test
(
    col1 INT UNSIGNED,
    col2 char(10),
    INDEX (col1)
);
```

Next, we loaded 500,000 rows of random data into both tables. We kept the numeric values in col1 for both tables less than or equal to 999,999. We then ran a battery of index-activating tests, including SELECT AVG(col1), SELECT MIN(col1), SELECT MAX(col1), SELECT COUNT(*), and simple filtering.

In all cases, operations on the numeric table were faster; in some cases, they executed more rapidly by several orders of magnitude. For a larger table, the results would be even more dramatic. Finally, in addition to saving index and data storage space, our revised strategy also should translate into faster index processing because MySQL will need to read fewer bytes to determine if a row contains the requested value. This will also help matters if the column in question is used for filtering and/or joining.

Finally, if your column does indeed contain a mixture of character and numeric data, and this information follows a consistent pattern, don't give up hope. Perhaps there is a way to separate them into their own columns. This possibility is discussed in the next chapter, which examines strategies for fast SQL.

Multicolumn Indexes

Like most other relational database management systems, MySQL lets you create indexes that span more than one column. These indexes come in handy when trying filter, join, or sort on a set of values contained in different columns.

Using the `customer_master` example from earlier in the chapter, suppose that you are trying to find a customer with the `last_name` of "Crane." In the absence of an index on this field, MySQL is forced to scan all rows in the table to find matching values.

What if you add a single index on this column? In this case, MySQL uses the index and jumps directly to all the appropriate records. However, suppose you really want to find a specific customer: "Ed Crane," and High-Hat Airways has many thousands of customers with the last name of "Crane." You need a faster, more selective way to locate this customer. This is an example of how a multicolumn index can greatly reduce the amount of searching MySQL must perform to find your results. Multicolumn indexes are usually much more selective than single-column indexes, even if the values in each column are fairly static.

You can create a multicolumn index as follows:

```
CREATE INDEX cm_last_first ON customer_master(last_name, first_name);
```

You could also specify this index when creating the table:

```
CREATE TABLE customer_master
(
    customer_id INT UNSIGNED AUTO_INCREMENT PRIMARY KEY,
    last_name VARCHAR(30) NOT NULL,
    first_name VARCHAR(30) NOT NULL,
        ...
        ...
        INDEX(last_name, first_name)
);
```

After the index is in place, finding "Ed Crane" should be very fast—MySQL uses the index as a shortcut to the relevant rows.

Unfortunately, many developers mistakenly introduce SQL that does not take advantage of these indexes. Take a look at a few examples:

- **Unanchored index access**—What is wrong with the following query?

```
SELECT *
FROM customer_master
WHERE first_name = 'Ed';
```

Our index begins with last_name and only then includes first_name; any database access that ignores last_name as a filter/join/sort value will likely render this index unusable. To use the index, you must reference the leftmost column(s).

- **Leading wildcard in index key**—Look at this query:

```
SELECT *
FROM CUSTOMER_MASTER
WHERE last_name LIKE '%rane'
AND first_name = 'Ed';
```

This query does indeed reference both indexed columns, but it uses a leading wildcard in the leftmost index column. This also forces a table scan to find appropriate rows. The following query, however, is still able to make some use of the index (via an index scan) to find rows with the correct last_name. Although this is still suboptimal, it is better than a full table scan:

```
SELECT *
FROM CUSTOMER_MASTER
WHERE last_name = 'Crane'
AND first_name LIKE '%Ed';
```

- **Incorrect order for sorting/grouping**—Look at the following query:

```
SELECT *
FROM CUSTOMER_MASTER
WHERE last_name LIKE 'Crane%'
ORDER BY first_name, last_name;
```

At face value, this query looks efficient. However, there is a problem with the ORDER BY portion of the statement. The index on last_name, first_name does nothing when you try to sort on a different sequence. In this case, MySQL is forced to perform a filesort to order the information correctly. Changing the ORDER BY to match the index yields much better performance. Filesort was discussed as part of Chapter 6's MySQL query optimizer exploration.

Partial Indexes

As you have seen throughout this chapter, indexes are great tools for speeding up database applications. However, they can also impose extra costs. The price for indexing is primarily related to additional storage consumption as well as degraded performance when making modifications that affect one or more index keys.

However, MySQL lets you have it both ways: You can take advantage of the speed gains offered by indexes while also conserving storage and processing resources. The secret is in creating indexes that take only partial values of a column into account. The following sections look at two examples in which this makes sense.

Similar Values

Given that the purpose of an index is to help MySQL quickly locate one or more rows based on a certain criteria, it's a good idea to ensure that the index is as selective as possible. As you saw earlier, a highly duplicate index is often worse than no index at all. But what should you do if you have a CHAR or VARCHAR column that blends fairly unique and static information?

For example, suppose that you have a table of product information:

```
CREATE TABLE product_info
(
    id INT UNSIGNED AUTO_INCREMENT PRIMARY KEY,
    product_code CHAR(30),
    product_catalog_description TEXT,
...
...
) ENGINE = MYISAM;
```

Our research tells us that the product_code column needs to be indexed, has the following layout, and is most unique in the ten leftmost bytes:

AAAAA-NNNN-AAAAAAAAAAAAAAAAAA

In other words, the AAAAA-NNNN portion of this column is relatively unique, whereas everything to its right is quite repetitive. In this case, it makes sense to only index that portion of the column that is most unique:

```
CREATE INDEX prod_info_left ON product_info(product_code(10));
```

This index is very selective, yet consumes up to two-thirds less disk resources while decreasing CPU load when the index is updated. Note that you can construct multicolumn indexes using the same restrictions.

TEXT/BLOB Values

When defining an index for a TEXT or BLOB column, you must specify a prefix that indicates how many bytes you want to be included in the index.

One great way to determine this is to create a sample table that matches the structure of your production table. Next, load a representative subset of production data into the table, create a test index on a portion of the column(s), and then run OPTIMIZE TABLE followed by SHOW INDEX. Keep an eye on the cardinality value for this test index. When it starts dropping significantly, you'll know that you should not make the index any narrower.

Another technique is to use a query to get insight into the ideal prefix size:

```
SELECT COUNT(DISTINCT LEFT(column_name, prefix_length))
FROM table_name;
```

Ascending Versus Descending Indexes

Currently, MySQL only supports ascending indexes, even if you mandate a descending sort in your index generation statement. However, at some point in the future you will be able to create indexes that are made up of a mixture of ascending and descending key values. For example, suppose that you want to track information about employees and their hire dates:

```
CREATE TABLE employee
(
    last_name CHAR(40),
...
    date_of_hire DATE,
...
    INDEX (last_name ASC, date_of_hire DESC)
);
```

This new functionality will add a great deal of speed and flexibility to queries that return large, sorted sets of data.

Storing Tables in Column-Sorted Order

Earlier in this chapter, you saw how both MyISAM and InnoDB have their own mechanisms to change the physical storage order for rows within a table. However, you have one additional sort option: By using the ALTER TABLE ... ORDER BY statement, you have control over how MySQL stores the physical data for your tables, regardless of whether an index is in place. For example, we created a sample table to hold transaction details:

```
CREATE TABLE transactions (
    transaction_id INT UNSIGNED AUTO_INCREMENT PRIMARY KEY,
    transaction_date DATETIME NOT NULL,
    customer_id INT NOT NULL,
    amount DECIMAL (5,2) NOT NULL,
    transaction_type ENUM ('Purchase','Credit')
) ENGINE = MYISAM;
```

Next, we filled it with 100,000 rows of random data, and then created a copy of the table, called transactions_sorted. Finally, we sorted the latter table by customer_id:

```
ALTER TABLE transactions_sorted ORDER BY customer_id;
```

Figure 7.6 shows the results of two queries against this information. The top query shows that the original transactions table is sorted by the primary key, but the bottom query (showing the altered transactions_sorted table) demonstrates that the table has been restructured in customer_id order.

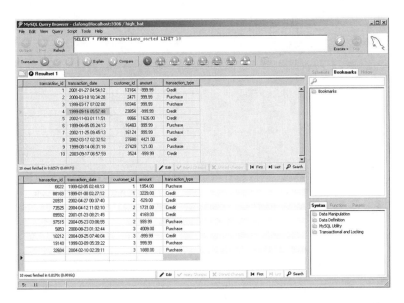

FIGURE 7.6   Resultsets from the same query taken from two tables stored in different order.

Although after data is added this table will not remain in this state (unless you rerun the ALTER TABLE statement), there can be usability advantages to storing a table in a meaningful order. If the table had been defined with InnoDB instead of MyISAM, this would have no effect: InnoDB always orders its data by the clustered key.

III

Optimizing Application Code

After learning how to understand and influence the MySQL optimizer, design your tables for speed, and create the right kinds of indexes on these tables, it's now time to turn your attention to developing the fastest possible MySQL-based solution.

Chapter 8, "Advanced SQL Tips," cites many examples showing how your choice of SQL can have a dramatic impact on your application's speed.

Chapter 9, "Developing High-Speed Applications," examines how to create the most efficient application logic. This includes taking advantage of MySQL's new stored procedures, managing transactions and concurrency, language-specific tips, and steps you can take to reduce unnecessary application overhead.

## 8

Advanced SQL Tips

MySQL offers developers many different options for building their applications, with the C, PHP, Java, and Open Database Connectivity (ODBC) APIs and connectors registering as some of the most popular. However, regardless of the connectivity method, it's vital that developers understand how to create the best possible SQL. This chapter does just that, focusing on two major subtopics: efficient data retrieval and optimal data modification.

Improving Searches

Slow queries are often the first and most visible sign of a sluggish database application. This section reviews how you can coax more performance out of your most listless queries.

One important topic that isn't covered here is how to speed up your searches on FULLTEXT information. Instead, this is discussed in more detail in Chapter 11, "MyISAM Performance Enhancement." This is because a number of crucial engine control variables have a direct impact on FULLTEXT search performance; these are best examined as part of our holistic examination of the MyISAM storage engine.

Leveraging Internal Engine Caches

Developers hoping to create high-performance MySQL-based applications are not alone in their efforts; MySQL offers a number of internal engine caching features that automatically leverage system memory to make information retrieval faster. These capabilities are discussed in great detail in Chapters 10, 11, 12 ("General Server Performance and Parameters Tuning," "MyISAM Performance Enhancement," and "InnoDB Performance Enhancement," respectively). For now, let's just describe them at a high level.

First, users of any MySQL engine can take advantage of the optional query cache. This cache stores queries and their related resultsets in memory. This can have dramatic benefits when your query profiles and resultsets are relatively static. You review how to exploit the query cache a little later in this chapter, with a much more detailed examination in Chapter 10.

Next, the MyISAM storage engine provides a sophisticated, memory-based internal structure known as the key cache. The key cache holds index information from your most frequently accessed tables. You can also use your own, different criteria to prepopulate this cache. In fact, you can create multiple caches, each with its own purpose. Regardless of how information enters the cache(s), MySQL is able to take advantage of the far greater speed of memory when performing operations using this data. You examine how to design, configure, populate, and tune this crucial MyISAM feature in Chapter 11.

Finally, the InnoDB storage engine has its own advanced memory-based caching technologies. The memory pool holds internal information, including data dictionary contents. Of greater interest to MySQL developers and administrators is the buffer pool, which holds both data and index information. Ideally, MySQL uses the buffer pool as often as possible to access as much InnoDB-based information as is available in the pool. Performing these operations in memory is far faster than working directly with the disk drives. However, MySQL administrators must understand how to set up and then optimally tune the buffer pool; this is a large part of Chapter 12.

Controlling Data Retrieval

MySQL offers a number of powerful extensions to the SQL standard that lets developers take a more active role in understanding and controlling how the database returns information to its clients. The following list looks at several of these innovations.

- **Bypassing other table operations**—Normally, a query waits its turn if other operations are making changes to the data in a table. However, you can elect to force MySQL to give your query priority by adding HIGH_PRIORITY to your SELECT statement, as long as there is no UNION involved:

```
SELECT HIGH_PRIORITY *
FROM customer_master
WHERE customer_id = 9930223;
```

It's nice to have the power to circumvent the normal procedures in a multiuser, multipurpose application. However, try to use HIGH_PRIORITY only in those situations in which you need instantaneous access to information and can afford to make other types of operations wait. A good example is building a query that uses a selective index (such as a primary key or unique value) to return results to a waiting user. In this kind of scenario, the goal is to give the user her information as quickly as possible, even if it means that updates or deletes to the same table take a little longer. Conversely, a bad place to employ HIGH_PRIORITY is in an application that has long-running SELECT statements and yet is update or delete intense: You could end up with many operations gated by your slow queries.

- **Estimating and limiting resultsets**—Suppose that you want to submit a query, but are afraid that it might return an enormous resultset or otherwise bog down the server. Of course, you can use the EXPLAIN command to see the optimizer's estimate, but what if you don't know the exact query until runtime?

Adding LIMIT to your query gives you some protection in these kinds of situations. For example, suppose that you want to find all transactions for a certain range of dates. However, you know that this has the potential to return a huge amount of information. In this case, simply adding LIMIT reduces the chances of a runaway query, as shown in Figure 8.1.

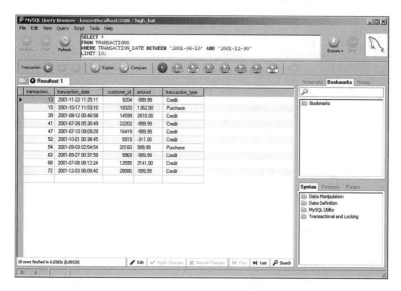

FIGURE 8.1   Using LIMIT to reduce the amount of returned information.

MySQL instantaneously returns the first 10 rows that match the query, and no more. If you then want the next 15 rows, simply change your LIMIT invocation to reflect your request, as shown in Figure 8.2.

It's important to be careful when using LIMIT, because you might inadvertently force the engine to perform unnecessary added work. Notice how the rows in the previous two queries are sorted. In this case, MySQL is returning the first 10, and next 15, rows in their physical order on disk, which in this case happens to be based on transaction_id. If you specify an ORDER BY on another column, MySQL is forced to perform additional computations before providing your results. Although it stops sorting as soon as it finds the number of rows you have requested, it still can be quite time consuming to complete the operation, largely negating the benefits of using LIMIT. See Figure 8.3.

Finally, try not to assume that the results from the EXPLAIN report for a relatively small LIMIT request will match the query plan for the entire query; MySQL might elect to use indexes for the LIMIT request yet perform a table scan for the full query.

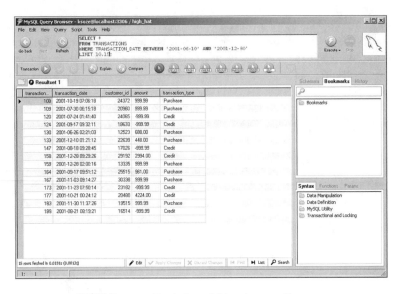

FIGURE 8.2   Retrieving additional rows with LIMIT.

FIGURE 8.3   An expensive query not helped by LIMIT.

Next, suppose that you want to get an idea of the size of the true resultset, but don't want to send all these returned values to the client (in case the results are enormous). The SQL_CALC_ROWS_FOUND option and FOUND_ROWS() function work in tandem with LIMIT to provide you with this information.

For example, let's construct a query of the transactions table that we know should be quite large. We'll add some directives to have the server process the full query but not return all the data to the client:

```
mysql> SELECT SQL_CALC_FOUND_ROWS *
    -> FROM transactions
    -> WHERE transaction_date BETWEEN '2001-01-01' AND '2001-12-31'
    -> AND amount BETWEEN 300 AND 500
    -> LIMIT 5;
+----------------+---------------------+-------------+--------+------------------+
| transaction_id | transaction_date    | customer_id | amount | transaction_type |
+----------------+---------------------+-------------+--------+------------------+
|            133 | 2001-12-10 01:21:12 |       22639 | 448.00 | Purchase         |
|            166 | 2001-05-09 09:14:44 |       16157 | 446.00 | Purchase         |
|            368 | 2001-02-19 03:52:29 |        3852 | 392.00 | Credit           |
|            551 | 2001-08-09 09:32:01 |         481 | 331.00 | Purchase         |
|            606 | 2001-12-03 05:05:55 |       23059 | 403.00 | Purchase         |
+----------------+---------------------+-------------+--------+------------------+
5 rows in set (1 min 56.16 sec)
```

Make no mistake: This query took some time to process. However, it only returned five rows to the client (in the order in which the table is stored on disk), so its bandwidth demands were minimal. As a developer, you can now retrieve the actual row count that would have been returned without the LIMIT clause:

```
mysql> SELECT FOUND_ROWS();
+--------------+
| FOUND_ROWS() |
+--------------+
|        97248 |
+--------------+
1 row in set (0.00 sec)
```

Armed with this information, you can take appropriate actions on your client, including warning the user, retrieving small blocks of data, and so on.

You can also block large data sets by utilizing SQL_BIG_SELECTS. To do this, set its value to 0, and provide a threshold value for MAX_JOIN_SIZE. When the optimizer detects a query that is likely to examine a number of rows greater than MAX_JOIN_SIZE, this option halts the information retrieval. In addition, you can set either the SQL_SELECT_LIMIT or --select_limit (for mysql) variables to restrict the maximum number of rows returned by a query. Note that a LIMIT clause within a query overrides this value.

- **Optimizing large GROUP BY/DISTINCT resultsets**—If you create a query that uses DISTINCT or GROUP BY and you know that the resultset is likely to be large, you can send the optimizer instructions about how to work through the results more efficiently. Adding SQL_BIG_RESULT to your query helps the optimizer decide whether to sort in memory or use a temporary table. For example, look at the query plans in Figure 8.4.

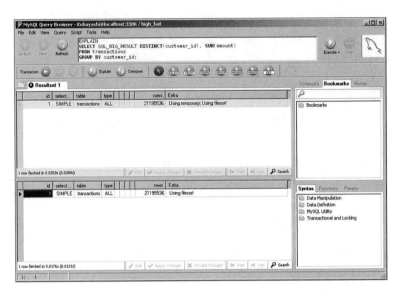

FIGURE 8.4   Using `SQL_BIG_RESULT` to invoke the filesort algorithm.

The only difference between the upper and lower query is that the lower query employs `SQL_BIG_RESULT`. Based on this information, the optimizer has decided not to create a temporary table, relying instead only on the filesort algorithm to sequence the large amount of retrieved data. When the two queries were run, this turned out to be very helpful: The lower query ran in less than half the time as the upper query.

However, be very careful when using `SQL_BIG_RESULT`: You might end up making things much worse! Look at the two query plans shown in Figure 8.5.

This query, which still processes many rows, only returns a few values in its resultset: the sum of transactions for each year for a certain set of customers. When run, the lower query, which employed `SQL_BIG_RESULT`, took 20 times longer to complete than the original, unmodified query! This highlights the importance of testing your queries against a realistic set of data before putting changes into production.

- **Forcing in-memory temporary tables**—MySQL generally attempts to use the fastest table structure possible when it's necessary to create a temporary table. If you know that your query won't be returning a large resultset, you can help MySQL decide to use an in-memory temporary table by including `SQL_SMALL_RESULT` with your query. Note that newer versions of MySQL have gotten better at making the right decision, thus avoiding the need for you to specify this option.

- **Query caching**—As you saw earlier, MySQL offers an optional, memory-based query cache that buffers already-retrieved information. By reducing the amount of processing necessary to return results, this cache can greatly improve performance. You discover how to configure and tune the query cache mechanism in more detail in Chapter 10.

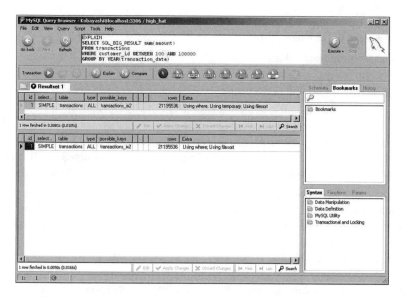

FIGURE 8.5   SQL_BIG_RESULT does not always mean faster queries.

You can control whether your query places its resultset in the query cache (assuming that the cache is enabled) by including SQL_CACHE or SQL_NO_CACHE with your SELECT statement.

For example, suppose that you are developing a customer support application that retrieves highly specific information such as the customer's profile or open cases. It's unlikely that multiple users of the application will need to see this data at or near the same time, so there's no reason to waste your limited cache space with the query's results:

```
SELECT SQL_NO_CACHE cm.*, ca.*
FROM customer_master cm, cases ca
WHERE ...
```

On the other hand, you might have a lookup table that you want cached so that others can read the cache rather than the disk:

```
SELECT SQL_CACHE sc.cost
FROM shipping_charges sc
WHERE ...
```

You should consider two additional notes about the query cache before the more in-depth exploration in Chapter 10:

1. Any changes to a table's data (such as with an INSERT, UPDATE, DELETE, or schema/index modification) cause the query cache for any data from this table to be flushed. For this reason alone, think carefully about the types of queries you want to cache.

2. You can configure whether results are cached by default; this is also discussed in more detail in Chapter 10.

- **Creating temporary tables**—Chapter 9, "Developing High-Speed Applications" delves into many concurrency considerations, including the interplay between locks (both table and row) and performance.

For now, note that if your queries that read MyISAM-based tables are taking a long time to complete, there's a good possibility that other database applications might have to wait for access to these tables. To release these locks more quickly, consider adding SQL_BUFFER_RESULT to your queries. Including this directive instructs MySQL to create a temporary table to buffer your query results, and thereby free any locks more quickly.

For example, the following query takes both a long time to process, as well as returns hundreds of thousands of rows from the transactions table. For these reasons, it is a good candidate for this instruction, especially if this large resultset needs to be transmitted to a client.

```
SELECT SQL_BUFFER_RESULT *
FROM TRANSACTIONS
WHERE transaction_date BETWEEN '2002-01-01' AND '2002-12-31'
AND amount BETWEEN 100 and 1000;
```

Reducing Security Costs

Security is a vital component of any well-designed relational database strategy. However, it's important to understand that security isn't free: There is a price to be paid whenever a client issues a request for database access. The more complex your security profile (that is, the privileges and permissions you have defined for access to your MySQL database), the longer it takes for MySQL to navigate through its internal security and resource control records to validate your request.

You can instruct MySQL to completely ignore your security profile by launching mysqld with the --skip-grant-tables option. However, this leaves your database completely unprotected, so it should be used with extreme caution.

Off-loading Processing Work

Spreading the data and processing load among several machines via replication is a great way to improve performance. Making good replication choices is the focus of Chapter 16, "Optimal Replication."

For now, imagine that your MySQL-based application performs both transactional processing and decision support tasks. Over time, the server becomes increasingly bogged down servicing both types of usages. In this case, it makes sense to replicate the information from the prime transactional server to one or more slave servers. The decision support users can then connect to the slave servers to run their reports without impacting performance on the prime, transactional server.

Boosting Join Performance

You reviewed several ways to make your joins more efficient as part of Chapters 6 and 7 ("Understanding the MySQL Optimizer" and "Indexing Strategies," respectively). These included the SELECT STRAIGHT JOIN request, the importance of indexing join columns, and taking advantage of the join_buffer_size parameter. The following sections look at some additional join improvement suggestions.

Join Column Consistency

In recent years, MySQL has greatly improved in its ability to accurately join data from columns that have been defined using different types. Nevertheless, it's important that you carefully design your tables so that join columns are consistent in both definition and size.

Numeric Versus Nonnumeric Queries and Joins

A common and potentially costly mistake frequently made by database designers and developers is to define columns as strings that truly only contain numeric information. The price of this miscalculation is paid whenever applications filter or join on these values.

For example, suppose that you are trying to design a new catering application for High-Hat Airways. As part of its ongoing and relentless cost-cutting strategy, High-Hat's catering division has invested in the newest artificial flavors and preservatives, increasing shelf life of meals from one week to six months. This means that meals need to be inventoried just like any other item. Two key tables are meal_header and meal_inventory:

```
CREATE TABLE meal_header
(
    meal_id CHAR(20) PRIMARY KEY,
    meal_description VARCHAR(40),
    ...
    ...
) ENGINE = MYISAM;

CREATE TABLE meal_detail
(
    airport_code INT,
    meal_id CHAR(20),
    meal_count SMALLINT,
    ...
    ...
) ENGINE = MYISAM;
```

As usual, you were given very little time to design this application. During your brief analysis, you observe that there are fewer than 1,000 different possible meals, yet you chose to define meal_id as a CHAR(20).

A commonly used query returns a listing of all meals, their descriptions, locations, and quantities:

```
SELECT mh.meal_description, mh.meal_id, md.airport_code, md.meal_count
FROM meal_header mh, meal_detail md
WHERE mh.meal_id = md.meal_id;
```

To join these two tables together on the 20-byte character `meal_id`, MySQL needs to evaluate the values in each table, byte-by-byte, up to 20 times per row. This can be very inefficient.

Given that you know `meal_id` is indeed always numeric, and always less than 1,000, it's a much better idea to define these columns as `SMALLINT(2)`, which only consumes 2 bytes. The performance and storage benefits are significant:

- You save 18 bytes of storage per row.
- You save 18 bytes of storage per index.
- Best of all, joining and filtering on this value consume much less CPU. MySQL only needs to compare 2 bytes (versus up to 20) to determine if a row is qualified for a filter or join.

Remember to be consistent when choosing data types for columns, especially those that are used for joins.

Substring Searches

After you've invested the time and effort to create the correct indexes, watch out for situations in which your database operations try to filter, join, or sort on substrings that are not anchored from the leftmost byte. These types of queries bypass your hard-earned indexes, and degrade into lethargic table scans.

It's easy to understand why this happens. Suppose that you are given the Manhattan white pages and told to find all people who have a last name beginning with "Mea." You quickly flip to the pages with entries that begin with "Mea," and then retrieve all names until you hit the initial last name beginning with "Meb." Fortunately for you, the phone book is indexed by last name, so locating correct entries doesn't take too long. To represent this in SQL, your syntax looks something like this:

```
SELECT *
FROM phone_book
WHERE last_name LIKE 'Mea%';
```

Now, assume that you're told to find all people with "ead" in their last name. How can you go about doing this? To be accurate, you have to go to the start of the book, and then laboriously read each one of the million+ entries, trying to find people who match your search criteria. In this case, the phone book's index on last names is useless. This kind of SQL looks like this:

```
SELECT *
FROM phone_book
WHERE last_name LIKE '%ead%';
```

Although the `last_name` column is indexed, the optimizer can't use it.

What should you do if you have many database operations that require substring filters? In these kinds of situations, if at all possible, you should simply split the string field into two or more additional, meaningful, and indexed fields. These extra indexes come with the standard cost of more disk space and slightly slower table writes, but they can have a dramatic impact on filter response.

For example, suppose that you're designing a revamped, multitiered, frequent flyer application for High-Hat Airways. This application will extend High-Hat's partnerships with other airlines, hotels, and car rental companies. This requires a renumbering of existing accounts. The revamped frequent flyer account numbers will be structured as follows:

AAXXBB-NNNNN

"AA" is a code that represents the region where the customer lives.

"XX" is the type of program that the customer has joined.

"BB" is a code that represents the partner that referred the customer to this new program.

"NNNNN" is a numeric sequence.

Suppose that the initial table and index design looks like this:

```
CREATE TABLE ff_new
(
    id INT UNSIGNED AUTO_INCREMENT PRIMARY KEY,
    ff_number CHAR(12),
    last_name VARCHAR(30),
    ...
    ...
);
CREATE INDEX ff_new_ix1 ON ff_new(ff_number);
```

If users want to construct database operations that filter on the `ff_number` field, everything should be fine, right? Not exactly. What happens if someone wants to find all customers that were referred by a particular partner?

```
SELECT *
FROM ff_new
WHERE substring(ff_number,5,2) = 'UA';
```

Even though there is an index on `ff_number`, MySQL is unable to use it; it must run a table scan to find all relevant rows. As you've seen, table scans are very expensive, so you should give serious consideration to a revised table design.

In this case, it makes sense to break the ff_number column into several indexed columns as follows:

```
CREATE TABLE ff_revised
(
    id INT UNSIGNED AUTO_INCREMENT PRIMARY KEY,
    ff_region_code CHAR(2) NOT NULL,
    ff_program_type CHAR(2) NOT NULL,
    ff_partner_code CHAR(2) NOT NULL,
    ff_sequence SMALLINT NOT NULL,
    last_name VARCHAR(30),
...
...
    INDEX (ff_region_code),
    INDEX (ff_program_type),
    INDEX (ff_partner_code),
    INDEX (ff_region_code,ff_program_type,ff_partner_code,ff_sequence)
);
```

This table design has several advantages over the old design:

- Each of the subcomponents of the old ff_number field has been given its own column and index. Users can now filter on any of these columns and make use of an index.

- A multifield index now combines all of the subcomponents into one index. You can use this index for searching and sorting.

- We've added growing room for the numeric ff_sequence field by changing it to a SMALLINT.

- For MySQL version 5.0 and beyond, you might be able to leverage the new index merge algorithms to rapidly process a table with multiple indexes. This feature is discussed in Chapter 6.

Improving Temporary Table Performance

MySQL automatically creates temporary tables in a variety of circumstances, including when sorting and grouping large sets of information. Aside from requesting an in-memory temporary table via SELECT SQL_SMALL_RESULT, and a number of server control variables set by your MySQL administrators, you don't have much control over the performance of these tables.

However, there might be situations in which you explicitly create temporary tables on your own. These typically involve a need to create and store a subset of information from larger tables for further processing or other specialized tasks. When you include TEMPORARY in your CREATE TABLE statement, MySQL creates a table that is visible to only your session. After your session closes, the temporary table is freed.

Under these conditions, you can indeed have a positive impact on system response. Make sure to

- **Follow good design practices**—Just because they're temporary tables doesn't mean you can throw caution to the wind when coming up with their designs. A badly designed temporary table functions just as poorly as one that needs to last for years.

- **Index appropriate columns**—See Chapter 7 for more details on this important topic. Depending on the size of your temporary table, it might make sense to first load the table with data and then create indexes.

- **Take advantage of MEMORY tables**—The benefits of these memory-resident structures are discussed in Chapter 4, "Designing for Speed." Consider configuring your temporary tables to use this storage engine if the tables aren't terribly large or if speed is of the essence.

- **Run OPTIMIZE TABLE when appropriate**—This command is discussed in Chapter 6. After you've populated (or otherwise heavily changed) a large temporary table, it's probably worth it to take the time to launch this command, especially if you plan for the "temporary" table to remain extant for some time, or if it will participate in complex joins with other tables.

Managing View Performance

Chapter 4 discusses the performance and application development benefits of views. Unfortunately, views have the potential to cause performance risks if not managed correctly.

The first example occurs when developers and users employ complex views when a simple query might suffice. For example, suppose that you are faced with the need to create a view that joins five tables using sophisticated join syntax, which unavoidably places a load on your MySQL server. However, this view provides real value and is necessary to realize all of the view-creation benefits discussed in Chapter 4.

The potential performance problem arises when developers and other users of your MySQL database decide to use the view to extract columns that happen to exist in only one or two of the base tables that make up the view. In this case, MySQL is forced to perform all of the underlying joins in the view, even though the necessary data could be retrieved much more quickly simply by reading only the necessary tables. For this reason, carefully consider the potential implications of views before creating them and notifying your developers and/or users.

The next potential performance issue occurs when users attempt to update a view. As you just saw, a simple-looking view can mask great complexity and resource consumption. Updates to this view can be very expensive. However, you do have some protection, as follows: If the query uses the LIMIT directive, and you are running MySQL 5.0.2 or newer, you can block updating of a view that does not contain all primary key columns from the underlying table by setting the updateable_views_with_limit system variable to 0/NO. When set to this value, MySQL blocks this kind of possible performance-impacting operation. If it is set to 1/YES, MySQL simply returns a warning.

Subqueries

Subqueries add tremendous power and flexibility to your SQL toolbox. Chapter 6 explores subqueries, including their impact on performance. If you decide to use subqueries, make sure that

1. They take advantage of indexes whenever possible.

2. They are not correlated. That is, they do not reference a table that has already been mentioned in a higher portion of the query. In certain cases, MySQL might be able to improve the performance for correlated subqueries. However, you are usually better off writing these types of queries in a different way.

Using Math Within SQL

As a database application developer building distributed solutions, you face many questions about where to deploy your data-processing logic. One common question relates to mathematical calculations: Should you embed them inside your SQL for running at the database server, or retrieve a larger set of information and then process the data in your application on the client instead?

Like many other decisions, there are strong advantages for either approach. Processing information on the client reduces the load on the server, but results in much more traffic between the database host and the client running the application code. If you're dealing with a widely distributed application with relatively poor connectivity, you run the risk of significant delays in transmitting all of this information. In addition, you might have no way of knowing the processing power of your clients; they might be unable to efficiently process this data after it arrives.

On the other hand, although running heavy calculations on the server can certainly reduce traffic and take load off of the clients, there are situations in which you might inadvertently force MySQL into inefficient server operations, particularly when joining between multiple tables. Take a look at the following simple example.

We created two basic tables to hold information about raw materials, and then loaded about 100,000 rows of random data. We're particularly interested in running simulations using the amount column, which is indexed in both tables:

```
CREATE TABLE materials_1
(
    id INT UNSIGNED AUTO_INCREMENT PRIMARY KEY,
    description CHAR(20),
    amount DECIMAL(5,2),
```

```
    INDEX (amount)
);

CREATE TABLE materials_2
(
    id INT UNSIGNED AUTO_INCREMENT PRIMARY KEY,
    description CHAR(20),
    amount DECIMAL(5,2),
    INDEX (amount)
);
```

Figure 8.6 shows the query plans for some single-table queries that perform calculations on amount.

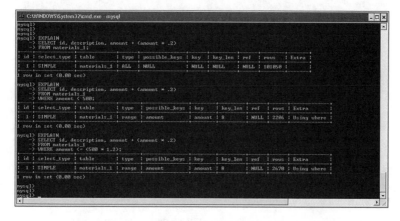

FIGURE 8.6   Query plans for math-based searches.

These query plans make sense: The first query forces a table scan because there isn't a filter, whereas the second and third queries are able to employ the index on amount to speed processing.

Now, take a look at Figure 8.7, which includes joins to the materials_2 table.

The first two query plans are expected: Because there is no filter, the first query forces a table scan, whereas the second query is able to use the correct indexes because there is now a filter. However, the third query is more interesting (and unexpected). By adding math to the join, we have forced MySQL to perform a table scan because it is now unable to use the index.

What should you do if you really need to perform math inside a join clause? One answer is found in MySQL 5.0 and beyond: stored procedures. You may be able to leverage these procedures for additional server-side runtime flexibility. You review all the efficiency benefits of stored procedures in Chapter 9.

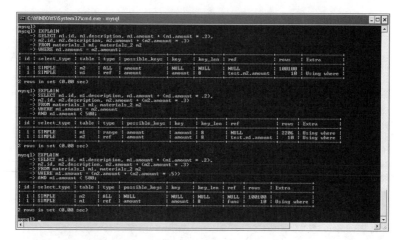

FIGURE 8.7   Multitable math-based query plans.

GROUP BY...WITH ROLLUP

Although server-side math might be expensive in certain situations, there are other times when you can take advantage of the ROLLUP modifier to GROUP BY. Typically, GROUP BY is used when you want to summarize information by major categories.

For example, suppose that you want to write a query that returns the sums of all transactions in the month of January for the last five years. You also want the query to sum up all of the values so that you don't have to perform this calculation on the client. This is where GROUP BY...WITH ROLLUP comes in handy:

```
SELECT YEAR(transaction_date) as 'Year', SUM(amount) as 'Total'
FROM transactions
WHERE YEAR(transaction_date) BETWEEN 2001 AND 2006
AND MONTH(transaction_date) = '01'
GROUP BY YEAR(transaction_date) WITH ROLLUP;
```

```
+------+----------+
| Year | Total    |
+------+----------+
| 2001 | 25572.01 |
| 2002 |  7162.00 |
| 2003 |  9400.00 |
| 2004 | 27403.99 |
| NULL | 69538.00 |
+------+----------+
```

GROUP BY and Sorting

Unless you specify otherwise, MySQL sorts your resultset in the same order as your grouping. For example, look at the following query:

```
SELECT YEAR(transaction_date) as 'Year', SUM(amount) as 'Total'
FROM transactions
GROUP BY YEAR(transaction_date);
```

In this case, your results are returned sorted by the year of the transaction. However, if this sorting is not important to you, append ORDER BY NULL to your query:

```
SELECT YEAR(transaction_date) as 'Year', SUM(amount) as 'Total'
FROM transactions
GROUP BY YEAR(transaction_date) ORDER BY NULL;
```

With this new directive, MySQL avoids the extra work to sort the resultset, which usually results in a modest performance gain. The increased performance is more noticeable if there are many distinct groups of results.

UNIONs

As a relatively recent addition to the MySQL product line, UNIONs are still fairly misunderstood. However, they can add tremendous value to your queries by dramatically speeding response. In addition, version 5.0 offers new query processing algorithms that further extend the power of UNIONs. This section reviews how you can make the most of this valuable database operation.

UNIONs are most helpful when you want to conduct a search on two or more filtered conditions that are typically separated by OR. Prior to MySQL 5.0, even if all filter columns are indexed, MySQL still conducts repeated table scans through the table using each filter and then merges the results to provide an answer. This can be excruciatingly slow.

Fortunately, MySQL introduced the UNION operator with version 4.0. This new functionality means that you can separate these types of queries with a UNION rather than an OR. By doing this, MySQL uses all relevant indexes in separate passes through the table, and then merges the results back at the end.

In version 5.0, things are even better. Its new query processing algorithms can take advantage of multiple indexes on the same table, even if they are separated by OR. However, there are still performance benefits for UNIONs in version 5.0, as you'll see in a moment.

For the next few examples, suppose that you have a multimillion row table containing customer information:

```
CREATE TABLE customer_master
(
    customer_id INT UNSIGNED AUTO_INCREMENT PRIMARY KEY,
    ff_number CHAR(10),
```

```
    last_name VARCHAR(50) NOT NULL,
    first_name VARCHAR(50) NOT NULL,
    home_phone VARCHAR(20),
    mobile_phone VARCHAR(20),
    fax VARCHAR(20),
    email VARCHAR(40),
    home_airport_code CHAR(3),
    date_of_birth DATE,
    sex ENUM ('M','F'),
    date_joined_program DATE,
    date_last_flew DATETIME
) ENGINE = INNODB;
CREATE INDEX cm_ix1 ON customer_master(home_phone);
CREATE INDEX cm_ix2 ON customer_master(ff_number);
CREATE INDEX cm_ix3 ON customer_master(last_name, first_name);
CREATE INDEX cm_ix4 ON customer_master(sex);
CREATE INDEX cm_ix5 ON customer_master(date_joined_program);
CREATE INDEX cm_ix6 ON customer_master(home_airport_code);
```

Now, assume that you need to locate all customer records for people with either the last name of "Lundegaard" or those who normally fly out of Minneapolis. Both the last_name and home_airport_code columns are indexed. However, look at the results of the EXPLAIN command for version 4.1.7:

```
mysql> explain
    -> SELECT last_name, mobile_phone, email
    -> FROM customer_master
    -> WHERE last_name = 'Lundegaard'
    -> OR home_airport_code = 'MSP'\G;

*************************** 1. row ***************************
           id: 1
  select_type: SIMPLE
        table: customer_master
         type: ALL
possible_keys: cm_ix3, cm_ix6
          key: NULL
      key_len: NULL
          ref: NULL
         rows: 1187067
        Extra: Using where
1 row in set (0.00 sec)
```

As predicted, this results in a table scan. On the other hand, if you separate these two conditions with a UNION, observe the new query plan:

```
mysql> explain
-> SELECT last_name, mobile_phone, email
-> FROM customer_master
-> WHERE last_name = 'Lundegaard'
->
-> UNION
->
-> SELECT last_name, mobile_phone, email
-> FROM customer_master
-> WHERE home_airport_code = 'MSP'\G;

*************************** 1. row ***************************
           id: 1
  select_type: PRIMARY
        table: customer_master
         type: ref
possible_keys: cm_ix3
          key: cm_ix3
      key_len: 50
          ref: const
         rows: 1
        Extra: Using where
*************************** 2. row ***************************
           id: 2
  select_type: UNION
        table: customer_master
         type: ref
possible_keys: cm_ix6
          key: cm_ix6
      key_len: 4
          ref: const
         rows: 53
        Extra: Using where
*************************** 3. row ***************************
           id: NULL
  select_type: UNION RESULT
        table: (union1,2)
         type: ALL
possible_keys: NULL
          key: NULL
      key_len: NULL
          ref: NULL
         rows: NULL
        Extra:
3 rows in set (0.00 sec)
```

This is much better: MySQL uses not one, but two indexes to get your answer more quickly. How much more quickly? The first table-scanned query was 17 times slower than the second, UNION and indexed query.

What happens in version 5.0? Look at the query plan for the original SQL with the OR:

```
mysql> explain
-> SELECT last_name, mobile_phone, email
-> FROM customer_master
-> WHERE last_name = 'Lundegaard'
-> OR home_airport_code = 'MSP'\G;

*************************** 1. row ***************************
           id: 1
  select_type: SIMPLE
        table: customer_master
         type: index_merge
possible_keys: cm_ix3, cm_ix6
          key: cm_ix3, cm_ix6
      key_len: 50,4
          ref: NULL
         rows: 240
        Extra: Using sort_union(cm_ix3,cm_ix6); Using where
1 row in set (0.00 sec)
```

This is much better than 4.1.7. MySQL is now able to use the index-merge algorithm to sort and merge the results from both parts of the query.

However, UNIONs still have value with version 5.0:

```
mysql> explain
-> SELECT last_name, mobile_phone, email
-> FROM customer_master
-> WHERE last_name = 'Lundegaard'
->
-> UNION
->
-> SELECT last_name, mobile_phone, email
-> FROM customer_master
-> WHERE home_airport_code = 'MSP'\G;

*************************** 1. row ***************************
           id: 1
  select_type: PRIMARY
        table: customer_master
         type: ref
possible_keys: cm_ix3
          key: cm_ix3
```

```
      key_len: 50
          ref: const
         rows: 1
        Extra: Using where
*************************** 2. row ***************************
           id: 2
  select_type: UNION
        table: customer_master
         type: ref
possible_keys: cm_ix6
          key: cm_ix6
      key_len: 4
          ref: const
         rows: 239
        Extra: Using where
*************************** 3. row ***************************
           id: NULL
  select_type: UNION RESULT
        table: (union1,2)
         type: ALL
possible_keys: NULL
          key: NULL
      key_len: NULL
          ref: NULL
         rows: NULL
        Extra:
3 rows in set (0.00 sec)
```

When we ran the two competing queries in version 5.0, the UNION was approximately 30% faster than the original statement.

As you develop or tune your MySQL-based application, be on the lookout for those cases in which including a UNION can both simplify and speed your SQL.

Sorting

It's an unfortunate fact that no matter how much work you put into planning your database and application, users will find a way to introduce unforeseen, resource-hogging requests, usually at a time when you're least prepared to service them.

New sorting requirements are one of the most common of these unplanned performance complications, especially when they involve nonindexed columns from enormous tables.

Suppose that you have a table that holds many millions of records of transaction detail:

```
CREATE TABLE transaction_detail
(
    transaction_id INT UNSIGNED AUTO_INCREMENT PRIMARY KEY,
```

```
    transaction_date DATETIME NOT NULL,
    amount DECIMAL (5,2) NOT NULL,
    transaction_type ENUM ('Purchase', 'Credit'),
    payment_ref VARCHAR(30),
    INDEX (transaction_date, amount)
);
```

A few weeks pass after the application has gone live, and now management wants a new report that shows all transactions, sorted first by the payment_ref and then by the transaction_date columns. This query is especially slow because there are no filter criteria and these columns are not indexed together.

What makes this situation even worse is that because the query returns all rows, MySQL needs to create a temporary table to hold the sorted results. It's very possible that you will run out of necessary resources, and the query will hang (or worse).

Even though you can't prevent new requirements, you can do some things to avert the potential side effects that these new situations typically introduce:

- **Design indexes to support required sorting**—Prevention is the best remedy for performance problems; do all that you can to get the true picture of your user requirements before events reach a crisis.

- **Build temporary indexes**—If you expect a periodic need for indexes to support additional sorting, consider creating these indexes and then dropping them when they are no longer necessary. Recognize, however, that building these indexes can take some time, so good planning is again a must.

- **Structure the query differently**—Perhaps the query can be rewritten to retrieve a smaller batch of data, which could then be recombined to create the full resultset.

- **Warn users**—If you give users the power to construct free-form queries and sorts, you must also warn them about the prospective danger of terrible performance if they're not careful. You might also want to programmatically intercede on their behalf.

- **Use LIMIT/SQL_BIG_SELECTS/SQL_SELECT_LIMIT**—As you saw earlier in this chapter, MySQL allows you to place restrictions on the size of your query resultsets. When retrieving data, this gives you much more control over how many records are returned by the database to your application.

- **Take advantage of replication**—The power of replication is discussed in Chapter 16. For now, if you're facing a performance challenge (like the current example), replication might help you shift some of the processing load to one or more alternative servers.

- **Tune the MySQL engine**—You can use several engine parameters to help improve large sorting operations. These include read_rnd_buffer_size, sort_buffer_size, and tmp_table_size, which are discussed later in Chapters 10, 11, and 12.

- **Use the MERGE storage engine**—This powerful capability is discussed in Chapter 4. It is especially suited for scenarios in which large volumes of data need to be processed on a fairly infrequent basis.

HANDLER

Many database application developers have also written or maintained applications that perform file-based I/O. These applications typically open a text or binary storage file, seek to a certain position, and then return results from the file to the invoking application.

These types of programs are often very fast and involve minimal overhead. For MySQL-based application developers, there might be times that this type of capability is useful. In fact, MySQL AB made this functionality available in both the MyISAM and InnoDB storage engines, beginning with version 4.0.3.

This section explores this new information retrieval option and pays special attention to ways you can take advantage of it to boost response, as well as some things to keep in mind if you decide to employ HANDLER.

Recall the simple table that tracks customer mileage transactions from Chapter 7:

```
CREATE TABLE customer_mileage_details
(
    customer_id INT NOT NULL,
    ff_number CHAR(10) NOT NULL,
    transaction_date DATE NOT NULL,
    mileage SMALLINT NOT NULL,
    INDEX (customer_id),
    INDEX (ff_number, transaction_date)
) ENGINE = MYISAM;
```

This table contains many millions of rows. Suppose that you need to create a data analysis application that has the following requirements:

- It needs to retrieve blocks of information as quickly as possible.
- Based on user input or other factors, it will likely "jump around" in the table.
- It is not concerned with concurrency or other data integrity issues.
- Cross-application table locking is not required.

With all these criteria in place, using HANDLER makes sense. The table would be opened as follows:

```
HANDLER customer_mileage_details OPEN;
```

Next, suppose you want to seek to the section of this table that matches a particular value for ff_number. Normally, a SELECT statement would trigger the optimizer to determine the correct query plan. However, HANDLER bypasses the optimizer, so you're on your own to pick the correct retrieval method:

```
HANDLER customer_mileage_details
READ ff_number FIRST WHERE ff_number = ('aaetm-4441');
```

```
+-------------+------------+------------------+---------+
| customer_id | ff_number  | transaction_date | mileage |
+-------------+------------+------------------+---------+
|       23782 | aaetm-4441 | 2001-12-21       |    4204 |
+-------------+------------+------------------+---------+
```

After you've found your place in the table, you now want to read the next 10 rows from this position:

```
HANDLER customer_mileage_details READ NEXT LIMIT 10;
```

```
+-------------+------------+------------------+---------+
| customer_id | ff_number  | transaction_date | mileage |
+-------------+------------+------------------+---------+
|       12934 | aaaoh-1730 | 2004-10-02       |   20645 |
|       19170 | aaawk-5396 | 2001-12-19       |    3770 |
|       18520 | aabas-1028 | 2000-12-17       |   14982 |
|       30396 | aabzt-5102 | 2003-03-20       |   18204 |
|       14363 | aacit-1012 | 1999-07-09       |    5111 |
|       16343 | aaclf-5747 | 2002-10-10       |    2030 |
|        7781 | aacqb-1420 | 2002-04-06       |   29931 |
|       29118 | aacwp-2267 | 2003-11-05       |   21146 |
|        3690 | aacys-7537 | 2004-09-14       |   14433 |
|        3750 | aadaa-7803 | 1999-07-04       |   27376 |
+-------------+------------+------------------+---------+
```

As mentioned earlier, this HANDLER call retrieves data in the physical order that the data is stored on disk (that is, in the MyISAM file). In this case, it is stored in ff_number, transaction_date order. Also, because the HANDLER is already open, the engine has minimal parsing and other overhead to process the statement.

When you've finished processing the information that you retrieved from the database (usually within your application logic), you should close the HANDLER:

```
HANDLER customer_mileage_details CLOSE;
```

Many more permutations and possibilities are available with HANDLER than just shown. If you decide to make use of it, be aware of a few important facts:

- Multicolumn indexes need to be referenced from the leftmost position, just as with a standard SQL statement.

- If you want to retrieve more than one row, you need to include the LIMIT option with your HANDLER call.

- Other users can access the table and insert, modify, or delete information that you are examining.

Improving Data Modification

In addition to internal storage engine features such as InnoDB's insert buffering capability, MySQL gives you a surprising amount of control over performance for INSERT, REPLACE, UPDATE, and DELETE operations.

Each storage engine's buffering mechanisms are explored a little later. For now, this section looks at some examples of how you can develop your applications to improve the speed of your data modifications.

First, you might decide at the server, connection, or statement level that you want these types of data modifications to take less precedence than query operations. To set this behavior as the default for your system, include --low-priority-updates when you launch mysqld. If you want this trait enforced by connection, issue a SET LOW_PRIORITY_UPDATES = 1 request. Finally, you can make this request by statement by including LOW_PRIORITY within your SQL syntax. After being set, all searches against the relevant table(s) must complete before making any modifications.

Improving INSERT

The following sections look at several options to boost performance for data-loading operations. Before getting started, note that Chapter 15, "Improving Import and Export Operations," is dedicated to import and export operations a little later in the book.

INSERT LOW_PRIORITY

You reviewed SELECT HIGH_PRIORITY earlier in this chapter. Recall that adding HIGH_PRIORITY to your queries forces MySQL to move them ahead of other processes that modify data.

On the other hand, when it comes to inserting information into a table, you just saw that you can elect to request that these inserts take a lower precedence than operations that are already reading from the table by simply adding LOW_PRIORITY to your INSERT statement. This causes the insert operation to wait until these reads are completed, including any reads that may have begun while the old reads are finishing.

Clearly, this can have a negative impact on an application that sees a mixture of relatively infrequent inserts with constant searches. Here is yet another example of when replication can add great value to your environment: You could set up a master to receive new data inserts, while directing queries against a replicated, more static copy of the master's database. Finally, note that the INSERT HIGH_PRIORITY option doesn't really increase INSERT priority per se; instead, it merely overrides the --low-priority-updates server option should it be set.

INSERT Versus INSERT DELAYED

Because the MyISAM engine only supports table-level locks, there might be situations in which an INSERT operation needs to wait if there are other users accessing the table at that moment. This is less of a problem than it used to be because MySQL now supports parallel SELECT and INSERT operations if there are no empty blocks in the middle of the table (that is, new rows are able to be stored in blocks at the end of the table).

However, for those situations in which there are empty blocks in the middle of your MyISAM table, you can instruct MySQL to queue your inserts via the INSERT DELAYED statement. From your database application's perspective, it's as if the data has been written into the table, when it, in fact, has entered a memory queue for writing as soon as the table is ready. This queue is shared by multiple clients, which also helps to improve performance.

For example, we created a MyISAM table, filled it with millions of rows of random data, and then deleted significant quantities of data from the middle of the table. After that was complete, we ran a simple INSERT DELAYED statement, which was accepted immediately by MySQL. Figure 8.8 shows what the MySQL Administrator reported after the insert operation was accepted.

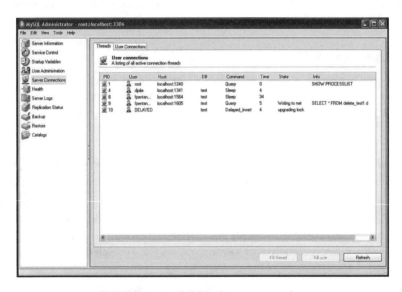

FIGURE 8.8   A delayed INSERT operation.

As you can see, MySQL has allocated a thread (PID 10) and is waiting until the query (PID 9) completes before actually writing the row to the table.

This convenience comes at a cost: MySQL must allocate some additional memory and threads to support this functionality. You are also unable to determine the last value of any columns that have the AUTO_INCREMENT attribute because the rows haven't really been written yet. There is also a risk of lost data if the server is abruptly shut down before the operation truly completes.

In summary, consider using INSERT DELAYED in situations when you

1. Are using the MyISAM engine

2. Have a heavily accessed table, with a mixture of INSERT, UPDATE, and DELETE operations

3. Can't afford to have your client applications block until their INSERT operations complete

4. Are confident that your mysqld process is not subject to undue interruptions or crashes, or if you can reconstruct and retry inserting information should the server crash

INSERT Versus INSERT ... ON DUPLICATE KEY UPDATE Versus REPLACE

If you are building a MySQL-based application that performs both INSERT and UPDATE operations, there will likely be situations in which you want the flexibility to insert a row if it doesn't yet exist (that is, there is no row with the same primary key in the table) but update the row if it already does (that is, a row with this primary key already present).

Beginning with version 4.1, MySQL enhanced the INSERT statement with ON DUPLICATE KEY UPDATE. Some readers might have heard of this functionality described as "UPSERT," which is an amalgamation of UPDATE and INSERT.

This new capability can help streamline your application as well as have a helpful impact on performance, especially for large tables that see frequent insert and update operations. Take a look at the following example.

Suppose that you create a table to track the current mileage totals for all customers:

```
CREATE TABLE customer_mileage
(
    customer_id INT PRIMARY KEY,
    current_mileage INT,
    ...
    ...
);
```

After this table is created, several different applications repeatedly access the table. Some create new customer_mileage records (including current_mileage), whereas others merely add some additional miles to the current_mileage column for existing customers.

If you erroneously issue an INSERT statement against this table when there is already an existing record, you receive an error, which you'll have to manage:

```
INSERT INTO customer_mileage VALUES (179939,5634);

ERROR 1062 (23000): Duplicate entry '179939' for key 1
```

However, the new INSERT functionality lets you write a single, flexible SQL statement that handles both INSERT and UPDATE operations:

```
INSERT INTO customer_mileage VALUES (179939,5634)
ON DUPLICATE KEY UPDATE current_mileage = current_mileage + 5634;
```

Note that if there is no row already present with this primary key, MySQL reports that one row is affected. However, if there is a row already resident, MySQL reports that two rows are affected.

Finally, to take advantage of this capability, your table needs either a primary key or at least one unique index.

Multirow Inserts

MySQL supports INSERT statements that create multiple rows. This can have a notable effect on performance, especially when inserting large quantities of information. Consider the following example.

High-Hat Airways has entered into a partnership with KramAir, one of Southeast Asia's most successful airlines. Part of this partnership includes mutual frequent flyer credit for all flights flown on either airline. Each month, KramAir sends a number of large files containing relevant details to ensure these credits. One of these files contains data that needs to be loaded into your flights table, which is defined as follows:

```
CREATE TABLE flights (
    flight_id INT UNSIGNED AUTO_INCREMENT PRIMARY KEY,
    flight_number SMALLINT UNSIGNED NOT NULL,
    flight_date DATE NOT NULL,
    flight_departure_city CHAR(3),
    flight_arrival_city CHAR(3)
);
```

Because KramAir is also a happy MySQL customer, it's easy for them to generate a multirow INSERT as part of their mysqldump operation. Chapter 15 explores mysqldump.

Without the multirow INSERT syntax, your SQL operations would look like this:

```
INSERT INTO flights VALUES (1,2358,'2006-03-09','SYD','KUL');
INSERT INTO flights VALUES (2,109,'2006-03-09','SIN','HAN');
INSERT INTO flights VALUES (3,9893,'2006-03-09','HKG','NRT');
INSERT INTO flights VALUES (4,642,'2006-03-09','ACK','KUL');
INSERT INTO flights VALUES (5,8845,'2006-03-09','BGK','SIN');
...
```

The multirow INSERT syntax is much more compressed (if a bit harder to read):

```
INSERT INTO `flights` VALUES (1,2358,'2006-03-09','SYD','KUL'),(2,109,'2006-03-
09','SIN','HAN'),(3,9893,'2006-03-09','HKG','NRT'),(4,642,'2006-03-09','ACK','KUL
'),(5,8845,'2006-03-09','BGK','SIN')...
```

To gauge the potential performance gains from introducing multirow inserts, we created a sample data set of 600,000 rows to be loaded into the flights table.

First, we created this table using the InnoDB storage engine. Next, we included a LOCK TABLE directive at the start of the load. Finally, we tested the difference between using a dedicated INSERT statement for each row as well as multirow INSERT statements.

To ensure that buffering was not a factor, after each test we dropped the table, stopped and restarted the engine, and re-created the table.

The results were dramatic: The time to complete the load when using single row INSERT statements was approximately thirtyfold longer than when rows were loaded in multiples.

Next, we conducted the same set of tests with the MyISAM storage engine. The results were quite a bit less dramatic, but still substantial: Single row INSERT operations took eight times longer than corresponding multirow INSERT statements.

Disabling Indexes

If you are using the MyISAM storage engine, you have the option of disabling index updates when loading large amounts of data into the table by running myisamchk with the --keys-used parameter. If you are exporting data via mysqldump, you can also specify --disable-keys when launching the utility. This is discussed in more detail in Chapters 7 and 15.

Improving DELETE

Most transactional applications generally don't delete large amounts of data in one operation; they typically remove a relatively small quantity of data in the context of a brief transaction. However, there are many other situations in which large-scale deletions happen. MySQL offers a number of performance-enhancing options that you can use to speed up these operations. The following sections review what these options are and how you can take advantage of them. Server parameters that affect deletion are not covered now because Chapters 10, 11, and 12 provide a significant amount of coverage.

DELETE LOW_PRIORITY

Add the LOW_PRIORITY option to your DELETE statement if you don't mind delaying your delete operation until all other active readers of the table have completed their access to the table. Note that after it starts, the DELETE operation consumes the same amount of resources even if you specified LOW_PRIORITY. Of course, this statement does not improve delete performance per se, but does reduce its impact on other activities.

DELETE QUICK

If you are 1) using the MyISAM storage engine and 2) attempting to delete a large amount of data, try including the QUICK option with your DELETE statement:

```
DELETE QUICK FROM transactions WHERE transaction_id BETWEEN 100000 AND 300000;
```

Choosing this option means that MySQL skips some internal index housekeeping steps when processing the delete. However, if these values are unlikely to be reinserted later, this increases the likelihood of table and index fragmentation because MySQL now bypasses the normal steps of merging that index leaves upon deletion. To reclaim this space, you eventually want to defragment the table and indexes via either the OPTIMIZE TABLE or myisamchk command.

To test the performance implications of DELETE versus DELETE QUICK, we first created a sample table and filled it with 10 million rows of random data:

```
CREATE TABLE delete_test
(
    col1 INT UNSIGNED AUTO_INCREMENT PRIMARY KEY,
    col2 CHAR(10) NOT NULL,
    col3 VARCHAR(200) NOT NULL,
    col4 BIGINT NOT NULL,
    INDEX (col3),
    INDEX (col4)
) ENGINE = MYISAM;
```

Next, we ran some DELETE tests. All tests deleted the same amount of data, using the primary key as a lookup. The only difference was that half the operations used DELETE alone, whereas the other half used DELETE QUICK.

Unfortunately, the results were inconclusive at best. In a significant number of situations, DELETE QUICK slightly degraded performance rather than enhancing it. Because the prime motivation for using DELETE QUICK is to dramatically improve performance, these tests indicate that it does not add tremendous value.

Nevertheless, it is possible that your specific table and index structure might benefit from employing DELETE QUICK; this is when experimentation on a test server that replicates your environment is invaluable.

DELETE, ORDER BY, and LIMIT

First introduced in version 4.0, the combination of DELETE, ORDER BY, and LIMIT gives you significant flexibility when deleting from very large tables. You can construct a delete operation that first sorts the potential deleted rows by criteria that you specify, and then deletes a limited number of rows to keep performance within acceptable parameters.

For example, using the transaction_detail table described earlier in this chapter, suppose that you want to delete the oldest 1,000 rows. Prior to this new combination of DELETE options, you would have needed to somehow figure out what the time stamp was for the oldest 1,000 rows and then include that value in our WHERE clause.

However, you can now write much simpler SQL:

```
DELETE FROM transaction_detail
ORDER BY transaction_date
LIMIT 1000;
```

It goes without saying, of course, that you will want your ORDER BY clause to make use of an index.

DELETE Versus TRUNCATE TABLE Versus DROP TABLE

MySQL offers a choice of several commands when you need to quickly remove large quantities of data from an existing table. Your actual choice depends on your storage engine as well as your particular processing need. Take a look at a few scenarios:

1. You are using the InnoDB storage engine and need to delete all rows in a large table. In this case, it is much faster to issue a DROP TABLE command and then re-create the table via CREATE TABLE, assuming you have sufficient permission. Otherwise, running a full DELETE on the table can generate tremendous transaction load on the database engine.

2. You are using the MyISAM storage engine, and need to delete all rows in a large table. MySQL offers the TRUNCATE TABLE command, which implicitly drops and then re-creates the table.

3. You are using any storage engine, and need to delete the vast majority (90%+) of rows in a table. In this situation, you might get better performance by first extracting the rows that you want to keep, placing them in a temporary table, and then dropping/re-creating the large table. After this is done, you can then reload the remaining rows back into the newly re-created table.

9

Developing High-Speed Applications

Up to this point, the book has been focusing on how to select a MySQL storage engine, design and index your tables, and write optimal SQL; coming up later are suggestions on how to tune your MySQL storage engines. Right now, it's time to pay attention to developing swift application software to make the most of your efficient MySQL database.

Because concurrency is so vital to good performance on a multiuser MySQL database server, this chapter begins by examining the interplay between concurrency considerations (such as locking and transaction isolation levels) and database responsiveness. After that topic has been explored, the chapter moves on to explaining how stored procedures, functions, and triggers all have a role to play in speeding your MySQL-based solution.

Developers building a MySQL-based solution have a surfeit of language and connector alternatives. To help these developers, regardless of their choice of application development technology, the chapter closes with a compilation of ideas to help improve application logic performance.

Before beginning this chapter, it's worth repeating an observation that has been made throughout the book: A well-performing MySQL-based solution begins with a good design, followed in turn by wise index deployment and optimal SQL. By the time application code is ready to be written, the performance characteristics of the solution have already been mostly predetermined.

In other words, world-class application logic bogs down when confronted with a horrendously structured database that suffers from incorrect indexing. On the other hand, the sloppiest application code often appears to be worthy of worldwide acclaim when, in fact, the database, indexes, and queries have been designed with performance in mind.

Understanding Locking

Concurrency refers to the ability of multiple database-accessing applications and processes to peacefully coexist at the same time, with no application consuming more than its necessary and fair share of system resources. Good concurrency is more conspicuous by its absence than its presence: No users ever complain when a system is highly concurrent, but imagine the noise when a key database resource is locked indefinitely.

What makes MySQL's locking behavior somewhat difficult to understand is that there are general MySQL locking concepts as well as InnoDB-specific notions. Further complicating matters is that although much of MySQL's locking activities happen automatically, developers can take many steps to influence these actions. To help address this potential confusion, this section explains locking from both the general and InnoDB perspectives, along with how SQL statements can drive locking activities.

General Locking Overview

To begin the locking discussion, it's a good idea to examine locks from the top-level perspective of MySQL itself, including the granularity of all available locks, the types of locks offered, and the concurrency options for these locks.

Lock Granularity

Each MySQL storage engine offers different levels of granularity for their locks. In decreasing granularity (that is, from largest lockable object to smallest), they are as follows:

- **Table locks**—Supported by the MyISAM, MEMORY, and InnoDB storage engines, these restrict access to an entire table. Their effects can be mitigated by the LOCAL and LOW_PRIORITY options available for READ and WRITE locks, respectively.

- **Page locks**—Provided by the BDB storage engine, these locks confine their effects to only those data and index details resident on a particular page. Because this chapter does not cover the BDB engine, page locks are not covered here.

- **Row locks**—A row-level lock hones in on a particular record, leaving all other rows within a table free for others to access and modify. The InnoDB storage engine offers this kind of lock: You can also obtain a table lock for an InnoDB-hosted table, but you should take care to first commit or roll back your transaction before explicitly releasing the lock via the UNLOCK TABLES command.

Lock Types

Broadly speaking, MySQL-level locks fall into one of two classes:

- **READ locks**—By placing a READ lock on a table (via the LOCK TABLES statement), you restrict other users from altering information in the affected table until you release the lock via the UNLOCK TABLES statement. If you have included the LOCAL option with your LOCK TABLES statement, other processes are able to execute concurrent, nonconflicting INSERT operations at the same time. After issuing a READ lock request, your application can count on no data changes (other than inserts if LOCAL was specified) for the duration of the lock.

- **WRITE locks**—Designed to safeguard data modifications, when issued a WRITE lock prevents all other processes from altering information in the table. By including the LOW_PRIORITY directive, you instruct MySQL to wait until all other activities that request READ locks have completed prior to obtaining your WRITE lock.

When to Explicitly Request Table Locks

In most cases, there are only two scenarios in which a database developer or administrator should intercede and overtly request one or more table locks. Before citing these cases, it's important that you recognize the risks inherent in this strategy. These dangers include greatly diminished concurrency as well as the potential for data-integrity problems should something go wrong in the middle of an operation.

The first setting occurs when it's vital that a series of database events happen without interference. This is typically handled in a transaction, but there might be times that you are using a nontransactional storage engine yet need this capability. In these cases, locking a table for the duration of your alterations effectively provides you with transactional behavior. However, because the built-in rollback features found in a transactional storage engine are lacking, it is not easy to undo any changes applied to your tables.

The second situation transpires when you want to coax additional performance from your MyISAM tables during large-scale operations. Locking these tables effectively reduces the amount of overhead necessary to complete these activities, but at the cost of significantly reduced concurrency.

InnoDB Locking Overview

Because InnoDB offers full transactional support, it stands to reason that its locking functionality is more substantial than that found across all MySQL storage engines. This is indeed the case: There are additional lock considerations and capabilities that developers should keep in mind when deploying applications that use this storage engine.

This section begins with an exploration of InnoDB's lock concurrency properties, and then moves on to explain (at a high level) some of InnoDB's locking algorithms. Because there is a strong interplay among locks, SQL statements, transactions, and transaction isolation levels, the section closes with an examination of how specific types of SQL statements and operations leverage locks.

Before starting the discussion, review the following two tables, along with rows from the first table. This chapter periodically refers to these very simple tables to help illustrate a concept.

```
CREATE TABLE vip
(
    id INTEGER PRIMARY KEY AUTO_INCREMENT,
    last_name VARCHAR(30) NOT NULL,
    vip_level ENUM ('Tin','Silver','Gold'),
```

```
    INDEX(last_name)
) ENGINE = INNODB;

CREATE TABLE vip_gifts
(
    id INTEGER PRIMARY KEY AUTO_INCREMENT,
    vip_id INTEGER NOT NULL,
    gift_date DATE NOT NULL,
    gift_description VARCHAR(80) NOT NULL,
    INDEX(gift_date),
    FOREIGN KEY (vip_id) references vip(id)
) ENGINE = INNODB;

mysql> SELECT * FROM vip;
+----+-----------+-----------+
| id | last_name | vip_level |
+----+-----------+-----------+
|  1 | Adir      | Gold      |
|  2 | Bass      | Silver    |
|  3 | Crocker   | Silver    |
|  4 | Dietrich  | Tin       |
|  5 | Egan      | Tin       |
|  6 | Fish      | Silver    |
|  7 | Lapexin   | Gold      |
|  8 | Ramystein | Tin       |
|  9 | Savedien  | Gold      |
| 10 | Zlotnick  | Gold      |
+----+-----------+-----------+
```

Lock Concurrency

Whether a lock is set implicitly by MySQL, or explicitly by a user or application, it has a number of characteristics. As you have seen, these include its scope (that is, granularity) as well as whether it is a read or write lock. For locks in the InnoDB storage engine, one additional property is its concurrency, which can be either exclusive or shared. An exclusive lock prevents any other users from obtaining the same kind of lock on the object in question. On the other hand, a shared lock means that other users can obtain the exact same type of lock at the same time.

Row-level Locking Scope

In Chapter 12, "InnoDB Performance Enhancement," which focuses on improving InnoDB performance, you learn that this engine internally stores all rows in a clustered index. In those situations in which you have not defined an index for the table, one is created for you automatically.

Many types of operations cause InnoDB to set row-level locks. Depending on the type of procedure under way, it chooses among several row locking tactics:

- **Locking the index entry for the row itself**—This is known as a "non-next-key" lock.

- **Locking the gap (that is, the space) in the index immediately prior to the row**— Known as a "gap" lock, this prevents other rows from being placed into that position for the duration of the lock.

- **Locking both objects**—This is known as a "next-key" lock.

Monitoring Locks

InnoDB offers detailed diagnostic information via the SHOW INNODB STATUS command. For example, look at the following open transaction, along with its associated entry in this command's output:

```
START TRANSACTION;
UPDATE vip SET vip_level = 'Gold' WHERE id BETWEEN 3 AND 5;

SHOW INNODB STATUS\G

...
------------
TRANSACTIONS
------------
Trx id counter 0 1061815858
Purge done for trx's n:o < 0 1061815856 undo n:o < 0 0
History list length 9
Total number of lock structs in row lock hash table 1
LIST OF TRANSACTIONS FOR EACH SESSION:
---TRANSACTION 0 1061815857, ACTIVE 3 sec, process no 20846, OS thread id 210858
6928
2 lock struct(s), heap size 320, undo log entries 3
MySQL thread id 8, query id 663 localhost Gabriel
...
```

Experimenting with the SHOW INNODB STATUS command is a worthwhile exercise for any MySQL designer, developer, or administrator. See the "Optimal Transactions" section of this chapter for numerous other examples of what this command's output looks like in problem situations.

SQL Statements and Locks

Many SQL statements cause InnoDB to place and release locks. Because this usually happens so quickly and smoothly, most developers and administrators never realize that this is transpiring. Exceptions to this rule can occur when a transaction is left running too long, for example. These problem transactions are discussed later in this chapter.

Even if your transactions are perfectly designed, however, it's important that you understand the locking implications of your SQL statements; this can have a significant impact on both your InnoDB server's performance and concurrency.

In increasing order of restrictiveness, these locks and the SQL statements that trigger them include the following:

- **Shared same-record lock**—This lock placed on the row in addition to any locks listed next.

    1. All data-modifying SQL statements.

- **Shared next-key lock**—By preventing insertions immediately adjacent to a given key, a next-key lock helps defend against data integrity problems. The following statements trigger creation of shared versions of this lock.

    1. `SELECT ... FROM`—This happens if the SERIALIZABLE transaction isolation level has been specified. Otherwise, no locking is done. Isolation levels are discussed in the following section.

    2. `SELECT ... FROM ... LOCK IN SHARE MODE`

- **Exclusive non-next-key lock**—The following statements require more restrictive locking.

    1. `INSERT INTO ... VALUES (...)`

    2. `SELECT ... FROM ... FOR UPDATE`

    3. `CREATE TABLE_X ... SELECT ... FROM TABLE_Y`—This lock is placed for rows in Table_X. If binary logging is enabled, Table_Y also receives a shared next-key lock.

    4. `INSERT INTO TABLE_X ... SELECT ... FROM TABLE_Y`—This lock is placed for rows in Table_X. If binary logging is enabled, Table_Y also receives a shared next-key lock.

- **Exclusive next-key lock**—Because of the possibility of data integrity problems, the following statements necessitate very restrictive locks.

    1. `SELECT ... FROM ... FOR UPDATE`

    2. `UPDATE ... WHERE`

    3. `DELETE FROM ... WHERE`

The preceding three statements have the potential to generate enormous amounts of locks if there is no index available for InnoDB to use to process the query. This is because InnoDB locks all of the rows it evaluated to identify the resultset. In the absence of the assistance provided by an index, this could equate to a table scan.

For example, suppose that the "vip" table listed previously had tens of thousands of rows, and you started a transaction that did not make use of an index:

```
START TRANSACTION;
UPDATE vip SET vip_level = 'Rust' WHERE vip_level = 'Tin';
SHOW INNODB STATUS\G
...
```

```
---TRANSACTION 0 1061815874, ACTIVE 9 sec, process no 20846, OS thread id 210858
6928 fetching rows, thread declared inside InnoDB 293
mysql tables in use 1, locked 1
4129 lock struct(s), heap size 240960, undo log entries 313915
MySQL thread id 8, query id 2012 localhost Gabriel Updating
update vip set vip_level = 'Rust' where vip_level = 'Tin'
...
```

Here's the SHOW INNODB STATUS output after the update operation finished, but before the transaction was closed:

```
...
---TRANSACTION 0 1061815874, ACTIVE 153 sec, process no 20846, OS thread id 2108
586928
26433 lock struct(s), heap size 1502528, undo log entries 2010022
MySQL thread id 8, query id 2319 localhost Gabriel
...
```

Look at the number of lock structures and undo log entries. This kind of open-ended, index-free operation can cause serious performance and concurrency problems. Try to ensure that these are rare in your MySQL environment.

Optimal Transactions

Transactions are a fundamental component in ensuring that data alterations are managed in a secure, consistent way. This section investigates how to apply solid optimization techniques to your transactions, combining their data integrity features with good performance.

As stated before, the BDB, NDB, and InnoDB storage engines all offer transactions. However, because this book does not explicitly cover the BDB engine, and because the NDB engine is covered in Chapter 17, "Optimal Clustering," this section exclusively focuses on InnoDB instead.

This section begins by clarifying a number of key transaction terms and concepts, and then moves on to exploring their costs and benefits. Finally, this section provides a collection of tips to help get the most speed out of your transactional operations.

Key Transaction Terms and Concepts

Before you can begin to choose an optimal transaction strategy for your server or application, you must first understand how transactions work, both standalone as well as in concert with other transactions. This section explores isolation levels, providing examples of each setting along with output from SHOW INNODB STATUS that you can use to comprehend what is happening on your MySQL server. A little later on, this chapter makes recommendations about selecting the correct isolation level.

Isolation Levels

Because modern relational database management systems are designed to support thousands of concurrent users, there must be some rules in place so that these simultaneous constituents can work without descending into chaos. These rules have been encapsulated into isolation levels, which dictate the concurrency behavior that each transaction undertakes, both solely as well as when encountering potential conflict.

MySQL offers all four of the isolation levels specified by the SQL standard. They include the following:

- **READ UNCOMMITTED**—Also referred to as "dirty read," this isolation level uses no locks when querying information with plain SELECT statements; on the other hand, UPDATE and DELETE statements employ locks. The scope of locking is dependent on the search conditions provided with the statement. If a unique search condition is passed in, InnoDB only locks the index records in question, and no others. On the other hand, if a range is passed into the statement, InnoDB is forced to apply additional locks to the gaps between records, reducing concurrency in the process.

    In the case of plain SELECT statements, any locks held by other active threads are disregarded and the data is retrieved anyway. Although fast and simple, this introduces the possibility of making a decision based on "phantom rows" (that is, information that can be rolled back to a different state than it was when originally retrieved by the READ UNCOMMITTED query).

    For example, assume that there are only two users (Bud and Lou) working on a MySQL server. Bud begins a transaction and inserts a row into the "vip" table shown earlier in this chapter. Lou has set a very permissive isolation level of READ UNCOMMITTED. Lou queries the table, and sees the row that Bud has just inserted, even though it is not yet committed. In fact, Bud is preoccupied at the moment, and has walked away from his desk, leaving the transaction open.

    At this moment, if Lou ran SHOW INNODB STATUS, you would see these transaction details about Bud and Lou's sessions:

```
---TRANSACTION 0 1061815303, ACTIVE 9 sec, process no 20247, OS thread id 2108386224
MySQL thread id 8, query id 668 Client292 LCostello
show innodb status
---TRANSACTION 0 1061815302, ACTIVE 17 sec, process no 20247, OS thread id
2108185520
1 lock struct(s), heap size 320, undo log entries 1
MySQL thread id 7, query id 634 Client142 BAbbott
```

    Perhaps Lou will make a decision about the row that Bud has inserted but not yet committed. If he does, there is a good chance that this decision will be wrong because Bud might decide to roll back the transaction.

    As it turns out, Lou decides to update the row that he sees in the table. He issues an UPDATE statement, but is surprised to see that the statement appears to take a very long time to execute. If he were to run SHOW INNODB STATUS again at that moment, he would likely be alarmed at what he sees:

```
---TRANSACTION 0 1061815879, ACTIVE 13 sec, process no 20846, OS thread id 21089
88336 starting index read
mysql tables in use 1, locked 1
LOCK WAIT 2 lock struct(s), heap size 320
MySQL thread id 14, query id 4425 Client292 LCostello Updating
update vip set vip_level = 'Gold' where last_name = 'Fields'
------- TRX HAS BEEN WAITING 13 SEC FOR THIS LOCK TO BE GRANTED:
RECORD LOCKS space id 0 page no 213046 n bits 80 index `last_name` of table `hig
h_hat/vip` trx id 0 1061815879 lock_mode X waiting
Record lock, heap no 12 PHYSICAL RECORD: n_fields 2; 1-byte offs TRUE; info bits
0
 0: len 6; hex 4669656c6473; asc Fields;; 1: len 4; hex 8000000b; asc    ;;
```

This output tells you that poor Lou won't be able to make his change until after Bud commits the transaction. Unfortunately, Bud has left the building, so no transaction commit will be forthcoming. In fact, several moments later Lou receives the following error:

```
ERROR 1205 (HY000): Lock wait timeout exceeded; try restarting transaction
```

Even with this permissive isolation level, Lou still received an error because data altering statements like he was trying to run still attempt to acquire locks, and open transactions can block these locks.

- **READ COMMITTED**—This isolation level is more restrictive than READ UNCOMMITTED, preventing others from seeing phantom rows. However, other data-modifying operations are treated the same as with READ UNCOMMITTED.

Continuing the preceding example, Lou has learned from the error of his ways, and has decided to use the READ COMMITTED transaction isolation level so as to never see a phantom row again.

As part of month-end processing, Bud runs a lengthy transaction that must update all rows in the table. At that moment, Lou needs to insert a single row into the table. Unfortunately, once again Lou is blocked from completing his work. Consulting SHOW INNODB STATUS, he sees the following:

```
---TRANSACTION 0 1061815882, ACTIVE 6 sec, process no 20846, OS thread id 210898
8336 inserting
mysql tables in use 1, locked 1
LOCK WAIT 2 lock struct(s), heap size 320
MySQL thread id 14, query id 4909 Client292 LCostello update
insert into vip (last_name, vip_level) values ('Hardy','Gold')
------- TRX HAS BEEN WAITING 6 SEC FOR THIS LOCK TO BE GRANTED:
RECORD LOCKS space id 0 page no 213044 n bits 80 index `PRIMARY` of table `high_
hat/vip` trx id 0 1061815882 lock_mode X insert intention waiting
```

```
Record lock, heap no 1 PHYSICAL RECORD: n_fields 1; 1-byte offs TRUE; info bits
0
 0: len 9; hex 73757072656d756d00; asc supremum ;;


-----------------
---TRANSACTION 0 1061815881, ACTIVE 31 sec, process no 20846, OS thread id 21087
87632
2 lock struct(s), heap size 320, undo log entries 6
MySQL thread id 15, query id 4922 Client142 BAbbott
```

Just as Lou is about to pick up the phone to ask Bud to finish his work, he receives another error from MySQL:

```
ERROR 1205 (HY000): Lock wait timeout exceeded; try restarting transaction
```

What happened this time? Because Bud was running a broad UPDATE process, InnoDB was forced to set locks to prevent other users from inserting information into the spaces between rows in the table. Lou's transaction fit that profile, so it had to wait until the transaction completed. Unfortunately, it ran out of time yet again because Bud's transaction took too long.

- **REPEATABLE READ**—Even more protective than COMMITTED READ, this isolation level ensures that all SELECT statements within a transaction see consistent results, even if the underlying data has changed in the interim.

  For example, suppose that Lou is running a simple query within a transaction, and is looking at a series of rows. A few moments later, Bud starts a transaction, makes a change to a particular row, and then commits his transaction. What will Lou see? Until he closes his transaction and then refreshes the data, it appears as if Bud never made his change. Known as a "consistent read," this uses InnoDB's multiversioning capabilities to provide a point-in-time view of information. If Lou were to run SHOW INNODB STATUS while his original transaction was still open, he would see the following entry of interest:

```
---TRANSACTION 0 1061815884, ACTIVE 26 sec, process no 20846, OS thread id 21089
88336
MySQL thread id 14, query id 5299 Client292 LCostello
Trx read view will not see trx with id >= 0 1061815885, sees < 0 1061815885
```

  The last line is interesting: It provides insight into which transactions will be "invisible" to Lou until he closes his active transaction.

- **SERIALIZABLE**—As the most protective isolation level, SERIALIZABLE blocks other threads from modifying information that has merely been viewed with a simple SELECT statement.

  For example, Bud has now decided that he doesn't want anyone to alter any of his data while he's reading it, even if he won't be making any changes at all. By setting his isolation level to SERIALIZABLE, InnoDB causes any other database access threads that

attempt to modify any of Bud's already-read data to pause. They won't be able to proceed until they either time out or Bud completes his transaction. Viewing SHOW INNODB
STATUS points this out:

```
---TRANSACTION 0 1061815888, ACTIVE 4 sec, process no 20846, OS thread id 210898
8336 starting index read
mysql tables in use 1, locked 1
LOCK WAIT 3 lock struct(s), heap size 320
MySQL thread id 14, query id 5603 Client292 LCostello Updating
update vip set vip_level = 'Tin' where last_name = 'Fish'
------- TRX HAS BEEN WAITING 4 SEC FOR THIS LOCK TO BE GRANTED:
RECORD LOCKS space id 0 page no 213044 n bits 80 index `PRIMARY` of table `high_
hat/vip` trx id 0 1061815888 lock_mode X locks rec but not gap waiting
Record lock, heap no 7 PHYSICAL RECORD: n_fields 5; 1-byte offs TRUE; info bits
0
 0: len 4; hex 80000006; asc     ;; 1: len 6; hex 00003f4a0626; asc   ?J &;; 2:
len 7; hex 800005c0020084; asc         ;; 3: len 4; hex 46697368; asc Fish;; 4: l
en 1; hex 02; asc  ;;
```

Setting Transaction Isolation Levels

You can set a serverwide default transaction isolation level policy by providing a value for
the --transaction-isolation option in your MySQL configuration file. Unless specified
otherwise, the default value is REPEATABLE READ.

You can also use the SET TRANSACTION ISOLATION LEVEL statement to control this behavior
globally or for a session. Remember that any active transactions don't have their isolation
levels changed by this statement; only new transactions are affected.

You can discover the global and session-level isolation levels currently in effect in several
ways:

```
mysql> SELECT @@global.tx_isolation;
+----------------------+
| @@global.tx_isolation |
+----------------------+
| REPEATABLE-READ      |
+----------------------+
1 row in set (0.00 sec)

mysql> SELECT @@tx_isolation;
+---------------+
| @@tx_isolation |
+---------------+
| SERIALIZABLE  |
+---------------+
1 row in set (0.00 sec)
```

```
mysql> SHOW VARIABLES LIKE 'TX%';
+---------------+--------------+
| Variable_name | Value        |
+---------------+--------------+
| tx_isolation  | SERIALIZABLE |
+---------------+--------------+
1 row in set (0.00 sec)
```

Cost of Transactions

It's important to note that in InnoDB, all activity happens within a transaction regardless of whether the developer or administrator overtly requests one. The AUTOCOMMIT option controls the mechanism by which these transactions are concluded. When set to 1, every database-affecting operation can be considered as occurring within its own transaction. On the other hand, setting AUTOCOMMIT to 0 means that a transaction remains open until either a COMMIT or ROLLBACK statement is sent by the client. Most applications that contain transaction-concluding logic (that is, whether to commit or roll back the transaction) elect to set AUTOCOMMIT to 0.

Naturally, transactions involve some extra costs. These costs chiefly involve additional writes to the binary log, as well as added memory consumption to keep track of the internal locks that InnoDB uses to maintain transactional integrity. Although neither of these costs is terribly burdensome, they do warrant consideration before opting for transactional support for a given table. This topic is explored in more detail in the next section.

Transaction Performance Suggestions

Before choosing whether to require that a table use transactions, it's useful to take a number of factors into account. Then, if you decide to stipulate that a given set of tables use the InnoDB storage engine, you can take several actions to improve overall transaction response. This section examines these decision criteria and suggestions.

Choosing the Right Storage Engine

Regardless of your AUTOCOMMIT configuration, InnoDB's transactional support incurs extra overhead. For this reason, it's smart to only use InnoDB as the storage engine for those tables that require the extra capabilities offered by transactions. Otherwise, using an engine like MyISAM is a better choice.

Even if a table requires transactional support, consider using a nontransactional table to hold historical or other nondynamic information.

Choosing the Right Isolation Level

Each of MySQL's four transaction isolation levels is appropriate in certain circumstances. This section describes the scenarios in which each isolation level is suitable:

- **READ UNCOMMITTED**—As you saw earlier, this isolation level uses the fewest number of locks, but opens up the possibility of seeing "phantom rows." Although potentially dangerous in highly dynamic, multiuser environments, it can safely be used in single-user situations, or when the table's data is static.

- **READ COMMITTED**—Applications that would benefit from this isolation level are those that cannot tolerate phantom rows but do not need the more protective capabilities of REPEATABLE READ.

- **REPEATABLE READ**—As MySQL's default, this isolation level is suitable for applications that require assistance in avoiding phantom rows, protection from other users altering information that is currently being modified by the current application, and the data reliability and point-in-time view provided by its consistent read guarantees.

  Dozens of types of applications fit this profile; a good example is a program that computes a result after examining a set of detail records, updates these detail records, and then revises a header record with this information. In this case, it's vital that the detail records remain consistent until they and their associated header record are updated and the transaction is committed.

- **SERIALIZABLE**—This highly restrictive isolation level should only be used for those transactions that cannot tolerate any changes to underlying data, even if the transaction is simply reading information without making any of its own alterations.

  Extending the example previously described, suppose that this application also examines detail data from another, secondary table via a simple SELECT statement, but that this newly read data is not touched in any way. Still, the developer does not want anyone to alter any rows in this secondary table that have been evaluated in computing the result for updating the header, even if those rows themselves are not updated. In this case, SERIALIZABLE would be the right approach, but it should be used with extreme caution: If the transaction examines many rows *and* is lengthy, there is a good chance other users and processes will encounter delays until this transaction closes and releases its locks.

Keeping Transactions Brief

Transactions do not improve with age; in most cases, they should be kept as brief as possible. There are a number of dangers introduced by lengthy transactions:

- **Degraded concurrency**—Combining a restrictive isolation level with a long transaction is a recipe for concurrency problems: You just saw how one inattentive user (Bud) kept his transactions open too long and caused another user (Lou) to make all kinds of incorrect decisions and encounter timeouts.

- **Resource consumption**—Although InnoDB is very efficient in its transaction-supporting resource allocation, a long-running transaction consumes these resources for greater amounts of time, reducing their availability for other users.

- **Rollback segment issues**—Chapter 12 discusses how InnoDB uses insert and update undo logs in its rollback segment to help ensure consistent views of information, even if transactions are under way. If a transaction runs too long, InnoDB is unable to free up these resources in the rollback segment, which could cause tablespace issues or other performance-degrading problems.

- **Deadlocks**—Over time, InnoDB has increasingly improved its ability to avoid deadlocks, and manage them when they do occur. Developers can do their part by keeping transactions as short as possible. In addition, for those sites using AUTOCOMMMIT = 1, consider setting innodb_table_locks to 0 to help reduce the frequency of deadlocks.

- **Rollback problems**—Although InnoDB uses good buffering techniques when handling big insert operations, a rollback of the same transaction does not benefit from this caching. This means that a rollback can take a very long time, even if the insert operation was proceeding rapidly. By definition, a short transaction has fewer modifications that might need to be rolled back.

Now that you've read the sorrowful litany of difficulties that can be spawned by lengthy transactions, what can you do to reduce the frequency of their occurrences?

- **Use the right isolation level**—As you saw earlier in this chapter, there are dramatic resource and concurrency differences among the four isolation levels. These differences can also affect transaction duration because a transaction that requires very restrictive concurrency might find itself pausing until other resources are released. Try to gain a good understanding of these isolation levels, and use the most permissive one you can without compromising your data's integrity.

  If you are new to either MySQL or transactions, you will reap large rewards from the relatively small investment of time it takes to experiment with multiple sessions, sample tables, and different transaction isolation levels.

- **Don't include user interface communication within the transaction**—One way to guarantee all kinds of transaction and other problems is to allow users to walk away from their computers while a transaction is waiting for information from them. Always prompt your users for all necessary input to complete, and only then start (and quickly finish) your transaction.

- **Use DROP TABLE or TRUNCATE TABLE rather than DELETE**—Chapter 8, "Advanced SQL Tips," reviews a variety of SQL performance-enhancing tips. One important suggestion contrasts the speed of a brute-force DROP TABLE/TRUNCATE TABLE compared with the more nuanced (and consequently slower) DELETE statement. These faster statements also consume much fewer resources, and greatly reduce transaction time.

Stored Procedures and Functions

By centralizing and then processing application logic on your database server, stored procedures and functions can yield significant operational improvements. This section looks at these potential advances, including when you should employ these features, and when you should not.

For those situations in which stored procedures or functions make sense, you should keep a number of issues in mind to ensure that they deliver the anticipated performance benefits. Because the book's purpose is not to serve as a programming reference for stored procedures or functions, there is not a grand overview of their syntax.

Before beginning, it's worth pointing out the basic differences between stored procedures and functions.

Difference Between Stored Procedures and Functions

These two MySQL features have much in common. Both accept parameters and can then take action based on these arguments. However, stored procedures and functions part ways in two significant manners:

1. Stored procedures might or might not return a result; functions must return a result, and this result and its type must be defined in the function's body. This requirement means that the developer of a function works in a somewhat more constrained way than her stored procedure-writing peer: There is less runtime freedom about what to return, along with its type.

2. Stored procedures can access tables; functions cannot. This limitation alone disqualifies functions from many situations, but there are still many cases in which they add value: The rich library of built-in functions provided by MySQL itself proves that point. One good example in which a function still makes sense is when you have a sophisticated algorithm that is used to help run your business. Even if this algorithm needs information from a table, you could retrieve the data in advance and simply pass it to the function, which would then perform its computations and return the results to the function invoker.

When to Use Stored Procedures or Functions

There are many compelling performance-related reasons to employ these capabilities. They include the following:

- **Specialization and consistency**—Stored procedures and functions lighten the workload on your application developers. Instead of each developer possibly "reinventing the wheel" each time a new operation is necessary, they are free to focus their expertise on writing the finest application code that they can. Meanwhile, the author of a stored procedure or function is better able to specialize and spend the time writing the best shared operations possible.

  This division of labor usually translates into tighter, cleaner, more consistent code in the client application as well as in the server-based procedure or function. In addition, this is less likely to cause performance problems or even fail.

- **Reducing client workload**—If your client computers are underpowered, overworked, or linked via a slow network connection, anything you can do to diminish the amount of local data processing goes a long way toward amplifying your applications' responsiveness.

- **Supporting disparate programming technologies**—By extracting key portions of your applications' logic and placing them into stored procedure or functions, you make it possible for application developers to work with a variety of different programming technologies yet still share access to these operations.

- **Reducing application complexity**—By definition, consolidating application logic reduces the number of "moving parts," making it easier to develop and debug software.

- **Decreasing network traffic**—Despite today's ever-increasing network performance, it's still a good idea to minimize traffic between your database server and your clients. By filtering out extraneous information prior to returning results, stored procedures and functions can reduce the amount of data flowing across your network (or the Internet) by orders of magnitude.

- **Security and secrecy**—Your application might consist of proprietary algorithms that you want to keep as private as possible. A server-based stored procedure or function gives users and developers access, while restricting their ability to examine the actual logic, just as views can be used to hide underlying table structures.

When Not to Use Stored Procedures or Functions

Like any powerful tools, there are times when stored procedures and functions are not an appropriate answer to your data-processing needs. These situations include the following:

- **One-off operations**—Generally, creating and deploying stored procedures and functions makes sense if they will serve multiple users and purposes. On the other hand, if you are solving a single problem within a solitary application, it might make more sense to code your solution within your application logic. However, keep an open mind and plan for the future: If this logic will indeed be of benefit in multiple situations, it might pay to encode it now as a stored procedure or function.

- **Overloaded database server**—If your database server is either overloaded or underpowered, adding additional processing work might only make things worse. In these types of circumstances, it's safest to plan on performing this work on the client, or spending the time or money to make the server more efficient. One compelling approach is to use MySQL's distributed computing technologies such as replication and clustering to off-load work from your server.

- **Advanced logic needs**—Although MySQL's implementation of stored procedures and functions is powerful, there might be times that you need the extra capacity and flexibility of a procedural language, such as C, C++, Java, and so on. In these cases, you might find it easier to solve your problem by using your application's native language, or creating a user defined function (UDF).

Stored Procedure Optimization

Now that you've seen when to turn to stored procedures and functions, as well as when to shun them, it's time to review a few important performance suggestions.

Don't Create Unnecessary Procedures/Functions

As you saw a moment ago, not every database operation is a candidate for adaptation to a stored procedure or function. Before you spend the time to make the conversion, and risk cluttering the server with unnecessary processing, think things over.

Follow Good Table Design and Query Practices

It might seem obvious, but a brand-new procedure or function that runs on your superfast database server will still fall flat on its face if the underlying table/index design is bad or you write subpar SQL.

As you develop your server-side logic, make sure to run the EXPLAIN command on all query statements, looking for any of the warning signs that were discussed in Chapter 6, "Understanding the MySQL Optimizer."

Watch for Extraneous Database Operations

As you go about developing your server-side stored procedure and function logic, always be watching for ways to streamline your code and reduce the quantity and complexity of your activities.

For example, a common stored procedure mistake is to encode a SQL statement within a loop when this statement could have easily been run only once outside of the loop. If the loop is run hundreds or thousands of times, it's easy to see the impact on performance of the unnecessary SQL calls.

Watch for Loops

Stored procedure developers can choose among a variety of looping statements, including the following:

- LOOP ... END LOOP
- WHILE ... END WHILE
- REPEAT ... END REPEAT

Like any other programming language, MySQL stored procedures are subject to the performance dangers of unnecessary looping. Before committing to running logic within a loop, be sure that there are no other, potentially more efficient ways to accomplish the same results.

Use Existing Built-in Functions

MySQL offers dozens of built-in functions, providing functionality ranging from mathematical to string to logical operations. Before you commence writing a complex stored procedure or function, see if any of the existing built-in functions can provide all or even part of the necessary capabilities that you seek.

Handle Errors

If your stored procedure encounters a problem, try to handle the error gracefully rather than aborting. To facilitate this behavior, MySQL offers two types of handlers: EXIT and CONTINUE, both of which are tied to MySQL error codes. You can create highly granular handlers that tie to specific error codes.

As their names imply, an EXIT handler abandons the current BEGIN/END block, whereas a CONTINUE handler tries to press on. Armed with this capability, you can embed sophisticated conditional logic into your stored procedures, logic that previously could only have been delivered within a client-side programming language.

Triggers

Triggers introduce basic server-side event handling and control to your MySQL database by intercepting database activity before it can affect underlying information. Data-modifying events (INSERT, UPDATE, or DELETE) can activate a trigger, which is then processed either before or after the data-modifying event.

For example, you might want to perform a server-side calculation on information before it's written into the database. This scenario is discussed momentarily.

Current Trigger Limitations

At the time of this writing, there are a number of restrictions on what your triggers may accomplish. They include the following:

- **No transactional support**—Your triggers cannot take advantage of InnoDB's transactional capabilities with the START TRANSACTION, COMMIT, or ROLLBACK statements. This can significantly impact your databases' integrity.

- **No table names**—You cannot explicitly name any tables within a trigger. This means, for example, that you cannot copy information from one table to another or even examine the contents of another table. Actions such as information or event logging aren't possible.

- **No stored procedure invocations**—You might be thinking that you can avoid the preceding limitations by invoking a stored procedure. Unfortunately, this isn't possible: You cannot use the CALL statement within your triggers.

Despite these limitations (many of which are addressed in upcoming versions), triggers can still add performance value to your application. The following section lists some situations in which you should consider them versus situations in which they are not warranted.

When to Use Triggers

From a performance perspective, the primary reasons to use triggers given today's restrictions are similar to those of stored procedures: to remove processing from clients and centralize it on the database server.

For example, suppose that you're developing an application that records purchases at High-Hat's new airport souvenir stands and then calculates the sales tax due among several government entities:

```
CREATE TABLE purchases (
    purchase_id INTEGER AUTO_INCREMENT PRIMARY KEY,
    iata_code CHAR(3),
    amount DECIMAL(5,2),
    federal_tax DECIMAL(5,2),
    province_tax DECIMAL(5,2),
    municipal_tax DECIMAL(5,2),
    vat DECIMAL(5,2)
);
```

You could encode this at the client, but this adds complexity and processing time, and might also introduce developer-caused inconsistencies if these calculations are written in two or more applications. Instead, you elect to use a trigger:

```
DELIMITER !!
CREATE TRIGGER t_insert BEFORE INSERT ON purchases
FOR EACH ROW
BEGIN
    CASE NEW.iata_code
...
...

        WHEN 'JFK' THEN SET NEW.municipal_tax = NEW.amount * .00235;
        WHEN 'LHR' THEN SET NEW.municipal_tax = NEW.amount * .00350;
        WHEN 'NYO' THEN SET NEW.vat = NEW.amount * .15;
...
...
    END CASE;
END!!
DELIMITER ;
```

You can now be assured that regardless of its source, any data that is inserted into the purchases table will have the proper taxes set. Of course, you are now responsible for keeping the trigger up to date.

When Not to Use Triggers

Whenever any new technology arrives, it's tempting to apply it in as many situations as possible. This is especially true with triggers. Even though they are currently quite constrained in terms of functionality, they can still streamline many types of operations and calculations.

However, triggers do add server-side overhead. The exact overhead amount is very dependent on the number and complexity of your triggers. For example, in the previous purchases instance, we added a trigger with eight options in the CASE statement. Next, we loaded 50,000 rows of random information via a series of INSERT statements. Overall, loading performance degraded by approximately 10%. For a large data-load operation, this might be significant. However, for an interactive transactional application, it's unlikely that the users would notice this overhead.

In general, don't let triggers serve as your last line of defense for data validation. The previous example shows a trigger setting a tax based on information provided at runtime. This is very different than a data integrity check, which might be faced with missing information. Given their limited capabilities, your ability to handle error conditions is quite constrained. Stored procedures are a much better choice for these kinds of activities.

Writing Efficient Application Code

If you have taken the time to design your database with performance in mind (including setting up proper indexes and defining queries correctly), you are a long way toward your goal of a fast MySQL-based solution. If you have also factored concurrency considerations into your application design, so much the better.

In fact, at the point when you actually need to write code, there is very little left to be done regarding performance from a purely database perspective. Of course, if you don't understand your application development technology, and introduce new performance problems at the application code level, then all bets are off.

The remainder of this chapter provides some development technology-neutral ideas about how your application code can take advantage of several MySQL server-based performance features. Most of these ideas are explored elsewhere in the book: This bolsters the just-stated argument that by the time you reach the software development phase, most of the optimization work is finished.

Finally, because ODBC is an extremely popular way of connecting database-neutral applications with a MySQL server, this chapter closes with a review of how to configure the MySQL ODBC Connector for maximum performance.

General Suggestions

To provide language-specific ideas for only one or two of the myriad MySQL APIs or connectors would shortchange the developers that use the others. To supply language-specific ideas for all of these major MySQL-friendly development technologies would expand this book substantially beyond its scope. Happily, most performance-enhancing suggestions happen to be independent of your choice of API or connector.

Persistent Connections

Chapter 14, "Operating System, Web Server, and Connectivity Tuning," calls out the high costs of repeatedly creating and dropping connections to the database.

When designing your application, consider its typical database usage pattern. Will the application frequently access the database, or will it periodically fire a burst of information at the MySQL server and otherwise not need its services? The answer to this question has a fundamental impact on how you should structure your database connectivity.

For those applications that need constant access to the database, try to employ persistent connections. From the point of view of the application logic, this simply means not closing a session only to reopen it a few moments later. From the server perspective, Chapter 10, "General Server Performance Parameters and Tuning," describes several variables that you can set to prevent idle sessions from being disconnected.

Prepared Statements

When you send a SQL statement to a MySQL database server, it must parse the statement to make sure that it contains valid syntax and is acceptable for use. This parsing exercise incurs overhead, whether the same statement is run once, twice, or three million times. To help reduce this overhead, MySQL 4.1 saw the introduction of prepared statement support.

When you issue a PREPARE directive combined with a candidate SQL statement, MySQL analyzes and validates its syntax. Assuming that all is well, you can then invoke that statement as often as you want via the EXECUTE statement. Because the statement has already been parsed, there is no need for MySQL to conduct the same exercise again.

For example, suppose you are writing an application that will update the purchases table that was shown previously. You expect the application to be run frequently by a large number of users, with a common activity being an update of the municipal_tax field, consistently using the following SQL statement:

```
UPDATE purchases SET municipal_tax = some value WHERE purchase_id = some value;
```

This is an excellent candidate for statement preparation, using the following steps. Note that although it is displayed here in standard SQL, it can also be handled through most of the development technologies currently used to build MySQL-based applications:

```
PREPARE prep_update FROM 'UPDATE purchases SET municipal_tax = ?
WHERE purchase_id = ?';

SET @new_muni_tax = 12.22;
SET @purchase_identifier = 200112;

EXECUTE prep_update USING @new_muni_tax, @purchase_identifier;
```

From this point forward, the only necessary steps are to change the variables and rerun the EXECUTE statement. This reduces overhead, as well as takes advantage of a faster, binary-based client/server protocol that is available to clients using prepared statements. You should note, however, that MySQL still must generate a query plan; this extraneous work should be addressed in an upcoming version.

Multirow INSERT Statements

Large-scale data export and import operations are the focus of Chapter 15, "Improving Import and Export Operations." For now, it's worth mentioning that grouping INSERT statements into multirow batches can deliver significant speed improvements, especially for larger data sets.

Again referring to the previous purchases table, the following is how a five-row INSERT would look when batched into a multirow statement:

```
INSERT INTO purchases(iata_code,amount,federal_tax,
province_tax,municipal_tax,vat)
VALUES
('SLC',17.42,.21,.03,0,0),('YYC',19.12,.33,.12,0,.09),
('ANC',33.99,1.12,.88,0,0),('ABQ',102.00,8.02,5.77,0,0),
('ARN',218.31,22.55,13.98,.74,11.00);
```

Although tedious to type out by hand, an application should have no trouble programmatically generating, and then benefiting from, this kind of statement.

ODBC Configuration

Before the introduction of the Open Database Connectivity (ODBC) standard in the early 1990s, application developers faced the odious choice of either developing specialized versions of their products that worked with databases from different vendors or creating their own database-neutral connectivity layer.

Fortunately, the ODBC standard, along with ancillary products that conformed to this new approach, greatly improved the lives of developers by freeing them from having to worry about the idiosyncrasies of each database platform. However, differences do remain among these platforms, and the combination of these disparities and the ODBC standard can affect responsiveness for applications that use the MySQL ODBC driver.

As a MySQL developer or administrator, you have the ability to affect some of these ODBC performance aspects via the MyODBC driver. While most of its parameters are aimed at compatibility issues, some of them do affect performance, as shown in Table 9.1.

TABLE 9.1   MySQL ODBC Driver Performance-Related Settings

Setting	Performance Implication
Use Compressed Protocol	This book explores the benefits of compressing the communication between database clients and the MySQL server in Chapters 10 and 14. Enable this setting if you want your ODBC-based applications to enjoy the same benefits.
Don't Cache Results	Generally, MySQL attempts to cache the results from your forward-only cursor so that they remain resident in memory. This is usually faster than forcing a call to the server to return rows. However, if your goal is a dynamic cursor or your result-set is likely to be very large, disabling result caching can conserve client-side memory.
Force Use of Named Pipes	Named pipes (for Windows-based servers) or sockets (for Linux/Unix-based servers) offer a potentially faster alternative to standard TCP/IP for communication between a MySQL database server and its associated client when the two are running on the same machine.

One final word about ODBC and MySQL performance: Be sure that ODBC driver tracing is turned off. Otherwise, the cost of generating the extensive diagnostic information provided during tracing can easily translate into an orders-of-magnitude response degradation.

IV

Optimizing and Tuning the MySQL Engine

MySQL offers dozens of settings and parameters that administrators can use to control all aspects of their database servers. The next few chapters examine these settings from a system response perspective. They also cite any server-generated status messages that can help us understand our environment's unique performance profile.

Chapter 10 delves into a collection of parameters that are useful regardless of your choice of database storage engine. Chapter 11, "MyISAM Performance Enhancement," provides focus on settings of interest to users and administrators of the MyISAM engine, followed by Chapter 12, "InnoDB Performance Enhancement," which is dedicated to the InnoDB server. Since disk access is crucial to a well-performing database platform, Chapter 13, "Improving Disk Speed," will examine ways to keep this vital component in tune. Chapter 14, "Operating System, Web Server, and Connectivity Tuning," takes a look at how MySQL interacts with your operating system, web server, and network, while Chapter 15, "Improving Import and Export Operations," is a discussion on improving import and export performance.

Finally, while the book always tries to prescribe the best possible settings for these parameters, please understand that it's usually not possible to make a hard-and-fast recommendation. There are numerous reasons for this, not the least of which is that every MySQL-based application and environment is unique. What works for one situation will be anathema to another. Therefore, this book tries to explain what these parameters do and how you can take advantage of them; the actual settings will vary and are best tested in your own environment.

10

General Server Performance Parameters and Tuning

Before getting started, it's worth mentioning again: The most productive steps you can take to help most poorly performing database applications is to look at their indexing, followed by their SQL and application logic, and then their database design and other structural factors. At the very bottom of the list are the engine and other settings that you're about to discover. However, these do have an impact, so it's worth spending some time learning more about them.

To make things even easier for administrators, the past few years have seen MySQL AB bundling several prebuilt, configuration files for various processing profiles. While not necessarily optimized for your specific environment, they may be used as an effective base for further tuning efforts. They include those in the following list:

- Minimal memory, relatively infrequent MySQL usage: `my-small.cnf`
- Minimal memory combined with reliance on MySQL, or larger memory for a multi-purpose system: `my-medium.cnf`
- Large memory server dedicated primarily to MySQL: `my-large.cnf`
- Very large memory server completely dedicated to MySQL: `my-huge.cnf`

It's worth your time to review these files, if for no other reason than to gain some ideas on the optimal ratios between the various server settings.

To help put the dozens of different general engine performance-impacting parameters and status variables into perspective, this chapter is broken into several portions:

- Connectivity
- Memory management
- Application control
- User resource control

Before exploring each of these topics, the following section first discusses the scope of these parameters and variables.

Server Settings Scope

Broadly speaking, MySQL's server variables fall into one of three camps:

- **GLOBAL variables**—These are settings that are in effect for the entire MySQL instance. They are typically specified as an input parameter to the mysqld process, or contained in the MySQL configuration file. A good example of a GLOBAL variable is the connect_timeout setting, which sets the serverwide policy on how long MySQL will wait to complete a connection from any client.

  Although GLOBAL variables affect the entire server, there are situations in which they might be overridden by a client.

- **SESSION variables**—These apply only in the context of a specific MySQL connection, and are usually thought of as very specific to a particular application or processing need. For example, the autocommit variable controls the behavior of transactional operations for a specific connection.

- **GLOBAL and SESSION variables**—Many GLOBAL variables can be modified to fit the particular processing needs of a session. For example, the bulk_insert_buffer_size variable allocates a particular amount of memory for large-scale data insertion operations. You can elect to have one value for the entire server, and then allow a connection to specify its own setting.

Connectivity

The database connection experience is often the first impression a user will receive of your MySQL server. This next section discusses a collection of performance-specific connection settings.

Creating a Connection

To perform work in a database, a client application must first issue a connect request. After a connection is established, the client performs some work and eventually disconnects (or is timed-out by the database). Use connect_timeout to specify the number of seconds that MySQL should wait when servicing a connect request from a client.

Be careful about setting this value too low, especially if your clients are connecting via a slow network, are prone to momentary network lapses, or are underpowered.

You also can choose to optimize a number of communication factors for clients and database servers. To begin, you have control over the size of messages sent from the MySQL engine to your client application. Use the net_buffer_length setting, specified in bytes, to set the initial message size. This variable works in tandem with max_allowed_packet: If a message is larger than net_buffer_length, MySQL automatically raises the limit up to max_allowed_packet, which can hold up to 1GB of information.

If your applications employ large TEXT or BLOB values, consider setting the max_allowed_packet high; you can keep the net_buffer_length value low, and MySQL automatically adjusts when necessary (and then downsizes afterward).

Because connections are supported via threads (more on threads a little later), every time a connection request is made, MySQL's main thread services the request and then launches a new thread (or retrieves one from the thread cache) to support the link. This usually happens almost instantaneously.

However, there might be rare occasions in which large numbers of connection requests are submitted at one time to the server. The back_log parameter designates how many connection requests will be allowed to queue up for servicing before the database engine starts ignoring them (and the client receives an error). After the number of connection requests drops below back_log, MySQL again allows these requests to enter the queue.

Recent versions of MySQL set this value to a default of 50. If you want to change it, try to estimate the maximum number of concurrent connection requests your server is likely to receive. It's important to understand that this is different than concurrent connections; we're only interested in the number of connections in the queue at the same time. After you arrive at a number, set back_log slightly larger than this value. Finally, note that if you try to make this value larger than the number of incoming TCP/IP requests that your server can handle, MySQL will simply use this server-controlled maximum number.

To control the number of actual concurrent client connections, use the max_connections variable. If you set it too low, users will receive an error like the one shown in Figure 10.1.

FIGURE 10.1   A failed connection attempt.

You can determine your ratio of good connects to aborted connects by examining the connections and aborted_connects status variables, respectively. For the overall connection high-water-mark, look at the max_used_connections status variable:

```
mysql> SHOW STATUS LIKE '%CONNECT%';
+----------------------+-------+
| Variable_name        | Value |
+----------------------+-------+
| Aborted_connects     | 49    |
| Connections          | 2191  |
| Max_used_connections | 117   |
| Threads_connected    | 58    |
+----------------------+-------+
```

These results tell us that approximately 2% of all connections attempted have failed since the server was started or the statistics cleared. Remember that you can clear this data with the FLUSH STATUS command; this is a good idea when trying to debug a performance or other problem. Even FLUSH STATUS is not immune to tracking: See flush_commands to track how many times the server statistics have been reset.

Managing a Connection

After a client is connected, you can configure MySQL to drop the session under several conditions:

- **Inactivity**—If a certain amount of time passes with no activity, you can instruct MySQL to end the conversation. In fact, you have two choices when determining this behavior:

  1. If your client is one that involves live user interaction with the database (typically, but not always, an application that presents a user interface), set the `interactive_timeout` variable to the number of seconds to wait before dropping the connection.

  2. If your client is more of a machine-to-machine application (that is, it doesn't present a user interface for direct database interaction), set the `wait_timeout` variable instead.

Because open, inactive connections still consume resources (and can affect performance for active sessions), be certain to set this value low enough so that these clients are disconnected on a timely basis. Clients who attempt to continue working on a closed session receive a message like the following:

```
ERROR 2013 (HY000): Lost connection to MySQL server during query
```

How can you be sure which of these two variables will take precedence in your environment? The only way to truly be sure is to know if the CLIENT_INTERACTIVE connection option has been set in the source code of the client. Obviously, if you don't have access to source code, you'll need to make an assumption and then test your hunch.

- **Errors**—The `net_read_timeout` and `net_write_timeout` parameters work in conjunction, with the former tracking the amount of seconds that MySQL has waited when reading from a client and the latter monitoring the length of time to write to the client. If either of these values is tripped, MySQL terminates the connection.

Try not to make these values too low, especially if your database clients and/or network are sluggish. Undersizing these parameters might cause valid connections to be dropped, possibly triggering long rollbacks if a transaction-enabled bulk loading operation is under way.

- **Interruptions**—The `net_retry_count` variable specifies the number of times you are willing to let MySQL attempt to recover from a communication interruption. If you want to block a repeatedly interrupted, troublesome client, use the `max_connect_errors` parameter. When tripped, it prevents any future connections from that client until you clear the blockade via the `FLUSH HOSTS` command.

To see how many sessions have been closed abnormally, view the `aborted_clients` status variable. To get a better idea of your overall communication volume with your database clients, consult the `bytes_received` and `bytes_sent` status variables.

Memory Management

As you have seen throughout this book, it's always best to have MySQL perform database operations within memory as often as possible, rather than initiate more expensive disk access. The following sections look at some of the available variables that you can stipulate to determine your server's memory behavior, as well as some general-purpose MySQL memory functionality.

Locking `mysqld` in Memory

As an administrator, you have the option to force the `mysqld` process to remain in memory, rather than face the possibility of swapping to disk should system resources become scarce. Typically, you detect this problem via your operating system monitoring tools, which report page faults or other indicators of memory issues.

To lock `mysqld` in memory, launch it with the `--memlock` option enabled. However, two conditions need to be met or this won't happen:

1. You must launch the `mysqld` process as root. This opens up a host of potential security problems, so think carefully before you choose this option.

2. Your operating system must support the ability of processes to perform this kind of operation. For example, this functionality is available on Solaris, Linux, and HP-UX.

Finally, by forcing `mysqld` to remain resident in memory, you introduce the prospect of other performance problems because a significant amount of RAM is now unavailable to other processes. It's a better idea to first investigate why the swapping is happening: Is the amount of memory currently installed on your server simply insufficient for the tasks at hand?

Thread Memory Settings

Threads are the internal process mechanisms that MySQL uses to perform work as well as communicate with connected clients. You can control a few settings, but it's quite likely that the default values are fine for most applications.

First, to determine your current thread status, use SHOW STATUS:

```
mysql> SHOW STATUS LIKE '%THREAD%';
+-----------------------+-------+
| Variable_name         | Value |
+-----------------------+-------+
| Delayed_insert_threads | 4    |
| Slow_launch_threads   | 0     |
| Threads_cached        | 9     |
| Threads_connected     | 27    |
| Threads_created       | 30    |
| Threads_running       | 18    |
+-----------------------+-------+
```

To see what all your threads are doing, run SHOW PROCESSLIST or view MySQL Administrator's Threads tab, as shown in Figure 10.2.

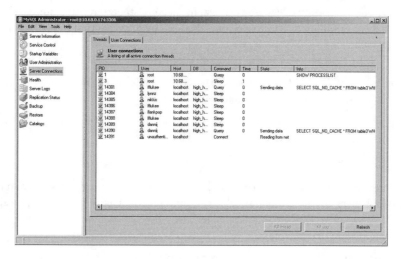

FIGURE 10.2   Active connection threads as reported by the MySQL Administrator.

Threads consume memory in several ways. The thread_stack variable specifies the amount of memory that each thread will be granted when it is started. Generally, this should be left alone. Administrators have another option with the thread_cache_size parameter: It specifies how many threads should be left alive and in the cache to service new connections.

Because there is a time and memory cost to creating new threads, you might consider boosting this value if your environment involves frequent new connections. For example, suppose that you are building a web server–driven application that typically sees numerous, short-lived database connections. Over time, you find that the values in both the threads_created and connections server status variables are growing quickly. This means that your thread cache is insufficient; new threads are being created very often. Raising the thread_cache_size setting might reduce some of this server overhead.

However, as you will see in Chapter 14, "Operating System, Web Server and Connectivity Tuning," it's an even better idea to figure out ways to reduce the number of database connection starts/stops; perhaps these connections can be pooled among multiple processes.

Finally, if you're running MySQL in a Solaris environment, you can use thread_concurrency to affect the operating system's thread consumption behavior. If you are running another operating system, you won't even see this variable.

MEMORY Tables

As you saw in Chapter 4, "Designing for Speed," on the MySQL storage engines, MEMORY (previously known as HEAP) tables are very fast, in-memory storage available for developers who need these capabilities. These tables are also used by MySQL itself for many smaller temporary tables.

As an administrator, you can decide how much memory you want to allocate for developer-generated tables by setting the max_heap_table_size variable. This value, measured in bytes, tells MySQL how large one of these tables can become.

How can you tell if you need to raise this value? A good way to make this decision is to see if any of your applications receive the following kind of error:

```
The table 'message_buffer_mem' is full,S1000,1114
```

For server-generated temporary tables, use the tmp_table_size setting instead. It also tells MySQL how many bytes a temporary table can consume in memory before being swapped out to a disk-based, MyISAM temporary table. These disk-based tables are obviously much slower than memory-based tables.

When setting these values, be careful not to give MySQL too much leeway: Memory is never free, and you might crowd out other system processes by consuming too much for your user and server-requested MEMORY tables.

Caching

Before discussing MySQL's general-purpose caching mechanisms, it's worthwhile to understand the differences among four crucial MySQL in-memory caches:

- **Buffer pool**—This cache holds index and data only for those tables specified to use the InnoDB storage engine. This is discussed more in Chapter 12, "InnoDB Performance Enhancement."
- **Memory pool**—This is a MySQL internal buffer that caches data dictionary and other server structures. It only benefits tables that use the InnoDB storage engine, so it is covered in Chapter 12.
- **Key cache**—This in-memory cache is used to buffer index information for only those tables that use the MyISAM storage engine; it is examined in more detail in Chapter 11, "MyISAM Performance Enhancement."
- **Query cache**—This cache holds queries and their results, and is of use to all MySQL users, regardless of their choice of storage engine.

Query Cache Overview

As you first learned in Chapter 7, "Indexing Strategies," each of MySQL's main storage engines (MyISAM and InnoDB) provides caches to hold index key values. For MyISAM, this cache is known as the key cache; the corresponding structure for InnoDB is the buffer pool, which also caches data.

MySQL also offers an optional, cross-engine query cache to buffer frequently submitted queries, along with their resultsets. If the cache is enabled, MySQL first consults the query cache and might find that the query and its results are already resident in memory. Because memory access is always faster than disk access, finding results in the query cache translates into significantly faster performance.

It's important to understand that many types of events either block usage of the query cache or cause it to be refreshed with new data the next time a query is run. Four very recurrent events include the following:

- **Data or table/index structure modifications**—MySQL needs to refresh the query cache if you change either the table/index structure or any of its data. For frequently updated tables (such as those that log transactional information), this happens all the time. In addition, all rows in the query cache that reference the table need to be refreshed, even those that are different than the row(s) that have been altered.

- **Different query statements**—MySQL does not look at the query cache if a new statement does not identically match a previously cached statement, including any upper- or lowercase variations. Obviously, different lookup values plugged in to WHERE clauses also skip the query cache.

- **Concluding a transaction**—When you issue a COMMIT (when using the InnoDB storage engine), MySQL invalidates the data in the query cache that references any of the InnoDB tables that were affected by the transaction.

- **Generating temporary tables**—MySQL is unable to utilize the query cache if your query explicitly or implicitly creates one or more temporary tables.

Despite all of these possible interruptions, the query cache is still very beneficial for performance. This is especially true if you want to improve response for queries that read relatively stable tables, such as those that provide lookup values or perform validation. You can track the number of times that MySQL has been able to read from the query cache by consulting the qcache_hits status variable.

The following sections explore how to enable, configure, and use the query cache.

Enabling the Query Cache

To begin, you must determine if your version of MySQL supports query caching:

```
mysql> SHOW VARIABLES LIKE 'HAVE_QUERY_CACHE';
+------------------+-------+
| Variable_name    | Value |
+------------------+-------+
| have_query_cache | YES   |
+------------------+-------+
```

In this example, the version of MySQL does support query caching, so you can now proceed to instruct MySQL to turn on the query cache. You do so by specifying a value for query_cache_size, either via SET GLOBAL or by including it in the MySQL configuration file:

```
SET GLOBAL VARIABLE query_cache_size = (64*1024*1024);
```

or

```
[mysqld]
Query_cache_size = 64M
```

If query_cache_size is set to zero, the query cache is disabled. You'll discover how to determine a value for this variable in a moment.

Your next decision is when you want queries to use the query cache. You have three choices when setting the query_cache_type system variable:

- **No access to the query cache**—Setting this variable to 0/OFF means that even though memory is allocated, no queries can benefit from the cache.
- **Implicit access to the query cache**—Setting this variable to 1/ON means that all queries consult the cache unless you include SQL_NO_CACHE with your SELECT statement. This is a smart setting for an application that primarily interrogates static tables; any other queries that search dynamic tables can be instructed to avoid the query cache with the SQL_NO_CACHE option.
- **Explicit access to the query cache**—Setting this variable to 2/DEMAND means that no queries access the cache unless you force this behavior by including SQL_CACHE with your SELECT statement. This is a good idea for those applications that contain a mixture of dynamic and static queries. In this case, you would add SQL_CACHE to statements that examine static tables so that they can benefit from the query cache; other types of queries would not even attempt to look at the cache.

You have the ability to set this behavior at the GLOBAL and SESSION level, which provides added flexibility.

Finally, note that you can enable and configure all variables for the query cache through the MySQL Administrator, as shown in Figure 10.3.

Configuring the Query Cache

After you've decided to enable the query cache, the next step is to pick a value for the amount of memory to allocate for caching. Whatever value you decide upon, the query_cache_size setting is where you specify your choice.

As with most memory settings, this is an art, not a science. You must balance the benefits of caching within the hard limits of available system memory, as well as consider the expected processing profile and load for the database server, all the while keeping in mind that performance can suffer if you excessively over- or underallocate memory. Making this decision even harder are the memory requirements of the MyISAM key cache combined with those of the InnoDB buffer pool—three caches all competing for the same scarce memory.

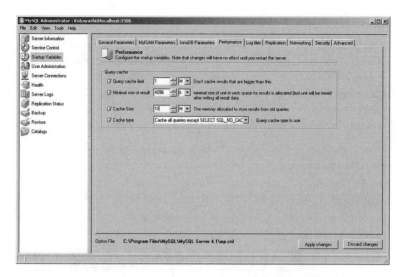

FIGURE 10.3   Configuring query cache variables through the MySQL Administrator.

In this situation, it's probably wisest to begin by allotting the smallest portion of memory for the query cache—between 5% and 10% of your system's memory. However, it's likely that you'll need to tune this number based on the real-world usage of your MySQL system. See the next section for more details on how to monitor important query cache statistics.

Your next decision is to determine the maximum amount of memory that you want to allocate within the query cache for an individual query's resultset. Queries with result sets larger than `query_cache_limit` will not be cached. Given the dynamic nature of the query cache's contents, the default of 1MB might be too large for many installations.

If you are in the mood for tinkering with some of the more esoteric query cache variables, a number of potential candidates are available for experimentation.

First, you can tune the internal buffers that MySQL uses to analyze, process, and store the queries whose results are then placed in the query cache. The `query_prealloc_size` variable sets the size of this buffer, whereas the `query_alloc_block_size` variable tells MySQL what size building blocks it should use to make up this buffer.

Both variables are usually fine with their defaults, but you can tune them upward if your queries are so large and/or complex that MySQL would otherwise be forced to perform an expensive memory allocation in the middle of parsing the query.

Next, you can tune the default block size that MySQL will use when allocating additional storage in the query cache. Think of the query cache as being constructed of chunks of memory in units of `query_cache_min_res_unit`. The default for this variable is 4KB. Although this setting should be sufficient for most environments, you can elect to raise it if the typical resultset is large or lower it if it's the opposite.

Monitoring the Query Cache

You have several methods at your disposal when monitoring the status of your query cache. Because a picture is worth a thousand words, the MySQL Administrator is the best tool to help you tune your query cache. Alternatively, you can combine the SHOW PROCESSLIST and SHOW VARIABLES commands to get an idea about what is happening. Take a look at a few sample reports to get an idea about how to tune the query cache. To make the most of these reports, output from the MySQL Administrator is combined along with SHOW VARIABLES.

Figure 10.4 appears to have a well-performing query cache (which has been defined with a query_cache_size of 16MB).

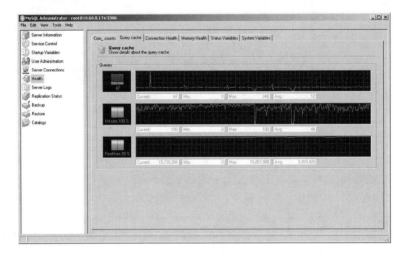

FIGURE 10.4   Well-performing query cache activity as reported by the MySQL Administrator.

```
mysql> SHOW STATUS LIKE 'qcache%';
+------------------------+----------+
| Variable_name          | Value    |
+------------------------+----------+
| Qcache_free_blocks     | 139      |
| Qcache_free_memory     | 15667648 |
| Qcache_hits            | 9057     |
| Qcache_inserts         | 2490     |
| Qcache_lowmem_prunes   | 0        |
| Qcache_not_cached      | 0        |
| Qcache_queries_in_cache | 1073    |
| Qcache_total_blocks    | 2289     |
+------------------------+----------+
```

How do you know that this is a well-performing query cache? There are several good indicators:

- The hit rate graph (middle graph) shows that most queries are being serviced by the query cache. There are two big drop-offs in the center of the graph. At that time, a big update operation was run that affected one of the tables, thereby temporarily dropping the hit rate as the cache needed to be refreshed.

- The query cache status variables all look good. In particular, the qcache_lowmem_prunes counter is zero. This means that MySQL has not had to purge any query cache values, which would be necessary if either the query cache was undersized or there was no consistency among the queries.

- A great deal of memory is still free in the query cache. In fact, you could probably remove some memory from the cache and run the experiments again. You know that you've lowered the memory far enough when you start to see the qcache_lowmem_prunes value climbing.

Unfortunately, something seems to have gone wrong in the second scenario, as shown in Figure 10.5.

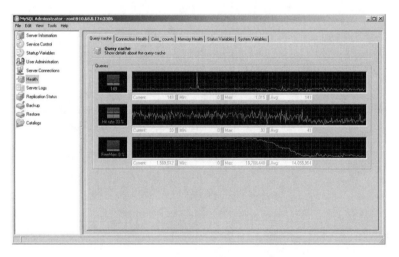

FIGURE 10.5   Degraded query cache performance as reported by the MySQL Administrator.

```
mysql> SHOW STATUS LIKE 'qcache%';
+------------------------+---------+
| Variable_name          | Value   |
+------------------------+---------+
| Qcache_free_blocks     | 189     |
| Qcache_free_memory     | 1915104 |
| Qcache_hits            | 9851    |
```

```
| Qcache_inserts         | 21227  |
| Qcache_lowmem_prunes   | 6098   |
| Qcache_not_cached      | 2744   |
| Qcache_queries_in_cache | 344   |
| Qcache_total_blocks    | 1505   |
+------------------------+--------+
```

What happened? Basically, this is a different processing profile. What started out (on the left of the graph) as a high-hit rate deteriorated as new connections came online. These connections both queried and updated large blocks of data in a number of tables. This had the effect of lowering the hit rate while increasing the amount of overhead that MySQL had to perform to find new space in the query cache: Note the high Qcache_lowmem_prunes value.

How could you make this situation better? You could add more memory to the query cache, but given the widely fluctuating query cache memory requirements of the application, it's quite likely that you would still see frequent query cache refreshes. Plus, you might waste precious memory at the same time.

A better idea is to try to identify those queries that are not likely to be able to take advantage of the query cache, and add SQL_NO_CACHE to their SELECT statements. By making that change, you save the query cache for only those queries that can benefit, as shown in Figure 10.6.

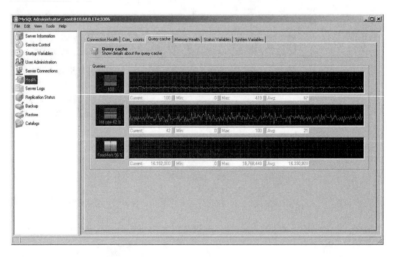

FIGURE 10.6   Query cache performance for a better-selected set of queries as reported by the MySQL Administrator.

```
mysql> SHOW STATUS LIKE 'qcache%';
+------------------------+----------+
| Variable_name          | Value    |
```

```
+------------------------+----------+
| Qcache_free_blocks     | 48       |
| Qcache_free_memory     | 16143808 |
| Qcache_hits            | 3953     |
| Qcache_inserts         | 5110     |
| Qcache_lowmem_prunes   | 0        |
| Qcache_not_cached      | 2861     |
| Qcache_queries_in_cache| 608      |
| Qcache_total_blocks    | 1268     |
+------------------------+----------+
```

The query cache hit rate is lower, but that's because many queries are not even bothering to work with the query cache, as evidenced by the Qcache_not_cached status indicator. Finally, given the large amount of free memory (Qcache_free_memory), you could probably safely give some back to the operating system.

Improving Table Scan Performance

As you saw earlier, table scans can be extremely expensive because MySQL must read each row to determine its results. In most cases, your goal should be to avoid them whenever possible. Unfortunately, this isn't always feasible, so to help boost performance in these situations, try tuning the read_buffer_size variable to reduce the number of time-consuming disk-seeks required for queries.

It's important to note, however, that MySQL uses the GLOBAL setting to allocate this memory to every thread that performs a sequential scan, whether the table has a thousand rows or a billion rows. It's not hard to imagine a scenario in which many connections are performing sequential scans through small tables, yet allocating (and wasting) large amounts of read_buffer_size memory. To be safe, try keeping this number reasonably low for the GLOBAL setting, and make it as large (or small) as necessary for the individual connection via the SESSION setting.

Improving Join Performance

Chapter 7, which was dedicated to making the most of your indexes, discussed why you should always place indexes on your join columns. However, there might be circumstances when you don't have an available index to speed a join.

As an alternative, you can use the join_buffer_size setting to request that each MySQL thread that works to process a nonindexed join set aside memory to help finish the join as fast as possible, with multiple join buffers set up when there are multiple nonindexed joins in a query.

Improving Sort Performance

Sorting large blocks of information via ORDER BY or GROUP BY can consume significant amounts of system resources. To help MySQL perform these operations in memory, specify a value for the `sort_buffer_size` variable. Each MySQL thread that is tasked with completing one of these tasks will request this many bytes from memory.

To test the impact of changing this parameter, we created a sample table to hold monetary transactions, as well as another identical table to receive extracted rows from our transaction table:

```
CREATE TABLE transactions
(
    transaction_id INT UNSIGNED NOT NULL,
    transaction_DATE NOT NULL,
    customer_id INT NOT NULL,
    amount DECIMAL(5,2) NOT NULL,
    transaction_type ENUM ('Purchase','Credit')
) ENGINE = MYISAM;
CREATE TABLE transaction_extract LIKE transactions;
```

Next, we loaded more than 21 million rows of random data into the `transactions` table. Finally, we created a simple query to place a sorting load on the engine:

```
INSERT INTO transaction_extract SELECT * FROM transactions ORDER BY amount;
```

We ran multiple tests, varying `sort_buffer_size` from 256K all the way up to 25MB. To ensure accuracy, we stopped and started the `mysqld` process between tests.

The results were conclusive, but not tremendously dramatic: The 25MB `sort_buffer_size` concluded approximately 25% faster than the 256K setting. However, look at some key status variables:

256K setting:

```
Sort_merge_passes          216
Sort_rows                  21195536
Sort_scan                  1
```

25-MB setting:

```
Sort_merge_passes          1
Sort_rows                  21195536
Sort_scan                  1
```

Allocating a bigger `sort_buffer_size` saved 215 merge passes for the sort algorithm, while everything else was identical between the two tests. In your own environment, a large (or rapidly growing) `sort_merge_passes` server status indicates that you should probably boost `sort_buffer_size`.

After the sort has been completed, MySQL uses the `read_rnd_buffer_size` variable to determine how much memory to allocate to finish processing the results. Before you get tempted to raise this value sky-high, remember that MySQL will apportion this memory to all clients, regardless of their sorting needs. As with the `read_buffer_size` variable discussed earlier, it's wiser to make the GLOBAL setting small, and raise it as necessary for any appropriate SESSION.

Binary Log and Caching

Recall that the binary log serves many purposes, including essential support for transactions and replication. To help improve performance, MySQL sets up a binary log cache for every connected client. As an administrator, you can configure the size of this buffer by setting the binlog_cache_size variable, which is applicable at the GLOBAL level.

How do you know if you have sized this variable correctly? Keep an eye on both the binlog_cache_use and binlog_cache_disk_use status variables: They count the number of times that your transactions were able to use the binary log cache and the number of times that the size of the transaction forced the creation of a relatively expensive temporary table. Your goal should be to keep the count of binlog_cache_disk_use as low as possible.

If necessary, you can also configure a not-to-exceed value for your binary log cache by specifying max_binlog_cache_size. However, the default of 4GB is probably sufficient for most environments.

You also have control over the binary log's internal memory structures for tracking transaction requests, via the transaction_alloc_block_size and transaction_prealloc_size. The former variable defines the memory block size for storing information about queries that participate in transactions, whereas the latter assigns an amount of memory that remains dedicated to this buffer after a query completes.

One final note about tuning binary log performance: You can stipulate how frequently the log is synchronized to disk. Remember that for a number of reasons, not the least of which is performance, MySQL performs binary log operations in memory, and then makes these operations permanent by synchronizing them to disk.

Administrators face a perennial dilemma: How should they balance the integrity benefits of frequent synchronization with the costs of these disk-based operations? Whatever your decision, use the sync_binlog GLOBAL server variable to instruct MySQL on how often to make these synchronizations. Values range from zero, meaning never synchronize, to one, meaning synchronize after each binary log change in memory, to higher numbers. For example, setting it to 10 means that synchronization will happen after the tenth write to the in-memory log.

Generally, it's wise to set this to one; the potential for minor performance degradation is not as costly as the possibility of lost data should the server crash prior to a disk synchronization.

Application Control

This section looks at how setting MySQL server variables can impact your MySQL-based application performance. First, to get a better idea of what activity is happening on your server, don't forget to consult the com status counters. These hold counts of the number of times various types of statements have been run. Figure 10.7 shows an example of a MySQL Administrator custom graph that was created to monitor transactions as well as INSERT/UPDATE/DELETE operations.

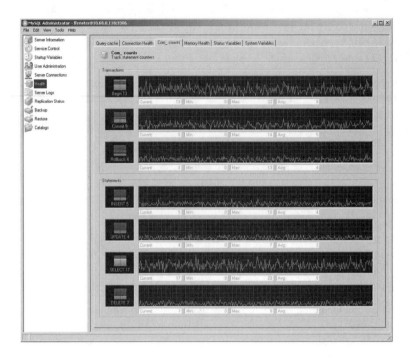

FIGURE 10.7   Monitoring statement counts via the MySQL Administrator.

The MySQL Administrator offers a tremendous amount of potential information, especially when various statistics are placed side by side into a graphical report.

Resources

MySQL connections claim system resources for all tables that they access. The table_cache parameter lets you dictate how many tables can be opened at one time for all applications that are using the database server. This is a very important parameter that you should carefully plan. Setting it too low means that MySQL needs to execute a series of expensive juggling maneuvers to satisfy all requests for table access. Specifically, it will close open tables so that requested tables may be opened. On the other hand, an excessive value means that you might run into operating system–specific resource constraints.

Fortunately, MySQL offers a very worthwhile diagnostic—the opened_tables status variable. Keep an eye on its value. A high number, especially if the server hasn't been running very long, means that MySQL is continually undertaking the expensive table juggling described above to satisfy these requests. Try raising the number in small increments, and then monitor `opened_tables` to see if your changes are having a positive impact. Recognize that you never want this number to exceed the `open_files_limit` variable, which apprises MySQL of the total number of file descriptors that your operating system will allow it to consume at any one time.

Optimizer Control

The MySQL query optimizer was reviewed in Chapter 6, "Understanding the MySQL Optimizer." One helpful capability of the optimizer is its capacity to take suggestions from application developers (in the form of special SQL directives) as well as parameters set by database administrators.

As you saw earlier, on occasion the optimizer might incorrectly choose table scans (that is, reading all rows in a table) rather than using an available index, especially if the cardinality of the index is low. However, by setting the `max_seeks_for_key` variable to a low number, the optimizer assumes that it is efficient to use the index after all. Before you change this setting, however, be certain to run EXPLAIN on your query and determine if any other factors could be at play.

For complex, multitable queries, it's possible that the optimizer could take longer to generate a query plan than to get the data itself. To help the optimizer from straying down the wrong path, leave the `optimizer_prune_level` variable to its default of one; this tells the optimizer to abandon work on unfinished query plans that start to appear inefficient rather than continuing to build the complete query plan.

The `optimizer_search_depth` variable provides guidance about whether the optimizer should pick a multitable query plan quickly, or evaluate all join permutations. In most cases, leave this value at zero unless you are having serious performance problems with a query. This setting means that the optimizer does its best to balance the benefits between a rapid versus comprehensive query plan search.

Chapter 6 explored the most recent enhancements to the filesort algorithm. This modified algorithm generally helps to elevate performance by retrieving results from the intermediate sorted collection, not the underlying table. However, this does introduce the potential for reduced performance if the row size is very large; precious buffer space can be crowded out by these big rows rather than just the key and row address information stored by the earlier incarnation of the algorithm.

To protect yourself from this possibility, try setting a limit by tuning the `max_length_for_sort_data`. If your result row size meets or exceeds this value, MySQL reverts to the earlier filesort algorithm.

Finally, the `range_alloc_block_size` parameter has the same purpose as other allocation block size variables already discussed, but in the context of memory management for enhancing faster range-based access to the database.

Concurrency

You reviewed the intricacies of MySQL concurrency management in Chapter 8, "Advanced SQL Tips," and Chapter 9, "Developing High Speed Applications." This section spends some time examining a collection of server variables that you can use to control several of these concurrency behaviors.

Delayed Insert

The discussion on improving INSERT performance discussed the optional DELAYED keyword that you can specify when loading rows into your tables. This directive instructs MySQL to allow other threads that are reading from a table to continue before it allows the INSERT to proceed. You have control over several facets of this behavior, as follows:

- **Number of threads to service INSERT DELAYED statements**—The max_delayed_threads parameter instructs MySQL to create no more than this many threads to handle delayed inserts. Setting it to zero completely disables delayed inserts, whereas a small number means that some delayed insert requests will actually be handled as standard INSERT statements.

- **Queue size**—You can configure the queue size for each table by tuning the delayed_queue_size variable. A larger value means that MySQL allows more rows to build up in this queue before delaying any new INSERT DELAYED requests.

- **Checking for waiting queries**—MySQL uses the delayed_insert_limit setting to determine how frequently to check for waiting queries while an INSERT DELAYED operation is under way.

  For example, if this value is set to 100, MySQL processes 100 delayed insert rows and then checks for any queries that are waiting for access. If it finds any, it allows the queries to complete and only then continues inserting any other delayed rows.

  Use this variable to help set the balance between the needs of your delayed inserts and those of your queries.

- **Thread termination**—You can control how many seconds the dedicated insert delayed thread remains alive and waits for new delayed insert rows by setting the delayed_insert_timeout variable. Keep several factors in mind if you decide to change the value from its default of 300, including the balance of insert and query operations, client connectivity speed, and delayed insert volume.

Unlocking Tables

As you have already seen, MySQL issues table locks under a number of conditions. Although they usually have minimal impact on others, they do have the potential to impact concurrency if not freed quickly enough. One way to get these locks freed sooner is to set the SQL_BUFFER_RESULT variable to one.

Under this setting, MySQL creates a temporary table to hold the results of a query, thereby freeing the base table lock more quickly. Before you go down this path, however, remember that there is a cost associated with creating temporary tables, so be careful to measure the performance differences introduced by this change.

User Resource Control

Some users have a natural talent for bringing the most efficient database servers to their knees, followed quickly by the responsible administrators. These users devour vast amounts of computing resources, but don't be too harsh on them: In many cases, they don't even know the damage they cause.

Luckily, MySQL administrators have several process restrictions options available when invoking the GRANT command to give users access to the database. These restrictions include the following:

- Connections per hour, via the MAX_CONNECTIONS_PER_HOUR setting
- Queries per hour, via the MAX_QUERIES_PER_HOUR setting
- Updates per hour, via the MAX_UPDATES_PER_HOUR setting

In the event that users are constructing their own queries or are using automated tools of dubious quality, set the max_join_size variable (either on mysqld startup or within your application code via the SET SQL_MAX_JOIN_SIZE statement) to prevent MySQL from completing this many disk operations or joins, such as those that might occur when unrestricted and/or nonindexed queries are sent to the server.

For example, look at how MySQL rejects this poorly constructed query:

```
mysql> set SQL_MAX_JOIN_SIZE = 1000;
Query OK, 0 rows affected (0.00 sec)
mysql> SELECT * FROM customer_master, customer_address;
ERROR 1104: The SELECT would examine more than MAX_JOIN_SIZE rows;
check your WHERE and use SET SQL_BIG_SELECTS=1 or
SET SQL_MAX_JOIN_SIZE=# if the SELECT is okay
```

This is when the query cache might help: If the results are already in resident in the cache, MySQL returns them to the user without triggering a resource consumption error. Another way to enable this bad query-blocking behavior is to set SQL_BIG_SELECTS to zero.

To get an idea of your environment's temporary table situation, monitor these three system status variables:

- created_tmp_disk_tables
- created_tmp_files
- created_tmp_tables

You can restrict the number of temporary tables that a client can keep open at one time by setting the max_tmp_tables variable. This will be fully enabled soon.

MyISAM Performance Enhancement

After completing the discussion of general-purpose tuning parameters, this chapter devotes attention to MyISAM-specific performance enhancement. This chapter is divided into three main sections:

- **Optimal MyISAM data storage**—Administrators have significant opportunities to squeeze more speed from MyISAM's use of data storage. This section begins by examining how to interpret some important statistics from the myisamchk utility, as well as improve its performance during table repair. Next, it looks at how to customize several key MyISAM settings to tune sort performance.

- **Taking advantage of memory for better MyISAM performance**—MyISAM offers a memory-based cache to hold index key values. Known as the key cache, this structure can have a dramatic impact on database speed, so this section spends a significant amount of time exploring its configuration, monitoring, and tuning.

- **Improving MyISAM operations**—After constructing the right data storage and memory caching strategy, your next goal is to manage how your applications make use of the MyISAM storage engine. The chapter closes by examining how to improve large-scale data operations, enhance concurrency, and get the most out of MyISAM's unique FULLTEXT search capabilities.

Optimal Data Storage

Prior to exploring how you can best configure MyISAM's data storage features, you can look at several key administrative reports and utilities at your disposal.

Table Reporting and Control

Recall that to help get a better understanding of the information MySQL tracks about MyISAM tables, the first part of Chapter 7, "Indexing Strategies," examined the SHOW INDEX output for a sample table, filled with 1.25 million rows, and then updated MySQL's internal statistics via OPTIMIZE TABLE. Of course, this command does much more than simply analyze and update statistics, including repairing any damage to the table as well as sorting index pages. To simply refresh statistics, you can use ANALYZE TABLE instead. In either case, here is the structure for this table:

```
CREATE TABLE demo_show_index
(
        col1 INT UNSIGNED AUTO_INCREMENT PRIMARY KEY,
        col2 VARCHAR(30) NOT NULL,
        col3 DATE NOT NULL,
        col4 ENUM ('Mercury', 'Venus', 'Mars', 'Earth', 'Jupiter') NOT NULL,
        col5 TEXT NOT NULL,
        col6 DATETIME NOT NULL,
        col7 BLOB NOT NULL,
        INDEX (col2),
        INDEX (col3),
        INDEX (col4),
        FULLTEXT (col5),
        INDEX (col6),
        INDEX (col7(150)),
        INDEX (col3,col2)
) ENGINE = MYISAM;
```

The following is a portion of the output from the SHOW INDEX command for this table:

```
mysql> SHOW INDEX FROM demo_show_index\G
*************************** 1. row ***************************
        Table: demo_show_index
  Non_unique: 0
    Key_name: PRIMARY
Seq_in_index: 1
 Column_name: col1
   Collation: A
 Cardinality: 1250000
    Sub_part: NULL
      Packed: NULL
        Null:
  Index_type: BTREE
     Comment:
```

Although this is helpful, you can get a much more informative report by running the myisamchk utility. Remember that myisamchk is designed to work only when the mysqld process is not running; otherwise you may corrupt your tables:

```
myisamchk -i demo_show_index

Checking MyISAM file: demo_show_index
Data records: 1250000    Deleted blocks:        0
```

```
- check file-size
- check record delete-chain
- check key delete-chain
- check index reference
- check data record references index: 1
Key:  1:  Keyblocks used:  98%  Packed:     0%  Max levels:  4
- check data record references index: 2
Key:  2:  Keyblocks used:  54%  Packed:    84%  Max levels:  4
- check data record references index: 3
Key:  3:  Keyblocks used:  81%  Packed:     0%  Max levels:  4
- check data record references index: 4
Key:  4:  Keyblocks used:  87%  Packed:     0%  Max levels:  3
- check data record references index: 5
Key:  5:  Keyblocks used:  83%  Packed:     0%  Max levels:  4
- check data record references index: 6
Key:  6:  Keyblocks used:  62%  Packed:     6%  Max levels:  9
- check data record references index: 7
Key:  7:  Keyblocks used:  68%  Packed:    70%  Max levels:  4
- check data record references index: 8
Key:  8:  Keyblocks used:  50%  Packed:    96%  Max levels:  4
Total:     Keyblocks used:  56%  Packed:    93%

- check record links
Records:              1250000   M.recordlength:        885   Packed:              0%
Recordspace used:        100%   Empty space:             0%  Blocks/Record:     1.00
Record blocks:        1250000   Delete blocks:           0
Record data:       1106732346   Deleted data:            0
Lost space:            937638   Linkdata:          4687784

myisamchk --verbose --description demo_show_index

MyISAM file:          demo_show_index
Record format:        Packed
Character set:        latin1_general_ci (8)
File-version:         1
Creation time:        2004-11-26 19:28:59
Recover time:         2005-05-27  5:40:42
Status:               checked,analyzed,sorted index pages
Auto increment key:           1  Last value:              1250000
Data records:           1250000  Deleted blocks:                0
Datafile parts:         1250000  Deleted data:                  0
Datafile pointer (bytes):     4  Keyfile pointer (bytes):       4
Datafile length:     1112357768  Keyfile length:        950180864
Max datafile length: 4294967294  Max keyfile length: 4398046510079
Recordlength:                67
```

```
table description:
Key Start Len Index    Type                    Rec/key        Root Blocksize
1   1     4   unique   unsigned long               1         1024     1024
2   5    30   multip.  char packed stripped      625     10260480     1024
3   35    3   multip.  uint24                    579     22009856     1024
4   38    1   multip.  binary                 250000     32770048     1024
5   49    8   multip.  ulonglong                   1     39958528     1024
6   57  150   multip.  varbin prefix BLOB          1     57952256     1024
7   35    3   multip.  uint24 prefix             579    344858624     1024
    5    30            char stripped               1
8   5   254   fulltext varchar packed          8621    364686336     2048
    1     4            float                       0
```

As you can see, these reports provide more extensive details about the table and its indexes than the SHOW INDEX command reviewed earlier. In fact, you'll get even more information if you pass in added "v" characters along with the -dv directive (such as -dvv). Additional items of interest from a performance point of view include the following:

- **Status**—You can see that this table has already received an integrity check as well as a full statistical analysis. In addition, the table has been sorted by the primary key.

- **Deleted blocks**—Recall that a MyISAM table can end up in a fragmented state after a period of data modifications in which blocks in the middle of the table are deleted. You can remove this fragmentation with OPTIMIZE TABLE. However, this is a new table that has not had any data alterations, so there aren't any deleted blocks.

- **Index key compression**—The packed portion of the report shows the percentage compression that MySQL was able to achieve on this key.

- **Index depth**—The max_levels section reports on the depth of the index B-tree—the number of non-leaf index nodes before reaching the leaf node. In the case of key number six, which is a large BLOB column that contains all unique values, the index is nine levels deep.

- **Datafile parts and Data records**—The ratio of these two numbers can provide insight as to the degree of fragmentation for this table. For example, if the number of Datafile parts significantly exceeds the number of Data records, then there is a good chance that the table is fragmented. On the other hand, equivalency between these two values means that the table has no fragmentation.

Storing a Table in Index Order

If you frequently retrieve large ranges of indexed data from a table or consistently sort results on the same index key, you might want to consider running myisamchk with the --sort-records option. Doing so tells MySQL to store the table's data in the same physical order as the index, and can help speed these kinds of operations. Alternatively, you can combine the ALTER TABLE statement with an ORDER BY a particular column option to achieve the same results.

For example, imagine that you have a table containing millions of rows of frequent flyer detail information:

```
CREATE TABLE customer_mileage_details
(
        customer_id INT NOT NULL,
        ff_number CHAR(10) NOT NULL,
        transaction_date DATE NOT NULL,
        mileage SMALLINT NOT NULL,
        INDEX (customer_id),
        INDEX (ff_number, transaction_date)
) ENGINE = MYISAM;
```

As you analyze usage patterns for the table, you realize that users typically employ the second index when running queries that locate and retrieve large blocks of consecutive rows. To speed access, you choose to have the table sorted by the second index:

```
myisamchk -v -R 2
```

From this point forward, all rows in the table will be stored in `ff_number`, `transaction_date` order until new rows are added. If you want to make this sequencing more permanent, consider running this command periodically.

This is just a fraction of the information that `myisamchk` provides. Although a full exploration of this vital utility is beyond the scope of this book, it's a good investment for any MySQL administrator to spend the time to learn more about `myisamchk`.

Table Maintenance and Repair

Table and index maintenance and repair are vital functions. The following sections look at a few examples of how to improve the speed of these necessary operations.

Compressing Tables

MySQL features a number of internal compression algorithms that can shrink the amount of space required by certain fields within indexes. However, administrators can also elect to compress an entire table by using the `myisampack` utility. Note that this option is only available for read-only tables, so a heavily updated transactional table is not a good candidate for compression.

Compression provides two main benefits. First, if your query uses either a primary key or unique index to locate a row, MySQL only decompresses the specific row in question. This happens very quickly and efficiently. Secondly, a compressed table consumes less disk space, freeing up resources for other uses.

If you still want to realize the benefits of compression from a frequently modified table, one idea is to occasionally create an empty MyISAM table, insert relevant records from your transactional table, and then compress the newly filled table. You can also elect to decompress a MyISAM table, fill it with additional data, and then rerun `myisampack` to recompress the table. However, these steps may be too time consuming if the table is very large or very frequently updated.

Parallel Index Creation

Although currently considered an alpha-quality feature, you may elect to have `myisamchk` build indexes in parallel. To do so, pass in the –p or --parallel-recover parameters. Another option would be to boost the value of the `myisam_repair_threads` server setting, which will affect the behavior of the REPAIR TABLE statement, forcing it to attempt index rebuilding in parallel.

In terms of choosing a value, don't raise this value to more than the number of CPUs found on your database server.

Defragmenting Tables

Over time, tables that feature variable length rows (such as those containing TEXT, VARCHAR, or BLOB columns) can become fragmented. This happens because these variable-length rows often span noncontiguous pages if there isn't available space on consecutive pages. Locating and retrieving this dispersed information taxes the database server. Fortunately, administrators have at least options to defragment these types of tables:

- **The OPTIMIZE TABLE command**—Periodically running this command causes MySQL to restructure the table, reclaiming space and removing fragmentation at the same time. Note that this statement locks the table for the duration of the process, so be mindful of when you choose to initiate defragmentation.

- **The `myisamchk` utility**—Like its preceding counterpart, you can use `myisamchk` to reclaim space and defragment the table. However, to run this command, you must shut down the database server, possibly inconveniencing your users.

- **The `mysqlchk` utility**—The main drawback of `myisamchk` is that you must shut down the `mysqld` process to avoid potential corruption. However, `mysqlchk` addresses this limitation, letting you keep your database server active while still defragmenting its tables.

Controlling Sorting Resources

MyISAM lets administrators dictate the amount of resources available for a number of important database operations, including sorting. The following list describes two ways to affect this behavior:

- **Setting up a memory buffer for sorting or creating indexes**—Provide a value for `myisam_sort_buffer_size` to control the amount of memory available to MySQL when either building a new index or sorting an index during table repairs.

  Because this variable is configurable at both the GLOBAL and SESSION levels, it's a good idea to leave the setting at its default globally; you can then raise it substantially for a session if you're about to embark on a significant table repair or big index creation operation.

- **Determining temporary storage selection during index creation**—This book has continually touted the fast processing benefits of working in memory versus on disk. However, there is at least one exception in which your goal should be to use the disk. This happens when you create or repair an index.

If MyISAM estimates that its temporary storage needs will exceed the value of `myisam_max_sort_file_size`, it performs the sorting necessary to build the index via the memory-based key cache. If you are experiencing sluggish performance when undertaking an index build or rebuild, try boosting this setting. However, be certain you have enough disk space before forcing MySQL to use a disk-based sort file.

Finally, if you want to ensure that MySQL uses your requested disk-based approach, make sure that the `myisam_max_extra_sort_file_size` variable is not set too low. In fact, it should be set to the same value (or even larger) as `myisam_max_sort_file_size`. Otherwise, MySQL might still elect to use the more costly key cache method of index creation. This determination is made as follows: If the sort file is larger than the `key_buffer_size` setting by `myisam_max_extra_sort_file_size` bytes, then use the slower keycache method.

How can you tell if you have indeed forced MySQL to use the disk-based method? Simply run either the MySQL Administrator or the SHOW PROCESSLIST command:

```
*************************** 3. row ***************************
      Id: 4
    User: enorton
    Host: db-server1
      db: high_hat
 Command: Query
    Time: 439
   State: Repair by sorting
    Info: create fulltext index cl_ix1 on customer_letters(letter_body)
```

If you have configured things correctly, you will see "Repair by sorting" in the "State" column rather than "Repair by Keycache." For administrators using `myisamchk`, you may force this behavior with either the –n/--sort-recover or –p/--parallel-recover options.

The correct settings can make an enormous difference when building a large index. This chapter's section on FULLTEXT indexing provides a dramatic example of this.

MyISAM and Memory

Aside from the engine-neutral server settings described in the preceding chapter, the MyISAM key cache is the primary memory-based structure that administrators can configure. This section explores its architecture, as well as how to set up, monitor, and tune its behavior.

Before getting started, recall that there actually are several memory caches built in to MySQL:

- **Key cache**—This is the cache that buffers index information for tables that use the MyISAM storage engine.
- **Buffer pool**—This is InnoDB's answer to MyISAM's key cache, except it holds both indexes and data. This is discussed more in Chapter 12, "InnoDB Performance Enhancement."
- **Memory pool**—This is a MySQL internal buffer that caches data dictionary and other server structures. It only benefits tables that use the InnoDB storage engine, so it is discussed more in Chapter 12.
- **Query cache**—This cache holds queries and their results, and is of use to all MySQL users, regardless of their choice of storage engine. This cache was discussed in Chapter 10, "General Server Performance and Parameters Tuning," in its review of general engine settings.

The Key Cache

Because accessing information from a disk drive is orders-of-magnitude more expensive than the same operation performed in memory, it's always beneficial to leverage memory and reduce the interaction between the database server and its related disks. The MyISAM key cache is specially designed for this purpose, and focuses exclusively on indexed information.

Although it's beyond the scope of this book to deliver a detailed architectural description of this highly sophisticated engine module, it's still worthwhile to explore it at a high level before discussing its configuration and monitoring.

It's best to think of the key cache as an optional, administrator-defined and configured block of memory that holds index information from one or more tables. The primary unit of storage is a block, which can contain index details from a single table or even a mixture of tables.

When attempting to create, update, or retrieve indexed information from a particular table, MySQL first looks into this cache to see if the relevant information is obtainable in memory. If it is, MySQL performs an extremely fast read from, or write operation into, the key cache. If not, MySQL identifies one or more key cache entries for replacement. These replacement candidates are then removed from the key cache; if their data or index information has changed, MySQL writes the new values back to disk. After they are out of the way, MySQL uses the space for the new information.

The following lists a few more significant facts about the key cache:

- **All index blocks are implicitly time stamped**—MyISAM uses a queue mechanism to store blocks. This lets MySQL know which blocks are the "oldest" (that is, are at the front of the queue and therefore have been present in the key cache for the longest amount of time). This is important because the key cache has limited space, and MySQL might need to swap out an existing block to make room for a new block. This is known as the "Least Recently Used" (LRU) approach.

- **Blocks might change while in the cache**—For example, if you change someone's last name from Smith to Smythe, and this column is indexed, the key cache's index block is updated. As soon as it becomes necessary to remove the updated block from the cache (to satisfy a new request), MySQL writes the updated block back to disk, thereby making the index change permanent.

- **As long as you have sufficient memory, you can elect to deploy multiple key caches in addition to the default key cache offered by MySQL**—This is typically done to separate different processing profiles into their own caches, a feature introduced in MySQL 4.1.

    For example, you can choose to create one key cache to support highly dynamic, transactional usage, and another designed for decision support, in which the data doesn't change very often. Separating the key caches means that these very different applications aren't likely to interfere with each others' usage of the key cache.

- **To improve concurrency, multiple threads may work with the cache all at once**—However, if changes are being made to a particular block, other threads that need to access the block need to briefly wait until the update is complete.

- **In addition to the LRU method driven by the ordered queue, MySQL offers an optional, sophisticated algorithm to control replacements in the key cache**—Known as the "midpoint insertion strategy," it distinguishes between different degrees of index block utilization, which has a significant effect on which blocks are identified for replacement.

- **When enabled, MyISAM divides the queue of potential candidates into two segments: a "hot" list (that is, blocks that are being heavily accessed and, hence, should remain in the key cache) and a "warm" list, containing less "popular" blocks**—Although this chapter doesn't devote a significant amount of explanation on this topic, its configuration is explored momentarily.

Configuring the Key Cache

Now that you've seen how the key cache works, this section discusses how to configure it and control its behavior. You'll create a group of sample key caches at the end of this section.

To get started, follow these steps:

1. Decide if you want to deploy multiple key caches, and if so, how many. Whether you employ one, two, or ten key caches isn't as important as understanding the important performance role they play, as well as how to configure, monitor, and then tune them.

2. Set the appropriate variables. You have several decisions to make for each of the key caches you create:

   - **Sizing the in-memory key cache buffers**—The key_cache_block_size setting determines how many bytes will make up each of the key cache buffers. The default of 1,024 bytes should be good enough for most applications; future releases of MySQL will make changing this parameter more meaningful.

   - **Allocating memory to your key cache(s)**—This is an important decision: Setting the key_buffer_size variable too low means that you won't realize the full benefits of key caching. Setting it too high wastes precious memory, and might introduce performance anomalies elsewhere.

     As stated previously, every environment is different, so off-the-cuff recommendations are hard to make. With that said, a good starting point is to allocate approximately 5%–10% of your system's main memory to your combined group of key caches; you can grant more space if your InnoDB memory requirements are low. It's always better to start small and then request more resources.

   - **Determine if you want to use the midpoint insertion strategy**—This optional algorithm was described earlier. If you don't want to employ this approach, simply ensure that key_cache_division_limit is set to 100. Otherwise, set it to be the desired dividing line between the hot and warm index block lists. For example, when set to 30%, MySQL ensures that the warm list contains no less than 30% of the blocks in the key cache, whereas the remaining blocks are associated with the hot list.

   Alas, some blocks are not meant to live out their existence in the hot list and face downgrading onto the warm list, where they will likely be quickly swapped out for a newer block. The key_cache_age_threshold determines how long a block can remain in the most-unused part of the hot list before it is cast out onto the warm list.

3. Associate your indexes with their designated caches. The CACHE INDEX statement does the actual assignment between your key caches and the indexes that will be placed in them. These key caches use structured system variables, which have scope only in the context of each key cache.

4. Decide if you want your key cache preloaded. MySQL gives you the choice of having your key cache loaded with data "on the fly" (that is, the key cache fills in as rows are requested from the server) or preloaded. If you decide to preload your key cache, use the LOAD INDEX statement. You can configure the amount of memory allocated for this load operation via the preload_buffer_size setting.

5. Monitor your key caches. You have a number of ways to keep an eye on your key cache performance. The most effective is by using the MySQL Administrator, which is explored in a moment.

6. If you want to clear the contents of your key cache(s), you can either stop and then restart MySQL or simply alter its `key_buffer_size` setting. When faced with this kind of request, MySQL synchronizes the key cache with the disk in an orderly manner, and then clears the cache's contents.

After identifying the steps to follow to configure your key cache, let's walk through an example. For the purposes of this illustration, let's use three caches: one key cache for OLTP-style access, one for DSS applications, and the default key cache.

Our database server has 4GB of memory, so using the 10% rule discussed earlier, you can allocate a total of approximately 400MB to the combined group of key caches:

- The default key cache will receive 256MB via the `key_buffer_size` parameter. You'll then preload the cache with indexes for your largest, widely accessed, mixed use table:

```
mysql> LOAD INDEX INTO CACHE customer_master IGNORE LEAVES;
+--------------------------+---------------+----------+----------+
| Table                    | Op            | Msg_type | Msg_text |
+--------------------------+---------------+----------+----------+
| high_hat.customer_master | preload_keys  | status   | OK       |
+--------------------------+---------------+----------+----------+
1 row in set (0.02 sec)
```

- Grant 75MB to both the OLTP and DSS key caches, assign the indexes from the appropriate tables to those caches, and then preload the indexes:

```
mysql> CACHE INDEX customer_address in dss;
+--------------------------+-------------------+----------+----------+
| Table                    | Op                | Msg_type | Msg_text |
+--------------------------+-------------------+----------+----------+
| high_hat.customer_address | assign_to_keycache | status   | OK       |
+--------------------------+-------------------+----------+----------+
1 row in set (0.01 sec)
mysql> LOAD INDEX INTO CACHE customer_address IGNORE LEAVES;
+--------------------------+---------------+----------+----------+
| Table                    | Op            | Msg_type | Msg_text |
+--------------------------+---------------+----------+----------+
| high_hat.customer_address | preload_keys  | status   | OK       |
+--------------------------+---------------+----------+----------+
1 row in set (0.00 sec)
mysql> CACHE INDEX transactions in oltp;
+----------------------+-------------------+----------+----------+
| Table                | Op                | Msg_type | Msg_text |
+----------------------+-------------------+----------+----------+
```

```
| high_hat.transactions | assign_to_keycache | status   | OK       |
+----------------------+-------------------+---------+----------+
1 row in set (0.01 sec)

mysql> LOAD INDEX INTO CACHE transactions IGNORE LEAVES;
+----------------------+--------------+---------+----------+
| Table                | Op           | Msg_type | Msg_text |
+----------------------+--------------+---------+----------+
| high_hat.transactions | preload_keys | status   | OK       |
+----------------------+--------------+---------+----------+
1 row in set (0.00 sec)
```

Monitoring and Tuning the Key Cache

After configuring your key caches, you can then create a set of MySQL Administrator graphs to help you understand its activities, as shown in Figure 11.1.

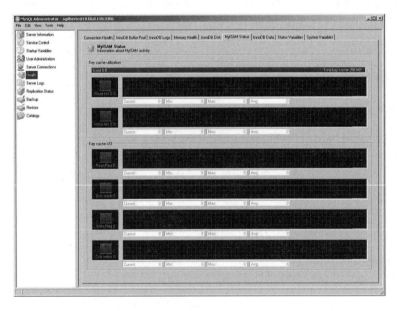

FIGURE 11.1   A collection of MySQL Administrator graphs designed to report about the key cache.

These graphs include information about the following:

- **Key cache consumption**—To determine how much of the key cache is currently being used, multiply the ever-changing value of key_blocks_used by the static key_block_size. Then, compare the result with the overall amount of key cache space, represented by key_buffer_size, yielding the current key cache resource consumption.

Use this bar graph to help determine if your key cache is sized correctly. For example, if it quickly fills up, there is a decent possibility that you need to allocate more memory, unless you are preloading the cache or your access patterns vary over time. On the other hand, if it remains relatively unused, you might be able to restore some of its memory back to the operating system or spread it to other MySQL caches. Remember to check these values over time; making a snap decision based on 10 minutes of activity is not wise.

- **Read hit rate percentage**—To determine the key cache hit rate (that is, the amount of times that MySQL was able to find the required information in the key cache rather than having to go to disk), use the following formula:

```
100-(^[Key_reads]/^[Key_read_requests])*100
```

How should you interpret these results? If you consistently see a high hit rate (in excess of 90%), chances are that your key cache is tuned efficiently.

A very low hit rate can mean that your key cache is undersized relative to your needs, and that you should allocate more memory. It's also possible, however, that your database is simply so big and/or accessed so randomly that MySQL can't efficiently place index information in the key cache. In this case, it's likely that no key cache will be big enough (unless your memory and data are equivalent in size), so your goal should be to boost the size of the key cache (along with the hit rate) with the understanding that it will never be perfect.

Finally, a hit rate of 99% or 100% might paradoxically mean that you have oversized your key cache, usually at the expense of another component of your server. When you see such high hit rates, consider gradually reducing the key cache's memory until you reach the point at which the hit rates begin to deteriorate.

- **Write hit rate percentage**—This graph measures the relationship between key writes (the number of key block writes to disk) and their associated key write requests (the number of key block writes into the key cache) as follows:

```
100-(^[Key_writes]/^[Key_write_requests])*100
```

Because key write operations typically touch a more dispersed, random set of data, it's natural to expect to see a lower cache rate than for read operations. You will notice exceptions to this rule for large-scale write operations, such as bulk data loads or large index creation.

- **Key cache reads versus disk reads**—The next two graphs display the varying number of times that MySQL was able to read information from the key cache (key_read_requests) rather than the disk (key_reads).

- **Key cache writes versus disk writes**—These next two graphs also track the number of times the key cache was used. In this case, the successful key cache write requests (key_write_requests) are contrasted with those that were written to disk (key_writes).

Be careful as you monitor your system: Unfortunately, there is no way to observe the hit rates for any nondefault key caches.

Take a look at a few real-life MyISAM activity profiles. In Figure 11.2, a series of read-only queries are run against a disparate group of MyISAM tables.

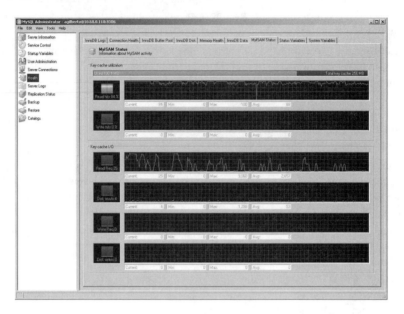

FIGURE 11.2   MySQL Administrator graphs showing key cache metrics on an active, read-intensive system.

As would be expected, there are only indicators of read activity; there are no write operations under way. In addition, according to this graph, a respectable hit rate is being received even though the key cache hasn't filled up. If this profile persists, you might be able to reduce the default key cache from its current 256MB level to somewhere around 200MB, and adjust the customized key caches as well.

Next, a mixture of read-focused and write-focused applications are launched, as shown in Figure 11.3.

Why is there such a disparity between the near-perfect read cache hit rate and the (apparently) awful write cache hit rate? Recall from earlier in this section that in the absence of large, sequential, key-affecting operations like bulk inserts or index building, write operations are typically more random and dispersed than read operations. Hence, the discrepancy between read and write cache hit rates.

Watch what happens in Figure 11.4, though, in which a series of write-intensive applications that update blocks of approximately 300 rows at a time are launched.

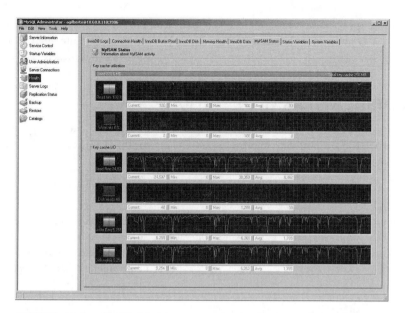

FIGURE 11.3   MySQL Administrator graphs showing key cache metrics on an active, mixed read-and-write system.

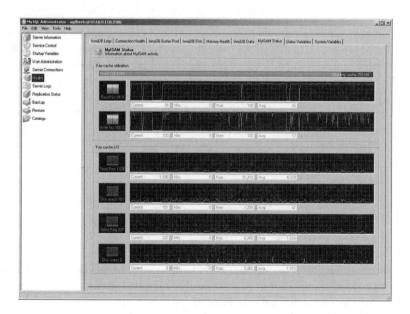

FIGURE 11.4   MySQL Administrator graphs showing key cache metrics on an active, write-intensive system.

Now you see great hit rates for both read and write access to the key cache. The writing applications' WHERE clauses are meeting with success in their quest to locate index information in the key cache, and MyISAM is able to buffer their updates in this cache as well.

Speeding MyISAM Operations

Now that you've examined how to make the most of MyISAM's disk and memory structures, this section devotes attention to improving performance for those applications that use this storage engine.

Loading Information

Operations that load data can consume massive amounts of time and system resources. Chapter 15, "Improving Import and Export Operations," which is dedicated to import and export processing, discusses general best practices for these types of procedures. For now, the following sections look at several key MyISAM-specific parameters that affect data load performance.

Specifying Table Size

Chapter 4, "Designing for Speed," reviewed the implications of tuning the average row length and row size parameters (AVG_ROW_LENGTH and MAX_ROWS, respectively) for MyISAM tables.

If you are unsure of what these values should be, but still want the option to create very large MyISAM tables, you can raise the value of the myisam_data_pointer_size parameter. Its default value of four (that is, 32 bits) translates to sufficient row pointer space to support a maximum table size of 4GB, assuming that your operating system allows a file this large. By raising it (to a maximum value of eight, or 64 bits), you increase the potential size of the table to a truly enormous value, but only for those tables created after the parameter has been changed; existing tables still face the previous size limitations. The trade-off is a slightly increased overhead cost for tables that are not this large.

Unless you really need automatic support for such big tables (such as for system-generated temporary tables that exceed 4GB), it's wise to just leave this parameter set to its default; you always have the option to raise the MAX_ROWS value or use MySQL's built-in RAID capabilities to support any necessary enormous user-created tables.

Delaying Key Writes

The MyISAM key cache was first mentioned in Chapter 7; this vital engine feature is discussed in more detail a little later in this chapter. For now, this section spends a moment discussing the benefits versus drawbacks of delaying key writes.

When you create a MyISAM table, MySQL gives you the option to request, by appending DELAY KEY WRITE=1 to your CREATE TABLE statement, that updates made to the key cache not be flushed to disk until the table is closed. Although this postpones the inevitable disk writing until it can be completed all at once, you do run the risk of lost or corrupted data should your server crash before the write has been completed. You can use the delay_key_write server variable to further configure this functionality.

For example, if it is set to OFF, MyISAM flushes the key cache when necessary, regardless of whether the table creator wanted delayed key writes.

Bulk Insert Buffering

MySQL offers special in-memory buffers for situations when you perform certain kinds of data loading operations for nonempty tables, such as multi-row INSERT, INSERT ... SELECT, and LOAD DATA INFILE statements. You can control the size of this buffer by setting the bulk_insert_buffer_size server variable.

To measure the performance impact of tuning bulk_insert_buffer_size, we created several empty MyISAM-based sample tables, composing each table with a variety of data types. To create a baseline performance measurement, we ran mysqlimport and loaded approximately 100 million records into each table.

Next, we deleted all rows from each table, set bulk_insert_buffer_size to zero (which canceled out the internal cache), restarted the server, and then reran mysqlimport. Interestingly, we saw no performance degradation when reloading these tables; it took the same amount of time as when the internal cache was enabled. Why? Quite simply, MySQL doesn't use this cache on completely empty tables. To take advantage of this cache, be certain that your tables contain some data, even if it is a single sample row that you will delete post-reload.

We then reran the test with each table containing only one row. With these settings, there was a dramatic difference in performance: This time, when the cache was disabled, the import operations took, on average, 40% longer than with an 8MB cache enabled. Finally, we tested the impact of larger caches. As you would expect, the law of diminishing returns set in; enormous values for this parameter did not translate into corresponding performance gains.

Deactivating Indexes

Deactivating index updates is one way to speed inserts of large amounts of data into an indexed MyISAM table. To do this, append --keys-used to myisamchk, along with a bitmask indicating the index that you want to deactivate. If you pass in a zero, all indexes are ignored when new data is inserted into the table.

After you have loaded your information, run myisamchk with the -r option to check the table's integrity and then rebuild the indexes.

Improving FULLTEXT Searches

Given that free-form, character-based data makes up a significant portion of the information tracked by many relational database applications, MyISAM's FULLTEXT search capabilities make it much easier to quickly locate and retrieve relevant results.

As entire books have been written regarding optimal search algorithms, this section primarily focuses on ways to advance the speed at which these specific types of searches operate.

Before getting started, how does MySQL implement FULLTEXT searches? First, your table must be designed to use the MyISAM storage engine, and cannot use MyISAM-based MERGE tables. Next, MySQL will only create FULLTEXT indexes for columns that are defined as CHAR, VARCHAR, or TEXT. The column cannot use the ucs2 character set. Finally, all columns in a single FULLTEXT index must have the same character set and collation. You can request these indexes as part of any of these operations:

- CREATE TABLE
- ALTER TABLE
- CREATE INDEX

To build the index, MySQL walks through the text in the identified column(s), breaking the text down into individual words that are then placed into the index, along with a pointer back to the data where the word is to be found. After the index is in place, you can then search it via the MATCH() function.

Now that we've briefly explained how these indexes are created and used, let's describe a scenario and then set up a sample table to help us illustrate how to design efficient FULL-TEXT queries.

For years, High-Hat Airways' executives have told the CEO that their airline's customer satisfaction metrics are the highest in the world. The CEO, thrilled with this ongoing customer contentment, decides to launch a contest to find the happiest High-Hat client. Customers will be encouraged to write letters to the airline, describing their best High-Hat experience. The winner of the contest will be determined by a panel of distinguished judges, who will award a fabulous prize—an entire wardrobe of High-Hat merchandise, from baseball caps to t-shirts to luxury slippers. These judges will use a web-based user interface to search the millions of expected entries for certain keywords and phrases, and then vote for their favorites.

As designer of the application, you create a new table to hold these entries:

```
CREATE TABLE customer_letters
(
        id INTEGER UNSIGNED PRIMARY KEY AUTO_INCREMENT,
        letter_date DATE NOT NULL,
        customer_id INTEGER NOT NULL,
        letter_body LONGTEXT NOT NULL
) ENGINE = MYISAM;
```

After determining your table design, as well as the fact that you need FULLTEXT search capabilities, how should you configure this capability?

Configuring FULLTEXT Options

You should keep several key parameters in mind as you set up your FULLTEXT search options:

- **Words to ignore**—MySQL maintains a list of words that are disregarded during FULLTEXT searches. For the curious and/or source code–literate, you can find these words in the `ft_static.c` file, found in the `myisam` directory:

```
#ifdef COMPILE_STOPWORDS_IN

/* This particular stopword list was taken from SMART distribution
   ftp://ftp.cs.cornell.edu/pub/smart/smart.11.0.tar.Z
   it was slightly modified to my taste, though
 */

  "a's",
  "able",
  "about",
...
...
  "yourself",
  "yourselves",
  "zero",
#endif

NULL };
```

  As entries begin to flow in, you are dismayed to observe that many of them are filled with rude remarks, obscenities, assertions about the matriarchal parentage of the CEO, and anatomically impossible suggestions.

  Clearly, it will be embarrassing to the company if the distinguished judges view these entries; more importantly, you might also get fired. Fortunately, MySQL lets you specify your own list of ignored words by simply setting the `ft_stopword_file` variable to point at this site-specific list, which should be in a similar format to the `ft_static.c` file as shown earlier in this section. After the list is in place and all existing FULLTEXT indexes rebuilt, the judges won't even see these uncouth entries in their search results.

- **Maximum word size**—By setting the `ft_max_word_len` variable, you can specify the maximum number of characters that MySQL will include in a FULLTEXT search.

- **Minimum word size**—You also have control over the minimum word length for FULLTEXT search. The default value of four might be too low for your site because there are many distinct three-letter words that would be legitimate search candidates. If you need to change this behavior, alter the `ft_min_word_len` setting.

  It's important to note that you need to rebuild your FULLTEXT indexes after changing any of the previous three parameters. To rebuild these indexes as quickly as possible, append the `QUICK` directive to the `REPAIR TABLE` statement.

- **Query expansion behavior**—Query expansion is an extremely helpful feature. When requested (via the WITH QUERY EXTENSION syntax), MySQL performs two search passes, using the most relevant matches from the initial resultset to find additional matches that the user might have wanted but was not able to correctly specify.

  You can control how many of the initial results are recursively fed back into the query expansion. By raising the ft_query_expansion_limit from its default of 20, MySQL passes additional values to the follow-on query, whereas a lower value means fewer results will be considered during the second pass.

Building FULLTEXT Indexes

The next important decision to make about FULLTEXT searching is what parameters to set and when to build the index. If you try to launch a standard FULLTEXT search without the proper index in place, MySQL returns an error:

```
mysql> SELECT * FROM customer_letters
    -> WHERE MATCH(letter_body) AGAINST ('appalled');
ERROR 1191 (HY000): Can't find FULLTEXT index matching the column list
```

You can still run queries against the underlying table; you can even use MATCH() in Boolean mode, but you are limited in your usage until the index is in place. Building a FULLTEXT index can take a very long time to complete, especially if the table is extremely large. For this reason, if at all possible it's wise to delay creating your index until the table is fully loaded. However, it's even more important that you correctly define your temporary sort settings (myisam_sort_buffer_size, myisam_max_sort_file_size, and myisam_max_extra_soft_file_size) when rebuilding your FULLTEXT indexes; these settings were described earlier in this chapter.

For example, we generated more than 4.5 million rows of random data and then loaded this information into the customer_letters table. The letter_body column contained, on average, 30 meaningful words.

After the table was built, we created a FULLTEXT index on the letter_body column. With our temporary sort settings defined correctly (that is, forcing the use of a disk-based sorting method rather than a key cache–based approach), it took three hours to build the index.

After the data was loaded and indexed, we then unloaded all information into a 4GB flat file. After dropping the table and restarting the server, we reloaded it with the FULLTEXT index already defined. It still took about three hours to complete the reload and index rebuild.

Finally, we lowered values of the temporary sort settings to levels at which MySQL would be forced to use the key cache method of sorting for index creation. After restarting the server, we dropped the table and then re-created an empty copy. It took 11 hours (more than three times longer than before) to finish the task of loading and indexing the table. This highlights how important it is to use the proper settings when building a FULLTEXT index.

Using the FULLTEXT Index

After you've created the index, how can you tell if it's being used? As with all MySQL queries, the EXPLAIN command provides the answer. Let's look at several queries and their associated plans.

This first example runs a simple search through the customer correspondence:

```
mysql> EXPLAIN
    -> SELECT * FROM customer_letters
    -> WHERE MATCH(letter_body) AGAINST ('incompetent')\G
*************************** 1. row ***************************
           id: 1
  select_type: SIMPLE
        table: customer_letters
         type: fulltext
possible_keys: cl_ix1
          key: cl_ix1
      key_len: 0
          ref:
         rows: 1
        Extra: Using where
1 row in set (0.00 sec)
```

You can see that this query will correctly use the FULLTEXT index to locate rows. Next, suppose that you want to take advantage of query expansion:

```
mysql> EXPLAIN
    -> SELECT * FROM customer_letters
    -> WHERE MATCH(letter_body) AGAINST ('incompetent' WITH QUERY EXPANSION)\G
*************************** 1. row ***************************
           id: 1
  select_type: SIMPLE
        table: customer_letters
         type: fulltext
possible_keys: cl_ix1
          key: cl_ix1
      key_len: 0
          ref:
         rows: 1
        Extra: Using where
1 row in set (0.00 sec)
```

Again, no surprises in the EXPLAIN output. Now, suppose that you want to find all rows that contain two different words:

```
mysql> EXPLAIN
    -> SELECT * FROM customer_letters
    -> WHERE (MATCH(letter_body) AGAINST ('delighted') AND
    -> MATCH(letter_body) AGAINST ('delicious'))\G
```

```
*************************** 1. row ***************************
          id: 1
 select_type: SIMPLE
       table: customer_letters
        type: fulltext
possible_keys: cl_ix1
         key: cl_ix1
     key_len: 0
         ref:
        rows: 1
       Extra: Using where
1 row in set (0.00 sec)
```

This is a good, efficient query plan; there are several other ways to achieve the same results. For example, you could also use a UNION statement:

```
mysql> EXPLAIN
    -> SELECT * FROM customer_letters
    -> WHERE MATCH(letter_body) AGAINST ('delighted')
    -> UNION
    -> SELECT * FROM customer_letters
    -> WHERE MATCH(letter_body) AGAINST ('unexpectedly')\G
*************************** 1. row ***************************
          id: 1
 select_type: PRIMARY
       table: customer_letters
        type: fulltext
possible_keys: cl_ix1
         key: cl_ix1
     key_len: 0
         ref:
        rows: 1
       Extra: Using where
*************************** 2. row ***************************
          id: 2
 select_type: UNION
       table: customer_letters
        type: fulltext
possible_keys: cl_ix1
         key: cl_ix1
     key_len: 0
         ref:
        rows: 1
       Extra: Using where
*************************** 3. row ***************************
          id: NULL
 select_type: UNION RESULT
```

```
        table: <union1,2>
         type: ALL
possible_keys: NULL
          key: NULL
      key_len: NULL
          ref: NULL
         rows: NULL
        Extra:
3 rows in set (0.00 sec)
```

What about cases in which you want results containing at least one of two words?

```
mysql> EXPLAIN
    -> SELECT * FROM customer_letters
    -> WHERE (MATCH(letter_body) AGAINST ('delighted') OR
    -> MATCH(letter_body) AGAINST ('delicious'))\G
*************************** 1. row ***************************
           id: 1
  select_type: SIMPLE
        table: customer_letters
         type: ALL
possible_keys: NULL
          key: NULL
      key_len: NULL
          ref: NULL
         rows: 4704049
        Extra: Using where
1 row in set (0.00 sec)
```

This is not what you want to see. MySQL performs an extremely expensive table scan for queries written this way. Fortunately, there are better ways to create OR queries:

```
mysql> EXPLAIN
    -> SELECT * FROM customer_letters
    -> WHERE MATCH(letter_body) AGAINST ('delighted delicious')\G
*************************** 1. row ***************************
           id: 1
  select_type: SIMPLE
        table: customer_letters
         type: fulltext
possible_keys: cl_ix1
          key: cl_ix1
      key_len: 0
          ref:
         rows: 1
        Extra: Using where
1 row in set (0.02 sec)
```

Boolean searches are also helpful for queries that need more flexible search criteria:

```
mysql> EXPLAIN
    -> SELECT * FROM customer_letters
    -> WHERE MATCH(letter_body)
    -> AGAINST ('+delighted +delicious' IN BOOLEAN MODE)\G
*************************** 1. row ***************************
           id: 1
  select_type: SIMPLE
        table: customer_letters
         type: fulltext
possible_keys: cl_ix1
          key: cl_ix1
      key_len: 0
          ref:
         rows: 1
        Extra: Using where
1 row in set (0.00 sec)
```

Finally, the following looks at a simple join between two tables, using a FULLTEXT search as part of the filtering criteria:

```
mysql> EXPLAIN
    -> SELECT cm.*, cl.*
    -> FROM customer_master cm, customer_letters cl
    -> WHERE cm.customer_id = cl.customer_id
    -> AND MATCH(cl.letter_body) AGAINST ('lawsuit')\G
*************************** 1. row ***************************
           id: 1
  select_type: SIMPLE
        table: cl
         type: fulltext
possible_keys: cl_ix1
          key: cl_ix1
      key_len: 0
          ref:
         rows: 1
        Extra: Using where
*************************** 2. row ***************************
           id: 1
  select_type: SIMPLE
        table: cm
         type: eq_ref
possible_keys: PRIMARY
          key: PRIMARY
      key_len: 4
          ref: high_hat.cl.customer_id
```

```
       rows: 1
      Extra: Using where
2 rows in set (0.02 sec)
```

MySQL processes this query as you would expect. In general, if you're new to FULLTEXT searches, always run EXPLAIN before launching a noteworthy query.

General FULLTEXT Performance Suggestions

To get the most out of your FULLTEXT searches, keep these suggestions in mind:

- MySQL AB continually releases newer software versions; generally, more modern versions have better FULLTEXT search performance.

- For consistency's sake, verify that the server and myisamchk utility are both informed about your wishes for any FULLTEXT configuration settings. If you fail to do so, myisamchk will use the default values, not your customized settings. To avoid this problem, define the settings with identical values in two places within your configuration file: under both the [mysqld] and [myisamchk] sections.

- It's a good idea to clear the query cache after changing your FULLTEXT settings or rebuilding your index.

- Use indexed columns beginning in the leftmost position. This rule was covered in Chapter 7's indexing review and Chapter 8's study of advanced SQL. The same regulation applies for FULLTEXT indexes.

- If possible, cleanse your data prior to loading it into your database. A FULLTEXT index is only as useful as the data that it catalogs. If your data set contains misspellings, abbreviations, and other inconsistencies, it makes FULLTEXT searches much harder to successfully invoke.

Concurrency Considerations

Chapter 9, "Developing High-Speed Applications," spent a considerable amount of time discussing concurrency. The following sections look at two MyISAM-specific settings that can affect concurrency and performance.

Concurrent Inserts

The concurrent_insert variable lets you dictate whether MyISAM allows simultaneous SELECT and INSERT statements on a table that has no empty space in its middle. For most applications, the concurrency-friendly default of ON is the appropriate choice.

Query Cache Locking

If you want to block other queries from seeing the contents of the query cache while another process has a write lock in place on a MyISAM table (but has not yet modified the table), set the query_cache_wlock_invalidate variable to ON/1. The main reason to restrict this behavior is if you are concerned that one of these other queries might suffer from very bad timing, and receive a stale, query cache–based result. Of course, once the lock-owning process has altered the table's data, the query cache is invalidated no matter what you do.

The more liberal, default setting of OFF/0 lets these additional queries continue to access the query cache, even if the underlying table is locked for writing.

InnoDB Performance Enhancement

Now that you've explored general MySQL database engine-tuning options, as well as specific things you can do to boost MyISAM performance, this chapter turns your attention to increasing the InnoDB storage engine's responsiveness.

This chapter begins by examining the InnoDB data storage architecture, as well as how to make all disk I/O operations as efficient as possible. Next, it studies how to leverage InnoDB's powerful memory management capabilities. Finally, it reviews several ways that administrators can provide guidance to InnoDB to improve operational activities.

Before this chapter begins, you should note the following important points:

- This chapter only focuses on those InnoDB server variables and status indicators that directly affect performance; it doesn't discuss unrelated InnoDB options.

- Although Chapter 9, "Developing High-Speed Applications," has already examined InnoDB-based transactions, locking, and concurrency, some of these observations are resurrected here.

- Instead of one dedicated section on InnoDB performance monitoring tools, SHOW INNODB STATUS and MySQL Administrator-based examples are interspersed throughout the chapter to help illustrate the suggestions.

- This chapter spends significant time examining the InnoDB buffer pool, which caches frequently used data and index content to help speed performance. Of course, even if you incorrectly undersize your buffer pool, it's quite possible that your operating system might end up caching this information anyway. However, for clarity's sake, this chapter doesn't examine the potential interaction between operating system and database caching.

- As stated previously, chances are that at least one of the preconfigured settings files that ship with InnoDB will go a long way toward delivering optimal performance in your environment. The best return on investment when analyzing response tuning usually is found in schema and index alterations; replication and/or clustering configuration is also very important.

InnoDB Storage Architecture and I/O

Before you can improve InnoDB's I/O performance, it's worthwhile to spend a little time understanding the core data storage structures and some key data management technologies for this engine. Note that Chapter 13, "Improving Disk Speed," explores disk tuning for all MySQL storage engines in much more detail.

To keep things as uncomplicated as possible, a number of internal InnoDB engine structures that are beyond the scope of this book are skipped here. In addition, for simplicity and clarity, we'll reprise our basic sample table from Chapter 7, "Indexing Strategies"; we periodically refer to this table as we explain how InnoDB stores information:

```
CREATE TABLE sample_names
(
    id INT UNSIGNED PRIMARY KEY AUTO_INCREMENT,
    last_name CHAR(30) NOT NULL,
    age SMALLINT NOT NULL,
    INDEX (last_name)
) ENGINE = INNODB;
```

Indexes

In addition to the general performance implications of your indexing strategy, InnoDB introduces an additional set of index capabilities. This section explores these InnoDB-specific features.

Clustered Indexes

To begin, this section examines how rows from the preceding schema will be structured. As mentioned earlier in Chapter 7, InnoDB automatically creates at least one index per table: This index is known as the clustered index. InnoDB creates this index even if the database designer has not defined a primary key.

In cases in which there is no primary key or other unique index, InnoDB automatically generates a unique, 6-byte value called the rowid. It's important to understand that the clustered index *is* the data; in a sense, the clustered index has double responsibility: first to store the data, and then to order it by the primary key, another unique value, or, as a last resort, the database-generated rowid.

Secondary Indexes

What about other indexes? How are they structured, and what is their relationship with the data found in the clustered index?

These additional indexes are known as "secondary indexes," and you can create as many of them as you need for an InnoDB table. Because our sample table schema definition requests an index on the last_name column, InnoDB creates one secondary index on this value. Each entry in the secondary index contains the primary key value from the clustered index, thereby facilitating linkage back to the data.

At this point, you've examined the lowest-level structures responsible for storing data and index information. The following section looks at the next-higher level of granularity: the page.

Pages

All information (data, indexes, and internal structures) in InnoDB reside on pages, which are set to 16K by default. In MySQL version 5.0.3, rows are now stored in a more condensed format. Despite the 16K page size and more optimal row storage layout, this doesn't mean that InnoDB completely fills each page with information. Instead, depending on your data access patterns, InnoDB might try to fill a page to more than 90% of its capacity. However, some pages might end up only being 50% full. If the amount of information on the page drops below this threshold, InnoDB performs internal shuffling and rebalancing to consolidate pages. Note that all of this activity goes on unbeknownst to the administrator.

Pages are then grouped into the next higher unit of organization: the extent.

Extents and Segments

An extent is defined as a sequential grouping of 64 pages. Placing these pages in successive order generally helps performance. InnoDB then organizes extents into segments.

Tablespaces

Tablespaces are the biggest data storage structures managed by InnoDB. They contain one or more data files (which themselves are composed of segments). You can configure these data files to automatically expand (until you run out of disk space) as your database grows. InnoDB uses tablespaces to store both data and index information. One shared tablespace is created when InnoDB is enabled. You can also dedicate a tablespace to a single table.

Transaction logs (which you explore a little later) reside in their own data files; they are not part of the tablespace.

A tablespace consists of at least one to possibly many disk files, which can exist on different drives. As you can see from Figure 12.1, tablespaces can become enormous, and let you bypass the file size restrictions imposed by many operating systems. Figure 12.1 shows an example of a tablespace that is made up of three files.

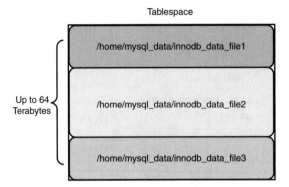

FIGURE 12.1   Tablespace comprised of three files.

Built-in Performance Enhancers

Before discussing how best to configure InnoDB, the following sections look at a few key performance-enhancing capabilities that require little or no intervention from administrators.

Insert Buffer

InnoDB sets aside a small portion of its buffer pool to diminish the amount of costly disk operations for certain types of inserts. When you change information that affects a secondary index (provided that this index is permitted to have duplicate values), InnoDB first writes the alteration into this buffered memory. Afterward, these modifications are written en masse to disk, which is much more economical.

Doublewrite Buffer

InnoDB employs the doublewrite buffer for two chief reasons. First, by initially writing data modifications into a special section of the tablespace, InnoDB reduces the risks of data loss should either the database or the server die unexpectedly. Paradoxically, these write delays can also minimize some expensive operating system disk costs by reducing the quantity of low-level I/O invocations.

Read Ahead

As your applications work with the database, InnoDB is continually monitoring utilization patterns. When it detects consistent sequential data read requests that are returning large blocks of information from a given table, InnoDB preemptively arranges to read additional information from this table into its buffer pool with the expectation that these rows will soon be needed.

Although more randomized data access presents a challenge in determining where the next set of requests will occur, InnoDB still attempts to set up prestaged reads.

Versioning

Recall from both our earlier review of the InnoDB row structure and Chapter 7 that this storage engine maintains an internal field in each row (within the clustered index) to track those transactions in which the row is involved. Each row also holds a link (called the roll pointer) to a structure known as the rollback segment, which comes into play should you need to either abort the transaction or provide a point-in-time view of your data. InnoDB is responsible for maintaining the contents of the rollback segment, but administrators have a job to do as well.

Without going into great detail, understand that an earlier view of data from a row might linger in the rollback segment's update undo log long after the underlying row has been changed or even deleted.

How is this possible? Because InnoDB relies on the rollback segment's update undo log for consistency and recoverability, it is unwilling to discard this crucial information until the transaction is completed. After this event takes place, InnoDB is then free to permanently delete this safety mechanism from the undo log, via an activity known as purging.

Here is yet another reason to keep your transactions as brief as possible; long-running transactions equal long-lived undo log contents.

The danger here is that InnoDB will fall behind, leading to a bottleneck for database modification operations or excessive disk space consumption. Here's where administrators can help. The `innodb_max_purge_lag` setting lets you instruct InnoDB to employ an invisible (to users and their applications) yet very effective delaying tactic when processing new or existing rows when there is a backlog of purge chores to work through.

Data Storage

Now that you've examined these key InnoDB internal assemblies and algorithms, the following sections investigate how to configure, monitor, and tune data storage for the most advantageous performance.

Configuring Data Storage

If you decide to use multiple tablespaces, InnoDB creates files with a suffix of '.ibd' to store their data, instead of using the shared tablespace. You can configure a ceiling for the number of open '.ibd' files by setting the `innodb_open_files` server variable, but the default value of 300 should suffice for most installations. In fact, you can even lower this parameter, with a minimum value of 10.

Another server setting that can probably be left untouched at its default value of 4 is `innodb_file_io_threads`. This controls the number of threads spawned to support InnoDB's disk operations. The one exception to this rule is if you are running a Windows-based server. If so, you might try boosting its value to see if it improves disk performance. As always, remember to change your values in small increments, and test only one alteration at a time.

As tables grow, it might become necessary for InnoDB to request additional space for the tablespace. If you have enabled and set values for the `autoextend` option in your configuration file, InnoDB attempts to increase the size of the last file in the tablespace. In Figure 12.1, this means that InnoDB tries to gain additional storage space in `/home/mysql_data/innodb_data_file3`.

How much space does InnoDB request? This is determined by the `innodb_autoextend_increment` server setting, which defaults to 8MB. If you are running a very dynamic, rapidly growing MySQL instance, you might want to boost this value to reflect the lively character of your environment. Keep in mind, however, that reclaiming space from an expanded file can be done, but is neither easy nor automatic. Also, if you run out of room on your file system, you receive a message similar to the following:

```
InnoDB: The database cannot continue operation because of
lack of space. You must add a new data file to
my.cnf and restart the database.
```

After the extension, your tablespace now looks like Figure 12.2.

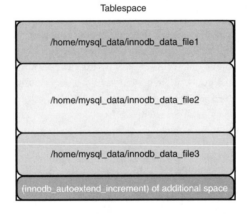

FIGURE 12.2   Additional space added to the tablespace.

To get an idea of the internal file structure and status of your tablespaces, examine the output of the `innodb_tablespace_monitor`, which also tells you if there are any problems with the tablespace. You can configure this report to be regularly written to mysqld's standard output via the CREATE TABLE statement:

```
CREATE TABLE innodb_tablespace_monitor (anyname INT) ENGINE = INNODB;
```

Here is some sample output:

```
===============================================
060610 11:35:54 INNODB TABLESPACE MONITOR OUTPUT
===============================================
```

```
FILE SPACE INFO: id 0
size 110720, free limit 109248, free extents 2
not full frag extents 2: used pages 49, full frag extents 15
first seg id not used 0 3051
SEGMENT id 0 1 space 0; page 2; res 1178 used 1030; full ext 15
fragm pages 26; free extents 0; not full extents 3: pages 44
SEGMENT id 0 2 space 0; page 2; res 1 used 1; full ext 0
fragm pages 1; free extents 0; not full extents 0: pages 0
SEGMENT id 0 3 space 0; page 2; res 1 used 1; full ext 0
fragm pages 1; free extents 0; not full extents 0: pages 0
. . .
. . .
SEGMENT id 0 15 space 0; page 2; res 160 used 160; full ext 2
fragm pages 32; free extents 0; not full extents 0: pages 0
SEGMENT id 0 3030 space 0; page 2; res 992 used 987; full ext 14
fragm pages 32; free extents 0; not full extents 1: pages 59
SEGMENT id 0 17 space 0; page 2; res 1 used 1; full ext 0
fragm pages 1; free extents 0; not full extents 0: pages 0
. . .
. . .
SEGMENT id 0 29 space 0; page 2; res 7264 used 7241; full ext 112
fragm pages 32; free extents 0; not full extents 1: pages 41
SEGMENT id 0 2902 space 0; page 2; res 1 used 1; full ext 0
fragm pages 1; free extents 0; not full extents 0: pages 0
. . .
. . .
NUMBER of file segments: 89
Validating tablespace
Validation ok
----------------------------------------
END OF INNODB TABLESPACE MONITOR OUTPUT
```

Monitoring and Tuning Data Storage

In addition to the data file space management information listed previously, with version 5.0.2, MySQL AB now offers extensive, easily accessed status variables that give valuable insight into activity in our data files. To highlight these new diagnostics, you can create a custom MySQL Administrator page that logically presents this information, as shown in Figure 12.3.

What do all of these graphs track? From top to bottom, they include the following:

- **Data read operations**—This graph monitors the changes in value for innodb_data_reads. Look for trends that tell you if the system is under particularly heavy or light read access.

- **Pending read operations**—The innodb_data_pending_reads value tracks a low-level internal status variable that counts the number of times that the database engine had to wait before gaining access to information within the underlying data file. You can track relative changes in this graph: If you see this number start to climb, it could indicate contention issues.

- **Data write operations**—The third graph corresponds to the first, except this new graph focuses on the changing number of data writes as indicated by `innodb_data_writes`.

- **Pending write operations**—Just as you're interested in the number of times MySQL had to wait before being granted access to read raw data, you can now track corresponding delays for write access by examining the `innodb_data_pending_writes` status variable. Again, a high or steadily rising number requires attention.

- **Doublewrite buffer operations**—This performance-oriented structure is described earlier in this chapter. To help us monitor its activity, the next two graphs look at the changing number of writes to the buffer (`innodb_dblwr_writes`), as well as the overall number of pages affected (`innodb_dblwr_pages_written`).

- **Fsync() operations**—Recall that MySQL uses the `fsync()` call to flush memory buffers to disk, thereby ensuring that the information persists. The final two graphs track the moving values of `innodb_data_fsyncs` and `innodb_data_pending_fsyncs`. These indicate the number of `fsync()` calls, as well as the number that are pending, respectively.

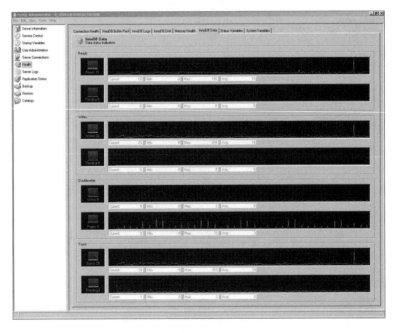

FIGURE 12.3   Custom MySQL Administrator graph highlighting new status variables.

An alternative to the MySQL Administrator is to run SHOW INNODB STATUS and locate the sections that describe disk activity:

```
----------
SEMAPHORES
----------
OS WAIT ARRAY INFO: reservation count 8568, signal count 5752
--Thread 2122673072 has waited at ../include/btr0btr.ic line 28 for 1.00 seconds the
    semaphore:
S-lock on RW-latch at 0x6767a2d4 created in file buf0buf.c line 470
a writer (thread id 2122673072) has reserved it in mode  exclusive
number of readers 0, waiters flag 1
Last time read locked in file not yet reserved line 0
Last time write locked in file buf0buf.c line 1675
Mutex spin waits 50498, rounds 388124, OS waits 4617
RW-shared spins 565, OS waits 277; RW-excl spins 2890, OS waits 1758
--------
...
...
FILE I/O
--------
I/O thread 0 state: waiting for i/o request (insert buffer thread)
I/O thread 1 state: waiting for i/o request (log thread)
I/O thread 2 state: doing file i/o (read thread) ev set
I/O thread 3 state: waiting for i/o request (write thread)
Pending normal aio reads: 122, aio writes: 0,
 ibuf aio reads: 0, log i/o's: 0, sync i/o's: 0
Pending flushes (fsync) log: 0; buffer pool: 0
7380 OS file reads, 10222 OS file writes, 9965 OS fsyncs
2 pending preads, 1 pending pwrites
3000.00 reads/s, 16384 avg bytes/read, 5000.00 writes/s, 5000.00 fsyncs/s
```

Chapter 13 considers numerous ways to improve overall disk performance.

Log Files

Log files are an essential building block of InnoDB's transaction support. These components facilitate several vital capabilities, including the following:

- **Crash recovery**—If your InnoDB server goes down unexpectedly, MySQL uses the logs during the next system launch as a way of reconstructing activity from the most recent good checkpoint (that is, disk synchronization) prior to the crash all the way to the final committed transaction.

- **Rollback**—Logs let InnoDB roll changes back to the beginning of a transaction should the need for a rollback arise.

Don't confuse these logs with the error, binary, or slow logs; instead, they are dedicated to helping the InnoDB storage engine provide a safe, consistent way to manage transactions.

Log File Configuration

As an administrator, you have several decisions to make about your InnoDB log file configuration. First, you should decide how many log files you want to employ. The default and minimum is two. If you want to initiate more log files, alter the `innodb_log_files_in_group` server setting.

After deciding how many log files you will create, the next step is to settle on how much space you want to allocate to each of your log files via the `innodb_log_file_size` setting. MySQL ships with this value set to 5MB, which is fine for relatively small databases. However, enterprise-class production databases require much bigger logs. With that said, how can you determine the correct value?

Smaller log files mean that MySQL frequently runs out of log space and often needs to run expensive checkpoints between the memory-based buffer pool and the disk-based log files. On the other hand, these compact log files translate into faster recovery because there are simply fewer transactions in them to work through upon startup.

However, given that crash recovery should be an infrequent event, it makes more sense from a performance viewpoint to make the log files large. In fact, you could set the aggregate group of log files equal to the size of the buffer pool. In this case, slow-running checkpoints are rare, but crash recovery takes a long time. For situations in which you have massive amounts of data to load and are very unconcerned about recovery, you might make these logs even larger.

Now that you've decided how many logs you want, along with how much space you are willing to allocate for them, the next step is to determine the size of the memory-based log buffer, which is represented by the `innodb_log_buffer_size` parameter. Ranging between 1MB and 8MB, it caches transactional information prior to its inscription in the disk-based log. Making the value larger means that InnoDB needs to perform fewer costly writes to the log. However, imagine the impact of a sudden, unplanned system failure to any memory-based, unwritten information still in the buffer. With that said, if your environment features sufficient memory and is not particularly failure-prone, it's a good idea to make this value as large as you can.

Finally, you have one more decision to make about your log buffer and files: What behavior should they follow when a COMMIT is issued? The `innodb_flush_log_at_trx_commit` setting offers the following alternatives:

- **Immediate flush to disk**—This is the safest approach: A setting of 1 means that as soon as InnoDB receives a COMMIT statement, it immediately flushes (that is, synchronizes) the memory-based log buffer and the disk-based log file.

- **Slightly delayed flushing to disk**—Setting this value to either 0 or 2 introduces a minimal delay into this process. When set to 0, the log buffer is written to disk every second, rather than when a transaction is committed. A setting of 2 means that a COMMIT forces a log buffer to log file write, but the log file is not written to disk unless a second has passed.

Log File Monitoring and Tuning

After sizing and configuring your logs, how can you determine if they are working optimally? As you saw earlier, beginning with version 5.0.2, MySQL AB has introduced numerous server status variables that make it much easier for administrators to gather the necessary statistics to make informed decisions about all aspects of their InnoDB environment, including the status of their logs. Using the MySQL Administrator, you can create a graph that pays particular attention to log file activity, as shown in Figure 12.4.

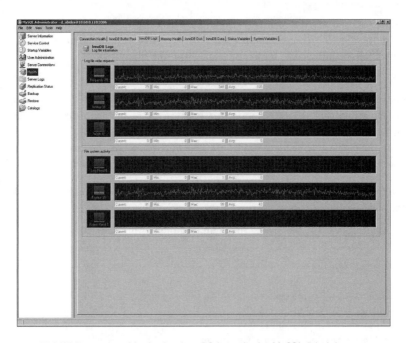

FIGURE 12.4   Monitoring InnoDB logs via the MySQL Administrator.

What can we learn from these graphs? From top to bottom, they include the following:

- **Number of log write requests**—By tracking the changing value of innodb_log_write_requests, you can observe how frequently your applications are making requests to etch information in the log.

- **Number of log writes**—Just as the first graph tracks the log write requests, the innodb_log_writes indicator reports on actual writes. If you observe a significant lag between the first and second graph, there might be a logging bottleneck.

- **Number of log waits**—InnoDB increments the `innodb_log_waits` status variable each time it needs to wait before writing to the log buffer. What causes this problem, and how can it be corrected?

  The primary reason for excessive log wait events is that the log buffer is undersized relative to the amount of operations that need to be written into the log. This can happen when loading large volumes of information, or during any time of significant transactional activity.

  If this is the case in your environment, the simplest corrective action possible is to boost the `innodb_log_buffer` setting. If you're concerned about the extra memory that this requires and/or the potential for lost data in the event of a system failure, note that you can always change it back to a lower value when the heavy data modification operations are complete.

- **Logfile/operating system interaction**—Because the disk-based log files are the eventual destination of the data modifications first recorded in the log buffer, it's a good idea to monitor the interaction between InnoDB and the file system. The next set of graphs highlight this relationship.

  First, you can watch the changing number of pending writes to the log file via the `innodb_os_log_pending_writes` indicator. Because the `fsync()` function is responsible for the actual disk writes, the next two graphs track the actual and pending number of times this function is being called from moment-to-moment. The two indicators are `innodb_os_log_fsyncs` and `innodb_os_log_pending_fsyncs`, respectively.

Based on these indicators, this appears to be a well-running InnoDB installation, at least from the perspective of logging.

You can also use SHOW INNODB STATUS to get an idea of your log activity:

```
---
LOG
---
Log sequence number 3 3165436224
Log flushed up to    3 3165435546
Last checkpoint at   3 3163280023
1 pending log writes, 0 pending chkp writes
9917 log i/o's done, 5000.00 log i/o's/second
----------------------
```

InnoDB and Memory

This section cites ways to configure, monitor, and tune InnoDB's advanced memory-based buffering and caching capabilities for optimal performance.

Buffer Pool

Most modern database servers take advantage of system memory to increase performance by reducing and/or delaying the amount of interaction with the much slower disk drives. InnoDB is no exception: Its buffer pool offers sophisticated data analysis and caching algorithms that translate to significant response enhancements.

The buffer pool contains many internal structures that determine what information is placed in the cache, how it is synchronized to disk, and what should be removed from the cache. The design and details of these internals are beyond the scope of this book, but it's important to understand that they exist and play a vital role in augmenting database speed.

Database administrators set a number of key server variables that control the overall size of the buffer pool, along with its behavior. The following sections look at how to configure, monitor, and tune this essential module.

Buffer Pool Configuration

The server variable that controls the amount of memory to be allocated to the buffer pool is `innodb_buffer_pool_size`. How much memory should you apportion to your buffer pool? The conventional wisdom ranges from 50% to 80% of all available memory, which is a good starting point. However, before picking a value, you should ponder several key considerations:

- **Server purpose**—You can safely allocate more memory to the buffer pool if your server is dedicated to MySQL. On the other hand, if your server is tasked with many responsibilities (for example, web server, application server, development, and so on), you should be careful not to consume more memory than is absolutely necessary.

- **Overall available system memory**—Even if your server is dedicated to MySQL, memory is still a finite resource. Devoting up to 80% of available RAM to the buffer pool can place a heavy tax on overall system responsiveness.

- **Processing profile**—A write-intensive database server has very different buffer pool needs than one that primarily retrieves information. This is one reason why it's so important to monitor your buffer pool; you might discover that you have allocated excessive memory to this cache, which penalizes other aspects of your server.

  If you're faced with the need to load a large amount of data, you might also decide to temporarily boost this value until after the load is complete.

- **Storage engine mix**—Finally, as you go about the task of deciding on a buffer pool size, it's vital that you consider your environment's unique blend of storage engines. For example, if you are heavily skewed toward the MyISAM storage engine, allocating abundant memory to the InnoDB buffer pool doesn't help things at all. In fact, it might make them worse. It's easy to imagine a scenario in which the InnoDB buffer and memory pool vie with the MyISAM key cache and all-purpose query cache.

Conversely, an InnoDB-intensive situation warrants an extra dose of buffer pool memory, but this might also cause conflict with other caches; this is especially true when the other caches themselves are oversized relative to their actual workload.

After settling on a buffer pool size, you then need to manage additional necessities for this cache. Given that the buffer pool is the main in-memory cache for InnoDB index and data information, two important requirements spring to mind:

- It's vital that altered pages are periodically persisted to disk. Otherwise, data will be lost if the system is unexpectedly shut down.

- There must be room in the pool for new data/index information to be loaded from disk and/or entered by user interaction with the database.

The `innodb_max_dirty_pages_pct` server variable helps satisfy both of these obligations. With a range from 0 to 100, it instructs the primary InnoDB thread to synchronize (that is, flush) dirty pages to disk. For example, if set to 80, InnoDB does not allow more than 80% of the pages in the buffer pool to be marked as dirty. Instead, it flushes enough pages to bring the dirty page percentage in line with this parameter.

However, in reality, it's fairly unlikely that adjusting this setting will make much of a difference in resolving a performance bottleneck. For example, if your system is configured with insufficient memory for the computing tasks at hand, the buffer pool page contention issue that you are attempting to address with this parameter is merely a symptom of the underlying problem: inadequate memory for the server's processing load.

In recent years, Microsoft introduced enhanced virtual memory capabilities into its server-side operating system. Known as Address Windowing Extensions (AWE), it gives administrators access to substantially larger amounts of memory than the previous limit of 4GB.

To make this memory available to the InnoDB buffer pool, just set the `innodb_buffer_pool_awe_mem_mb` to the amount of additional memory that you want to use, with a limit of 64GB.

Chapter 10, "General Server Performance and Parameters Tuning," explains the differences among MySQL's in-memory caches. Recall that in addition to the buffer pool, InnoDB also employs a cache (known as the memory cache) to accumulate RAM-based information about database structure as well as other internal details.

As an administrator, you have control over the size of this cache by setting the `innodb_additional_mem_pool_size` parameter. If you are running a very large and/or complex database and insufficient memory is assigned to the memory cache, MySQL requisitions supplementary memory from the operating system. In most cases, however, the out-of-the-box default value should suffice.

Buffer Pool Monitoring and Tuning

To help give you a better idea of how well your buffer pool is being used, you can create a collection of custom MySQL Administrator graphs that use the status variables introduced in version 5.0.2, as shown in the following two examples. The first explores a number of buffer pool–specific indicators, whereas the second reports on InnoDB page and row operations.

To begin, Figure 12.5 shows an example of monitoring a 256MB buffer pool's state just after InnoDB has started, but prior to any activity.

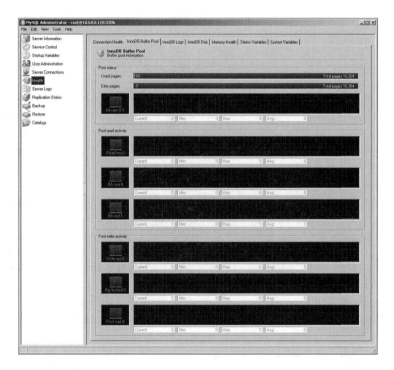

FIGURE 12.5   Monitoring a quiet InnoDB buffer pool.

Because the next part of this chapter also refers to this custom MySQL Administrator graph, take a moment to explore its components. From top to bottom, they include the following:

- **Buffer pool used pages**—This bar graph tracks the value of `innodb_buffer_pool_pages_data` (the total number of pages in use) versus the total amount of available buffer pool space, represented by `innodb_buffer_pool_pages_total`.

  Notice how much space is available in the buffer pool after starting the server, but before any activity. At this point, any used pages are controlled by InnoDB for its own internal purposes.

- **Dirty pages in the buffer pool**—Recall that a dirty buffer pool page is simply a page where the underlying data or index has been modified, so it must eventually be written

back to disk to preserve database integrity. This is tracked via
`innodb_buffer_pool_pages_dirty`, again comparing it to the total amount of space in
the buffer pool: `innodb_buffer_pool_pages_total`.

- **Buffer pool hit rate**—This is a very important graph, one that serves as the foundation
  of determining whether the buffer pool is sized correctly for your needs. The formula
  used for this graph is as follows:

  100-(100*(^[`innodb_pages_read`]/

  ^[`innodb_buffer_pool_read_requests`]))

  What does this mean? This simply tracks the proportion of page reads that were satis-
  fied by examining the buffer pool, rather than by going to disk.

  A high value means that MySQL was frequently able to find what it needed from the
  buffer pool; a lower number shows that the buffer pool did not contain the necessary
  data as often as possible. Some examples of buffer pool hit rates are shown a little later
  in this chapter.

- **Buffer pool read requests**—This graph monitors the changes from moment to
  moment of the `innodb_buffer_pool_read_requests` value. It helps you to see if you are
  experiencing spikes or lulls in demand for access to information in the buffer pool.

- **Buffer pool sequential read-ahead activity**—As you saw earlier, InnoDB offers
  sophisticated algorithms to determine if a program is requesting significant amounts of
  sequential data, typically via a table scan. To monitor this activity, you can check the
  relative values of the `innodb_buffer_pool_read_ahead_seq` status variable. A rising trend
  means that InnoDB is performing more table scans.

- **Buffer pool random read-ahead activity**—InnoDB's read-ahead algorithm is also useful when the user is requesting large amounts of nonsequential information. You can
  monitor this by watching the value of `innodb_buffer_pool_read_ahead_rnd`.

- **Write requests into the buffer pool**—To examine the relative rates of buffer pool
  modifications, you can track the continually changing values of the
  `innodb_buffer_pool_write_requests` status variable.

- **Buffer pool pages flushed**—As discussed earlier, MySQL periodically synchronizes
  pages from the buffer pool to disk: This ensures that data is not lost. To watch the relative amounts of page synchronization activity, you can screen the value of
  `innodb_buffer_pool_pages_flushed`.

- **Number of waits for space in the buffer pool**—If there is insufficient space in the
  buffer pool, InnoDB needs to wait until a buffer pool flush event has occurred before it
  can write information onto a newly freed page. The `innodb_buffer_pool_wait_free` status variable counts the number of times this type of undesirable episode has happened.
  A high value here means that your buffer pool is undersized for your needs.

  The error log receives a message similar to the following one if InnoDB has repeated
  difficulty in finding free blocks in the buffer pool:

```
061230 15:55:47InnoDB: Warning: difficult to find free blocks from
InnoDB: the buffer pool (285 search iterations)! Consider
InnoDB: increasing the buffer pool size.
InnoDB: It is also possible that in your Unix version
InnoDB: fsync is very slow, or completely frozen inside
InnoDB: the OS kernel. Then upgrading to a newer version
InnoDB: of your operating system may help. Look at the
InnoDB: number of fsyncs in diagnostic info below.
InnoDB: Pending flushes (fsync) log: 0; buffer pool: 0
InnoDB: 241586 OS file reads, 279151 OS file writes, 48757 OS fsyncs
InnoDB: Starting InnoDB Monitor to print further
InnoDB: diagnostics to the standard output.
```

If you prefer character-oriented utilities, you can run SHOW INNODB STATUS. The section of its results that's relevant for the buffer pool is as follows:

```
BUFFER POOL AND MEMORY
----------------------
Total memory allocated 317682874; in additional pool allocated 1529728
Buffer pool size    16384
Free buffers        1
Database pages      16298
Modified db pages  57
Pending reads 63
Pending writes: LRU 0, flush list 2, single page 0
Pages read 343297, created 572, written 22277
1.00 reads/s, 0.00 creates/s, 0.00 writes/s
Buffer pool hit rate 999 / 1000
```

In Figure 12.6, a collection of heavy read-oriented processes is started; you can examine what things look like in the buffer pool.

A second group of graphs, which focus on InnoDB page and row access, are shown in Figure 12.7.

This second page tracks the following indicators:

- **Pages created**—The innodb_pages_created status variable tells us how many pages InnoDB is creating within the buffer pool. These pages are created when you insert new data or index values. Being interested in the trend, you can track relative values.

- **Pages read**—The innodb_pages_read status variable was described earlier. Recall that its purpose is to track the number of pages that InnoDB was able to find in the buffer pool; relative values are tracked here as well.

- **Pages written**—InnoDB increments the innodb_pages_written counter each time it writes (and then flushes) an InnoDB page.

- **Rows inserted/read/updated/deleted** —These important indicators are tracked by watching the innodb_rows_inserted, innodb_rows_read, innodb_rows_updated, and innodb_rows_deleted status variables, respectively.

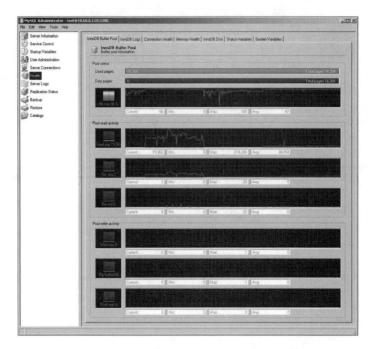

FIGURE 12.6   Buffer pool activity for a read-intensive server load.

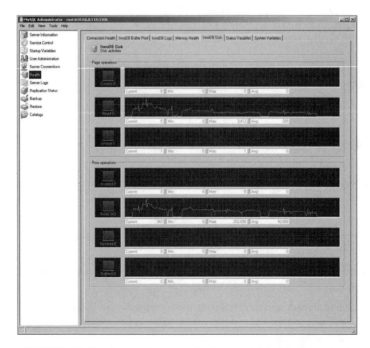

FIGURE 12.7   Page and row activity for a read-intensive server load.

The SHOW INNODB STATUS command generates a character-based counterpart to these graphs:

```
--------------
ROW OPERATIONS
--------------
8 queries inside InnoDB, 0 queries in queue
Main thread process no. 7818, id 1839139760, state: sleeping
Number of rows inserted 10552, updated 0, deleted 0, read 14515057
5000.00 inserts/s, 0.00 updates/s, 0.00 deletes/s, 9000.00 reads/s
----------------------------
```

Observe that the graphs correctly reflect the heavy read activity on the server, whereas all indications of write activity are quiescent. You can see good buffer pool cache hits, especially when InnoDB is performing large, sequential read operations (particularly prevalent on the left one third of the graphs).

Although you can see a good hit rate, if this was the typical activity profile for your server, it might be worthwhile to boost the size of the buffer pool to allow even more pages to be cached. However, make sure to let your statistics accumulate over a meaningful period of time before finalizing this kind of change.

To balance the load, you can introduce a collection of database processes that perform significant amounts of data alterations, as shown in Figure 12.8.

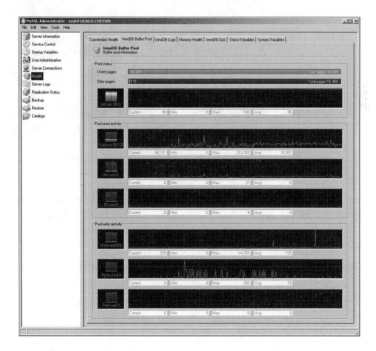

FIGURE 12.8   Buffer pool activity from a more balanced server load.

Things are still going well: The buffer pool cache hit rate remains very high, pages are being synchronized to disk regularly, and there have been no waits for the buffer pool to be flushed. With a consistent hit rate of 99%, in fact, you might even be able to reduce buffer pool memory if it didn't significantly lower the caching percentage. Again, however, it's important to let enough time pass before making such a change.

Finally, you can completely flip the processing profile of your server by converting its primary workload into CREATE/UPDATE/DELETE operations, as shown in Figure 12.9.

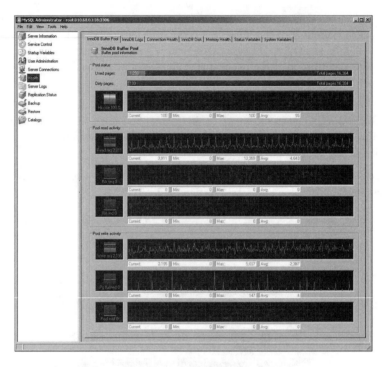

FIGURE 12.9   Buffer pool activity for a write-intensive server load.

The buffer pool cache rate is high, but observe how there aren't many used pages in the cache. Assuming that this pattern holds up over time, this is a good indicator of a situation in which a relatively small amount of data is heavily accessed (and consequently placed into the buffer pool) to support other operations.

A good example of this kind of scenario is a lookup table that drives data alterations in other tables. If this was the typical profile of your server, you could probably reduce the size of the buffer pool given its underutilization. Meanwhile, the write performance appears optimal: Page flushing is proceeding normally, and there have been no wait states on the buffer pool.

The previous three examples all show a well-configured, smooth-running buffer pool. How can you tell if you should alter your buffer pool settings? There are several key symptoms that indicate a problem:

- **Very low buffer pool cache hit rate**—Generally, but not always, a consistently low value for this indicator means that InnoDB is laboring harder than necessary: Instead of finding information in the superefficient buffer pool, it must perform the time-consuming task of retrieving data from the disk. If you can spare the memory, it is wise to augment the buffer pool with more resources and then carefully monitor the cache hit rate, along with any possible side effects.

  Unfortunately, if your database is very large, and/or features hard-to-predict access patterns, you might have to accept that your cache hit rates may never get very high.

- **Very high buffer pool cache hit rate**—Paradoxically, a consistent, very high (95%+) buffer pool cache hit rate might mean that you've allocated too much memory. Because memory is never free, you might be shortchanging other equally needy structures, such as the key cache, query cache, or the operating system itself. If any of these other system components are complaining of insufficient memory, consider gradually decreasing the amount of memory dedicated to the buffer pool.

  Of course, another explanation for the sky-high hit rate might be that your databases are simply relatively small in comparison to available memory. In this case, you might just have to accept your good fortune.

- **Excessive buffer pool waits**—The `innodb_buffer_pool_wait_free` indicator lets us know how many times InnoDB's buffer pool access threads had to pause while awaiting already-resident pages to be flushed to disk.

  If you observe a steadily (or rapidly) rising value for this server status variable, it's likely an indicator that you are shortchanging your buffer pool; slowly increasing its size is a good idea.

An Alternative to the Buffer Pool

Before leaving the subject of the InnoDB buffer pool, it's worth taking a moment to discuss one possible alternative to using InnoDB tables and their associated buffer pool: MEMORY tables.

These types of tables (formerly known as HEAP) are discussed during Chapter 4, "Designing for Speed." Recall that they are extremely fast and based completely in memory. Although they have numerous restrictions and limitations that keep the number of potential replacement scenarios relatively low, one very useful situation in which you can substitute them for InnoDB tables is when you have large, static lookup tables that you want to be always present in memory.

For example, suppose you are building an application that will rely on a very large, relatively unchanging table to provide lookup values. You are concerned that because of heavy system activity, it's likely that data from this table will frequently be pushed out of the buffer pool to make room for other information, thereby slowing the application. Under these circumstances, you could permanently store the underlying data in an InnoDB or MyISAM table, and then load a corresponding MEMORY table when your server boots, application starts, and so on. Your application clients would then look to this MEMORY table to find their lookup values. Assuming that there's sufficient memory to both store all data and index information in the MEMORY table and, thereby, avoid swapping or other resource contention, all necessary lookup data will be resident in memory.

InnoDB Operational Control

Before leaving the chapter on InnoDB tuning tips, this section takes some time to explore some additional operational-specific settings that you can use to regulate server responsiveness.

Thread Performance

MySQL uses the `innodb_thread_concurrency` setting to gate the number of simultaneous active operating system threads supporting the InnoDB engine. With a default value of 8, it usually can be left alone. However, if you are running a database server with a combined total of greater than eight CPUs and disk drives, try boosting this value to match the sum of these critical components.

By raising the setting, you are instructing MySQL to request additional threads. However, these supplementary threads aren't fully utilized if there aren't sufficient CPUs and disk drives.

Improving Concurrency

You completed a holistic review of concurrency, locking, and transactions during Chapter 9. Recall that newer MySQL versions are more adept at detecting and correcting deadlocks. However, if you are running an older version, MySQL relies on the `innodb_lock_wait_timeout` setting, specified in seconds, to help it determine when a deadlock is under way.

If you believe that your older MySQL server is particularly susceptible to these kinds of problems, try lowering the value to cause deadlocks to be discovered and fixed sooner, or, even better: Take the time to upgrade to a newer version.

Improving Large-Scale Operations

Chapter 15, "Improving Import and Export Operations," cites numerous ways to help coax added performance from these costly processes. For now, there are a few key things to remember:

- You can specify that your MySQL data export process generate relatively few (but very fast) multirow `INSERT` statements rather than a large collection of traditional single-row `INSERT` statements.

- Data-loading speed is significantly better if your input file is already sorted in primary key order.

- Whenever possible, disable expensive foreign key and unique checks when loading large volumes of data into InnoDB. To do this, set `FOREIGN_KEY_CHECKS` and `UNIQUE_CHECKS` to zero.

- Automatically committed transactions are expensive: They require frequent, costly disk flushes. For large-scale data load operations, remember to set `AUTOCOMMIT` to zero.

Speeding Up Shutdown

You should note one final topic regarding InnoDB-specific performance. When enabled (the default), the `innodb_fast_shutdown` parameter instructs InnoDB to bypass the potentially expensive tasks of purging internal memory structures and then merging insert buffers. This does not affect data integrity; InnoDB still inscribes any pertinent buffer pool pages onto disk.

Improving Disk Speed

This book has continually pointed out the benefits of rapidly processing information in memory whenever possible, rather than incurring the higher costs of disk interaction. However, eventually the piper must be paid, and the disk must be accessed. This chapter discusses a number of steps that administrators can take to keep these performance-draining disk charges as low as possible.

The chapter is divided into three major sections. The first provides general (that is, MySQL storage engine and operating system–neutral) suggestions on how to accelerate disk performance. The next section presents MyISAM and InnoDB-specific recommendations for getting the most out of your disk drives. Finally, the chapter closes with a collection of operating system–specific ideas on reducing disk overhead.

General Suggestions

The following suggestions are grouped together because of their cross-platform, cross database engine validity.

Deploying the Fastest Possible Disk Drives

Although the cost per gigabyte for disk drives continues to plunge, there are still price premiums for faster drives in any storage capacity compared to their more lethargic cousins. As you plan out your hardware purchase or upgrade, carefully consider making the investment in drives with lower seek times than average. Although you pay more initially, the return on investment is quite dramatic; a slower disk drive continually hurts performance.

Configuring Memory Caches Correctly

It seems self-evident, but the best way to reduce the cost of disk access is to simply reduce or eliminate as much disk access as possible. MySQL's specialized memory caches do an excellent job of letting the database server spend more time working within memory-based structures rather than having to continually interact with the disk drive.

Any MySQL administrator who is serious about improving disk performance (or any other type of performance, for that matter) should take the time to learn more about MySQL's memory caches, including their configuration, monitoring, and management. These topics are all covered in detail in Chapters 10, 11, and 12 ("General Server Performance and Parameters Tuning," "MyISAM Performance Enhancement," and "InnoDB Performance Enhancement," respectively).

Implementing a RAID Strategy

A redundant array of independent (or inexpensive, depending on your budget) disks (RAID) lets administrators spread the processing load among multiple disk drives, while also helping to reduce the risk of catastrophic data loss should something happen to a particular disk drive.

It's best to think of RAID as a collection of different disk usage strategies, rather than a single, monolithic technology. Multiple classes, or levels, of RAID usage are available.

It stands to reason that because disk access is usually the most expensive and time-consuming portion of a database-driven application, anything you can do to reduce or optimize these operations translates into dramatic benefits. By spreading the load among multiple drives, RAID technology helps to diminish the inevitable blockages caused by disk operations.

RAID is actually the tip of the iceberg when it comes to modern, sophisticated fault tolerance and disk performance enhancement technologies. Numerous additional options are at your disposal, including the following:

- Storage area networks (SAN)/Network area storage (NAS)
- Journaling file systems
- Logical volume management

These technologies typically coexist with RAID, although they might not be aware of each other. Rather than embarking on an extensive storage review, this chapter stays focused on RAID.

As an administrator, you have a number of decisions to make when implementing a RAID strategy. The following sections look at the various RAID levels, as well as situations in which they are most appropriate. A little later, this chapter covers methods of spreading the load among multiple disk drives without employing a RAID strategy.

RAID 0

Also known as disk striping, this RAID level simply divides data among two or more disk drives that appear as a single unit to the application. The primary benefit of RAID level 0 is the load balancing brought about by spreading the work among multiple drives. However, serious data loss is likely if even one of the level 0 disk drives is damaged.

If you already have an effective replication and backup strategy in place, RAID 0 might suffice for a significant portion of your data. This level ensures faster performance, and your replication/backup policies mean that you will have a way to restore information should you experience a severe disk failure.

In summary, RAID 0 provides an easy-to-implement load balancing strategy that is unfortunately hampered by its lack of true fault tolerance.

RAID 1

Commonly referred to as mirroring or duplexing, RAID level 1 sees all disk writes to a particular drive copied to all other appropriate drives in the RAID set. For example, if there are four disks (identified as A through D), when information is written to disk A, RAID level 1 means that drives B, C, and D also receive mirrored copies of this data.

These extra writes add some performance overhead, but this is more than offset by RAID level 1's enhanced data security. In addition, read operations (which make up the bulk of most database applications) can be split among these drives, also yielding increased speed. Some installations feature a dedicated channel (known as "disk duplexing") among the drives in the RAID set, which offers even better performance and security capabilities.

In summary, RAID 1 is the simplest RAID storage subsystem architecture; it also incurs the highest disk overhead of all RAID configurations.

This RAID level is a good choice for data that would be lost forever in the event of a disk failure. However, the next RAID level represents the best choice.

RAID 0+1

As its name implies, this RAID level takes the performance benefits of RAID 0 and combines them with the data security features of RAID 1. The result is a fast and secure solution, especially tailored for those environments that see large, sequential database loads.

This speed and data safekeeping comes at a price: the financial outlay to buy the extra disks necessary to keep copies of the data. However, the cost per gigabyte of disk drives continues to plummet, so the financial impact of this approach is ever-decreasing.

Several other combinations and permutations of RAID levels are availble, but RAID 0, 1, and 0+1 are the most relevant for this book's purposes.

Implementing RAID

After deciding to deploy a RAID implementation, your next step is to establish the exact strategy that you will follow. Again, administrators must choose among several options:

- **Hardware-based RAID**—Numerous RAID-aware disk controllers are on the market today. These controllers are usually more expensive than standard devices, and are typically closed solutions, meaning that they aren't easily portable among different systems. However, they do provide increased speed and simplicity.

- **Operating system software-based RAID**—Choosing this kind of RAID strategy entails using either built-in or add-on software that is tied very closely to your particular operating system. This is usually less expensive than the cost of acquiring specialized controllers and fast disk drives. In fact, it's often possible to let older, less-expensive disks participate in this type of configuration. However, these price and flexibility benefits can translate into some additional configuration work for the administrator.

- **MySQL software-based RAID**—If your build of MySQL supports it, you can instruct MySQL to divvy a MyISAM table's data among multiple disk files by supplying values for the RAID_TYPE portion of the CREATE TABLE statement. This effectively implements a RAID strategy unbeknownst to the operating system or hardware, and is primarily useful when attempting to surmount disk file size limitations that can affect your environment. Realistically, if you want RAID, you should choose between the hardware and operating system–based approaches described previously.

Distributing Temporary Directories

You just learned how executing a well-planned RAID strategy can distribute the disk process load among multiple storage devices. As you saw, however, setting up a RAID configuration requires some planning and careful action to ensure success. Luckily, when it comes to temporary files, administrators have a fast, easy way to distribute these files among multiple drives, regardless of whether RAID is in place.

Commencing with MySQL 4.1, the tmpdir server variable lets you instruct MySQL to use, in a round-robin fashion, a collection of devices for its temporary file needs. Before embarking on this journey, however, make sure that the drives cited when you configure this variable are indeed on separate disks. Otherwise, this alteration will have minimal performance benefits because you really haven't distributed the load.

MyISAM Suggestions

For administrators supporting MyISAM-based tables, a few simple, yet effective, disk performance-improvement strategies are worth exploring.

Symbolic Links

Spreading the disk-processing burden among multiple drives helps diminish the performance expense of relying on a single disk drive for all the work. Because MyISAM databases consist of individual file system–based objects, one way to achieve this distribution is to use symbolic links.

Symbolic links can apply to the entire database, in which case the database appears to be on one drive when it is, in fact, on another disk. For administrators on Linux or Unix, symbolic linking granularity can also be set lower, affecting individual tables and indexes.

Prior to version 4.0, symbolic links carried an increased risk of undesirable events if you inadvertently ran certain database maintenance operations, such as OPTIMIZE TABLE or ALTER TABLE. These risks are somewhat mitigated in newer versions, but symbolic links do require some thought when it comes to database management, particularly for backup and restore. You can even elect to place data and index files on the same drive, or separate them onto different hardware. In the absence of RAID, this latter strategy achieves maximum diffusion of information and is likely to be a very simple, yet responsive solution.

Table Compression

Although it's not a viable solution for all database applications, consider using the myisampack utility to compress tables containing read-only or infrequently updated information.

The performance benefits from this tactic typically accrue from the reduced amount of disk operations necessary to locate and retrieve a particular set of information, even taking the extra CPU costs of decompressing the data into account.

InnoDB Suggestions

As part of its sophisticated database management capabilities, InnoDB offers numerous internal disk performance-enhancing features. However, there are still several steps that administrators can take to squeeze additional disk speed from their InnoDB instance.

Choosing the Right autoextend Setting

Chapter 12 cited InnoDB's ability to request additional chunks of disk space from the operating system when growth necessitates expansion. The autoextend variable (from my.cnf) or innodb_autoextend_increment setting (available in the 4.0 products in version 4.0.24 and the 4.1 products in version 4.1.5) specifies the size of this supplementary storage. However, its default of 8MB is quite low for many of today's data-intensive applications.

The danger of making this value too low is that your last tablespace file can end up with dozens of 8MB segments of disk storage scattered across the entire drive. Solving this avoidable splintering requires a time-consuming and user-inconveniencing full disk defragmentation. A better choice is to spell out a more realistic value for this setting when creating the tablespace. At worst, stipulating too large a value wastes disk space, which is generally a better risk than facing the discomfort of defragmenting a tablespace.

Using Raw Devices

MySQL allows you to allocate raw disk partitions for use in an InnoDB tablespace. What exactly is a raw disk partition? How does it correspond to a "normal" disk partition? How can you decide between the two?

Unlike a "normal" disk partition, which has been set up in accordance with the rules of the operating system, a raw disk partition is simply a section of disk that has not been formatted to the standards imposed by an operating system. From the viewpoint of the operating system, it is simply an unallocated disk drive, or even just a sector of a drive. This anonymity lets MySQL bypass the standard operating system calls to the file system, which can result in better speed.

From a purely performance perspective, raw partitions are better than standard disk partitions for at least two key reasons:

- **Lower overhead**—Raw partitions let MySQL bypass all of the necessary, yet time-consuming, operating system mechanisms that typically are involved when reading or writing data on a standard partition. This reduced overhead should benefit your applications.

- **Contiguous disk space**—As described in several places in this chapter and entire book, disk fragmentation taxes system response and is to be avoided. However, by definition, a raw partition's disk space is contiguous because there are no other entities or processes to claim a portion of the partition, inserting their own proprietary information into the mix.

Because nothing in life is free, there are costs associated with raw partitions. Paradoxically, the biggest cost is complexity: It simply requires more planning and thought to carve out a chunk of disk space and "hide" it from the operating system than to simply give the entire disk over for it to manage. In addition, a raw partition, if not managed and secured correctly, could be overwritten at any time by another administrator, or even a user with extra permissions. Generally, operating systems do a decent job of blocking such gross data alterations on those partitions that are under operating system control. For raw partitions, that job falls to you, the administrator.

Alternative Disk Writing Methods

Recall from Chapter 12's discussion on InnoDB architecture and optimization that InnoDB leverages a collection of memory-based structures to increase concurrency and performance. Periodically, these structures are synchronized (that is, flushed) to disk, thereby making any data alterations permanent.

Administrators employing Linux or Unix can tune the `innodb_flush_method` setting to specify the method InnoDB will take when flushing data to disk. Normally, InnoDB uses the `fsync()` system call to handle this work. However, benchmarks on a variety of Linux and Unix platforms suggest that altering this setting to other values (`O_DSYNC` or `O_DIRECT`) can improve InnoDB's interactions with the file system.

Unfortunately, other benchmarks and tests suggest possible issues when moving away from the default `fsync()` operation, so alter this setting only after careful experimentation and after backing up your information.

Table Defragmentation

In several earlier chapters, this book described the burdens disk fragmentation imposes upon performance. MyISAM offers the myisamchk utility to defragment tables; what choices are available to InnoDB administrators?

Aside from the many operating system–based defragmentation tools (which usually affect the entire disk drive or segment), or the OPTIMIZE TABLE statement explored in Chapter 6, "Understanding the MySQL Optimizer," InnoDB administrators can use either the ALTER TABLE statement or data export/import to achieve table-level defragmentation.

For example, suppose that you have a very dynamic table, one that sees abundant data modification each day. Because its usage pattern is so active, you suspect it has become fragmented.

Issuing a simple ALTER TABLE statement:

```
ALTER TABLE customer_master ENGINE = INNODB;
```

instructs MySQL to rebuild the table, squeezing out any fragmentation in the process. Be aware that if the table uses a different storage engine, this statement will now switch its storage to InnoDB. You can monitor the progress of this operation via MySQL's traditional management tools, as shown in Figure 13.1.

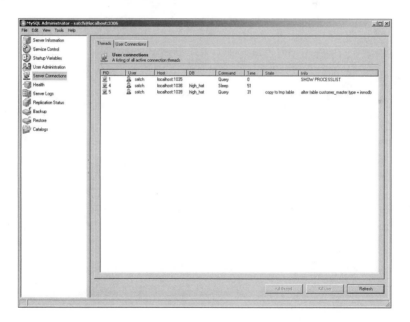

FIGURE 13.1   InnoDB table defragmentation in process.

This job takes quite a while for tables of any significant size. Note that data is still available for queries while the table is being rebuilt, although it's likely that access to the table will be much slower than normal.

Unloading the table via `mysqldump` and then reloading it is a more involved path to the same result.

Operating System–Specific Disk Suggestions

After configuring your MySQL instance, you have one more step on your quest toward the fastest disk setup possible. This section closes the chapter by looking at the interplay between MySQL and the two most popular operating systems (Linux/Unix and Microsoft Windows), particularly as related to disk responsiveness.

Linux/Unix Suggestions

As you will see in a moment, there are a collection of steps that Linux/Unix administrators can take to boost performance. However, a word of warning: If used improperly, these suggestions can hurt responsiveness or, even worse, data integrity.

Using `hdparm`

Used to check and set a variety of disk access parameters, the `hdparm` command can be of use for those installations running Linux with ATA or (E)IDE drives. Administrators can customize any of the following performance-affecting capabilities:

- Read-ahead
- Noise control
- Power management
- Defect detection and management
- Sector modes
- Read-only
- Benchmarking

As is the case with any advanced, low-level alteration, this command has the potential to do damage (to both system response and data) as well as good, so be sure to save a complete copy of your data before embarking on any amendments, and only make one change at a time.

File System Options

The `mount` command offers a number of options that you can use to coax some additional performance from your disks:

- **Asynchronous capability**—Asynchronous access is usually faster, and can be enabled via the `-o async` option.
- **Disabled time stamping**—Use the `-o noatime` setting to eliminate the work involved in updating the file access time stamps.

- **Integrity checking**—You can control startup integrity checking for the ext2 file system type via the check option.

- **Journaling**—The ext3 file system has a number of mount commands that affect journaling behavior.

Windows Suggestions

For graphically minded administrators, Windows servers offer a number of helpful utilities to clean, tune, and otherwise speed up your disk drives.

Disk Cleanup

During the course of normal system activity, it's likely that your disk drives will become cluttered with unneeded files. These files can be by-products of software installation, operating system upgrades, or any number of other temporary activities. Although these files don't directly affect performance, it's a good idea to periodically remove them from your system.

The Disk Cleanup utility can be of great help in finding and then deleting these extraneous files. This application can be found under the System Tools menu within the Accessories submenu. Before removing any files, it conducts a complete analysis of your system and then presents you with a report listing candidates for deletion (see Figure 13.2).

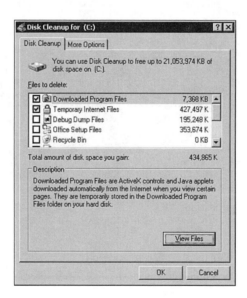

FIGURE 13.2   The Windows Disk Cleanup utility.

Defragmentation

Over time, information stored on your Windows-based server will become fragmented. This fragmentation adds an ever-increasing performance penalty to all applications that use data from the disk drive. Naturally, this includes MySQL. Most flavors of Windows now ship with a collection of helpful utilities and tools, including software to help restore order to your disk drives by reducing fragmentation.

To defragment your disks, choose the Disk Defragmenter option from within the Computer Management application. One useful feature of this utility is that it first analyzes your data and makes a recommendation before launching the potentially time-consuming task of defragmentation, as shown in Figures 13.3 and 13.4.

FIGURE 13.3   The Windows Disk Defragmenter.

Based on the combination of this analysis/recommendation and your own availability, you can make an informed decision about whether this is the right time to start the defragmentation process.

Finally, it's a good idea to include regular invocation of this application in your administrative tasks. Its frequency is very dependent on the levels of system and database activity that your site experiences.

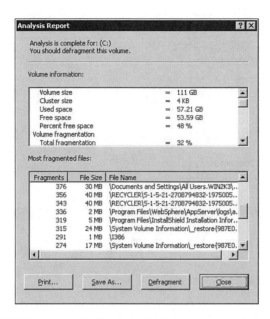

FIGURE 13.4   The Windows Disk Defragmenter analysis and recommendation.

Operating System, Web Server, and Connectivity Tuning

Most MySQL database servers are just one component in an overall computing strategy that depends on other advanced technologies, such as complex, modern operating systems, web servers, and application servers. In addition, all these computers rely on a network infrastructure to communicate with clients and among themselves.

This chapter reviews considerations for these ancillary technologies, particularly those that have significant consequences for MySQL responsiveness. The first section examines the interplay between the most popular MySQL-supporting operating system (Linux/Unix and Microsoft Windows), as well as how administrators can configure these operating systems to leverage faster throughput from MySQL.

Because web-based applications make up such a noteworthy portion of MySQL's installed base, the subsequent section looks at tips for setting up the right topography, one that efficiently mixes web and database servers. After the server topography is in place, this section continues onward, providing a series of tips for configuring web servers for optimal MySQL support, especially as related to environments that use PHP.

Finally, because distributed applications rely so heavily on connectivity, the chapter closes by explaining ways to reduce or optimize connections and their associated network traffic. This yields both faster applications as well as happier users.

Operating System Considerations

As the underlying platform upon which your MySQL database resides, it's imperative that your server operating system be as efficient as possible. This section examines ways to perk up the two most popular operating systems for MySQL servers: Linux/Unix and Microsoft Windows. Because discretion is the better part of valor, this book takes no sides and makes no attempt to broker or mediate the religious war between aficionados in each camp. Instead, it assumes that the reader has already made a decision. Actually, it's likely that many readers will be managing both flavors of operating system.

Assumptions

This book assumes that if you are tasked with administering a database server, you are familiar with the operating system–specific monitoring and management tools for your environment. For more details on these tools, see Chapter 2, "Performance Monitoring Options." In addition, it's a good idea to use these tools to help first get your computer to a stable, decently performing baseline prior to undertaking some of the MySQL-specific alterations described in this chapter.

Linux/Unix

In keeping with their commitment to open source solutions, many MySQL administrators have chosen to deploy their database servers on one of the many available flavors of the Linux operating system. Other administrators have instead opted for the Unix operating system.

Regardless of your choice of operating system, a number of variables are under your control that can help improve MySQL's performance on your platform. This section reviews these options, with the assumption that you do not want to make major kernel modifications. If you are inclined to embark on that path, check the MySQL website for a list of platform-specific kernel alterations.

Upgrading to a Recent Kernel

On Linux systems, MySQL relies on a number of key kernel features found in more recent versions. In the absence of these capabilities, your performance might be adversely affected. These kernel enhancements include the following:

- Multithreading support
- Exploiting symmetric multiprocessors
- SCI Sockets (for faster communication among clustered database servers)

If at all possible, it is wise to upgrade your kernel to at least version 2.4.

Disabling Unnecessary Services

In their understandable rush to move from operating system installation to production, many administrators choose default packages and values for their Linux or Unix platforms. Unfortunately, any time saved during installation is paid back with interest after the server goes live: Many unnecessary software packages have been installed, and numerous extraneous processes are now a permanent part of the server landscape.

These processes represent a perpetual tax on server response because administrators are often reluctant to break a working system to remove a potentially unneeded component. Consequently, think carefully before installing any of the following server packages or processes on your platform:

- Remote shell
- BIND
- DNS server
- FTP
- Mail

This list is far from comprehensive; there are loads of other candidates for elimination from your server. Take the time to excise them from the picture before going live.

Windows

Although Linux is often the first operating system that comes to mind when you think of a MySQL-based server, in fact Windows-based platforms represent a significant percentage of MySQL's installed base.

This section surveys a collection of tips that can help remove performance bottlenecks from any MySQL server hosted in a Windows environment.

Running the Right MySQL Server Process

In older (prior to version 4.1) releases of MySQL, Windows administrators had to take care to choose the correct server process for optimal MySQL performance. Things have been made simpler in more recent versions. Table 14.1 provides a list of factors to help you decide which version of the MySQL server process to launch.

TABLE 14.1   Selection Criteria for the MySQL Server Process

Feature	Process
InnoDB support, no debugging	mysqld
Windows NT, 2000, XP with named pipes	mysqld-nt
InnoDB plus BDB	mysqld-max
InnoDB plus BDB plus named pipes	mysqld-max-nt
Debug version, including InnoDB and BDB	mysqld-debug

Choosing the Right Operating System

Over time, Microsoft has released many variations of the Windows operating system. Some of these varieties are more appropriate than others for a relational database server such as MySQL. Whether you are purchasing and configuring a new computer, or repurposing an existing machine, try to select a Microsoft operating system designed to run as a server.

Microsoft also issues frequent Windows updates, often designed to address bugs, security gaps, and so on. After your server has been deployed, it's important to keep track of these patches.

Disabling Extraneous Services

When you install Windows, you are provided with many choices about what operating system components to enable. It's natural for a harried administrator to elect to install everything, rather than taking the time to carefully evaluate each option, just like their Linux- and Unix-administering peers. This can lead to a computer loaded with automatically launched services that add no value to a MySQL database, yet drain memory and CPU resources.

For example, look at the following small subset of available Windows services, and think if any of them would add any value to your database server:

- Bluetooth Support Service
- Universal Plug and Play Device Host
- Help and Support
- Infrared Monitor
- Office Source Engine

It's not an exaggeration to state that the preceding list of five services represents a tiny proportion of all of the potentially unnecessary Windows services. This can be especially dramatic if you have pressed a previously configured computer into service for MySQL: There might be dozens of unnecessary software packages and services already installed and running.

Watching Out for Spyware

In an ideal world, your Windows-based MySQL database server will run on its own pristine, dedicated machine, free from the distractions of other chores and activities. Unfortunately, in the real world, MySQL databases are often resident on machines that play many roles, not only that of a database server. The real world also sees rampant infestation of Windows-based computers with performance and privacy-damaging spyware.

If your database server computer is used for any web browsing at all, or if a user (perhaps you?) might have downloaded software from other sources, it's worth the time and effort to run one of the many free or commercially available utilities to check for spyware.

Web Server Performance Considerations

A very large percentage of MySQL AB's customer base combines MySQL database software along with the Apache web server and PHP scripting language to produce inexpensive, yet powerful web-based solutions. This section provides suggestions on how to enhance performance in these configurations. Because the Microsoft Internet Information Services (IIS) also sees heavy usage for web-based MySQL applications, this chapter also reviews performance-related tuning for that web server.

This section begins with server-independent topology, communication, and PHP configuration proposals before moving on to Apache-based and then IIS-centric suggestions.

Optimal web server design and PHP techniques merit their own, dedicated books. Consequently, this section simply attempts to provide easily implemented performance tips for these technologies; administrators who want to employ more sophisticated or specialized tuning strategies are encouraged to first make these simple alterations before embarking on that path.

In keeping with this book's attempt to service as broad-based a clientele as possible, this section does not spend much time exploring some of the more advanced (and potentially costly) load-balancing and caching products on the market, nor does it focus on purely web server performance–related issues.

Choosing the Right Server Topology

When designing your web and database server configuration, the first decision you face is where to run each of these important processes. For web servers that see relatively low hit rates, it might be sufficient to run both processes on the same hardware. However, even these small implementations benefit from a multi-CPU server; any division of labor can only help these CPU-intensive web and database server applications.

This single-computer topology will not scale for larger, more heavily trafficked sites. In these cases, it's imperative that you place the web and database servers on their own, dedicated machines. To reduce unnecessary overhead, you should also review the operating system configuration suggestions found earlier in this chapter.

Multiserver Configurations

When designing a multiserver topology, administrators often wonder how to determine the ratio of web to database servers that will yield optimal performance. The exact ratio is highly dependent on the usage patterns and site-specific stress levels that will be placed on the web and database servers, as well as the capacity of these computers. However, with these caveats in mind, it is still possible to provide some general guidelines on how to calculate the correct proportion of computing technologies.

An example of a well-designed, thorough study can be found at http://office.microsoft.com/en-us/assistance/HA011607741033.aspx. Although this capacity planning guide does not focus on MySQL, it does illustrate a solid methodology as well as the number of variables that should be taken into consideration when embarking on this kind of research.

In this case, the research shows that the optimal ratio of web to database servers is roughly 4:1. That is, for every four web servers, you should deploy a database server. Although total throughput can, of course, be increased by adding additional web and database servers, the ratio of these servers should remain at approximately 4:1. For example, if you want to utilize 12 web servers, you will need 3 database servers to preserve the 4:1 ratio.

Realistically, if your web application environment boasts more than 10 web or database servers, it's probably astute to look at either a commercial or open source load-balancing solution. You might also implement caching or other techniques to equitably divide the workload. Chapters 16 and 17 ("Optimal Replication" and "Optimal Clustering," respectively) review MySQL technologies designed to help in these kinds of situations.

Fast Interserver Communication

Regardless of your choice of web and database server topography, it's critical that the communication between these computers be as fast as possible. This means using the most rapid networking technologies that you can afford and taking any necessary steps to remove communication impediments.

For example, if your web and database servers are resident in the same facility, they should communicate on a speedy, dedicated local area network (LAN) using the fastest network cards possible. Broader wide area networks (WANs) should be avoided if feasible. Unless the communications among these computers is not secure, time-consuming encryption technology such as Secure Sockets Layer (SSL) should obviously be avoided.

General PHP Suggestions

Among its many uses, PHP has proven to be an enormously popular method of connecting web servers to MySQL databases. This section examines techniques you can use to improve PHP performance.

Correctly Building PHP

If you are building your PHP installation from source code, rather than downloading a binary distribution, you have several ways to improve performance when you compile your PHP instance, including the following:

- Disabling debugging, by including the `--disable-debug` option
- Allowing PHP to make inline optimizations by providing the `--enable-inline-optimization` directive
- Using shared memory sessions for PHP versions 4.20 and newer by specifying `--enable-mm=shared`

Correctly Configuring PHP

If your server-side PHP applications are likely to consume significant amounts of processor time or memory, it's essential that you configure your PHP initialization file correctly.

In particular, make sure that the `max_execution_time` configuration parameter is set to a large enough number to accommodate your likely CPU utilization. Otherwise, you (or an unhappy user) will eventually see a message that looks something like this:

```
[usr3292@DBSERVER3 apps]$ PHP Fatal error:  Maximum execution time of 3 seconds
exceeded in /apps/mysql/user_logger.php on line 41
```

Also, remember to allow for enough memory utilization by providing a good value for `memory_limit`. The following message indicates a PHP-based memory problem:

```
PHP Fatal error:  Allowed memory size of 256000 bytes exhausted
(tried to allocate 32000 bytes) in Unknown on line 0
```

Finally, if you have elected to use shared memory for session handling (see the earlier section about building PHP), make sure to add `session.save_handler=mm` to your PHP initialization file.

Caching PHP

A standard, unmodified PHP installation requires that before a given script can be run, the server must incur the overhead of accessing, loading, parsing, and, finally, compiling the script. These steps are taken because it's possible that a script might change between invocations. However, this is generally not the case in most situations. These costs can add up, especially for sites that see heavy traffic accessing a relatively small number of scripts.

To address this bottleneck, a number of commercial vendors and open source projects (including Zend, ionCube, and APC) have released products that cache PHP scripts. By caching scripts in shared memory, these offerings help reduce the load on the web server, allowing better throughput and higher client service levels. A collection of independent and vendor-provided studies have estimated that PHP performance can improve by more than 40% when this caching technology is employed.

If your environment sees heavy PHP workloads, it's worth your time to investigate the current state of the market for these tools.

Your PHP applications might also benefit from server-side cursors or prepared statements; both topics are discussed in Chapter 9, "Developing High-Speed Applications."

Apache/PHP Suggestions

With a market share approaching 70% (see http://news.netcraft.com/archives/web_server_survey.html for the latest statistics), Apache dominates the web server category. This section provides several ideas on how you can get more responsiveness out of your selection of this technology, especially when PHP is involved.

Before beginning, keep in mind that the right server topology (that is, the optimal balance of web and database servers) can go a long way toward reducing or even eliminating

Apache/PHP performance problems. If you haven't yet done so, it's a good idea to read that section of this chapter before starting your web server performance improvement odyssey.

Understanding Your Potential Bottlenecks

Your ability to tune an Apache/PHP environment is highly dependent on your unique processing profile. For sites that see heavy downloading of static HTML pages, the network is typically the bottleneck. Large, static, graphically heavy pages can consume vast amounts of bandwidth even though your web and database server might be underutilized; users might report a sluggish server when, in fact, the problem lies entirely with the network. Reducing the amount of graphics or taking any other steps to make these pages smaller should help take some of the burden off the network. HTML compression (built in to most modern browsers) can also be a factor in improving things.

On the other hand, a dynamically generated PHP-intensive environment can strain your CPU while your network goes virtually unused. For these situations, your best bet might be to make more use of static web pages, saving dynamic PHP page generation for only those situations in which it is absolutely necessary. Perhaps these pages can be generated on other servers or during off-hours. Adding extra processors can also be useful.

Clearly, before you can possibly remedy any Apache/PHP performance problems, you must understand where the problems lie. Fortunately, as you saw in Chapter 2, numerous tools are available that you can use to spot the bottleneck and then take action.

Upgrading to a Recent Version

It's logical to expect a continual stream of performance enhancements given the speed at which open source software improves. Apache is no exception to this rule. Before starting on a time-consuming optimization project, consider upgrading to a more recent version such as the 2.0 series.

Build Suggestions

If you are building your Apache instance from source code instead of downloading a binary, make sure that you only incorporate relevant and necessary modules for your site. Many administrators make the mistake of including too many of the dozens of potential Apache modules into their instance. If your compilation creates a static executable, these extra modules will make the executable larger.

Configuring Your Apache/PHP Environment

After you've set up the correct ratio of web and database servers and then downloaded and (optionally) built Apache and PHP, it's time to configure your environment for optimal performance.

Table 14.2 lists a number of important settings and parameters that impact the speed of your Apache/PHP instance.

TABLE 14.2   Performance-Affecting Apache/PHP Settings

Setting	Purpose
HostNameLookups	When enabled, this parameter instructs Apache to perform a potentially expensive reverse DNS lookup to resolve the client's IP address to a name. Unless this kind of data is vital for you, leaving it set to its default disabled value is a good idea.
KeepAlive	Later, this chapter discusses the costs associated with building and closing connections, both to the database server as well as the web server. Enabling this setting and then having clients request persistent connections can help reduce these costs by keeping sessions alive longer, rather than forcing the client to make repeated connections. Note that it only makes sense to use persistent connections when your web pages and other content are static.
KeepAliveTimeout	You just learned how persistent connections can yield better web server performance by allowing connections to remain active for longer amounts of time. However, if allowed to live too long, these idle yet persistent connections can squeeze out legitimate, active session requests. Setting this parameter to a reasonable value helps Apache close down truly idle sessions, freeing their resources for other users. The default value of 15 seconds might be fine for a web application that sees relatively frequent user activity (that is, intrasession navigation). However, some applications might require more user "think time"; in these situations, the default value might terminate a session that was not really idle. Estimating or observing representative usage patterns goes a long way toward identifying a reasonable value.
MaxKeepAliveRequests	In cases in which persistent connections have been chosen, this parameter places a cap on the number of keep alive requests a single connection can make. Be careful not to make it too low: Depending on your specific activity profiles, a value between 250 and 1,000 should suffice.
MaxClients	This parameter determines how many clients can connect to the web server at one time. For multithreaded Apache servers, this value affects the number of threads launched; it controls the number of child processes for nonthreading servers. For very busy sites, it's a good idea to gradually raise this value while keeping an eye on performance. If you decide to alter this parameter, you might also need to update the ServerLimit parameter.
MaxRequestsPerChild	This setting places a ceiling on the number of requests a child process or thread can serve before being terminated. It's smart to leave this value at its default of 1,000: There will likely be less child threads/processes remaining when system activity slows, and any problem threads/processes will disappear in short order.

Other Apache parameters of interest to administrators are `StartServers/StartThreads`, `MinSpareServers/MinSpareThreads`, and `MaxSpareServers/MaxSpareThreads`.

Internet Information Services (IIS)/PHP Tips

Although the combination of Apache and PHP represents the most frequently seen web server and scripting technology combination, there are sites running PHP in conjunction with IIS. This section describes several steps that administrators for these environments can take to increase overall performance.

Improving Common Gateway Interface (CGI) Performance

Typically, PHP on IIS makes use of the Common Gateway Interface (CGI). However, several traits of CGI (including its continual process creation) have been identified as performance bottlenecks. Fortunately, the FastCGI open source solution (available from PHP version 4.05) addresses many of these issues, leading to dramatic response advances.

As of version 4.3.0, standard PHP downloads (available from www.php.net) include the libraries for FastCGI. For the inquisitive, the FastCGI source code is also available from the same website. If you run heavy PHP volumes on IIS, it's a good idea to explore the benefits of incorporating FastCGI into your environment.

Tuning IIS

Microsoft offers a collection of helpful tools to control IIS performance. Although not directly correlated to PHP response, it's still worthwhile to briefly describe these features. Because the correct settings for these parameters is so dependent on your site-specific hardware, processing, and network bandwidth profiles, this book does not make blanket recommendations. Instead, use these tools as part of an overall performance enhancement strategy, and remember to continue to change only one variable at a time.

To begin, administrators can place a restriction on the amount of information flowing between clients and this web server (bandwidth throttling) as well as specify an upper limit to the number of active connections (see Figure 14.1).

Other important performance-related settings control how much time will pass before a session is terminated (connection timeout) as well as whether a user can invoke multiple, sequential requests within the same session (HTTP Keep-Alive). See Figure 14.2.

Earlier in this chapter, you saw how HTTP compression can help boost performance by reducing network traffic. IIS administrators can elect to compress both static and dynamic content (see Figure 14.3). One comprehensive study of the challenges and benefits of HTTP compression can be found at http://www-106.ibm.com/developerworks/web/library/wa-httpcomp/.

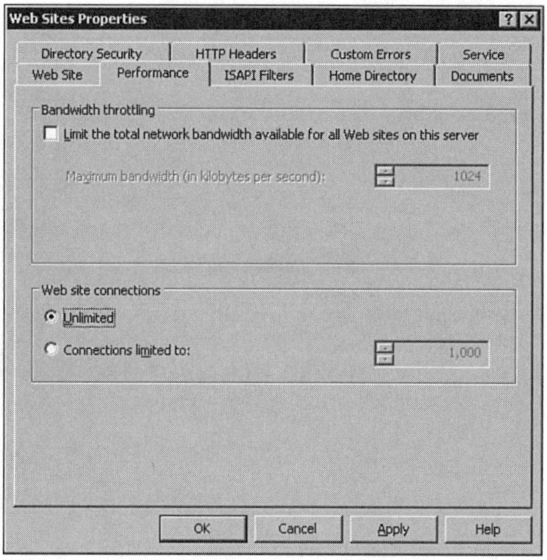

FIGURE 14.1   Setting limits on bandwidth and website connections.

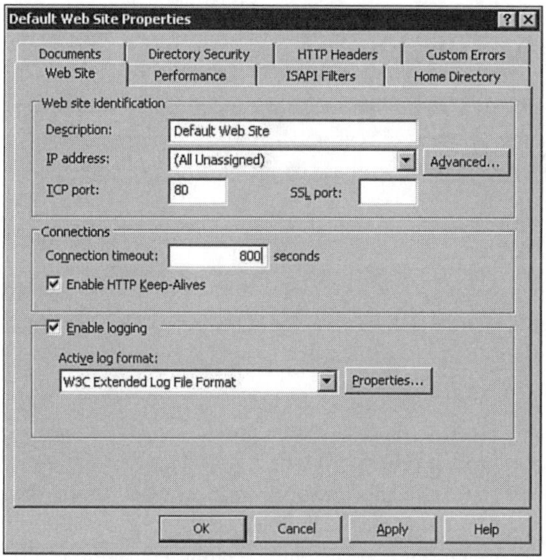

FIGURE 14.2   Setting connection timeout, enabling HTTP Keep Alive.

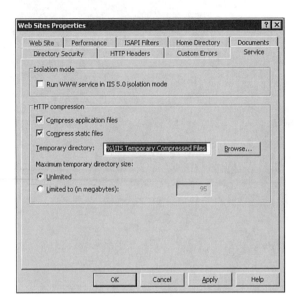

FIGURE 14.3   Enabling HTTP compression.

Connectivity Tuning

Chances are that your MySQL server does not exist in isolation; it's likely that other computers connect to it for a myriad of reasons, including accessing and updating information. This section examines ways to make these connections more efficient.

Protocol Choices

Depending on your platform, MySQL offers a number of different protocols for communication between clients and the database server. This section looks at each of these major choices, as well as when to employ them for optimal speed.

TCP/IP

So much of today's computing relies on TCP/IP that it's natural that the first choice of many administrators is to turn to this protocol. In most cases, this is the right choice. In fact, it is the only choice if the database client and server are not resident on the same machine. Even if they are on the same machine, computers running certain older versions of Windows have no option but to use this protocol.

When the database client and server run on the same machine, administrators' choices become more interesting. The next sections cover these alternatives. If you elect to employ these other options and have no need for TCP/IP, you can disable this protocol by launching your server with the `--skip-networking` directive. As a side benefit, this setting also improves security because remote users cannot log in to the database.

Named Pipes

Administrators can choose the named pipe protocol for Windows-based computers with the database server and clients both present on the same machine. To launch the server with named pipes enabled, specify `--enable-named-pipe` when starting MySQL.

In terms of performance, there is some debate as to whether named pipes are better than TCP/IP. When faced with conflicting information, the wisest approach is to test both alternatives in your own unique environment. If you don't have the time or patience to run these tests, this is probably one of those cases in which the status quo (TCP/IP in this instance) is the better choice.

Sockets

These Linux/Unix counterparts to the Windows named pipes can be selected as the protocol for clients and servers running on the same computer by specifying `localhost` in the connection string.

Shared Memory

Long a fixture of other database platforms, MySQL introduced shared memory connections in version 4.1 for Windows servers. Note that this is only relevant if the clients are running on the server. However, shared memory connections typically are very fast—it's hard to beat memory for speed.

Regardless of your choice of protocol, you can use the `--protocol` directive (with available options of TCP, PIPE, SOCKET, and MEMORY) when launching the client.

Scalable Coherent Interface (SCI)

One final protocol merits mention: SCI. Used in conjunction with clustering, this technology can greatly boost the communication speed among servers participating in a NDB Cluster. This protocol is discussed in more detail in Chapter 17's examination of clustering.

Costs of Hostname Resolution

To ensure that a new client has the right to connect to your database, MySQL performs a series of steps to validate this client. Part of this validation includes looking up the hostname of the client and then matching it against the internal grant tables.

However, depending on the multithreading capabilities of your operating system, it's possible that the act of looking up the hostname can cause a bottleneck; similar operations might have to queue until the search has been resolved. This problem can be exacerbated if your DNS lookup service is slow.

If you are concerned that these lookups might be causing undue delays, and if your clients have known, static IP addresses, one alternative is to simply use these IP addresses when granting access:

```
GRANT ALL PRIVILEGES ON high_hat.* TO 'melvin'@'218.22.192.244';
```

If you elect to follow this route, you must also tell MySQL not to perform the DNS lookup by launching mysqld with the --skip-name-resolve option enabled.

Of course, if you have no way of knowing these IP addresses in advance, hard-coding numeric IP addresses don't solve the problem. In this kind of situation, you can follow still other approaches, including finding a faster DNS server or increasing your name caching. A truly radical approach is to use --skip-grant-tables, which disables verification of client connections via the grant tables. Of course, this also disables GRANT and REVOKE, so it is an extremely drastic measure.

Costs of Creating and Destroying Connections

Chapter 10, "General Server Performance and Parameters Tuning," provides a general MySQL engine tuning review and describes all of the internal work that MySQL must perform to satisfy an incoming connection request. To reiterate, a number of key internal structures and buffers must be initialized and staged so that the new connection can be supported correctly.

Given this overhead, anything you can do to either consolidate or eliminate the number of new connection requests translates into less work for the database server.

Let's look at a simple "before-and-after" example to give you an idea of the impact of excess connection management loads for the server. To begin, assume that this sample application is served by a single web server in contact with a single database server. A collection of PHP processes are running on the web server, responsible for measuring, recording, and tracking a variety of statistics (page visited, time spent per page, and so on). The web server is heavily loaded, so the database is accessed frequently.

The "before" application was developed to minimize its connections to MySQL; every time a new instance of the web application is launched, the PHP script creates a new connection and registers key information (date, time, IP address, and so forth). After this data has been committed into MySQL, the PHP script drops the connection.

Can you see the inefficiency here? Contrast this scenario with one that keeps the connection alive, inserting rows as needed. To illustrate the costs of this extra work, two sample PHP scripts were written and then benchmarked. The "after" script, which used a persistent connection to MySQL and inserted 100,000 rows, ran four times faster than the "before" script, which had to wade through the same amount of work while continually opening and closing database connections.

Costs of SSL

Just as TCP/IP is the foundation of the communication that makes the Internet possible, SSL technology is the groundwork of much of the Internet's security.

MySQL administrators can employ SSL to reduce the likelihood of undesired eavesdropping on their client-to-server connections. This security comes at a cost: There are extra configuration tasks for the administrator, and both sides of the connection must expend additional CPU cycles to encrypt and then decrypt message traffic.

However, if your clients and database servers communicate over an open network, you really have no choice but to implement SSL. Fortunately, MySQL gives you the flexibility of using SSL on a per-connection basis. Given that option, it's wisest to mandate SSL for only those clients that are not connecting securely. Other clients can continue using their default connections.

If SSL performance is a big concern for your environment, consider one of the many SSL accelerator appliances now available. These devices off-load the time-consuming encryption/decryption tasks, thereby unburdening your server.

Improving Import and Export Operations

MySQL's import and export functionality offer tremendous convenience and reliability for the database administrator, especially for those faced with maintaining sizable databases. However, they are also unparalleled in their ability to be both painfully slow for the administrator as well as an aggravating source of widespread system sluggishness for all users. Fortunately, MySQL lets you have more control than you might realize when it comes to these types of activities.

This chapter investigates the most optimal procedures to follow when performing any kind of large data movement operation. This chapter begins by researching how to make exports as fast as possible. Next, it reviews the flip side of the export process: speedily importing copious volumes of information into a MySQL server.

Speeding Data Exports

You have some choices when exporting information from your MySQL server. Your first choice is to pick a binary or text-based method. If you are simply interested in backing up information for a potential restoration at some point in the future, the more rapid binary format is your best choice. On the other hand, if you want the platform independence and interoperability of text-based data, choose this kind of approach, although it will run more slowly than its binary counterpart for large amounts of information.

Although `mysqlhotcopy` is a great tool for performing database backups in binary format, it is currently not available on several key platforms, nor is it particularly designed for data import and export. Consequently, this chapter devotes most of its attention to the powerful and versatile `mysqldump` utility for text-based usage, especially as invoked from a shell prompt. The MySQL Administrator backup utility also provides a handy graphical user interface for many of the same types of text-based data import and export operations, with the added convenience of schedule control.

The MySQL Administrator backup utility lets you define repeatable projects and then gives you fine-grained control over which elements will be affected (see Figure 15.1).

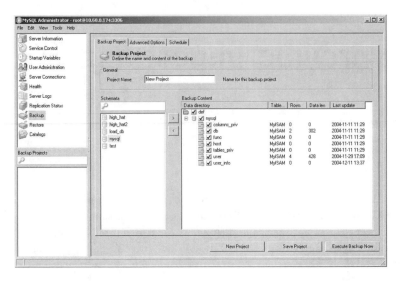

FIGURE 15.1   Choosing a table for backup in the MySQL Administrator.

Once a backup project has been defined, you may fine-tune how the operation will proceed (see Figure 15.2).

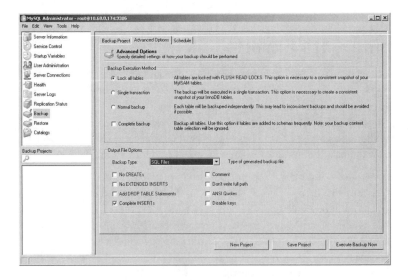

FIGURE 15.2   Managing details of the backup operation.

After defining and configuring your backup, you may specify a schedule for execution (see Figure 15.3).

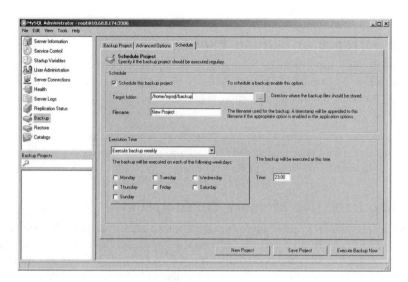

FIGURE 15.3   Selecting a repeatable execution schedule for a MySQL Administrator backup.

Because the primary focus is on performance optimization, this chapter avoids an exhaustive overview of all possible options. Instead, it describes several scenarios, along with the correct invocation to make them run as quickly as possible. It's also important to note that certain mysqldump directives, such as --opt, actually include several other options. However, to keep things simple, any relevant options are specifically cited, regardless of whether they're included "for free" as part of other options.

Finally, it's important to decide what you want to do when it comes time to reload this exported information. You can choose between the SQL script generated by mysqldump or the mysqlimport utility (and, optionally, its corresponding LOAD DATA INFILE statement).

Your answer will determine the correct data exporting tool. Generally, if you want to back up and then copy or restore an entire database and don't want to use a binary format, first run mysqldump, and then import the information using the generated SQL script. However, you can reap performance benefits from exporting information with SELECT ... INTO OUTFILE and then loading this data with either mysqlimport or LOAD DATA INFILE.

If you decide to use these commands for full database backups, you need a little more preparation, primarily in the area of reliably automating the table generation process followed by launching mysqlimport/LOAD DATA INFILE.

We ran a battery of tests on a variety of tables to gauge the efficiency differences between the two options. We found that the SELECT ... INTO OUTFILE/LOAD DATA INFILE (mysqlimport) pairing generally ran 25% to 30% faster than the mysqldump alternative. Others have reported much more dramatic performance differences between the two choices.

The Importance of Regular Exports

Even though this book's primary mission is to help improve MySQL productivity, it's worth mentioning how important it is to combine the power and control of binary backups (including InnoDB's transaction logs where applicable) with regularly scheduled, ASCII-based exports.

Whether you use mysqldump or SELECT ... INTO OUTFILE, the extra safety realized by running these exports (and safeguarding their results) protects you from possible data integrity damage due to circumstances beyond your control.

Avoiding Excessive Memory Consumption

This book has continually stressed how important it is to take advantage of in-memory processing to speed database access. However, several exceptions to this rule exist. One of these arises when exporting large amounts of data. If you forget to include either the -quick or --opt directives when launching mysqldump (especially in older versions), MySQL attempts to retrieve the data export into memory before sending it on to its destination.

For a small database, this isn't a problem. However, for a more voluminous database (or smaller amount of memory), you run the risk of crowding this finite resource with export results. Be aware of this possibility when launching your data retrieval process. Fortunately, more recent versions of MySQL include this option as a default.

Concurrency and Exports

Generally, it's developers who focus on concurrency issues when building their applications. Database administrators also consider concurrency because they want their data load operations to have minimal impact on other users. Recall that concurrency and performance were discussed earlier as part of Chapter 9, "Developing High-Speed Applications," review of optimal application design. However, database administrators also need to keep concurrency in mind when running data extraction.

In particular, you should decide whether you want to lock your tables (via the --lock-tables attribute) or treat the export as one distinct transaction (via the --single-transaction attribute). The --single-transaction attribute is only meaningful as long as the storage engine is InnoDB.

Which should you choose? Much depends on the amount of data to be exported, along with the transactional and concurrency demands on your database. For example, although opting for the --single-transaction tactic runs a slight risk of added undo space requirements, this is more than offset by the increased concurrency supplied by letting you avoid locking your tables. Although `mysqldump` operates very quickly, if your database is large, it still may take quite some time for this utility to finish its work. If you chose `--lock-tables`, database users may experience severe concurrency problems until the operation finishes.

From the perspective of concurrency alone, `--single-transaction` represents the better choice in most cases.

Retrieving Subsets of Information

The `mysqldump` utility offers administrators increasingly fine levels of granularity when deciding what to export. You might elect to export all of your databases, a single database, or even a single table with one database. In fact, you might even create a more selective extract: a set of rows from within a single table.

To export a subset of a table, include either the `--where` or `-w` directives with your `mysqldump` request. For example, if you want to export only those transactions older than January 1, 2003, request the following:

```
[mysql@DBSERVER1 /tmp/results]$ mysqldump -w=transaction_date<=2003-01-01
high_hat transactions
```

The results include your WHERE directive:

```
...
...
--
-- Dumping data for table `transactions`
--
-- WHERE:  transaction_date<=2003-01-01
...
...
```

Be aware that the `--where` option can be a bit finicky, especially when it comes to quote placement; you might need to experiment to get it just right for your query. If your query criteria don't include any spaces or special characters (such as those that might confuse the operating system into thinking that you are making a request of it), you can even omit quotes.

Also remember that you should ideally have the right indexes in place to help the export run more quickly, especially if the export is run regularly.

Copying Table Structures Without Data

As described in Chapter 1, "Setting Up an Optimization Test Environment," it's important to replicate your production schema, data, hardware, and configuration environment when performing optimization tests. However, there might be times when you don't want or need all of your data, but do want the correct schema.

One quick way to create identical copies of your schema without all associated data and indexes is to specify the --no-data option when running mysqldump:

```
[mysql@DBSERVER1 /tmp/results]$ mysqldump --no-data high_hat

-- MySQL dump 8.23
--
-- Host: localhost    Database: high_hat
---------------------------------------------------------
-- Server version        5.0.2-alpha-max-log

--
-- Table structure for table `awards`
--

CREATE TABLE awards (
    award_id int(10) unsigned NOT NULL auto_increment,
    customer_id int(10) unsigned NOT NULL default '0',
    award_date date NOT NULL default '0000-00-00',
    miles_deducted int(10) unsigned NOT NULL default '0',
    origin char(3) NOT NULL default '',
    destination char(3) NOT NULL default '',
    PRIMARY KEY  (award_id)
) ENGINE=MyISAM DEFAULT CHARSET=latin1;
...
...
```

You can even request a single table:

```
[mysql@DBSERVER1 /tmp/results]$ mysqldump --no-data high_hat customer_master
```

This option creates an identical, empty schema (including index definitions) that you can deploy on any MySQL server. The following section looks at how you can speed up index re-creation on the destination system.

Delaying Index Re-creation—MyISAM

When copying large tables between systems, it is usually more advantageous to load all data first, and only then rebuild your indexes. Otherwise, you might find that it takes much longer to complete the reloading on the destination system because each row loaded requires index maintenance even though MyISAM offers algorithms to quickly perform this index work for empty tables when using LOAD DATA INFILE. To delay these indexing operations, specify --disable-keys when running mysqldump.

Note that this option is only effective for MyISAM tables; if you specify it for InnoDB tables, MySQL still performs the laborious task of updating indexes in real time. Also, in earlier versions of MySQL, it was necessary to run several different commands, including launching myisamchk, to achieve the same results; passing this flag is much less cumbersome.

```
[mysql@DBSERVER1 /tmp/results]$ mysqldump --no-data --disable-keys
high_hat customer_master
```

When chosen, this option embeds directives into the output stream. These commands instruct MySQL to rebuild the indexes after all data has been loaded:

```
CREATE TABLE awards (
  award_id int(10) unsigned NOT NULL auto_increment,
...
...
) ENGINE=MyISAM DEFAULT CHARSET=latin1;
...
...
/*!40000 ALTER TABLE `awards` DISABLE KEYS */;
...
INSERT INTO awards VALUES (98481,30018,'2003-09-05',50000,'ORD','LGA');
INSERT INTO awards VALUES (98482,26818,'2001-10-25',100000,'PDX','LHR');
INSERT INTO awards VALUES (98483,13293,'2003-03-19',50000,'ALB','PHX');
...
...
/*!40000 ALTER TABLE `awards` ENABLE KEYS */;
```

Delaying Index Re-creation—InnoDB

Due to architectural differences between MyISAM and InnoDB, delaying index re-creation when loading InnoDB tables won't benefit import performance. However, there are still a number of significant steps that you can take to make imports run faster.

For example, one handy InnoDB feature is its disabling of foreign key constraint checks for the data export/import process. With these constraint checks in place, there's a good chance that your reload process might fail if rows are inserted out of sequence. This topic is discussed later in the chapter.

Also, if at all possible try to export your information in primary key order; reloading will proceed many times faster by simply following this basic directive. If you are unable to make this happen during export, consider sorting the file prior to reloading.

Preparing for Data Reload

You'll discover the most optimal ways to import information in a moment. However, there are a number of performance-enhancing suggestions you can make while generating your export. These simple suggestions can make a big difference when it comes time to reload your exported data.

Multirow INSERT

To begin, you can request that mysqldump generate an export file that inserts multiple rows as part of each INSERT operation. This helps boost the speed of reloading the information later, while keeping the size of the extract file smaller. For example, contrast the following small samples of the traditional and multirow versions of this output:

```
INSERT INTO awards VALUES (1,28565,'2001-08-01',75000,'ORD','SFO');
INSERT INTO awards VALUES (2,6850,'2001-05-25',75000,'MSP','CDG');
INSERT INTO awards VALUES (3,10665,'2001-09-06',50000,'SIN','SEA');
INSERT INTO awards VALUES (4,11347,'2001-03-22',50000,'IAD','RIO');
```

versus

```
INSERT INTO awards VALUES (1,28565,'2001-08-01',75000,'ORD','SFO'),(2,6850,'2001-05-
25',75000,'MSP','CDG'),(3,10665,'2001-09-06',50000,'SIN','SEA'),(4,11347,'2001-03-
22',50000,'IAD','RIO');
```

To request a multiple row insert, simply specify --extended-insert when you launch mysqldump:

```
[mysql@DBSERVER1 /tmp/results]$ mysqldump --extended-insert high_hat awards
```

To make these multirow SQL commands as big and efficient as possible, provide a large value for max_allowed_packet when you launch mysqldump. However, be certain that this value doesn't exceed the size of the same variable on the server.

INSERT DELAYED

In Chapter 8, "Advanced SQL Tips," review of optimal SQL tactics you saw how INSERT DELAYED takes advantage of memory buffering to boost multiclient access to a MyISAM-hosted table. If you want to employ delayed inserts when reloading information, specify --delay when you run mysqldump.

Remember that this does come with a price—additional memory consumption. Generally, you should only request it for those tables that are likely to be accessed (in read/write mode) by other clients at the same time the reload is happening. You will receive a much better return on investment by using multi-row INSERT statements as seen earlier in this chapter.

Locking Tables

Locking your target tables is one simple way to reduce overhead (and boost performance) when reloading large blocks of data. By including --add-lock with your mysqldump command, MySQL embeds a LOCK TABLES ... WRITE directive after the CREATE TABLE statement, but before the INSERT operations.

After the inserts have been completed, MySQL appends UNLOCK TABLES to release the table lock. By delaying key buffer flushes until when the lock is released, MySQL is able to reduce overhead and boost loading speed.

You examined the impact of locks on multiuser database concurrency earlier; use this directive wisely when loading information onto heavily accessed database servers.

Using SELECT ... INTO OUTFILE

At the beginning of this chapter, you learned how the SELECT ... INTO OUTFILE/LOAD DATA INFILE SQL statement pair can extract and then import information more quickly than the mysqldump/mysqlimport utility pair.

If you choose the SQL route, simply generate your SELECT statement as follows:

```
mysql> SELECT * FROM flights WHERE flight_id < 100 INTO OUTFILE '/tmp/flights'
```

Take a look at some of the contents of the resulting file:

```
[mysql@DBSERVER1 /tmp]$ head flights
```

```
1       2358    2003-03-09      IAD     MSP
2       109     2002-11-12      LGW     CDG
3       9893    2001-10-30      PHX     KUL
4       642     2004-07-23      ROM     FRA
5       8845    2002-08-11      SFO     SJO
...
...
```

As you saw earlier, this type of file loads in approximately one-quarter to one-third less time than the collection of SQL statements created by mysqldump.

Improving Network Performance

If you are planning to extract data from one machine and then insert the same information onto another machine in real time across your network, be certain that your MySQL communication variables are set to handle this type of task as efficiently as possible. These parameters (including net_buffer_length, max_allowed_packet, net_retry_count, and so on) are discussed in Chapters 10, "General Server Performance and Parameters Tuning," and 14, "Operating System, Web Server and Connectivity Tuning."

In addition to tuning these parameters, you might also pass --compress to utilities such as mysqldump and mysqlimport. This requests that they make use of compression (if available) to reduce the amount of traffic flowing across your network. When you consider the amount of repetitive information typically found in most ASCII data streams, compression might be able to squeeze significant volume from this communication. From the parameters listed above, --compress is likely to have the most impact.

Accelerating Data Loading

The first part of this chapter discussed how you can speed up the data extraction process, as well as prepare the results for a quick reload into their destination. This section changes focus and looks at how to insert large quantities of information into MySQL as quickly as possible.

The majority of this section explores the performance-specific aspects of the mysqlimport utility. Because this utility nearly directly corresponds to the LOAD DATA INFILE SQL statement, this statement is specifically included as part of the review.

Finally, if you are running your MySQL server with binary logging enabled (to help with data recovery and/or replication), you might also elect to use the mysqlbinlog utility to extract data-manipulation statements from the log. You can then feed them into the mysql utility to re-create information on the same (or another) database server. However, since this is typically used for other purposes such as point-in-time recovery, this is a much more unwieldy and complex approach than simply using the utilities mentioned previously.

Managing Concurrency

Loading hefty volumes of information has the potential to cause significant concurrency disruption issues for other users of your database. From the users' perspective, it will appear as if your system has ground to a halt. In fact, performance might be fine, but all resources are dedicated to the data-loading process and these users are blocked. The following sections look at two ways to minimize these inconveniences when running LOAD DATA INFILE.

LOW_PRIORITY

During Chapter 8's exploration of optimal SQL you saw how the LOW_PRIORITY attribute, --low-priority-updates server variable, and SET LOW_PRIORITY_UPDATES command causes a data-modification operation to wait until no other threads are reading a table. This also has value when running LOAD DATA INFILE, especially for MyISAM tables: The loading halts until these other threads are through, but once started it will proceed until completion. However, your load process might end up being delayed for a long time if many lengthy queries are already under way.

CONCURRENT

You examined how to take advantage of MyISAM's concurrent insert capabilities in Chapter 11, "MyISAM Performance Enhancement." For now, note that supplying the CONCURRENT keyword with your LOAD DATA INFILE statement causes MySQL to append this new information to the end of the table, as long as no free blocks are in the middle of the table. Other applications will then be able to retrieve information from the table in spite of your data load.

Finally, note that LOW_PRIORITY and CONCURRENT are mutually exclusive when loading data into MyISAM-based tables.

Handling Errors

During Chapter 5, "Using Constraints to Improve Performance," you learned how MySQL uses primary keys and UNIQUE constraints to guarantee data integrity. Later, in Chapter 8, you examined how you can take advantage of "upsert" (update or insert) functionality by using the REPLACE SQL statement rather than INSERT. This is much simpler than writing logic to handle situations in which a record's primary key or unique identifier is already present in the database.

Both mysqlimport and LOAD DATA INFILE give you the same flexibility and control. By including --replace when you launch the import, you request that MySQL overlay any existing, primary key or uniquely identified rows with new data from the input file. Conversely, the --ignore directive instructs MySQL to simply bypass the values from the input file when it encounters a potential primary key or unique index breach.

Although these directives are very helpful, it's also important to comprehend the underlying reason(s) why your soon-to-be-loaded data violates your well-planned integrity constraints. This could be a symptom of a larger database design difficulty or data cleansing issue.

Engine-Specific Tips

Up until now, this chapter has focused on general, cross-engine import and export suggestions. At this point, it's time to look at engine-specific recommendations to boost performance. Note that many of these proposals were first offered during the book's earlier chapters dedicated to MyISAM and InnoDB tuning (Chapters 11, " MyISAM Performance Enhancement," and 12, "InnoDB Performance Enhancement," respectively).

MyISAM

You reviewed MyISAM's many optimization features earlier in Chapter 11. Two tuning parameters bear repeating here: bulk_insert_buffer_size and myisam_max_sort_file_size.

The bulk_insert_buffer_size variable is used to control the amount of memory devoted to MyISAM's large-scale-operation internal cache. With a default value of 8MB, it can significantly improve response time when loading data into a MyISAM-based table, as long as the table is not completely empty.

In the context of a LOAD DATA INFILE operation, the myisam_max_sort_file_size variable controls the amount of space that a temporary file consumes while MySQL rebuilds any relevant indexes. The max_extra_sort_file_size setting also plays a part: If you set either of these values too low, MySQL might elect to use a slower, key cache–based algorithm to recreate these indexes. Aside from the possibility that the temporary file necessary to support a large, heavily indexed table might fill your file system, there's little reason to make this value any smaller than the default found in newer versions of MySQL.

In addition, remember to configure the myisam_sort_buffer_size setting to be large enough to accommodate your index rebuilding.

Finally, don't be afraid to alter some vital engine settings just for the duration of your load operation. For example, consider making the key_buffer and myisam_sort_buffer_size variables much larger. By raising these values to a very high percentage of available memory, you help MySQL perform much more of its data import work in memory.

InnoDB

The effort involved in validating foreign key constraints is a big potential performance bottleneck when reloading InnoDB tables. In addition, it's possible that legitimate rows will be rejected because tables are inadvertently reloaded (and the foreign key checks are executed) in the wrong order.

For example, you might have written your reload script to first load records for a child table, followed by its parent. This triggers many error messages when the data is, in fact, valid. The risks of these types of false issues multiply when your database includes many cross-referencing foreign keys.

To avoid this kind of problem, use the LOAD DATA INFILE statement and disable foreign key validation by entering SET FOREIGN_KEY_CHECKS = 0 prior to loading information. Of course, for administrators using mysqldump, you saw earlier that this utility now disables foreign key checks when extracting information.

InnoDB's rich transaction capabilities were discussed in Chapter 12. Recall that overhead is associated with every COMMIT statement, which might become substantial when loading massive blocks of information. To avoid this prospective bottleneck, be certain to disable AUTOCOMMIT (via SET AUTOCOMMIT = 0) prior to launching any large-scale import operation. For small tables or multiple-value inserts, you might not notice any benefit; it is the most sizable tables as well as single-value inserts that should see the most noticeable improvement.

It's also a good idea to disable the checking of any unique constraints during data loading, as long as you're confident that your data is clean. To do this, enter SET UNIQUE_CHECKS = 0 for the session that is doing the import. When disabled, InnoDB is then free to leverage its insert buffer for mass operations by grouping secondary index writes into larger units.

V

Distributed Computing

In the next two chapters, you survey MySQL's essential capabilities that allow you to distribute your database processing load among multiple servers.

To begin, you delve into MySQL's easy-to-implement, yet powerful replication functionality. After reviewing how to coax the most possible speed out of this technology, you discover the dramatic performance benefits possible by employing MySQL's clustering facilities.

Optimal Replication

Introduction

MySQL's replication features allow you to quickly and easily spread your processing load among multiple database servers. This chapter focuses on the performance aspects of replication. It begins by briefly explaining how this vital technology works, along with some tips you can use to decide if replication is right for you.

Next, you examine several replication scenarios, starting with several very basic topographies, and then explore how these can scale to more complex configurations. Finally, this chapter discusses how to optimize your replication performance.

Entire books have been written on distributed computing, load balance, and database replication theory and topographies. However, the purpose in this chapter is simply to

1. Describe scenarios in which replication might help improve your MySQL performance.
2. Understand how to tune MySQL replication for optimal performance.

This chapter avoids the intricacies of initial setup and customization, except in those situations in which these decisions might have an impact.

How Does Replication Work?

Replication is actually quite straightforward. At its core, it merely involves an administrator picking a server to act as the master, and then registering one or more slave servers to receive updates from the master. Each slave server is responsible for contacting the master server. This master server records all data manipulation statements in a binary log, which is then fed in a stream to any slave(s) that contact the master. The slave computers then play back these statements locally, thus updating their own data copies accordingly.

In addition, a slave can, in turn, act as a master to other servers. This lets you construct sophisticated chains of replication servers.

Obviously, there are many steps to follow to correctly configure and use replication, but the preceding discussion describes it accurately at a high level.

Is Replication Right for You?

Replication is a wise strategy if any of the following are relevant in your MySQL environment:

- **High availability**—The data stored on your MySQL server needs to be accessible 24 x 7.
- **Frequent backups**—To protect against data loss, you often back up your databases.
- **Mixed processing profiles**—Your MySQL database server must field requests from online transaction process (OLTP) and decision support system (DSS) users.
- **Abundant, low-performance computers**—Your organization might not have the fastest computers, but they have lots of them.
- **Widely dispersed users**—Your MySQL users are spread among multiple locations.
- **Modular application code**—Your MySQL-based applications can be easily altered to read data from the slave servers while writing data to the master.

Creating a Replication Strategy

Now that you've seen some circumstances in which replication might help boost responsiveness, let's look at a collection of processing scenarios. To make these more meaningful, let's return to our friends at High-Hat Airways as they roll out a homegrown reservation system. To make these replication opportunities more understandable, we won't cite any of the modern processing appliances (for example, intelligent routers, load balancers, shared storage devices) that would likely be found in this kind of environment. In fact, for now we'll omit one of the most compelling MySQL features: clustering; clustering performance topics are explored in Chapter 17, "Optimal Clustering."

To begin, the Java-based reservation system serves internal reservation agent users based at High-Hat headquarters. Some of these users connect via PC-based sessions, whereas others connect using dumb terminals. These users directly connect to an application server, which, in turn, connects to the MySQL server (see Figure 16.1).

As time passes, this configuration proves to be problematic. In particular, the delays caused by the necessary nightly backups translate into lost revenue and user frustration. High-Hat administrators decide to experiment with MySQL's replication features. This first trial simply consists of reproducing the main database server's information on a secondary, backup server. This backup server does not need to be as modern, fast, or expensive as the primary server. It simply needs a sufficient disk, network bandwidth, and a backup device (see Figure 16.2).

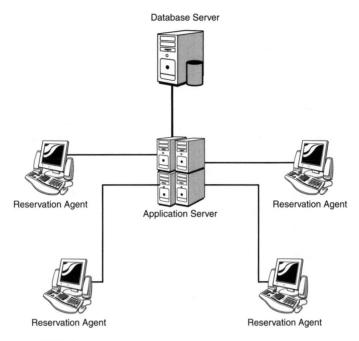

FIGURE 16.1   The initial reservation system configuration.

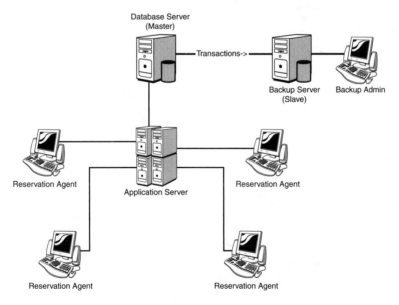

FIGURE 16.2   The original environment with replication enabled for backup.

This replication strategy yields immediate benefits. First, High-Hat now has increased their data security simply by duplicating it to another machine. Second, backups no longer need to be delayed to off-hours; they can be conducted from the secondary server at any time during the day.

However, like all computing solutions since the beginning of time, this new architecture soon needs performance enhancements. High-Hat recently invested in sophisticated data analysis software to support their fleet of expensive MBAs. These highly paid, finance department–based experts are running enormous queries that consume abundant system resources, in the middle of the day no less. In fact, ticket sales have begun to suffer: Many customers are hanging up on the reservations agents before their bookings are complete.

Fortunately, after you've done the research to successfully implement a single master/slave pair, adding additional slaves is quite easy. In this case, you can simply add a new slave server to your replication topography (see Figure 16.3).

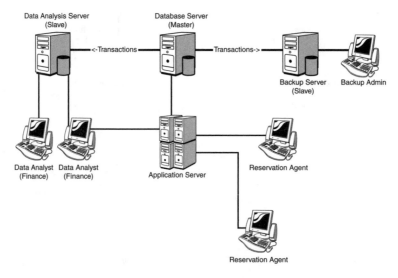

FIGURE 16.3 Replication extended to support users in another department.

Now, data analysts can run queries against a near-instantaneous copy of the production database.

Aside from running endless queries that bog down production servers, the data analysts also create value-added aggregations and compilations of information in their own database. This database resides on the data analysis slave, yet other users throughout the company want access to this information. In particular, the marketing department wants access to this derived data to help formulate new campaigns. After a while, these new demands bog down the data analysis server.

In this situation, it's easy to configure the data analysis server to simultaneously play the role of both master and slave (see Figure 16.4).

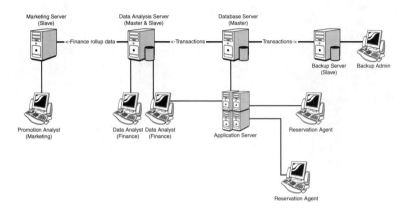

FIGURE 16.4   Departmental database server now functions as both a master and a slave.

How is this possible? Recall that the primary database server is replicating reservation information onto the finance server. Users on that server are creating their own information in a separate database. It's this latter database that is then replicated down the line. In fact, the marketing server could act as a slave to both the finance and primary servers, as long as it was registering interest in different databases (or at least different tables in the same databases) on these servers.

Finally, High-Hat's new web-based customer self-service portal is designed to let customers manage many of the tasks previously handled by reservation agents. However, management wants these agents and customers to perform real-time updates of the primary database, without resource conflicts. Replication might help here as well.

In this type of situation, you can design the web-based application to read information from a slave server yet write updates back to the primary server (see Figure 16.5).

As you've seen in the previous examples, you can create sophisticated replication interchanges throughout your organization. In fact, replication slaves can even be hosted by separate entities; the data interchanges can be encrypted to protect against eavesdropping. Optimal replication security is examined a little later in this chapter.

Now that you've seen how to design a replication strategy, it's time to review how to remove as many performance bottlenecks as possible.

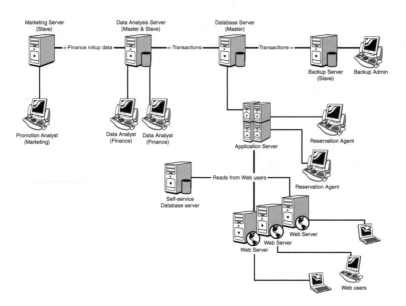

FIGURE 16.5   Reads serviced by a replicated server, while writes are performed on the original database server.

High-Performance Replication

As is the case with engine tuning, replication speed is largely dependent on the quality of the work you did when you designed your databases and selected an indexing strategy.

With those caveats stipulated, MySQL replication performance suggestions can be categorized into one of three classes: network, master, and slave.

Network Considerations

The quality and speed of your network has the biggest potential impact on replication responsiveness; MySQL replication is, at its core, a distributed record-and-playback mechanism.

A slow or already overloaded network is likely to have trouble digesting the traffic generated by replication. If you have no way to improve your network or reduce competing traffic load, one idea is to take the slave servers offline until times when your network is running with a lightened load. You don't need to worry about the slaves losing their place; they reconnect to the master and resynchronize. Of course, this presents two potential concerns:

- **Stale data**—If the slave server is offline for days or even minutes (for a very active master), it will certainly be out-of-step with the most accurate data. This is definitely an issue in transactional systems, although generally less of a problem for decision support.

- **Delaying the inevitable network overhead**—Even if you postpone heavy network traffic by taking the slave servers offline, you run the risk of an enormous strain on the network when replication resumes.

The MySQL Administrator provides details on network activity. The following example examines the network traffic for a master server. In this case, only two activities are under way. First, the server is being used to log visits to a website, so there is a steady trickle of data updates. Second, the server is replicating its information to a slave server. This accounts for most of the network traffic (see Figure 16.6).

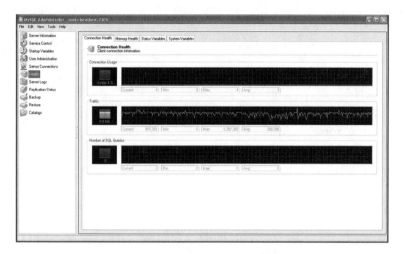

FIGURE 16.6   Network traffic in a replicated environment.

Compression and Replication

One way to reduce network traffic is to employ a compression algorithm. By enabling the `--slave_compressed_protocol` server variable, you instruct MySQL to compress replication traffic if both master and slave are able to support this capability.

Encryption and Replication

Security is always a hot topic in distributed computing, and MySQL replication is no exception. Administrators might elect to enable encryption via SSL. This requires that the master server be configured correctly, and all slaves wanting to connect to the master need to provide several additional parameters to be able to understand the encrypted traffic.

Should you incur the extra processing and network costs imposed by encryption? The answer is very dependent on the profile of your replication topography:

- If all relevant servers are on the same physical network (such as in the same building or on the same campus), and you're not concerned about any internal unauthorized snooping, encrypted replication probably isn't worth the extra costs.

- If even one slave server will communicate with its master via the public Internet, you should definitely enable encryption on the master, and then encrypt communication with that slave. It would be very easy for someone outside your organization to reverse engineer your database structure and, more importantly, information by simply eavesdropping on the replication messages.

  Also, recall that master servers are unaware of who will connect to them, and, consequently, make no "special arrangements" for any particular slave servers. This is important: *Any* slave using a nonsecure connection means that the master and that slave need to bear the costs of encryption. This kind of scenario might warrant investing in a virtual private network (VPN) or other wire-level security mechanism (see the next item in this list).

- If you use the public Internet for communication but also employ VPN technology, you are already benefiting from secure encryption. Adding even more data scrambling might be redundant, unless you're concerned about someone already authenticated on your VPN eavesdropping on your data streams.

Timing and Error Handling

MySQL offers two important settings to control how slave servers behave when encountering network issues. The first parameter, --slave-net-timeout, instructs the slave to wait a specified number of seconds for additional data from the master before timing out or aborting its read.

If the threshold passes, the slave treats the connection as broken, and tries to reconnect. The amount of time that is allowed to pass before this attempt is controlled by the second parameter, --master-connect-retry, which is set to a default value of 60 seconds.

Try to keep your network's unique circumstances in mind when setting these parameters. For example, if a slave is connected via a low-speed and/or unreliable dial-up, you might want to increase the --slave-net-timeout setting. Setting it too low might cause the slave to think that the connection is broken when, in fact, it is simply a bandwidth or other session problem that will pass momentarily.

Master Server Performance Considerations

As the source of all replicated information, it's important that your master server be as efficient as possible. The next section reviews several suggestions toward that goal.

Monitoring the Master

MySQL offers a collection of server status variables and graphs (via the MySQL Administrator) to help give you a better idea of what is happening in your replication environment. You saw Figure 16.6's network activity graph earlier. At this point, take a look at two additional graphs.

The first graph provides some details about the master server, including its status, log file, and position within the binary log (see Figure 16.7).

FIGURE 16.7   Status information for the master server.

The next example shows thread activity on the master, including information about its replication actions (see Figure 16.8).

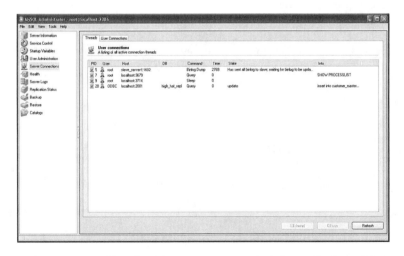

FIGURE 16.8   Thread activity on master server, including replication activity.

You can also use the SHOW MASTER STATUS command to get an idea of what's happening on the master server from an examination of its binary log files.

```
mysql> SHOW MASTER STATUS\G
*************************** 1. row ***************************
            File: high_hat_main-bin.000009
        Position: 155326663
    Binlog_Do_DB:
Binlog_Ignore_DB:
1 row in set (0.00 sec)
```

The SHOW MASTER LOGS command gives you an overview of the current collection of binary logs stored on this master:

```
mysql> SHOW MASTER LOGS;
+-------------------------+
| Log_name                |
+-------------------------+
| high_hat_main-bin.000001 |
| high_hat_main-bin.000002 |
| high_hat_main-bin.000003 |
| high_hat_main-bin.000004 |
| high_hat_main-bin.000005 |
| high_hat_main-bin.000006 |
| high_hat_main-bin.000007 |
| high_hat_main-bin.000008 |
| high_hat_main-bin.000009 |
+-------------------------+
9 rows in set (0.00 sec)
```

Running SHOW BINARY LOGS would provide the same details; the two commands are synonymous.

If you're curious about what operations are being processed during replication, you can view the contents of the binary log by running the SHOW BINLOG EVENTS command. Be careful when launching this request: Unless you restrict the amount of returned data, you could be swamped with information:

```
mysql> SHOW BINLOG EVENTS IN 'high_hat_main-bin.000003' LIMIT 100\G
*************************** 1. row ***************************
    Log_name: high_hat_main-bin.000003
         Pos: 4
  Event_type: Start
   Server_id: 1
Orig_log_pos: 4
        Info: Server ver: 4.1.8-nt-max-log, Binlog ver: 3
. . .
. . .
```

```
*************************** 94. row ***************************
    Log_name: high_hat_main-bin.000003
         Pos: 10551
  Event_type: Query
   Server_id: 1
Orig_log_pos: 10551
        Info: use `high_hat_repl`; insert into transactions(transaction_date,cus-
tomer_id,amount,transaction_type)
 values('2004-07-03 01:15:08',11045,2,'Purchase')
*************************** 95. row ***************************
    Log_name: high_hat_main-bin.000003
         Pos: 10724
  Event_type: Query
   Server_id: 1
Orig_log_pos: 10724
        Info: use `high_hat_repl`; SET ONE_SHOT
CHARACTER_SET_CLIENT=8,COLLATION_CONNECTION=8,COLLATION_DATABASE=33,COLLATION_SERVER
=33
. . .
. . .
```

Implementing Best Tuning Practices

It stands to reason that a badly tuned master server will see its performance problems reflected on its slaves. For an example, a poorly designed indexing strategy on the master translates into sluggish queries, not only on the primary server, but also on all slaves that receive replicated information from this machine. The same holds true for other key design and configuration decisions, such as database structure and engine parameters.

For this reason alone, it's important that you take the time and apply sufficient effort into optimization when designing your database, application code, index, and engine configuration.

Only Log Necessary Information

As you saw earlier, as one of its many roles, the binary log is the mechanism that MySQL uses to replicate data from master servers to their associated slaves. Data manipulation activity on the master is written into this log, which is then read and performed by slaves.

In many cases, you will want your slaves to look just like their master. However, what if you have master server activity that you don't want to replicate to slaves? For example, suppose that the same server is managing production, test, and development databases. Replicating the test and development databases is a waste of time and bandwidth. To reduce this unnecessary overhead, you can restrict which databases participate in the binary log (and associated replication) via the --binlog-ignore-db setting in your master server's MySQL configuration file.

With this parameter set, MySQL does not log any data modifications to these databases on the master, but it does log activity from all other databases. Slaves that connect to this master do not see any data alterations: It is as if these ignored databases don't exist. This absence of logging and replication also reduces network bandwidth consumption; statements that aren't logged can't be replicated.

Conversely, you can explicitly name any master databases that you want logged and replicated via the `--binlog-do-db` setting. This is the inverse of `--binlog-ignore-db`: When set, MySQL only logs and replicates those databases cited by `--binlog-do-db`. Be careful when using these options: There are potential side effects for statements that embed database names, rather than simply specifying USE their SQL.

Both of these parameters have partners with similar purposes on the slave servers. The `--replicate-do-db` and `--replicate-ignore-db` parameters are discussed a little later.

Managing Slave Resources

Just because a server is acting as a slave doesn't mean that database administrators are freed from their responsibility to tune the machine, including its caching settings. In fact, slave server platform capabilities often vary widely, and are also frequently less powerful than their masters. This means that it will likely be hard to come up with a "one size fits all" configuration. In this environment, proper tuning and monitoring is crucial. Monitoring is reviewed in a moment. For now, take a look at some configuration guidelines.

- **Follow standard configuration best practices**—Assuming that your master servers' database structures and application code/queries should already be optimized (for example, well-thought-out schema and indexes design, performance-tuned database access logic) prior to launching a replication strategy, your chief remaining responsibility is to configure your slave servers for optimal engine performance.

  Much of this book has discussed how to leverage MySQL's unique collection of performance settings. When configuring your slave servers, it's a good idea to revisit the relevant sections (for example, general engine tuning, server-specific recommendations, disk configuration). In practice, you might find that the best course of action is to simply use one of the preset configuration files supplied by MySQL.

- **Manage the relay log**—Relay logs are a vital element in replication. In a nutshell, the slave connects to the master and requests that the master server send the contents of its binary log to the slave. When the slave receives this information, it promptly records this data in the relay log. Then, the slave reads the relay log and applies the changes, thereby completing the replication cycle.

  You have control over the maximum size of a single relay log (via the `--max-relay-log-size` setting), the entire relay log group (via the `--relay-log-space-limit` setting), as well as rotation policies (via the `--relay-log-purge` setting). However, from a purely performance-related perspective, there are very few settings that concern the relay log.

Most importantly, it's a good idea to place the relay logs on the fastest file system available, as long as there is sufficient space to store these crucial files. This helps with load balancing as well, especially if there are heavy volumes of replicated data being processed at the same time as extensive user access to the replicated data on the slave server. By default, MySQL places these logs in the data directory. To change this location, configure the `--relay-log` startup setting.

- **Manage temporary storage**—MySQL creates a number of temporary files when processing the relay log. To boost disk performance, it's wise to place these temporary files on the fastest device possible, just as you do for the relay logs. To specify this location, provide a value for the `--slave-load-tmpdir` setting.

Monitoring the Slave

After you've set up a replication strategy and configured your master and slaves, MySQL offers a number of helpful tools and utilities to help you monitor the slave's health and performance.

First, even though a server is functioning as a slave doesn't mean that you can't make use of the standard monitoring tools such as the MySQL Administrator. For example, look at the following two screenshots. In the first case, observe the internal replication threads at work (see Figure 16.9).

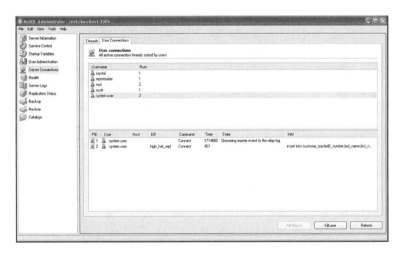

FIGURE 16.9   Connection activity on a slave.

However, this server has other responsibilities. In particular, it contains its own rollup databases that are being scrutinized by users employing business intelligence tools (see Figure 16.10).

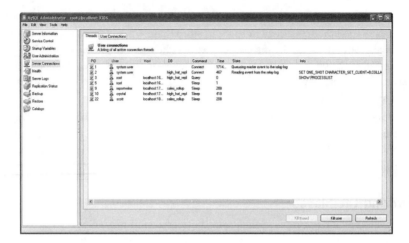

FIGURE 16.10   A diverse set of activities running at the same time on a slave
server.

For the character-minded, the SHOW SLAVE STATUS command provides practical information
for administrators:

```
mysql> SHOW SLAVE STATUS \G
*************************** 1. row ***************************
              Slave_IO_State: Waiting for master to send event
                 Master_Host: high_hat_main
                 Master_User: root
                 Master_Port: 3306
               Connect_Retry: 60
             Master_Log_File: Replication-2-bin.000009
         Read_Master_Log_Pos: 155326663
              Relay_Log_File: slave_server1-relay-bin.000004
               Relay_Log_Pos: 155440260
       Relay_Master_Log_File: Replication-2-bin.000009
            Slave_IO_Running: Yes
           Slave_SQL_Running: Yes
             Replicate_Do_DB: high_hat_repl
         Replicate_Ignore_DB:
          Replicate_Do_Table:
      Replicate_Ignore_Table:
     Replicate_Wild_Do_Table:
 Replicate_Wild_Ignore_Table:
                  Last_Errno: 0
                  Last_Error:
                Skip_Counter: 0
         Exec_Master_Log_Pos: 155326663
             Relay_Log_Space: 1229182150
```

```
        Until_Condition: None
         Until_Log_File:
          Until_Log_Pos: 0
      Master_SSL_Allowed: No
      Master_SSL_CA_File:
      Master_SSL_CA_Path:
         Master_SSL_Cert:
       Master_SSL_Cipher:
          Master_SSL_Key:
    Seconds_Behind_Master: 11
1 row in set (0.00 sec)
```

Slave Server Performance Considerations

The next section provides a collection of proposals to help your slave servers deliver optimal performance.

Sharing the Workload

With today's commodity-priced hardware and continually dropping bandwidth costs, often the easiest and most cost-effective way to improve an individual slave server's responsiveness is simply to add additional slaves to your environment.

After you have multiple slave servers in place, you can configure your clients to connect to a specific server, using whatever performance criteria you like as the deciding factor. You can even chain replication servers together, configuring a slave to act as a master to additional slave servers.

If you are concerned about erroneous updating of slave servers, use the --read-only option in the slave's configuration file. When present, this blocks any local updates of the slave server by any users lacking the SUPER privilege.

Only Replicate Necessary Data

You just reviewed how the --binlog-ignore-db and --binlog-do-db parameters affect what gets logged on the master server. Slave servers have their own parameters that affect their processing of replicated information. The --replicate-do-db and --replicate-ignore-db settings determine whether the slave will reproduce actions for a given database.

For example, suppose that a master server logs activity from all databases. However, because of operational, disk, or CPU resource issues, you decide not to process activity from a particular database on a slave server. In this case, you include --replicate-ignore-db in this slave server's configuration file. Note that the slave server still receives traffic for this unwanted database: It is inscribed in the master's binary log, after all. The slave will ignore these directives, however. If you want to eliminate the traffic altogether from the point of inception, use the --binlog-ignore-db directive on the server.

Slave servers have even more discretion over what to replicate. The `--replicate-do-table`, `--replicate-ignore-table`, `--replicate-wild-do-table`, and `--replicate-wild-ignore-table` settings give administrators fine-grained control over which tables to process and which tables to ignore. However, if used incorrectly or inconsistently, these settings can introduce data anomalies into your slave server database.

Reducing Overhead

Taking the time to minimize your slave servers' overhead delivers two notable performance advantages. First, because the slave server is running more efficiently, it simply takes less time to complete the replication process. Second, a more efficient slave server can assist more users more quickly. The following takes a look at a few simple things you can do to diminish this processing burden.

First, recall that Chapter 11, "MyISAM Performance Enhancement," discussed the MyISAM engine and that MySQL gives you the option to defer key buffer synchronization to disk until a table is closed, rather than every time an index is updated. The overhead savings can be significant, especially when the master server (and, hence, the slave server) are subject to very frequent data updates. You can control this behavior via the `--delay_key_write` server setting.

Speaking of MyISAM, you can instruct MySQL to only use this rapid storage engine on one or more slave servers. To do so, include the `--skip-innodb` and `--skip-bdb` directives on your configuration file. When these options are enabled, MySQL replicates all master tables, regardless of their storage engine, into its most efficient disk-based storage engine: MyISAM. Note that this introduces the potential for transaction and referential integrity anomalies should something fail during replication. The InnoDB and BDB storage engines will be able to maintain integrity; MyISAM will not.

Finally, during Chapter 8's ("Advanced SQL Tips") appraisal of optimal SQL, you learned that MySQL gives you the option to set data modification priority (INSERT/UPDATE/DELETE) below that of queries. When you include the `--low-priority-updates` directive in your slave's MySQL configuration file, database readers take precedence over database writers. However, be aware of one potential latency-causing side effect: The slave server(s) might not be able to catch up on its replication work in a timely manner if the query load is very high.

Optimal Clustering

Introduction

Just as MySQL's open source architecture and liberal licensing terms have revolutionized the relational database market, MySQL Cluster's reliability, performance, and scalability capabilities let organizations with limited software and hardware budgets enjoy the same database processing power and dependability previously restricted to very large enterprises.

This chapter examines ways that you can exploit MySQL Cluster's capabilities to pry additional speed and consistency from your hardware and software, while charting a realistic plan for future growth. This chapter begins by explaining how clustering works, including a synopsis of key terms and concepts. The next section can be used as a guide to help determine if clustering is right for you and your unique data-processing needs.

After completing that task, this chapter examines some clustering strategies, with special attention on best practices. Finally, the chapter closes with a review of how to configure MySQL Cluster in your environment, with a particular focus on the performance ramifications of your choices.

Before beginning, it's a good idea to keep several facts in mind about the content found in this chapter:

- Clustering is a highly complex topic, with many variables combining to determine the optimal structure and configuration for a given environment. To do the theme full justice would require an entire book. This chapter simply attempts to provide an overview and a start to your clustering journey, while citing key performance considerations; comprehensive coverage requires much more space than is available here.

- In the best of circumstances, performance recommendations are highly subject to the vagaries of each installation's site-specific configuration and processing profile. Given the copious potential permutations of node relationships, this is especially true with clustering; consequently, this chapter makes relatively few absolute recommendations about parameter settings. Instead, it points out which of these variables might have the most relative impact on performance. The final arbiter is you—the MySQL administrator.

- Numerous utilities and other programs can be used to set up, monitor, and manage a MySQL cluster. Except as needed to illustrate a point, this chapter does not explore these modules, nor does it cover more than a relatively small percentage of all the MySQL Cluster settings: Only those variables that directly impact performance are reviewed.

- At the time of this writing, clustering is supported in the 4.1 production versions of MySQL. You should note that the 5.x series will feature substantial new capabilities that will have a dramatic and positive impact on performance. The result of these improvements will make clustering more appropriate in many more situations.

How Does Clustering Work?

Before beginning an exploration of how to employ this technology to enhance performance, it's worthwhile to spend some time defining some key clustering terms and concepts.

Although you can visualize a MySQL cluster in many ways, at its core it is simply a group of computers all working together to provide you with information as quickly as possible, with much higher levels of availability and failure resistance than a single database server could offer. Each computer fulfills at least one of three specialized roles, which are discussed momentarily.

Nodes

In the context of a MySQL cluster, a physical, tangible computer is known as a "host." The role that it plays is described as a "node," which is a logical rather than a physical concept. Three classes of node are available, as described in the following three sections.

SQL Node

Previously known as client, or API node, this is merely a MySQL database server, just like you use for all of your other MySQL needs. The difference here is that this database process uses a specialized storage engine (NDB), which is responsible for the physical storage of information on another type of server: the data node, which may also be referred to as the "storage" node. In effect, the SQL node has outsourced the task of looking after data to the data node.

Clients (such as enterprise applications, query editors, tools, and so forth) continue to contact the SQL node to serve their data needs, which, in turn, looks to the data node for help. To these clients, however, there is no difference between a "normal" MySQL installation and a clustered installation, except that information access should be more reliable when clustering is employed.

Data Node

This node, alternatively described as the storage node and formerly known as the database or DB node, has the important job of keeping information in memory as well as periodically making any data alterations permanent on disk. As you have seen throughout the book, any time you can take advantage of in-memory processing usually means better performance: This is a key benefit of clustering.

In addition, data nodes work together to keep redundant copies of information on different nodes. This also serves as one of the cornerstones of clustering, and helps give it its high availability and fault-tolerant reputation.

Management Node

This node has the least glamorous job: administration. It is responsible for launching and shutting down all other types of nodes, keeping track of their configuration, logging data alterations, and backing up and possibly restoring information.

One task that is not performed during communication *among* the nodes is security and permission checks; these still happen *within* the SQL node, however. This distinction is important, and serves to highlight the assertion you will see shortly: Clustering should happen on its own dedicated network.

Shared-Nothing

This term does not refer to the communal attitudes and beliefs of a group of stingy loners; instead, it accurately describes the clustering architecture scenario in which each node runs on its own separate host. The host is dedicated to this node and is not shared by any other nodes. Although not mandatory, it offers the highest degree of protection from unanticipated problems: The loss of one node does not translate into a catastrophic failure unless that node was the only one of its kind.

Cluster Clients

Whether written by you using one of the many MySQL-friendly languages or connectors, purchased commercially, or acquired via open source, these standard database-accessing applications don't need to know that they are addressing a cluster. At the end of the day, these cluster clients are the ultimate beneficiaries of your investment in a MySQL cluster, reaping the performance and reliability gains from your distributed computing strategy.

Storage Engine

Chapter 4, "Designing for Speed," described the specialized roles that each MySQL storage engine plays. In the case of MySQL Cluster, the NDB storage engine is the only choice. This engine is designed for distributed processing, and provides full transactional support.

Transporter

Now that you've seen what role each node plays along with where the cluster client fits in, you might wonder how these nodes are made aware of each others' existence, and how they communicate. This is the job of the transporter, which is simply the designated communication protocol used to transmit information within the cluster. Note that the transporter is not responsible for communication between the SQL node and actual clients: This is a separate configuration setting.

There are currently four varieties of the supported transporter, briefly summarized in the following sections. Configuring these transporters is reviewed a little later.

Shared Memory

Although beneficial from a performance perspective but not desirable from the viewpoint of fault tolerance, it is indeed possible to have a single host run multiple types of nodes. In these kinds of circumstances, MySQL Cluster is able to employ a shared memory transporter, which provides for extremely fast internode communication.

TCP/IP Local

If multiple nodes are running on the same computer, you can elect to use the TCP/IP protocol as the transporter for local communication among these nodes.

TCP/IP Remote

Naturally, TCP/IP support is also available to serve those clusters when the nodes are spread among multiple hosts. It should be noted, however, that node-to-node communication in the 4.1.x series of production servers is not optimized; this will be much better in the 5.x series of MySQL products.

Scalable Coherent Interface (SCI)

This new technology shatters the 100-MBPS speed limit; computers can now communicate at speeds up to 10 times faster. This speed comes at a price, however: Additional hardware and more complex configuration need to be in place before this transporter is ready for your nodes to use.

Data Distribution

One technique that the NDB storage engine and MySQL Cluster use to greatly boost fault tolerance and availability is to automatically spread data among multiple data nodes. The next section explores how this information is allocated.

Fragment

To facilitate this data distribution, tables are divvied up into chunks that are known as fragments in a process that is invisible to the administrator. These fragments (also known as partitions) are then available for distribution for redundancy's sake. In a moment, you will see how this works.

Replicas

After the NDB storage engine has created and populated fragments from a given table, these objects are then distributed among multiple data nodes, assuming, of course, that you have deployed more than one data node. These copies are known as replicas, and MySQL Cluster currently allows up to four replicas for a given fragment.

Checkpoints

In any distributed computing environment, there needs to be a mechanism to establish a commonly agreed upon system state. Without this mechanism, each computer would have its own interpretation of reality. Although this freedom might boost the computers' individuality and self-esteem, it's not likely to improve the mood of the users.

Fortunately, MySQL Cluster uses an event known as a checkpoint, which is responsible for ensuring consistency among the nodes participating in the cluster. There are two types of checkpoints, described in the following sections.

Local Checkpoint

A local checkpoint is responsible for guaranteeing that data alterations on a given node are, in fact, written to disk, making them permanent. A little later in this chapter, you'll see ways to help control the frequency of these events.

Global Checkpoint

Just as a local checkpoint's scope is the transactions within a single node, a global checkpoint is in charge of making sure that transactions across the cluster are in a consistent state.

Is Clustering Right for You?

Chapter 16, "Optimal Replication," examined the costs and benefits of replication and a number of requirements that you could use to decide whether these benefits were worth the effort. It's now time to do the same with regard to clustering.

- **High availability**—The data stored on your MySQL server needs to be accessible 24 x 7.

- **Abundant, low-performance computers**—Your organization might not have the fastest computers, but they have lots of them.

- **Reliability**—You are very interested in keeping your information as dependable as possible; the loss of even a single record in an aborted transaction is a big concern.

- **Speed**—As a reader of this book, interest in this final criteria will likely apply to you. However, you should note that a MySQL Cluster–based database's read performance might be slower than a corresponding standalone system's when the 4.1.x series is deployed. On the other hand, write performance might be faster. In any case, version 5.x should yield dramatically faster results.

Clustering Versus Replication

Given that both clustering and replication spread the data and processing loads among multiple systems, how can you determine which technology to employ? Note that these two approaches are not necessarily mutually exclusive, but for simplicity's sake, this chapter treats them as if they are.

The Case for Replication

The following list highlights some of the advantages of choosing a replication strategy rather than employing clustering. This is only a partial list, primarily focusing on performance differences.

- **Simplicity**—Although setting up a MySQL cluster is not difficult if you plan and follow instructions, deploying replication is easier and generally requires less work.

- **Broader operating system support**—Currently, the list of operating systems supported for clustering is smaller than those supported for replication. One glaring omission is Windows; if your MySQL installation relies on this operating system, you need to wait before rolling out clustering.

- **Query cache support**—As you saw in Chapter 10, "General Server Performance and Parameters Tuning," the query cache can leverage the power of memory-based processing by storing already-run queries and their results in RAM. This feature is not supported in a MySQL cluster.

- **More optimal query plans**—In certain conditions, you might need to coach the query optimizer into recommending a better query plan via the FORCE INDEX or USE INDEX commands. Furthermore, the MySQL query optimizer was not designed for distributed operations, so there can be performance-affecting issues when clustering.

- **Better range scans**—InnoDB and MyISAM are both more efficient when processing range scans. These scans might make up a significant portion of your database activity.

- **FULLTEXT indexing support**—As you saw in Chapter 11, "MyISAM Performance Enhancement," FULLTEXT indexes can make information stored in your MyISAM-based tables much more accessible.

The Case for Clustering

The preceding section makes a compelling case for using replication rather than clustering to achieve your distributed database goals. What are some arguments in favor of clustering?

- **Availability**—Although replicated (slave) servers contain copies of the master's data, these slaves are generally not meant to be updated. Consequently, the loss of the master can disrupt the transactional nature of most database-reliant applications. Conversely, a clustered environment can more gracefully handle interruptions to individual servers, or even groups of servers. This helps increase overall availability, yielding a more dependable solution.

- **Better speed**—By storing all database information in memory and reducing the overall amount of disk access, MySQL Cluster can significantly increase performance. In version 4.1.x, this is especially true for write-intensive applications; read-intensive applications might see degraded performance. Version 5.x will introduce numerous features to address this problem.

- **Consistency**—MySQL Cluster delivers enhanced consistency because updates to one data node are reflected nearly instantaneously on all other data nodes within the cluster.

- **Transaction reliability**—As you saw in the preceding item, the fact that updates to one data node are reflected elsewhere translates into more reliable transactions. Unlike replication, in which there might be some latency between an alteration on the master and its reflection on slaves, a clustered environment should see its transactions created and executed in multiple places at once.

Creating a Clustering Strategy

With major clustering terms and concepts defined, it's now time to look at strategies and best practices you can employ to set up the right clustering environment.

This section provides an important discussion about the performance-related capabilities of the 4.1.x and 5.x series of MySQL Cluster, followed by some ideas on defining the right cluster topology.

Choosing the Right Version

As previously stated several times in this chapter, dramatic performance differences exist between different versions of MySQL Cluster. Perhaps the easiest way to view these differences is as follows: Version 4.1.x delivers high availability but might hurt performance, whereas version 5.x will address these performance issues through a collection of enhancements. These enhancements include the following:

- **Parallelism**—MySQL 5.x will do a much better job of leveraging data nodes to work in parallel, retrieving information much faster than before.

- **Data node–based filtering**—Prior to version 5.x, MySQL returned raw results to the SQL node, which, in turn, filtered these results. Newer versions will do a better job of filtering these results on the data node itself; this will greatly reduce expensive network traffic.

- **Better range queries**—In Chapter 6, "Understanding the MySQL Optimizer," you saw how the version 5.x series was able to utilize multiple indexes to retrieve results faster. The same holds true for queries across a cluster.

In spite of these performance challenges with version 4.1.x, it's still worthwhile to explore MySQL Cluster, if for no other reason than to gain experience and prepare for upgrading to version 5.x.

Cluster Topology

Whenever configuring a distributed computing environment, it's natural to wonder how to allocate servers, or in the case of MySQL Cluster, hosts and nodes.

This is yet another example of the site-specific nature of performance tuning: What works for a read-intensive search engine might be anathema to a site that processes thousands of data-modifying transactions per second. Administrators must strike a balance between the high-availability benefits brought about by deploying numerous redundant data nodes and the added network costs that these extraneous nodes incur.

With that said, consider a few suggestions that should be appropriate in the majority of situations in which MySQL Cluster is deployed.

- **Define at least two management nodes**—As you just saw, the management node is responsible for critical oversight of the MySQL Cluster; defining an additional node provides supplementary protection should the first management node fail.

- **Define at least two data nodes**—One technique used by MySQL Cluster to achieve high availability is to break tables into fragments and then distribute those fragments among multiple data nodes. This is only possible if enough data nodes have been defined.

- **Define enough SQL nodes to support your workload**—Recall that the SQL node is simply a standard MySQL database server that is able to leverage the added capabilities of the NDB storage engine. Although these nodes don't have the intense workload of the data nodes, it's still important to configure enough of them to support the expected demands from your clients. Note that in future versions, additional processing work might be pushed down to the data node level from the SQL node; it's likely that this will change the ideal ratio among nodes.

Configuring MySQL Cluster for High Performance

Now that you've learned how MySQL Cluster works, its key concepts, and scenarios in which it can be exploited to boost performance, it's time to review those settings and variables that can have the most impact on the speed at which your cluster operates.

This section begins by citing some clustering best practices that are independent of any other considerations. After exploring that topic, the chapter moves on to surveying the specific options for better networking, followed by how to configure performance-related transport options. Next, it proceeds on to considerations to help deploy a better management node before examining details about the data node. Finally, the section and chapter close with some ideas for the SQL node.

General Clustering Best Practices

No matter what clustering software version or topology you select, you can follow several best practices to get better performance from your MySQL cluster.

Employing Primary Keys

As you have seen throughout the book, a primary key makes it possible to find a record with a single read. Make sure that all of your tables have a primary key defined. If not, the NDB storage engine automatically creates one, but it's likely that this artificial key won't be meaningful for your application.

Grouping Insert Operations

If your cluster operations consist of many small data-altering transactions, the sheer amount of network traffic can bog down performance even if the network is fast. In cases in which you are inserting large amounts of data, try to batch the INSERT statements into big groups. If possible, try to use the LOAD DATA INFILE statement, which produces even better results.

Using Appropriate Indexes

Many portions of this book have cited the importance of indexes; clustering is no exception to this rule. In fact, it can be argued that the potential damage caused by a badly designed index strategy is multiplied by the number of nodes in a cluster. Remember to use the EXPLAIN command to get a better idea of how your queries are using indexes, if at all.

Spreading the Load Among SQL Nodes

Recall that from the perspective of the ultimate client (such as an application), there is no such thing as a cluster. Instead, the client simply connects to a MySQL server as always, and then issues requests against the database. In fact, the client is connecting to a node in the cluster—the SQL node in this case.

The SQL node, in turn, employs the distributed processing capabilities of the cluster to access or alter data. Load balancing at this level is built in to MySQL Cluster. However, the same is not the case for clients connecting to the SQL node. In this situation, it's the responsibility of the administrator to employ load balancing, round-robin access, or other methods of spreading the work among multiple SQL nodes.

In the absence of a work distribution strategy, it's quite possible that a given SQL node might be overloaded with user requests while another SQL node sits idle. Fortunately, many open source and commercial solutions can solve this problem.

Protecting Your Data

In Chapter 13, "Improving Disk Speed," you saw how MySQL derives performance and availability benefits by leveraging any of the disk-based data-preserving technologies, such as RAID, mirroring, and so on. The same holds true for information stored in MySQL Cluster; even though data remains resident in memory, it is also periodically logged to disk during checkpoints. Any steps that you can take to increase the integrity of this disk storage will help improve your MySQL cluster's ability to survive a severe hardware failure.

MySQL Cluster also offers backup and restore; it is well worth your time to learn how to use these utilities to help safeguard your information.

Network Considerations

Because internode communications are so vital in a well-tuned MySQL Cluster, this section examines this important topic.

Running on a Dedicated Subnet

Don't let other, nonclustered computers clog your cluster communication network with irrelevant chatter. Instead, connect all nodes in your MySQL cluster onto their own, private subnet. Only the SQL node needs to be directly accessible by cluster clients from your broader network; all communication *among* cluster nodes should be shielded from interference.

Using Numeric IP Addresses

You are free to use traditional names for all of the hosts that run the nodes that make up your MySQL cluster, but why force an unnecessary DNS lookup on these hosts? Instead, consider referencing these nodes by their numeric IP addresses. If you must use names, at least create entries in the /etc/hosts file on each host to provide a faster way for the host to translate between the name and its associated IP address.

Being Security Conscious

Earlier in this chapter, you learned that when communicating among themselves, nodes do not consult the standard MySQL permissions. In addition, all traffic among these hosts is sent in the clear: There is no encryption for this type of communication.

Both of these facts mean that a MySQL Cluster administrator has extra security responsibility, especially as it relates to network access because that traffic can be easily intercepted and managed.

Transports

Recall from earlier in this chapter that the transport is the actual communication protocol used by all the nodes in the cluster to converse. This section looks at each of the transports to explore performance-specific settings. It pays particular attention to how SCI sockets can make a huge difference in communication speed.

TCP/IP

Even though this is the most commonly used protocol for clustering and the Internet at large, surprisingly, few configuration settings are available. For the book's purposes, two come to mind:

- **SendBufferMemory**—If set too low, there is a risk that the TCP/IP buffer can overfill and fail. The primary potential consequence of setting it too high is memory wastage.
- **Checksum**—By switching this parameter from its default of 0 (disabled) to 1 (enabled), MySQL computes a checksum for these internode messages, which adds overhead to the communication process. Generally, it can be left alone at its default (disabled) value, especially if all internode communication is happening on a closed, nearby subnet.

Shared Memory

Shared memory is a transport option for those computers that are hosting multiple nodes. As you saw earlier, running several nodes on one machine partially defeats the purpose of clustering. However, if you decide to follow this approach, you can control two key performance-related settings:

- **ShmSize**—This parameter controls how much shared memory is allocated to each connection's shared memory segment. If set too low, there is a risk that this buffer might not have enough space to service the connection's request, whereas a too-high setting wastes memory. The default value of 1MB should suffice in most cases.
- **Checksum**—By switching this parameter from its default of 0 (disabled) to 1 (enabled), MySQL computes a checksum for these in-memory messages. Given that in-memory corruption is an extremely rare event, it likely can be left alone at its default (disabled) value.

SCI Sockets

At the beginning of this chapter, you saw how the new SCI technologies can dramatically improve communication among nodes. You also read how this transport requires specialized hardware and considerable additional configuration compared to standard TCP/IP.

With that said, you can control two parameters to help this transport run as efficiently as possible:

- **Checksum**—If you are concerned about potential message corruption, change this parameter from its default of 0 (disabled) to 1 (enabled). If enabled, MySQL computes a checksum for all messages sent between nodes using this protocol. However, the extra processing cost is probably not worth the derived benefits; LAN-resident message corruption is typically a very rare event.

- **SharedBufferSize**—With a default value of 1MB, this parameter is used by MySQL to create a memory-based area for internode communication. Unless you are really pressed for memory, it's probably wisest to leave this setting untouched. On the other hand, if your processing environment sees substantial amounts of concurrent data insertion, and you have available RAM, consider slowly raising this amount for extra memory benefits.

Management Node Considerations

This section examines optimal configuration of your management node, along with ways to monitor its status.

Logging

Because all data modifications are logged, and disk access is typically one of the most severe performance impediments, it stands to reason that anything you can do to improve the speed at which logging operates should reflect in overall cluster response.

One key logging parameter is the `LogDestination` setting, which tunes a variety of aspects of this capability. Try using the `FILE` option and setting it to the fastest available file system.

Arbitration

When something goes wrong (such as one or more nodes dying) in a MySQL cluster, arbitration refers to the decisions made by a predesignated node that instruct the other nodes how to proceed. Two important parameters affect arbitration; they each have a peripheral impact on performance.

The first, `ArbitrationRank`, tells MySQL whether this node may never act as an arbitrator (value of 0); whether this node is a high-priority arbitrator (value of 1); or whether this node is a "last-choice" arbitrator (value of 2). Management nodes should have a setting of 1; optionally, you may elect to grant a SQL node a setting of 2, but this should be done sparingly and only for redundancy's sake. Otherwise, SQL nodes should have a value of 0.

The second, `ArbitrationDelay`, tells MySQL to wait a specified number of milliseconds before responding to an arbitration request. There is little reason to change this value from its default of 0 (that is, instantaneous response).

SQL Node Considerations

As the node that interfaces with client applications, it's important that your SQL node work as efficiently as possible. This section examines how to configure the relatively few number of SQL node parameters to realize the best performance.

Arbitration

As you saw in the previous section that discussed the management node, the `ArbitrationRank` and `ArbitrationDelay` settings control the location and behavior of potential arbitrators for the cluster. As stated earlier, your best bet is to set ArbitrationRank to 0, thereby leaving the SQL nodes out of the arbitration loop. Only when you absolutely need an additional potential arbitrator should you set it to 1 or 2.

Batching

In certain query conditions such as index range scans or table scans, MySQL attempts to optimize data access by retrieving large chunks of information from a given table. For these situations, MySQL Cluster provides administrators with tools to configure the size of these chunks (also known as batches).

The BatchSize setting spells out the number of records per batch. With a range zero to 992, there is a lot of room for you to experiment with different settings. Here is yet another example of how understanding the MySQL optimizer's output can help an administrator do a better job of configuring their server. The BatchByteSize setting provides an alternative method (that is, actual size in bytes) of tuning the batch buffer.

Finally, the MaxScanBatchSize value acts as a throttle to prevent all nodes from flooding the network with batched results from a particular query. You have great leeway in tuning this setting; potential values range from zero to the default of 256KB all the way up to 16MB. If your environment sees lots of table or index range scans, and your clustering network is private and offers ample bandwidth, consider raising this value to take advantage of this speed. Otherwise, leave it at a relatively low number if network capacity is a concern.

Data Node Considerations

Now that you have seen how to configure the management and SQL nodes, it's time to look at setting up and tuning the most complex component in a MySQL cluster: the data node. For consistency's sake, try to employ servers with equivalent processing, memory, and storage capabilities as data nodes: It's not a good idea to have wildly divergent computers serving as data nodes. In addition, keep these settings alike on all nodes.

In terms of providing sufficient memory for clustering, note that each data node needs enough capacity to hold the database size times the number of replicas, divided by the number of data nodes.

After your data nodes are in place, you can then shape your settings to meet your site-specific needs. The balance of this chapter reviews a number of these variables, paying particular attention to those that directly affect performance. For clarity, they are organized by major functional area.

Capacity

MySQL Cluster administrators have numerous settings at their disposal to specify the operational and metadata capacities of their environment. Some of the most important parameters include the following:

- `MaxNoOfConcurrentScans`
- `MaxNoOfLocalScans`
- `BatchSizePerLocalScan`
- `MaxNoOfAttributes`
- `MaxNoOfTables`
- `MaxNoOfIndexes`
- `MaxNoOfOrderedIndexes`
- `MaxNoOfUniqueHashIndexes`
- `MaxNoOfTriggers`

If any of these variables are set too low, there is a risk of resource contention. For this reason, it's wise to leave them at their defaults unless you are sure that an alteration makes sense in your environment.

Timing

Timing plays a vital role in keeping all nodes in a cluster in sync; numerous settings are available for administrators to tune their MySQL Cluster's site-specific behavior. In most cases, however, the default values are sufficient. This is true for many of the "heartbeat" and timeout settings, such as:

- `ArbitrationTimeout`
- `TimeBetweenWatchDogCheck`
- `HeartBeatIntervalDbDb`
- `HeartBeatIntervalDbApi`
- `TransactionInactiveTimeout`
- `TransactionDeadlockDetectionTimeout`
- `TimeBetweenInactiveTransactionAbortCheck`
- `TimeBetweenLocalCheckpoints`
- `TimeBetweenGlobalCheckpoints`

The same can be said for those parameters that help throttle the number of data or index pages written to disk during checkpoints or startup, including the following:

- `NoOfDiskPagesToDiskAfterRestartTUP`
- `NoOfDiskPagesToDiskAfterRestartACC`
- `NoOfDiskPagesToDiskDuringRestartTUP`
- `NoOfDiskPagesToDiskDuringRestartACC`

One parameter that can definitely benefit from alteration is `StartFailureTimeout`. This setting places an upper limit on how long MySQL Cluster waits for a data node to start before giving up. The default value of 60,000 milliseconds (that is, 60 seconds) is probably insuffi-cient for a large site: It can take significantly longer for a data node to complete the startup operation. You might need to dramatically raise this value to meet your needs.

Memory

By storing all data within memory, MySQL Cluster is able to deliver substantially faster per-formance than a more traditional, disk-based database architecture. This section reviews those memory settings that can affect performance. As you saw earlier, the correct settings for these values are highly dependent on your own unique processing profile.

One initial decision you can make is to instruct MySQL Cluster not to register any data alterations to disk by enabling the Diskless setting. This in-memory clustering reduces overhead, but exposes you to complete data loss should your server go down unexpectedly.

During Chapter 10's discussion of general database settings, you saw how MySQL adminis-trators may elect to force mysqld to remain in memory, generally immune to the swapping that other processes face. The same holds true on the data nodes: The LockPagesInMainMemory setting (disabled by default) instructs the operating system not to swap the data node process to disk. If you are confident that you have enough memory so that other processes won't unduly suffer, consider enabling this parameter.

The DataMemory and IndexMemory each control how much memory is allocated for data and indexes, respectively. In addition to the typical storage requirements for this information, there is also overhead ranging from 16 bytes all the way up to more than 50 bytes, depend-ing on whether the information contains data or index content. To arrive at the ideal setting for your environment takes some calculation; you can also use the time-tested trial-and-error approach to arrive at the correct value. It's probably better to slightly overallocate memory than to deprive MySQL Cluster of the space it needs.

Memory allocation also plays a role in efficient online backups. Administrators can set the BackupDataBufferSize, BackupLogBufferSize, BackupMemory, and BackupWriteSize variables. The defaults for all of these settings are probably fine; if you have memory to burn you might try raising them.

Transactions

Transactions make it possible for MySQL Cluster to offer enhanced data reliability and con-sistency across multiple nodes. This section discusses performance-related transaction set-tings. Most of these settings are best left alone, unless your processing profile features many parallel query or data alteration operations. Settings that conform to this rule are MaxNoOfFiredTriggers, MaxNoOfConcurrentIndexOperations, and TransactionBufferMemory.

On the other hand, if your environment sees relatively few transactions and those transac-tions are relatively small, you can safely lower the MaxNoOfConcurrentOperations setting. If the opposite is true, consider raising its value. As usual, if you are unsure, just leave it at its default.

An environment with copious nodes and periodic very large transactions benefits from an increase to the MaxNoOfLocalOperations setting. Otherwise, it should be left untouched.

Finally, the MaxNoOfConcurrentTransactions default value of 4096 is generally sufficient. To determine if this is so for your site, estimate the total number of transactions likely to be active across all data nodes at any one time. Should all of the data nodes crash but one, the remaining node would need this setting to be greater than or equal to the new transaction workload.

Logging

Transactions are the mechanism that MySQL Cluster uses to keep information synchronized; logging is the process that transactions themselves use to ensure consistency.

Because log records are first buffered in memory and then written to disk, several parameters are available to determine the amount of memory available for this caching. These settings include UndoDataBuffer, UndoIndexBuffer, and RedoBuffer. Their default values will likely suffice in most environments; setting them too low triggers MySQL Cluster error states, whereas setting them too high wastes memory.

One vital logging-related parameter is NoOfFragmentLogFiles, which is used to allocate space for the node's REDO logs. Allocated in batches of 64MB, these logs are used to restore data to a consistent state should a transaction abort. If set too low, there is a strong possibility that MySQL Cluster will be forced to automatically abort transactions that alter data. If set too high, disk space is wasted. The default value of 8 translates to 512MB of REDO log storage. Here again, the dangers of a too-high setting are far outweighed by the risks of a too-low setting.

VI

Case Studies

Throughout the chapters, this book has tried to illustrate how a host of complex and inter-related design, development, and configuration decisions ultimately determine MySQL's performance in your environment. These judgments are made by a wide variety of individuals, including database designers, developers, and administrators, and span the entire life cycle of your MySQL–based solution.

Changes in one category can potentially ripple through the complete MySQL environment, often causing unanticipated side effects. This is one key reason that performance tuning is an art, rather than a science. The balance of the book looks at multifaceted case studies that embody this reality.

As with all of the other examples, the goal is to keep these case studies as uncluttered and simple as possible. This means that the illustrations are far cleaner than in the real world. Nevertheless, we always strive to communicate the underlying lessons in each case study.

One area in which the case studies do closely mimic the real world is in the solutions section. In reality, database designers, developers, and administrators typically face many choices when designing, developing, deploying, and tuning their MySQL-based solution. It's not easy knowing which path to follow. To help illuminate this problem, several of the examples include multiple potential actions. In fact, some of these actions conflict with each other: Your only choice is to make the best-educated selection possible, and then carefully monitor your results.

In terms of how to proceed through the section, note that every case study can stand alone; there are minimal interrelationships among them. However, you'll find several associated problems within each case study, just as real-world performance difficulties seem to come in groups.

To get the most from these case studies, look at each one separately, and try to come up with a holistic solution. See if your performance fixes match those suggested by the book.

## 18

Case Study: High-Hat Delivers!

To augment his already-stellar decision-making skills, High-Hat Airways' CEO employs a diverse squadron of soothsayers, astrologists, and fortune tellers. For months, these experts have been pushing him to enter the lucrative package shipment marketplace. The CEO has been reluctant; he can't exactly explain why, but he's been waiting for a signal. Finally, the sign arrives in the form of a dream: rows of singing cardboard boxes, each stuffed with cash. The next morning, the CEO summons his executive team to an emergency meeting to deliver the great news: High-Hat is entering the shipping business!

With lightning speed, High-Hat's IT department springs into action. Impending layoffs are delayed. Vacations are canceled; several projects nearing completion are put on hold as the entire team works around the clock to realize the CEO's dream.

This Herculean effort pays off: An entire package tracking application infrastructure is built and deployed worldwide in a matter of weeks. Of course, QA is a bit behind; performance testing isn't even a consideration.

Initially, the new package tracking service is a hit. Wall Street raises earnings estimates, and many executives receive bonuses. The previously delayed IT layoffs now proceed, adding even more to the bottom line.

From a systems perspective, everything appears fine. The new applications have relatively few issues. Results are accurate, and response time is reasonable. During the course of the first month, however, things begin to change. Mysterious reports, detailing sporadic yet horrendous application performance problems, start arriving daily from High-Hat's far-flung empire. Rumors of severe problems leak out to financial analysts, who promptly cut earnings estimates, thereby decimating the stock price. Several executives are demoted, while numerous midlevel managers are moved from their offices into tiny cubicles.

A desperate CIO calls you late one night. High-Hat is very sorry about laying you off, and wants you to return to help overcome these problems. After renegotiating your compensation package, you're ready to go back to work.

Being an astute performance-tuning expert, you know that the first task is to accurately cata-log the problems. Only then can you proceed with corrections. Your initial analysis separates the main problems into the following high-level categories.

Problem Queries

After looking into the query situation, you realize that, basically, two types of problem queries exist. The first is encountered when a user tries to look up the status of a shipment. However, it is not consistent: It appears to happen sporadically for most users. The second problem query happens to everyone whenever they attempt to accept a new package for shipment.

Package Status Lookup

Internal employees and external website users have begun complaining that it takes too long to look up the shipping status for a package. What makes this more perplexing is that it doesn't happen all the time. Some queries run very fast, whereas others can take minutes to complete.

The principal tables for tracking package status include the following:

```
CREATE TABLE package_header (
    package_id INTEGER PRIMARY KEY AUTO_INCREMENT,
    dropoff_location_id SMALLINT(3),
    destination_location_id SMALLINT(3),
    sender_first_name VARCHAR(20),
    sender_last_name VARCHAR(30),
...
    recipient_first_name VARCHAR(20),
    recipient_last_name VARCHAR(30),
...
    recipient_fax VARCHAR(30),
...
    INDEX (sender_last_name, sender_first_name),
    INDEX (recipient_last_name, recipient_first_name),
    INDEX (recipient_fax)
) ENGINE = INNODB;


CREATE TABLE package_status (
    package_status_id INTEGER PRIMARY KEY AUTO_INCREMENT,
    package_id INTEGER NOT NULL REFERENCES package_header(package_id),
...
...
    package_location_id SMALLINT(3) NOT NULL,
```

```
    activity_timestamp DATETIME NOT NULL,
    comments TEXT,
    INDEX (package_id)
) ENGINE = INNODB;
```

Diagnosis

As an experienced MySQL expert, you know that MySQL offers a number of valuable tools to help spot performance problems. One of them is the slow query log, as discussed in Chapter 2, "Performance Monitoring Options." By simply enabling this log, you can sit back and wait for the troubled queries to make their presence known.

Sure enough, after a few minutes you see some candidates:

```
# Time: 060306 17:26:18
# User@Host: [fpembleton] @ localhost []
# Query_time: 6  Lock_time: 0  Rows_sent: 12  Rows_examined: 573992012
SELECT ph.*, ps.* FROM package_header ph, package_status ps WHERE
ph.package_id = ps.package_id AND ph.recipient_fax like '%431-5979%';
# Time: 060306 17:26:19
# User@Host: [wburroughs] @ localhost []
# Query_time: 9  Lock_time: 0  Rows_sent: 0  Rows_examined: 5739922331
SELECT ph.*, ps.* FROM package_header ph, package_status ps WHERE
ph.package_id = ps.package_id AND ph.recipient_fax like '%785-4551%';
# Time: 060306 17:26:21
# User@Host: [nikkis] @ localhost []
# Query_time: 9  Lock_time: 0  Rows_sent: 0  Rows_examined: 5739922366
SELECT ph.*, ps.* FROM package_header ph, package_status ps WHERE
ph.package_id = ps.package_id AND ph.recipient_fax like '%341-1142%';
```

Now that you've found what appears to be a problem query, your next step is to run EXPLAIN to see what steps the MySQL optimizer is following to obtain results:

```
mysql> EXPLAIN
    -> SELECT ph.*, ps.*
    -> FROM package_header ph, package_status ps
    -> WHERE ph.package_id = ps.package_id
    -> AND ph.recipient_fax like '%431-5979%'\G
*************************** 1. row ***************************
          id: 1
 select_type: SIMPLE
       table: ph
        type: ALL
possible_keys: PRIMARY
         key: NULL
     key_len: NULL
         ref: NULL
        rows: 521750321
```

```
            Extra: Using where
*************************** 2. row ***************************
            id: 1
  select_type: SIMPLE
        table: ps
         type: ref
possible_keys: package_id
          key: package_id
      key_len: 4
          ref: high_hat.ph.package_id
         rows: 1
        Extra:
2 rows in set (0.00 sec)
```

This output provides the answer: MySQL is performing an expensive table scan on
package_header every time a user searches on recipient fax. Considering the sheer size of
the table, it's apparent that this leads to very lengthy queries. It also explains the sporadic
nature of the query problem: Most status queries use some other lookup criteria.

When you interview the developer of the query, you learn that this query exists to serve customers, who might not always know the area code for the recipient fax. To make the query
more convenient, the developer allowed users to just provide a phone number, and he places
a wildcard before and after the number to find all possible matches. He's aghast to learn that
this type of query frequently renders existing indexes useless.

Solution

When faced with a large-table query that is not correctly taking advantage of indexes, you
have two very different options: Fix the query or add a new index. In this case, it's probably
easiest and wisest to just correct the query. The application logic should force the user to
enter an area code and fax number. In combination, these two values will be able to employ
the index:

```
mysql> EXPLAIN
    -> SELECT ph.*, ps.*
    -> FROM package_header ph, package_status ps
    -> WHERE ph.package_id = ps.package_id
    -> AND ph.recipient_fax like '516-431-5979'\G
*************************** 1. row ***************************
            id: 1
  select_type: SIMPLE
        table: ph
         type: range
possible_keys: PRIMARY,recipient_fax
          key: recipient_fax
      key_len: 30
          ref: NULL
         rows: 1
```

```
        Extra: Using where
*************************** 2. row ***************************
           id: 1
  select_type: SIMPLE
        table: ps
         type: ref
possible_keys: package_id
          key: package_id
      key_len: 4
          ref: high_hat.ph.package_id
         rows: 1
        Extra:
2 rows in set (0.00 sec)
```

As you saw earlier during the review of MySQL's optimizer in Chapter 6, "Understanding the MySQL Optimizer," version 5.0 offers better index utilization. In this case, the developer might elect to allow the user to query on several area codes. The new optimizer capabilities mean that MySQL can still take advantage of the index:

```
mysql> EXPLAIN
    -> SELECT ph.*, ps.*
    -> FROM package_header ph, package_status ps
    -> WHERE ph.package_id = ps.package_id
    -> AND ((ph.recipient_fax like '516-431-5979')
    -> OR (ph.recipient_fax like '212-431-5979'))\G
*************************** 1. row ***************************
           id: 1
  select_type: SIMPLE
        table: ph
         type: range
possible_keys: PRIMARY,recipient_fax
          key: recipient_fax
      key_len: 30
          ref: NULL
         rows: 2
        Extra: Using where
*************************** 2. row ***************************
           id: 1
  select_type: SIMPLE
        table: ps
         type: ref
possible_keys: package_id
          key: package_id
      key_len: 4
          ref: high_hat.ph.package_id
         rows: 1
        Extra:
2 rows in set (0.00 sec)
```

Shipping Option Lookup

To wring more profit from its shipping service, High-Hat implemented a complex pricing mechanism, with thousands of possible prices based on weight, distance, potential value of the customer, currency, language, and so on. All of this information is stored in a single, vital lookup table:

```
CREATE TABLE shipping_prices (
    price_id INTEGER PRIMARY KEY AUTO_INCREMENT,
    price_code CHAR(17) NOT NULL,
    from_zone SMALLINT(3) NOT NULL,
    to_zone SMALLINT(3) NOT NULL,
    min_weight DECIMAL(6,2) NOT NULL,
    max_weight DECIMAL(6,2) NOT NULL,
    ...
    price_in_usd decimal(5,2) NOT NULL,
    price_in_euro decimal(5,2) NOT NULL,
    price_in_gbp decimal(5,2) NOT NULL,
    ...
    price_in_zambia_kwacha DECIMAL(15,2) NOT NULL,
    price_rules_in_english LONGTEXT NOT NULL,
    price_rules_in_spanish LONGTEXT NOT NULL,
    ...
    price_rules_in_tagalog LONGTEXT NOT NULL,
    price_rules_in_turkish LONGTEXT NOT NULL,
    ...
    INDEX (price_code),
    INDEX (from_zone),
    INDEX (to_zone),
    INDEX (min_weight),
    INDEX (max_weight)
) ENGINE = MYISAM;
```

Users are complaining that it takes too long to look up the potential price to ship a package. In several cases, customers have either hung up on the High-Hat sales representative or even stormed out of the package drop-off centers.

Diagnosis

Given how frequently this data is accessed by users, it seems that it should be resident in memory most of the time. However, this is not what your analysis shows.

The first thing you check is the size of the table and its indexes. You're surprised to see that this table has hundreds of thousands of very large rows, which consumes enormous amounts of space and makes full memory-based caching unlikely.

The next observation that you make is that this is a heavily denormalized table. This means that when a High-Hat representative retrieves the necessary rows to quote a price to a customer in France, each row that she accesses contains vastly larger amounts of information (such as the price in all currencies and shipping rules in all languages), even though this data is irrelevant in her circumstance.

Finally, you examine the query cache to see how many queries and results are being buffered in memory. You're disappointed to see that the query cache hit rate is very low. However, this makes sense: Recall that if two queries differ in any way, they cannot leverage the query cache.

Solution

The underlying problem here is that the database design is horribly inefficient: Had the designers done a better job of normalization, there would be reduced memory requirements for the essential lookup columns; extraneous columns would not even be included in most result sets. Alas, a database redesign is out of the question, so your next course of action is to make the best of a bad situation and help MySQL do a better job of caching information given the dreadful database design.

Often, the least aggravating and time-consuming approach to raising cache performance is to simply plug more memory into your database server. However, in this case, the server has no more storage capacity, so you need to come up with an alternative strategy. The only remaining choice is to focus on MySQL configuration.

You have several choices when deciding how to cache heavily accessed tables containing critical lookup information that is infrequently updated.

- **Switch to a MEMORY table**—These fast, RAM-based tables were explored in Chapter 4, "Designing for Speed," overview of MySQL's storage engines. If there was sufficient RAM, you could theoretically load the entire shipping_prices table into memory. However, there isn't enough storage, so this option is not workable.

- **Increase utilization of the key cache**—As you saw in Chapter 11, "MyISAM Performance Enhancement," the MyISAM key cache leverages memory to hold index values, thereby reducing costly disk access. However, memory is already a precious commodity on this server, so it's unlikely that you'll be able to extract some additional RAM from your administrators. In addition, this isn't an index problem; instead, the fault lies with the sheer amount of data in each row.

- **Make better use of the query cache**—As you have seen, the query cache buffers frequently used queries and result sets. However, there are several important requirements before a query can extract results from this buffer. One crucial prerequisite is that a new query must exactly match already-cached queries and result sets. If the new query does not match, the query cache will not be consulted to return results.

  In this case, you know from your analysis that there is a high degree of variability among queries and result sets, which means that even the largest query cache won't help.

- **Employ replication**—Recall from earlier in this chapter, the replication discussion that significant performance benefits often accrue by simply spreading the processing load among multiple machines. In this case, placing this fundamental lookup table on its own dedicated machines is very wise. Because there are no other tables with which to contend, it will have the lion's share of memory, so caching hit rates should be somewhat improved.

The application will then be pointed at this server to perform lookups, which should require minimal code changes. However, given the mammoth amount of data found in this table, it's vital that the replicated server have sufficient memory and processor speed to effectively serve its clients. Last but not least, these large rows have the potential to crowd your network, so it's important that the replicated server be placed on a fast network with ample bandwidth. If not, there's a real risk that you might trade one performance problem for another.

Random Transaction Bottlenecks

You've saved the most difficult-to-pin-down performance obstacle for last. The IT help desk receives high volumes of support calls at sporadic times throughout the day. During these periods of intense activity, users complain of system response problems across the board. These delays affect everything from saving new transaction records to updating existing package status details to running reports. To make matters worse, there doesn't appear to be a correlation with user activity load: Some of the most severe slowdowns happen during off-peak hours.

Diagnosis

Fortunately, when faced with such a fuzzy, hard-to-define problem, you have a wide variety of tools at your disposal. These range from operating system monitors to network traffic indicators to MySQL utilities. In circumstances in which there doesn't appear to be a consistent problem, it's often best to arrive at a diagnosis by the process of elimination. You can work through a list of possible causes of the transient performance issue:

- **Insufficient hardware**—If your server is underpowered, it's likely that this deficiency is most prominent during periods of peak activity. That isn't the case here. To be certain, it is wise to turn on server load tracking and then correlate that with MySQL response issues.

- **Network congestion**—This is a little harder to rule out, but the performance problems are not always happening during busy hours. Still, a slight possibility exists that some user or process is hogging the network at seemingly random times, which incorrectly gives the appearance of a MySQL problem. Matching a saved trace of network activity with reports of performance problems goes a long way toward completely eliminating this as a possible cause.

- **Poor database design**—Performance problems are the norm, rather than the exception, if the database designers made key strategic errors when laying out the schema. The same holds true for indexes: Generally, an inefficient index strategy is easy to identify and correct.

- **Badly designed queries**—Given the broad constituency that is complaining about these sporadic slowdowns, it seems unlikely that a single protracted query, or even a group of sluggish queries, could be the culprit. The slow query log goes a long ways toward definitively ruling this out.

- **Unplanned user data access**—The widespread availability of user-driven data access tools has brought untold joys into the lives of many IT professionals. Nothing can drag a database server down like poorly constructed, Cartesian product-generating unrestricted queries written by untrained users.

  Aside from examining the username or IP address of the offending client, it's difficult to quickly identify these types of query tools within the slow query log or active user list. However, by asking around, you learn that a number of marketing analysts have been given business intelligence software and unrestricted access to the production database server.

Solution

Now that you've established that decision support users are likely the root cause of these issues, you look at several alternatives at your disposal to reduce the impact of this class of user. Think of the choices as the "Four R" strategy: replication, rollup, and resource restriction. The following list looks at these choices in descending order of convenience.

- **Replication**—This is, by far, the most convenient solution to your problem. Dedicating one or more slave servers is a great way to satisfy these hard-to-please users. There will be some initial setup and testing, but no code or server settings need to be changed, significantly minimizing the workload for developers and administrators.

- **Rollup**—Another way to diminish the negative performance impact of open-ended reports is to aggregate and summarize information into rollup tables. This approach requires no application or configuration changes, but it does necessitate some effort on your part, and might not completely solve the resource contention issues. Moreover, reporting users will be faced with a lag between live data and their view of this information.

- **Resource restriction**—MySQL offers a variety of mechanisms to constrain user resource consumption. These options were discussed in Chapter 10, "General Server Performance and Parameters Tuning," exploration of general engine configuration. They include `max_queries_per_hour`, `max_updates_per_hour`, `max_connections_per_hour`, `max_join_size`, `SQL_BIG_SELECTS`, and `max_tmp_tables`.

This is the least desirable approach. First, it likely requires configuring these settings at either a global or session level. Second, there is a significant possibility that these changes will prove ineffective in your particular environment.

Implementing These Solutions

Now that your first paycheck from High-Hat has cleared and you've decided how to address these problems, what's the safest course of action to implement your solutions? You reviewed this topic in general during Chapter 1, "Setting Up an Optimization Test Environment," exploration of setting up a performance optimization environment.

In the context of the problems identified in this chapter, it's wise to execute changes in the following order:

1. **Package status query correction**—Correcting the application to force entry of an area code when looking up packages by recipient fax number correctly employs the relevant index and eliminates the costly table scans currently plaguing users. This is a low-risk, high-reward alteration.

2. **Roll up tables for business intelligence query users**—These users are wrecking performance at unpredictable intervals. Because you don't have the authority to lock them out of the system, it's a good idea to aggregate data for them in rollup tables. This is lower risk, and requires less work than the next step, replication.

3. **Replicate information for business intelligence query users**—This is the ideal solution for the problem of end-user query writers, but it does require some work on your part (and introduces some minimal risk of "collateral damage") to implement.

4. **Replicate the `shipping_prices` table to a dedicated server**—This change goes a long way toward reducing resource contention on the primary server. Just like its counterpart for business intelligence users, this type of activity comes with its own setup costs and risks. In this case, you must change application logic to point at the right server, which entails work as well as establishes some hazards if you miss a reference in your software.

## 19

Case Study: Friends Fly Free-for-All—A Promotion Gone Wrong

Thanks to your stellar consulting work in helping High-Hat Airways solve the devastating performance problems introduced by its new package-tracking application (see Chapter 18, "Case Study: High-Hat Delivers!"), you are now the official MySQL performance expert for the airline. Of course, there is no budget to increase the number of billable hours that you can work with the airline, but the CIO assures you that in the event of another big performance crisis, you will be the first person called.

That call arrives several weeks later from the CIO's replacement. Apparently, something went terribly wrong with a promotion the airline ran just after you finished your analysis. According to the new CIO, several members of the senior management team had stock options that were to be vested soon. Wall Street airline analysts had just raised their profitability forecast, but there was a good chance that High-Hat would miss the new target. Missing these estimates by even one penny per share would likely mean that the executives' eventual seaside retirement villas would instead be found several miles inland, and would feature half the planned square footage. Clearly, this could not be allowed to happen.

The senior vice president of marketing had a brilliant idea: High-Hat would immediately run an amazing airfare sale, one that would likely sell hundreds of thousands of new tickets and boost results for that quarter. To keep reservation agent overtime costs down, all ticket sales would be done over the Web, and would be nonrefundable. Some new software would have to be written, but this was just a mere detail.

The CIO proceeded to describe how the timing for this airfare sale could not have been worse. There was very little notice, so everything had to be rushed. During the last round of cost-cutting (following your success in solving the shipping problems), many IT employees had been furloughed. The austerity measures had even affected the number of available web and database servers in production. Although the previous CIO had begged for it, there was no money allocated for load-balancing hardware or software. Finally, despite significant pleas for reconsideration, much of the development of the new functionality to support the web-only ticket sale was outsourced to a company owned by the CEO's brother-in-law.

The airfare sale was announced at noon on a Monday, with the first flights available on Wednesday. Things immediately got off to a rocky start by 1:00 p.m. on Monday when customers began calling the reservation agents to complain about how slowly the website was performing. Some customers couldn't even access the site. Others were able to get in, but couldn't make a reservation. Finally, and worst of all: Numerous customers made a reservation and provided their credit card numbers, but did not receive an acknowledgment from the website.

If Monday and Tuesday were bad, Wednesday was horrendous. Gate agents were astonished to see large jetliners leaving with only two or three passengers on board. Ironically, dozens of other flights were oversold by 300, 400, or even 500 percent. To make matters worse, all ticketed passengers received boarding passes, regardless of whether the flight was oversold. This meant that every seat on these flights needed to hold anywhere between one and five occupants at the same time. This made for some very bad PR, as television news crews around the world descended upon airports to report the results of various onboard melees and donnybrooks as between 600 and 1,000 people attempted to squeeze into 200 seats on each airplane.

The aftermath of this fiasco saw the filing of dozens of lawsuits along with the immediate dismissal of the CIO and most of his team. The replacement CIO contacted you; there is much work to be done.

As you did during your last optimization exercise, your first task is to inventory the problems and then set out to diagnose and solve these issues. Based on what you have learned so far, you decide to classify these problems into two categories: server availability and application/transaction issues.

Server Availability

Even though it has been several weeks since the airfare sale disaster, it is still difficult to piece together exactly what triggered the apparent massive server outages. What is known is that the website slowdowns began within three minutes of the fare sale announcement, and that it got progressively worse as the day wore on.

Diagnosis

Fortunately, in spite of the conflicting anecdotal reports you are receiving from all constituencies, many tools and utilities can shed light on these kinds of problems. High-Hat Airways is an enthusiastic user of these technologies, so a trail of events should exist that you can use to reconstruct what happened as well as deliver a recommendation on how to prevent it from occurring again.

Observations

When evaluating an apparent serverwide performance crisis, it's not a bad idea to start with the tools provided by the operating system. Because the servers in question are running Linux, you have a broad set of technologies at your disposal, as described in Chapter 2, "Performance Monitoring Options." These include the sar, free, and vmstat utilities, which focus on system activity, physical memory, and virtual memory, respectively.

As it turns out, you are able to obtain historical records from all of these utilities from the time of the server problems. They were unanimous in their output: The servers were under tremendous load, with CPU utilization in the 90%–100% range. In addition, memory was incredibly scarce, which forced Linux to continually perform extremely expensive swapping.

Next, you turn your attention to the role MySQL's configuration might have played in the debacle. You know that the client applications were running elsewhere; the database servers were dedicated to MySQL alone. This eliminates the possibility of server-side conflict among applications, so any performance problems on the server will likely be tied directly back to MySQL.

MySQL itself offers a collection of helpful utilities, tools, and logs. These include the general query log, slow query log, and MySQL Administrator; all were described in Chapter 2.

Alas, these logs don't always help very much in a case like this: It's hard to identify a problem query when all queries are running slowly. This again indicates a systemic, serverwide problem. However, examining the MySQL server configuration delivers some interesting results.

It appears that these servers have been configured with generous memory allocation to the key buffer. The query cache and buffer pool are each substantially smaller. What makes this especially bad is that with the exception of a few ancillary tables that use the MyISAM storage engine, the vast majority of tables on these servers use InnoDB. You also observe that the administrators have also elected to lock the mysqld process in memory; the servers launch with the --memlock option enabled.

When you last reviewed the airline's MySQL performance issues (see Chapter 18), you suggested that High-Hat look at replication as a way of distributing information so that casual and report-driven users could work with near real-time data without interfering with operations. In the interim, your recommendation was implemented: Numerous slave servers are now deployed in production.

Solution

With your research and analysis complete, it's now up to you to deliver some specific advice to help prevent this kind of server failure from happening again.

Hardware

Based on the server overloading that you saw from examining the output from the Linux utilities, you recommend that High-Hat make the investment in additional server computers; if these computers can sport multiprocessors, that's even better. In addition, you advocate that each server (both existing and new) receive a generous memory upgrade to help reduce or eliminate the swapping problem. Finally, you advise more active monitoring of these utilities; it might be possible to intercept the next problem before it spirals out of control into a full-blown crisis.

MySQL Configuration

In Chapter 11, "MyISAM Performance Enhancement," you saw that the key cache is a section of memory used to buffer index information from tables that use the MyISAM storage engine. On the other hand, Chapter 10, "General Server Performance and Parameters Tuning," described how the query cache stores frequently used queries and results regardless of the storage engine being used. Finally, Chapter 12, "InnoDB Performance Enhancement," discussed InnoDB's reliance on the buffer pool for its own caching.

Because, in this case, your servers are heavily slanted toward InnoDB, it would be smart to deallocate memory from MyISAM-focused structures and instead use that memory for InnoDB as well as engine-neutral caching features.

Finally, you determine that locking `mysqld` in memory might not be the wisest choice if the servers don't have enough RAM to begin with. Instead, you opt to try to let the operating system manage its own memory.

Topology

The replication architecture that is currently deployed goes a long way toward reducing the query processing strain on master servers. However, it does nothing to spread the write load, nor does it address what happens during a major master server outage. Although database users might be able to connect to a replicated slave server, it will not be very easy for them to make updates.

For these reasons, you recommend deploying MySQL Cluster for any applications that need high availability. First described in Chapter 17, "Optimal Clustering," MySQL Cluster can coexist with replication, delivering an even better, faster-performing solution. To help isolate the impact of any potential node failures, you counsel a 1:1 ratio between nodes (SQL, data, or management) and hosts (that is, the computer that runs the node). To better spread the burden, you also propose a 2:1 ratio of SQL nodes to data nodes with a round-robin or other load-balancing technology serving to connect clients with a SQL node. You also recognize that this ratio might need to change as MySQL AB continually enhances MySQL Cluster's capabilities; more processing might eventually be done on the data nodes themselves.

Application and Transaction Issues

With the server availability problem tackled, your next job is to examine what, if any, issues can be found with the reservation system and its transactions. Once again, reports range from "hung" programs and browsers to cryptic error messages that flash by before the user had a chance to write them down.

What is known for sure is that somehow the airline's data integrity became badly damaged: The combination of nearly empty departing jumbo jets juxtaposed with the sight of police riot squads clearing mobs of hundreds of people away from oversold airplanes confirms that assertion.

Diagnosis

When faced with application or transaction issues, it's natural to want to dive in and start reading code. A better approach is to attempt to take advantage of any diagnostic tools or reports to help narrow your search. In this case, the SHOW INNODB STATUS command will likely provide useful clues. Fortunately, a quick-thinking system administrator repeatedly ran this command during the height of the crisis, and kept copies of its output. You would like to thank her, but she was terminated along with many others, so this will have to wait.

Observations

Poring through the output, you notice a pattern. You see the same type of message about transactions and locks:

```
---TRANSACTION 0 1291, ACTIVE 58 sec, OS thread id 3632 starting index read
mysql tables in use 1, locked 1
LOCK WAIT 2 lock struct(s), heap size 320
MySQL thread id 16, query id 1150 webserver19 10.68.0.19 webclient Updating
update flight_seats set seat_number = '23B' where reservation_id = 7944 and
flight_date = '2006-06-10'
------- TRX HAS BEEN WAITING 58 SEC FOR THIS LOCK TO BE GRANTED:
RECORD LOCKS space id 0 page no 52 n bits 456 index `PRIMARY` of table `high_hat
/flight_seats` trx id 0 1291 lock_mode X waiting
Record lock, heap no 2 PHYSICAL RECORD: n_fields 6; 1-byte offs TRUE; info bits
0
 0: len 4; hex 00000001; asc     ;; 1: len 6; hex 000000000508; asc     ;; 2:
len 7; hex 800000002d0084; asc     - ?;; 3: len 3; hex 8f9f04; asc  ? ;; 4: len
4; hex 80003cfd; asc    <?;; 5: len 3; hex 30396f; asc 09o;;
```

Something is definitely wrong here—no transaction should wait 5 seconds, much less 58 seconds for a lock to be granted. Few users will be so patient.

It appears that this transaction originates in the "change your seat" portion of the web application. Reading the code, you observe the following processing sequence, expressed here in pseudocode:

```
Start the transaction
Display a list of seats to the user
Wait for their input
Update the flight_seats table with the new seat request
Commit the transaction
```

You also notice errors like the following sprinkled through the output:

```
------------------------
LATEST FOREIGN KEY ERROR
------------------------
060604 21:51:23 Transaction:
TRANSACTION 0 1061815959, ACTIVE 32 sec, process no 20846, OS thread id 21087876
32 inserting, thread declared inside InnoDB 500
mysql tables in use 1, locked 1
22 lock struct(s), heap size 2496, undo log entries 1
MySQL thread id 73, query id 1584835 10.68.0.132 hberson update
insert into customer_flights(customer_flight_id,customer_id,flight_id)
 values(20321,23304,11472)
Foreign key constraint fails for table `high_hat/customer_flights`:
,
  CONSTRAINT `customer_flights_ibfk_1` FOREIGN KEY (`customer_id`) REFERENCES `c
ustomer_master` (`customer_id`)
Trying to add in child table, in index `customer_id` tuple:
DATA TUPLE: 2 fields;
 0: len 4; hex 00005b08; asc    [ ;; 1: len 4; hex 00004f61; asc    Oa;;

But in parent table `high_hat/customer_master`, in index `PRIMARY`,
the closest match we can find is record:
PHYSICAL RECORD: n_fields 15; 1-byte offs TRUE; info bits 0
 0: len 4; hex 00005b5a; asc    [Z;; 1: len 6; hex 00003f4a068f; asc    ?J  ;; 2:
len 7; hex 800005c00207a2; asc          ;; 3: len 0; hex ; asc ;; 4: len 0; hex ;
asc ;; 5: len 30; hex 317a686f756b71787333386a713537327678327361316637323727473
68; asc 1zhoukqxs38jq572vx2sa1f7272tsh;...(truncated); 6: len 8; hex 683867346d3
73977; asc h8g4m79w;; 7: SQL NULL, size 0 ; 8: len 14; hex 6a367a786e78747838337
0786d76; asc j6zxnxtx83pxmv;; 9: len 19; hex 7a32616933696961306a65346b71727a357
961; asc z2ai3iia0je4kqrz5ya;; 10: len 3; hex 727573; asc rus;; 11: len 3; hex 8
fa243; asc   C;; 12: len 1; hex 01; asc  ;; 13: len 3; hex 8fa110; asc     ;; 14:
 len 8; hex 800012356f8be2e0; asc    5o   ;;
```

Finally, as part of your normal review of the application, you discern a pattern of frequent, explicit temporary table creation. A statement to build one of these tables typically looks like this:

```
CREATE TABLE tmp_customer_master_address
AS SELECT cm.*, ca.address1 FROM customer_master cm, customer_address ca
WHERE cm.customer_id = ca.customer_id
AND cm.last_name = 'Meadows' AND cm.first_name = 'Charles';
```

After being built, these tables can hold large collections of rows, depending on the uniqueness of the name combination. They are then further searched before being dropped. You do notice, however, that most columns in this temporary table go unused.

Solution

Using the results from SHOW INNODB STATUS has saved you a tremendous amount of time, helping you hone in on the source of many problems without having to wade through thousands of lines of application code.

Transaction Timeouts

As currently defined, at least two serious problems exist with the transaction you saw earlier:

1. No transaction should ever be allowed to be open and awaiting input from a user. The user could walk away from the application, meaning that the transaction could remain active indefinitely unless specific timeout behavior was defined.

   As you saw in Chapter 9, "Developing High-Speed Applications," lengthy transactions can wreak havoc in any number of ways. In this case, other transactions are blocked from working with information currently accessed by this transaction. Their applications appear to "freeze," and eventually time out, returning an error similar to the following:

   ```
   ERROR 1205 (HY000): Lock wait timeout exceeded; try restarting transaction
   ```

   The scope of the locking problem can be even larger, depending on transaction isolation level and breadth of information access.

   In this case, you recommend the following high-level application processing flow:

   ```
   Display a list of seats to the user
   Wait for their input
   Start the transaction
   Make sure that the seat request is still valid (that is, no one else has taken it in
       the interim)
   If it is still valid
           Update the flight_seats table with the new seat request
           Commit the transaction
   Else
           Warn the user
           Roll back the transaction
           Redisplay the list
   End if
   ```

   This tactic protects you from endless transactions that also lock key data resources: This should go a long way toward reducing complaints of "hung" applications.

2. There is an even more fundamental issue here. Based on what you have seen and heard, you are concerned about the overall quality of the application logic. It appears that

developers (many of whom are outsourced and don't really understand the airline's business) have been given wide latitude to implement their solutions in whatever way they want.

The foreign key errors from SHOW INNODB STATUS provide an additional proof point that something is awry in these applications. A safer, more consistent, and often better-performing approach is to put critical business logic on the server within centrally available, stored procedures.

As seen in Chapter 9, stored procedures add value in numerous ways. The most appealing benefits in this situation are stored procedures' consistency. A specialized group of professionals could be charged with writing a collection of key business-based, stored procedures. Taking referential integrity and other deep knowledge of the airline's business and database into account, they would likely write well-designed procedures. These procedures would define all relevant transaction isolation settings, as well as be responsible for starting and committing or rolling back the transaction.

Other developers would simply make invocations against these procedures. The application flow might now look something like this:

```
Display a list of seats to the user
Wait for their input
Invoke the appropriate stored procedure
If the stored procedure returns an error
        Warn the user
        Redisplay the list
Else
        Notify the user of success
End if
```

Although this is not a panacea, it would definitely help standardize and centralize much of the business logic for the airline. Added benefits include improved performance and reduced network traffic.

Given the low quality of the application code you have already reviewed, you recommend a more in-depth study of all the transactional and referential capabilities of the software involved in the ill-fated airfare promotion: It's a necessary step in tracking down the root causes of the over- and underbooking problems.

Temporary Storage

Your investigation showed that temporary tables are being created all the time, and that these tables effectively serve as small subsets of information used for follow-on queries. At least four problems exist with these tables; luckily, all of these issues have solutions.

- **They are not specified as temporary**—The TEMPORARY keyword is omitted from the CREATE TABLE statement. As Chapter 8, "Advanced SQL Tips," describes, this means that name conflicts with other users are very likely, especially given the widespread usage of these statements. This is an easily implemented change: Simply include this directive when creating these kinds of tables.

- **They are not indexed**—Just because a table is not meant to be permanent doesn't mean that it doesn't need proper indexes. Depending on data and usage patterns for the temporary tables, it might be necessary to create relevant indexes to help speed their processing. Small, short-lived tables probably don't need indexes, but these tables appear to hold large amounts of data, making a stronger case for indexes.

- **There are better storage engines for them**—Unless they need the protection afforded by transactions, it might not be necessary to incur the overhead of the InnoDB storage engine for these temporary tables. Perhaps they can be stored in MyISAM or even using the MEMORY engine, assuming enough RAM is available to service the entire user community.

- **There are better ways to get information**—Ultimately, this is the question that needs to be addressed: Are there better means to obtain a meaningful subset of information, as shown in the table creation query? The answer is definitely yes.

For example, a view could be created to hold only those columns necessary for the task at hand. The application code would then query against the view, returning a smaller set of information. Alternatively, a stored procedure could exist on the server. Taking last_name and first_name as input parameters, it could do all necessary processing, returning only relevant information to the client. In both of the preceding solutions, the end result is that the client performs much less work; the network also sees less traffic.

## 20

Case Study 3: Practice Makes Perfect

Several weeks have passed since the disastrous airfare sale described in Chapter 19, "Case Study: Friends Fly Free-for-All—A Promotion Gone Wrong." The new CIO has settled in and begun a large-scale optimization project. You did such a good job on the previous two projects that you've been tapped to lead the task group. Surveying the user and technical groups tells you that things are better, but still far from perfect. Some of the old problems still remain, and some new issues have cropped up.

In particular, High-Hat Airways recently scrapped its partnerships with other airlines such as Germany's Kleine Sitzfluglinien, Spain's Vuelos Incómodos, and the French carrier LAD (Ligne Aérienne Désagréable). The old program has been replaced with a new group of partners. Being primarily composed of second-tier fast-food restaurants, dry cleaners, and laundromats, these new partners do not have the cachet of the original group, but they offered better financial terms. Their customers will be able to earn one High-Hat mile for every dollar spent in these establishments. However, because it takes at least 25,000 miles to earn a free trip, it will take decades for many of these new plan members to earn a trip. Nevertheless, the revamped program is a hit with a whole new constituency, many of whom have never even flown.

Within 30 days of the program's launch, massive data files containing information about the partners' customers, along with their mileage-earning purchases, began arriving. The first problems related to the files themselves; most were incorrectly formatted and were unable to be loaded. This caused no end of aggravation for the reservation agents, who had to field thousands of calls from irate new program members demanding to know why the few dozen miles they earned eating fast food during the last month aren't in their accounts yet.

Eventually, the data files are correctly formatted and successfully loaded each night. This introduces another, more intractable issue—it simply takes too long to import this information.

You also learn that the clustering solution you recommended has had mixed results: Database server availability is much higher, but many users are complaining of terrible query performance.

Finally, you had counseled High-Hat to start using MySQL 5's stored procedures as a way of centralizing business logic while improving performance. The good news is that the referential integrity and other problems that had plagued the airline have largely disappeared. The bad news is that some of the stored procedures are perceived as running more slowly than the client-side application logic they replaced.

Other problems also exist, but because the users are complaining most loudly about the preceding three problems, you decide to make solving them your priority.

Data Importing

Large-scale data imports often cause serious headaches for administrators. Fortunately, MySQL offers numerous ways to make these jobs more predictable and less exciting.

Diagnosis

Every night, transaction summary data from each partner is first loaded into a work table. A batch operation then processes all rows in the table, granting the appropriate credit to each partner's customer within the main High-Hat customer database. The work table (partner_transactions) and another relevant table are defined as follows:

```
CREATE table partners
(
    partner_id INTEGER PRIMARY KEY AUTO_INCREMENT,
    partner_name VARCHAR(40)
) ENGINE = INNODB;

CREATE table partner_transactions
(
    partner_id INTEGER NOT NULL,
    ff_account CHAR(10) NOT NULL,
    last_name VARCHAR(50) NOT NULL,
    first_name VARCHAR(50) NOT NULL,
    transaction_date DATE NOT NULL,
    daily_total DECIMAL (5,2) NOT NULL,
    PRIMARY KEY(partner_id,ff_account,transaction_date),
    INDEX (partner_id),
    INDEX (ff_account),
    INDEX (last_name, first_name),
    INDEX (transaction_date),
    INDEX (daily_total),
    FOREIGN KEY (partner_id) REFERENCES partners(partner_id)
) ENGINE = INNODB;
```

Now that you know the high-level information flow, what is the best way to proceed? First, when faced with a group of sluggish data import processes, pick one on which to focus your energies, rather than working on all of them in parallel. After this file has been identified, you should start by looking at the process that created the import file, followed by the file itself, and only then turn your attention to the import process and server configuration.

Observations

Using the order of analysis listed in the preceding section, here are your observations:

- After speaking with the partner (who also uses MySQL), you learn that when generating the file, they sort the transactions by amount. Looking at their data file confirms this report.

- The data file consists of individual INSERT statements; each statement records a single mileage-qualifying purchase for a particular member.

- After the file is received at High-Hat, the import operation is run on a different machine than the database server. Both machines are on the same secure network, but are separated by 2,000 kilometers. Furthermore, Secure Sockets Layer (SSL) is used between the client and database server.

- The database server is dedicated to running the import process; no other applications are running at the same time. No server parameter configuration changes are made: The database runs with the same settings as during normal operation.

Solution

Your research really paid off: The partner and High-Hat can make several easily implemented yet very powerful changes to facilitate information loading. All of these concepts are discussed at length in Chapter 15, "Improving Import and Export Operations." For this situation, the suggestions are categorized into the following areas:

- **Export file generation**—The partner can undertake two steps to make things better:
  1. **Generate the export file in the order of the High-Hat primary key**—Because InnoDB stores the table in the order of either your or a system-generated primary key (known as the clustered index), this reduces the amount of reorganization necessary to complete the load operation. This can have a dramatic impact on performance.
  2. **Generate the data file so that multiple INSERT operations are performed within the same batch**—Grouping these activities together can speed the importing process.

- **Import server configuration**—You can employ several tactics to help your import server handle information more efficiently:
  1. **Run the import closer to the database server**—Loading large volumes of information is time consuming enough. Having to send this data over a widely distributed network doesn't help. In fact, if enough resources are available, try to run the import process on the same machine as the database server: This reduces network traffic costs to zero.

2. **Avoid SSL**—Regardless of whether you are able to alter your network topology, you can speed things up by disabling SSL. Because both machines are on the same, secure network, there is no need to incur the extra cost of encrypting and then decrypting information.

3. **Temporarily alter InnoDB engine settings**—If it doesn't cause problems for other users or processes, you can allocate a very large percentage of system memory to the InnoDB buffer pool as well as increase the log buffer size (via the `innodb_buffer_pool_size` and `innodb_log_buffer_size` settings, respectively). Granting extra space to these memory-based structures helps InnoDB perform more work in memory, rather than on disk. You can also reduce disk I/O by boosting the size of InnoDB's log files via the `innodb_log_file_size` setting.

- **Import process**—During your diagnostic work, you noticed two glaring problems with how the import process is handled. Your recommendations include the following:

  1. **Reduce the number of indexes**—The `partner_transactions` table is heavily indexed. As you talk with the developers, you learn that the primary key is really the only necessary index. Because this is the case, you request that the other indexes be removed from the table definition: There is no need for InnoDB to do the work of keeping all of them up to date.

  2. **Disable foreign key validation**—To ensure data integrity, the `partner_transactions` table references the `partners` table. However, it's probably safe to assume that the partner will send you accurate information in this field, thus obviating the need for an expensive foreign key lookup for each imported row. To disable these lookups, be certain to enter SET FOREIGN KEY CHECKS = 0 prior to starting the import. The same holds true for uniqueness checks: They can be disabled by using SET UNIQUE CHECKS = 0.

Clustering

Recall Chapter 19's description of what went wrong when High-Hat launched its web-only airfare sale. The reduced number of servers could not handle the load. In fact, some crashed, which led to severe performance and availability problems. At that time, you recommended using MySQL's clustering capabilities to help improve response and availability.

Although availability is definitely improved, users are noticing considerable query delays. From their perspective, not much has improved, so your recommendation needs to be revisited. This is not surprising to you because you know that every clustering situation is different and is subject to periodic optimization review.

Diagnosis

As you know from Chapter 17, "Optimal Clustering," MySQL Cluster employs a sophisticated network of specialized nodes; each node is dedicated to one of three roles:

1. **Management**—As its name implies, this node is responsible for administrative and other tasks that are vital to the health of the cluster.

2. **SQL**—This node, which services the actual users for the cluster, is nothing more than a standard MySQL server that happens to use the NDB storage engine to store its information on the data node.

3. **Data**—This node looks after the actual information, including distributing redundant copies across the cluster onto other data nodes.

High-Hat elected to place each node on its own computer, or host. This is the safest approach from the perspective of high availability because a crash of a particular host won't take down more than one node.

To get an idea of what is happening in the cluster, you use the tools provided by MySQL to look for any error conditions or other anomalies. These include the management client (ndb_mgm) as well as evaluating the cluster logs. You also employ network management tools to get an idea about any potential bandwidth issues.

Observations

Poring through MySQL's clustering diagnostics doesn't show anything remarkable: Everything appears normal. However, monitoring the network's traffic levels presents a different picture.

Traffic appears to be directly correlated with the number of queries under way at one time. Even a simple query causes a spike in network traffic. When multiplied by the number of active users on the network during the workday, this leads to severely degraded performance.

Solution

This is an all-too-common case in which there is no "magic bullet" that will solve all problems. The fundamental issue is that in version 4.x, MySQL and MySQL Cluster still contain components that are not fully "distributed-aware." For example, there is currently no filtering on data nodes. This means that running a simple query from a SQL node causes one or more data nodes to send all rows to the SQL node for filtering. This is very inefficient: Imagine the extra traffic from the following basic, primary key–driven query that is run against a three-million row table:

```
SELECT * FROM customer_master WHERE customer_id = 129212;
```

In this case, the data nodes gather and send all rows from the customer_master table back to the requesting SQL node. The SQL node, in turn, filters out the 2,999,999 extraneous rows, returning the one correct row to the requesting client. Version 5.x of MySQL Cluster will feature data node–based filtering, which should go a long way toward improving query performance. The same holds true for MySQL Cluster's parallelism capabilities, which are used to take advantage of the parallel processing power afforded by the multiple computers that usually make up a cluster.

However, you need to make some recommendations given the current configuration and software version, so they are broken out as discussed in the following sections.

Node Realignment

Given that version 4.x sends massive amounts of query-driven traffic between the data and SQL nodes, why not put the two nodes on the same computer? That way, this communication occurs in shared memory. However, the price of this transformation is paid in availability: A host failure now takes out two nodes rather than one.

Transport Alteration

Chapter 17 described the various transports available for MySQL Cluster traffic. One interesting new transport is Scalable Coherent Interface (SCI), which uses new hardware to improve network communication speed by up to 10 times. This is still slower than shared memory, but allows High-Hat to maintain a separation of nodes onto dedicated hosts.

Using Replicated Slave Servers for Queries

The potentially least-intrusive tactic is to direct query-hungry users and applications to a replicated server. Remember that MySQL Cluster and replication are not mutually exclusive: They can both coexist in the same environment. These read-only operations could take place on a replicated slave server, which would deliver all of the built-in performance benefits offered by MySQL; users would still need to make their data updates elsewhere, however.

Stored Procedures

As part of your previous optimization work, described in Chapter 19, you suggested that High-Hat move toward centralizing its business logic in server-based, stored procedures. You felt that this would produce higher-quality applications, especially given the frenetic turnover and related lack of development discipline in the airline's IT department.

High-Hat took your advice and began converting significant portions of client-side application code into server-side, stored procedures. Almost immediately, the inconsistencies that had plagued their applications and data became much rarer. However, first developers and then users began noticing performance degradation for several of the applications that employ these new stored procedures, as well as some other applications that do not.

Diagnosis

Deciphering an apparent stored procedure performance problem is often far simpler than tackling a server configuration problem. All that is necessary is to look at the stored procedure code, along with any SQL invoked from the procedure; the EXPLAIN command helps with that task as well. Stored procedures are discussed in Chapter 9, "Developing High-Speed Applications."

Observations

Many of the stored procedures that you evaluate appear normal. However, several other procedures seem to follow the same design pattern. They typically

1. Set transaction isolation level to SERIALIZABLE.

2. Start a transaction.

3. Conduct a range search on a single table (table A) using one or more of the stored procedure's parameters.

4. For each fetched row from table A, declare cursors to look up information in three other tables (tables B, C, and D).

5. When all the relevant rows from all tables (tables B, C, and D) have been retrieved, update an internal variable.

6. After all the rows from table A have been fetched, divide this internal variable by the number of fetched rows to yield a result.

   - Insert a single row into a statistical table, using the value from the preceding step.

   - Commit the transaction.

Solution

Several performance and concurrency problems exist with this stored procedure design pattern. You present your recommendations in the following two categories.

Transactions

The preceding example, as well as the other procedures, appears to be not particularly sensitive to minor data alterations. Despite this indifference, the transaction isolation level is set to a superstrict value of SERIALIZABLE. Recall from Chapter 9 that this isolation level effectively blocks other processes from altering any rows that have been evaluated during the course of this transaction, regardless of whether these rows have even been changed. Given the large number of rows spread across multiple tables, there is a good chance that this procedure is negatively impacting users throughout the system. In addition, this procedure's demanding isolation level means that it will likely run into obstacles and be forced to wait for other operations to finish.

For this kind of transaction, the default isolation level of REPEATABLE READ would suffice. In fact, an even less restrictive isolation level would probably be fine. It can also be argued that the transaction should not even start until immediately before the INSERT statement. In this case, any less-restrictive isolation level change will likely yield a better-performing procedure that treads more lightly on other users and processes.

Processing Options

By failing to use basic joins and built-in functions, the authors of these procedures have been forced to reinvent the wheel. Aside from the waste of valuable development time, it's likely that their implementations will not be as speedy as the MySQL query engine and library of functions. You recommend that this group of stored procedures be rewritten to leverage the power of SQL and functions such as AVG(), freeing the developers to focus on application logic.

Index

How can we make this index more useful? Email us at indexes@samspublishing.com

M

management nodes, clustering, 343

arbitration issues (MySQL Cluster), 352

logging issues (MySQL Cluster), 352

mass storage devices, performance analysis, 10

master servers

replication speed

logging parameters, 335-336

monitoring information, 332-336

tuning practices, 335

role in replication, 325-329

SHOW BINARY LOGS command, 334

SHOW BINLOG EVENTS command, 334-335

SHOW MASTER LOGS command, 334

SHOW MASTER STATUS command, 334

math queries, calculation operations

GROUP BY, WITH ROLLUP statement, 168

performance guidelines, 166-169

max allowed packet setting (database connectivity), 213

max connections setting (database connectivity), 214

max length for sort data variable, 229

max used connections setting (database connectivity), 214

MaxClients setting, Apache/PHP performance configuration, 303

MaxDB storage engine, 45

selection criteria, 70

MaxKeepAliveRequests setting, Apache/PHP performance configuration, 303

MaxRequestPerChild setting, Apache/PHP performance configuration, 303

memory

buffer pools (InnoDB), 271

alternatives to, 279-280

configuring, 271-272

innodb buffer pool pages data value, 273

innodb buffer pool pages dirty value, 273

innodb buffer pool pages flushed value, 274

innodb buffer pool read ahead value, 274

innodb buffer pool read requests value, 274

innodb buffer pool size, 271-272

innodb buffer pool wait free value, 274

innodb buffer pool write requests value, 274

innodb max dirty pages pct, 272

monitoring, 272-279

problem indicators, 279

tuning, 272-279

in-memory caches, 218

buffer pools, 218

key cache, 218

memory pools, 218

query cache, 218-225

in-memory processing, data export rules, 314

Linux utilities

free, 41

vmstat, 41

MEMORY tables, 218

mysqld process (locking), 216

performance analysis, 10

thread status, 216-217

memory caches

disk drives, correct configuration of, 283-284

MyISAM, 239

buffer pool, 240

key, 240-248

memory pool, 240

query, 240

memory pools

in-memory caches, 218

indexes (InnoDB), 137

MyISAM, 240

MEMORY storage engine, 44

selection criteria, 66-67

MEMORY tables, 279-280

memory settings for database connectivity, 218

MERGE storage engine, 44

selection criteria, 67-69

mirroring (RAID 0), 285

MMC Performance Monitor, 36

monitoring

InnoDB, data storage, 265-267

key cache (MySQL Administrator reports)

consumption, 244-245

metrics graphs, 246, 248

read hit rate percentages, 245

reads versus disk reads, 245

write hit rate percentages, 245

writes versus disk writes, 245

log files (InnoDB), 269-270

master servers, replication performance, 332-335

query caches, 222-225

slave servers, health of, 337-339

mount command, drive performance parameters, modifying (Linux), 290-291

mpstat utility (Linux), 40

Q

network performance parameters, 319

SELECT, INTO OUT-FILE statement, 319

table locking, 318-319

REPEATABLE READ isolation level, 194

replicas

data distribution, node storage, 345

databases, performance analysis, 12-13

slave server data replication

query usage, 384

—replicate-do-db parameter, 339

—replicate-do-table parameter, 340

—replicate-ignore-db parameter, 339

—replicate-ignore-table parameter, 340

replication

distributed computing technology product, 45

performance issues

master servers, monitoring, 332-336

master servers, tuning practices, 335

master servers, when to log, 335-336

network considerations, 330-332

slave servers, configurations, 336

slave servers, data criteria, 339-340

slave servers, monitoring, 337-339

slave servers, overhead reduction, 340

slave servers, relay logs, 336-337

slave servers, resource management, 336-337

slave servers, shared workloads, 339

slave servers, temporary file storage, 337

query processing work, off-loading, 160

servers, master selection, 325-326

strategies

design of, 326-329

transaction bottlenecks (High-Hat Airways case study), 367

usage criteria, 326

versus clustering, 346

resolving High-Hat Airways scenarios

application failures, 375-377

large-scale data importation problems, 381-382

server clustering problems, 383-384

server outages, 372

stored procedure problems, 385-386

transaction failures, 375-377

resource consumption, transaction lengths, 197

resource restriction strategy for transaction bottlenecks (High-Hat Airways scenario), 367

results (testing), 17

resultsets (queries)

DISTINCT statement, 157-158

estimating, 154-157

GROUP BY statement, 157-158

limiting, 154-157

retrieving data exports from table subsets, 315

returned columns, reducing for query performance, 79-80

returned rows, reducing for query performance, 80-81

rollbacks, transaction length, 197-198

rollup strategy for transaction bottlenecks (High-Hat Airways scenario), 367

row locks, 186

rowid values, clustered indexes (InnoDB), 260

rows

locking scope (InnoDB), 188-189

tables

data handling (HANDLER statement), 175-176

specifying, 71-73

rows column, EXPLAIN command (optimizer) output, 110

rules, constraints

benefits, 85-86

DEFAULT, 85, 90-91

ENUM, 85, 92

FOREIGN KEY, 85, 88-90

function of, 85

NOT NULL, 85, 90-91

PRIMARY KEY, 85-87

SET, 85, 92-93

UNIQUE, 85-86

S

sar utility (Linux), 40

Scalable Coherent Interface (SCI)

connectivity tuning, 307

sockets, clustering issues (MySQL Cluster), 351-352

transporters (nodes), 344

schemas (tables), copying without associated data for export purposes, 315-316

searches (queries), performance tips, 153

data retrieval, controlling, 154-160

internal engine caches, leveraging, 153-154

How can we make this index more useful? Email us at indexes@samspublishing.com